Oracle Design

Oracle Design

Dave Ensor and Ian Stevenson

O'REILLY™

Cambridge · *Köln* · *Paris* · *Sebastopol* · *Tokyo*

Oracle Design
by Dave Ensor and Ian Stevenson

Copyright © 1997 O'Reilly & Associates, Inc. All rights reserved.
Printed in the United States of America.

Published by O'Reilly & Associates, Inc., 101 Morris Street, Sebastopol, CA 95472.

Editor: Deborah Russell

Production Editors: John Files and David Futato

Printing History:

March 1997:   First Edition.

ISBN: 1-56592-268-9

Table of Contents

Preface

Why did we write this book? For some time, we've both felt strongly that people underrate the importance of Oracle design and that a book devoted exclusively to this topic was sorely needed. Despite our common conviction, we came to this point from somewhat different directions.

Ian was motivated to write this book after being involved in the design phase of several Oracle projects for both Version 6 and Version 7. He began to notice that the same questions and problems would arise time and time again. But the conclusion reached for similar questions varied from project to project. It simply wasn't possible to say firmly that one solution was right and another wrong. Indeed, each solution might well have been the best possible one for the particular project concerned. He wanted to create a repository of information where he could record the reasoning that went into making a particular design decision. Then, in the future, he (and others) could refer to this repository when they were faced with a similar problem. It didn't take long to make the leap to believing that a book would be the best medium for sharing this hard-won design experience with others in the Oracle community.

Dave spent many years leading Oracle's Worldwide Performance Studies Group. In doing this work, he found, again and again, that Oracle performance problems had a similar root cause. They usually weren't the result of defective build techniques or poor Oracle tuning. Most often, they were the consequence of project teams having made the wrong design decisions. This is not to say that the "traditional" causes of performance problems never apply. But it is simply the case that many projects can *never* perform well because of defective design decisions. It was against this background that Dave wrote a one-day seminar called "Designing for Oracle7" which he presented to audiences around the world. However, even that seminar did not provide a foolproof recipe for design. In writing it, Dave discovered, like Ian, that each case needed to be judged on its own merits against each of the precise requirements of the project and the precise technical environment in which that project was carried out.

If there are no firm rules, why attempt to write a book on the subject? And, come to think of it, why are there so few books about design available on the market? To answer the second question first, we believe that the difficulty of being unable to present categorical answers (even to basic questions such as "Should every table have a primary key?") has deterred many authors and publishers who believe that readers will only be able to cope with technical material if there are nice, neat, absolute answers to all of the questions they ask. It just isn't so.

We have two very good reasons for writing this book:

1. On all of our projects, we've spent valuable time pursuing possibilities that were nonstarters—in other words, they were never going to work out, no matter what we tried. Had we known this, we could have eliminated them from the outset and saved some precious time.

2. As we grew in experience, we found that it was invaluable to have even rough notes from previous projects giving the potential advantages and disadvantages of possible design techniques. Even experienced designers sometimes overlook an option that might be used to solve a particular problem. So we concluded that having some type of reference, however non-absolute, would be an invaluable tool in forcing us to think along different lines.

Essentially, this is *our* book in the sense that *we*—and people much like us—will be using it to do our daily work. We'd like you to share in the benefits we've derived from our previous, sometimes difficult, but always instructive experiences.

Relational database design can be very frustrating. Seemingly simple business requirements might translate into complex design problems. Often you go full circle, considering various options that might satisfy a business requirement, only to come back to the original proposal—by which time you're so confused that you can't remember what your original objections were to that proposal. You feel that you're making no forward progress, and depression sets in. Even with this book as your companion, such dark days are occasionally inevitable. Just remember that we all go through these dreadful design experiences and that eventually you'll see the light at the end of the tunnel.

The real purpose of this book is to help you *work smarter, not harder*. We want to help you get some real benefit out of the efforts that you're going to have to put into design.

Why Oracle?

One of the first questions our publisher asked us was, "Why a design handbook for Oracle? Why not one for all relational databases? Is Oracle so different?" This remains a very important question, and one that we're anxious to answer.

All design, not only the design of computer applications, is about making the best use of the materials and technology available to you. Oracle7 has a number of specific and unique technical characteristics that you will need to take into account when you're selecting a design solution. A good portion of this book is devoted to discussions of these features. In many cases, we propose tests that you may want to perform in your own environment before you select a specific design approach.

We don't pretend that this book will make you a successful Oracle designer overnight. Sadly, there is no substitute for experience. One of the hallmarks of the very best designers is that they are still learning all the time. What we've set out to create here is a framework in which you can design in a more structured and controlled environment. Each chapter presents alternatives for major design decisions and highlights advantages and pitfalls. Of course, each decision will still rest with you, but we hope that you'll be better armed to justify that decision.

Oracle7 is now a mature product. From the time of Oracle Corporation's original announcement of this product, it was clear that the system marked the beginning of a general trend within Oracle to take the business rules' intelligence out of the application (or user interface) and put it in the database (or server). This evolution means that substantially more time now needs to be spent in database design than was the case for an Oracle Version 6 project or a 3GL project. Building should now be a simpler task, particularly if the design is good. Once the application build phase has started in earnest, it becomes difficult and costly to correct any bad decisions that were made during design.

Poor design decisions can lead to a long and frustrating development period and are often ultimately reflected in the poor quality of the eventual system. In fact, if the design is bad enough, there may never *be* an eventual system or, if there is, it may be a rather sick beast. When you are designing a system, always take the usability and performance of the system into account. If you are told that response time doesn't matter or that "We'll fix it later on," we advise you to argue the case. Fixing a design shortcoming or a bug in a production system is an extremely costly exercise. Attempting to solve performance problems by "throwing more hardware at them" works, in our experience, only on low-end systems; even there, it's never a guaranteed fix.

Remember too that the lasting user perceptions of any application are usually determined by users' experiences during the first week they use the system. The performance and user response time associated with any new computer system, together with its ease of use and robustness, make the difference between user acceptance and rejection.

In summary, these are the goals we should have for any design process, and the goals we'd like this book to help you reach: to provide, at the time the system is launched and throughout the life of the system, the required:

- Functionality and adaptability
- Throughput
- Response time
- Availability
- Ease of use
- Security

Structure of This Book

This book is separated into five parts, as described below. Although we'd like you to read every word, we know that some readers may not want to read the book from cover to cover; even those who read a large amount of the material may not do so in the order presented. To accommodate you, we've tried to make the chapters within the book fairly self-contained and to minimize the number of cross-references. Experienced designers and those who have good experience of project life cycles may find that they can skim some of the earlier chapters (notably Chapters 1 and 2), which introduce these subjects. Those who have used the recent versions of Oracle7 might be able to skip Chapter 2. Many of the chapters that describe specific technologies may be relevant only if you are working on a design that uses the particular feature. Distributed database (Chapter 12) and data warehousing (Chapter 13) are examples of such specific areas.

Part I: *Getting Started with Oracle Design*

- Chapter 1, *Introduction*, introduces the various phases of project development—in particular, strategy, analysis, design, and build; it provides a simplified example of a real project that illustrates the various project phases and deliverables.

- Chapter 2, *Why Is Design So Important for Oracle?* focuses on Oracle, describing the special design issues and itemizing the most important features of Oracle7; it also takes a look ahead to Oracle8.

- Chapter 3, *Data Modeling*, looks carefully at data modeling; it defines classic relational database terms like entity, relationship, and third normal form (3NF); and it itemizes the deliverables that the analysts must deliver to the designers so they can do the job of turning the conceptual data model into a logical data model.

Part II: *Designing the Database*

- Chapter 4, *Deciding When to Denormalize*, examines specific techniques for denormalizing the data in the database to improve performance.

- Chapter 5, *Choosing Datatypes and Nulls*, defines the various Oracle datatypes, describes how to choose the most appropriate datatypes for objects in the database, and explores the thorny issues of what null means and how nulls should be treated.

- Chapter 6, *Choosing Keys and Indexes*, discusses how to choose the best keys for your particular database.

- Chapter 7, *Dealing with Temporal Data*, explores a specific problem with Oracle and other relational databases—they don't adequately support time-series (temporal) data. It suggests a number of Oracle-specific techniques that you can use to overcome restrictions on this type of data.

- Chapter 8, *Loading and Unloading Data*, explores the various ways that you can populate your Oracle7 database from external data sources. It also discusses how to extract data from the Oracle7 database.

- Chapter 9, *Deciding on Object Placement and Storage*, looks at some of the most important physical aspects of database design, such as sizing and file placement.

- Chapter 10, *Safeguarding Your Data*, covers the topics of backup, archiving, auditing, and security.

Part III: *Designing for Specific Architectures*

- Chapter 11, *Designing for Client/Server*, applies Oracle7 design methods to the client/server model. We examine a variety of techniques for distributing the processing to optimize performance and usability.

- Chapter 12, *Designing for Distributed Databases*, takes the data distribution model a step further and looks at the why and how of distributed databases. We examine the various options available with Oracle7 and consider which should be employed in various scenarios.

- Chapter 13, *Designing for Data Warehouses*, looks at the steps involved in setting up and maintaining a data warehouse. We look at dimensional modeling and the various techniques involved in getting the data into the warehouse and extracting it out again.

- Chapter 14, *Designing for Parallel Processing*, describes parallel processing concepts, looks at practical applications of Oracle's Parallel Query Option and Oracle Parallel Server, and discusses such technologies as disk striping and RAID.

Part IV: *Designing the Code Modules*

- Chapter 15, *Introduction to Code Design*, describes the basic concepts of code module design.

- Chapter 16, *Determining Where to Locate the Processing*, looks at an innovative way of partitioning the logic of an application.

- Chapter 17, *Metrics, Prototypes, and Specifications*, describes the formal side of code design; in particular, this chapter focuses on how you can ensure that your modules meet the requirements.

- Chapter 18, *Locking*, contains information that will help you minimize contention within your applications.

- Chapter 19, *Selecting the Toolset*, compares the merits of the various categories of front-end products that can support an Oracle back-end.

- Chapter 20, *Designing Screens, Reports, Batch Programs, and More*, deals with specific design issues for screens, reports, batch programs, error handling, navigation, and online help.

Part V: *Appendixes*

- Appendix A, *Off-the-Shelf Packages*, compares the merits of buying a packaged solution with those of developing a complete application from scratch.

- Appendix B, *Tricks of the Trade*, focuses on three specific design techniques. We suggest a method for avoiding the annoying "mutating table" problem in Oracle7 triggers; we look at the problems presented by the imminent change of century (the millennium problem); and we take a brief tour into the extensible world of SQL.

About Our Readers

This book assumes prior knowledge of Oracle, although readers with experience using another relational database management system (RDBMS) who are making the transition to Oracle should find much of the book useful. It doesn't matter if your experience to date is mostly in the area of development or database administration. All we are really looking for is familiarity with the terms and concepts used in this book. We also presuppose a basic knowledge of a development project life cycle.

How will this book help you as a designer? We have attempted to provide you with a framework for your design and a checklist of common design issues. The book won't necessarily provide all the answers. We hope, though, that when you are performing a specific design task, you'll turn to this book. It will help you identify a number of questions which you otherwise might not have considered; we hope that it will also give you pointers that will help you resolve your design problem. We also hope that the book will provoke thought and discussion, will serve as a reference for important issues, and will help ensure the completeness of your design.

Which Oracle?

Most of what we say applies to all releases of Oracle7. In the few cases where this is not so, we indicate clearly which versions it does apply to. And what about Oracle8? At the time this book went into production, the product hadn't yet been announced. Naturally, we expect that Oracle8 will pose new problems as users start using new features. We also hope that Oracle8 will provide solutions to some of the shortcomings discussed in this book. In any case, we are confident that the great majority of our recommendations will continue to apply.

NOTE   What we refer to as simply Version 7.2 might well be called Oracle7 Release 7.2 in Oracle's own documentation. Throughout this book we refer to Oracle7 (and occasionally to Oracle6 and Oracle8), and we refer to the different releases of Oracle7 as *versions* since that is how most users refer to them. Oracle Corporation prefers the term *releases.*

Conventions

The following conventions are used in this book:

Italic
> is used for file, variable, and function names. It is also occasionally used for emphasis and to highlight key terms when they are first introduced.

Bold
> is used in headers.

`Constant width`
> is used for code examples.

UPPERCASE
> in code examples, indicates Oracle keywords.

lowercase
> in code examples, indicates user-defined items such as variables and parameters.

punctuation
> in code examples, enter exactly as shown.

indentation
> in code examples, helps to show structure but is not required.

.
> In code examples and related discussions, a dot qualifies a reference by separating an object name from a component name.

fixed<*variable*>
> in code examples and related discussions, part of a string or data item is fixed, and another part is variable.

Entity models
> are drawn using the *Information Engineering Methodology (IEM)* conventions.

About the Examples

We considered including a diskette or a CD-ROM with this book but decided against doing so because the code examples are relatively short and self-contained. However, if you want to obtain a machine-readable version of a specific program example in this book, you can do so by accessing the O'Reilly Web site. Examples are also available via anonymous FTP. For information on all of O'Reilly's online services, consult the backmatter at the end of this book.

Comments and Questions

We would welcome any comments you have about anything you read in this book. We view design as an imprecise science and accept the fact that there are many solutions to design problems. We especially want to hear from you if you've encountered a problem similar to one we discuss in this book and have a solution we've missed.

Please address comments and questions concerning this book to the publisher:

> O'Reilly & Associates
> 101 Morris Street
> Sebastopol, CA 95472
> 1-800-998-9938 (in the U.S. or Canada)
> 1-707-829-0515 (international or local)
> 1-707-829-0104 (FAX)

You can also send us messages electronically. See the advertising insert at the back of the book.

Acknowledgments

Many people have contributed to this book. First of all, we appreciate the encouragement and professional, friendly advice from the people at O'Reilly. In particular, we would like to record our appreciation of the efforts of Debby Russell, our editor; Mike Sierra, the O'Reilly tools specialist who solved many conversion and production problems for us; John Files and David Futato, the production editors for the book; Danny Marcus, the proofreader; Chris Reilley, who created the figures; Edie Freedman, who designed the cover; Nancy Priest, who created the interior format; and Seth Maislin who developed the index.

Many thanks to our reviewers, Mark Daynes, Barry Goodsell, Graham Wood, Martin Cantwell, Steven Feuerstein, and Mark Gurry for their constructive comments and reviews.

Many of our esteemed colleagues over the years have unwittingly contributed to this book. Much of what we learn comes from talking to associates, often casually at the coffee machine. Ian would particularly like to thank Andrew Mackley for his contribution to the data warehouse chapter.

Ian would like to put on record his thanks for the support and encouragement of his wife Brenda and his children Todd and Tara, especially for putting up with the long hours when he was shut in his office working.

Dave would like to thank Ian, who had the original idea for this book and who invited him to be coauthor. He also thanks his wife Mefus for putting up with him while the book was being written (and, also for putting up with him for the previous 27 years).

I

Getting Started with Design

This part of the book introduces the process of Oracle design. Design encompasses three major areas: the design of database objects, the design of code modules (for screens, reports, etc.), and the design of strategies for dealing with specific environments or technologies (e.g., client/server, data warehouse).

- Chapter 1, *Introduction*, introduces the various phases of project development—in particular, strategy, analysis, design, and build; it provides a simplified example of a real project that illustrates the various project phases and deliverables.

- Chapter 2, *Why Is Design So Important for Oracle?* focuses on Oracle, describing the special design issues and itemizing the most important features of Oracle7; it also takes a look ahead to Oracle8.

- Chapter 3, *Data Modeling*, looks carefully at data modeling; it defines classic relational database terms like entity, relationship, and third normal form (3NF); and it itemizes the deliverables that the analysts must deliver to the designers so they can do the job of turning the conceptual data model into a logical data model.

1

Introduction

This book is about database design—in particular, the design of Oracle databases—and some elements of the code that accesses them. How much does design matter? A lot. Performance usually makes or breaks a computer system, and design is central to good performance. If your database isn't well-designed from the start, it will be almost impossible for your applications to run efficiently. Even the most powerful hardware and software, and the most highly tuned code, won't make up for a poor or incomplete design. Design will also improve the chances that the system meets the original requirements and will ensure that what you intend to build is achievable, given the constraints that will inevitably be imposed upon you. Finally, good design will make it much easier for you to maintain your application, to change the way things work, and to add new features.

What Is Design?

What is design and when do we perform it? Design encompasses three major areas:

1. The design of the specific database objects that will be implemented in a database. For Oracle, these include such objects as tables, views, indexes, and stored procedures, functions, and packages.

2. The design of the specific screens, reports, and programs that will maintain the data in the database and allow inquiries against that data.

3. Under certain circumstances, the design must also be concerned with the specific environment or technology—for example, the network topology, the hardware configuration, and the use of a client/server, parallel processing, or distributed database architecture.

In an ideal world, you will be able to construct a database design that is utterly clear and logical and that achieves the best possible performance for your system. But design, like every other part of life, is all about tradeoffs and informed decision-making. Here is a real-world definition of design:

> Design is the business of finding a way to meet the functional requirements within the specified constraints using the available technology.

What are these constraints? Every project has some absolute requirements— usually, the maximum amount of elapsed time that can be consumed by the project, and the maximum amount of money that can be spent on it. A project may also have a myriad of other inconvenient requirements and limitations. As a designer, your job is to do the best job you possibly can within this structure— and to point out where tradeoffs can be made and where they will seriously jeopardize the success or quality of the project.

Although design is a vitally important task, it hasn't always received the attention it deserves. One problem is that the design of a database isn't as structured a task as the analysis of a project's requirements or the building of the application. You'll find many books on project analysis and development, but very few on design. (We're out to remedy that!)

There is one very common misconception about design—that it is a single and discrete phase of a project, falling neatly between the analysis and build phases. Very often, in books about project development, you'll see a diagram such as the one in Figure 1-1 of the so-called "waterfall method."

The reality is that a project simply can't be pieced together in such an idealistic way. For one thing, there is a wide overlap between the phases of a project. For another, design doesn't begin and end in such a clear way; it often continues through the test and implementation phases of the project.

In the next section, we'll present a case study of an actual (but much simplified) project. We'll look briefly at each phase of the project (strategy, analysis, design, build), and introduce some important terms and concepts along the way. We'll examine these in a lot more detail in later chapters.

A Case Study

In this example, let's look at a car rental company that wants to implement a new pricing strategy using discounts and loyalty bonuses. The mainframe system is already bursting at the seams and can't be further enhanced to provide the new functions. A new project to replace the aging technology with an Oracle database and a *graphical user interface (GUI)* front-end seems like a good idea! The company appoints a project manager, and we're on our way.

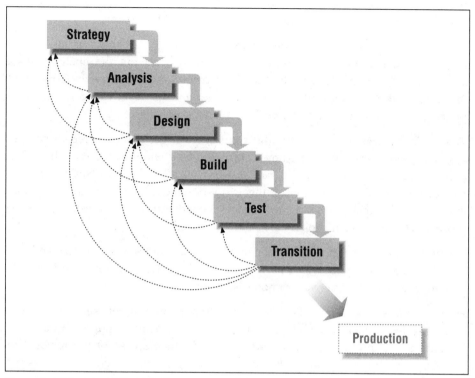

Figure 1-1. The waterfall method

Strategy

The first thing the new project manager does is to commission a *strategy study*. The main purposes of this study are to determine the true scope and goals of the project, and to produce high-level entity and function definitions. To be successful, strategy studies require highly experienced business analysts with frequent access to senior management. It is senior management who will have to approve the funds for the later stages of the project, and it is vital that their expectations of the results are carefully recorded.

The strategy phase involves heavy interaction with key users and business experts, extracting information from them and presenting it back to them in a formalized way to ensure a thorough and unambiguous understanding of the requirements. This may be done in a number of different ways—for example, as a series of one-to-one interviews and/or as general workshops. In our example, the analysts speak to the CEO, the Marketing VP, the Customer Services Manager, right down to the clerk on the hire desk. They learn about the business need to introduce special discounts for frequent customers and the introduction of a fourth category of rental car (minibus). They also hear about flexible payment schemes and special offers. In short, they learn what the business is all about and where it should be going if its computer systems would only let it.

Once the main part of the strategy study is complete, a technical architect (or a team, though it usually only takes one person) can set out the likely technical approach and the approximate hardware, software, and development costs. With this additional information, the project manager and his team can go back to the project sponsors with the *deliverable* from the strategy phase.

This is a clear statement of *what* the sponsors will get if they agree to proceed (scope), *when* they will get it (timescale), and *how much* it will cost them. The presentation should quantify the benefits as well as the costs ("this project will pay for itself in 18 months"), and if this is not done, or worse is not possible, then it may well be that there are no tangible benefits and the project should not proceed. However, such projects are often approved.

In our car rental scenario, the senior management endorse the findings and says that they are willing to wait one year and spend $1.2 million to achieve the requirement. The report covers (among other items):

- Constraints, risks, and critical success factors. Service targets such as response times and system availability, once validated as being genuine requirements and not simply nice to have, are constraints. In the case of the rental company, the timescale to introducing new pricing plans is a critical success factor as any significant slippage in schedule may mean a loss of market share.[*]

- The required functions, and possible future requirements, such as allowing rental cars to be booked via the World Wide Web.

- The entities required to support those functions.

This is also the time and place to state clearly what elements are *not* going to be included in the scope of the project. For example, in our car rental example, we state that management reports against our data are not in the scope of the project and will have to be dealt with as a separate project.

What is the outcome of this sample strategy phase? The conclusion is that we are going to go ahead with the project. The cost of *not* going ahead with the project is that the organization will not survive since all the competitors are introducing more flexible pricing schemes and thus are becoming more competitive.

Now that we have a clearly defined scope and a budget to play with, we move into the analysis phase.

---

[*] The last point about time constraints is not uncommon. Project managers of Year 2000 projects can tell you all about immovable timescales!

Analysis

The analysis phase is a detailed investigation of the required business processes (*functions*) and the information required to execute those functions (*entities* with their *attributes* and *relationships*). We'll give a quick overview of this phase in this section, and will provide more detail in Chapter 3, *Data Modeling*.

Even during the analysis phase it is important to articulate the requirements in general terms. By "general" we don't mean vague. What we mean is that no assumptions should be made about the computer system. This isn't easy to do. If (like us) you are a designer or programmer at heart, then you will find it extremely hard not to think in terms of "this screen" or "that table." Many programmers find it deeply mysterious that the most successful analysts are incapable of writing code (even though they usually claim that they could write some if they had to). The reason is simple: their inability to cut code means they don't waste time and effort in analysis trying to work out how to design the system.

Analysts capture and document two distinct but related forms of information:

* *Functions*—information about events and processes that occur in the business

* *Entities*—information about "things of significance to the organization about which something is known"

Two of the classical outputs from analysis are:

* The *function hierarchy*, which breaks down the processing into functions, or things that are done

* The *entity relationship model*, which captures all the entities, their attributes and the relationships between them

Figure 1-2 shows part of the functional decomposition and illustrates how we break down the billing process into a series of smaller steps until they cannot be sensibly split any further (at this point they are considered *atomic*). Each of the headings shown in this figure would normally be accompanied by a short description of the function. The atomic functions will ordinarily have a more detailed description of their purpose.

Figure 1-3 shows a simple entity model for our car rental system, in the form of an *entity relationship diagram (ERD)*. Pictures such as this one help enormously with understanding and documenting the system. Modeling techniques and the conventions behind this diagram are the main subject of Chapter 3. In a complex system, the ERD of the entire model will almost certainly be about as easy to read as a single-page map showing every star visible from the Northern Hemisphere! We recommend that you break it down into a number of small diagrams, each one depicting a relatively self-contained subject area of the model.

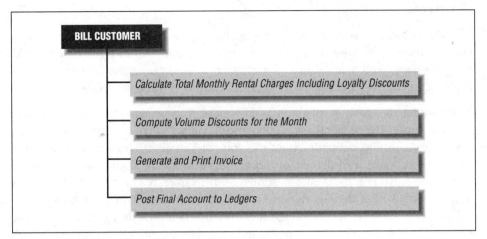

Figure 1-2. An extract from a functional decomposition

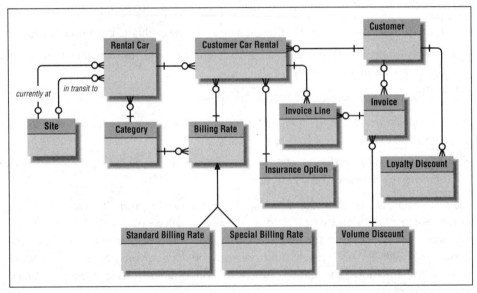

Figure 1-3. An entity relationship diagram

WARNING   We keep seeing serious omissions in design and code which result from designers and programmers using diagrams that do not tell the whole story. So if you are going to use incomplete or partial models, please make sure that you show the off-page connectors and that you provide some idea of where they go.

Each entity should have a description of what it is, a set of attributes with properties and descriptions, and a unique identifier that tells us how to distinguish one occurrence from the others.

WARNING   Time, however, for another warning. It is dangerous to show entity relationships without naming them since readers then have to assume the nature of the relationship and can get it wrong. For simplicity, we have only named two of the relationships in Figure 1-3, those which relate rental car to site. In a different rental company it might also be necessary to show other relationships between these two entities, such as *originally delivered to* and *nominally based at*.

During analysis we also need to capture any *business rules*. These aren't functions as such; rather, they are immutable facts about the operation that must be obeyed at all times by the system. In our example, some sample business rules might be:

- The special discount rates may not be applied on vehicles less than one year old.

- The total discount (loyalty + volume) may not exceed 40% of the net invoice amount.

Other outputs in frequent use include *entity life histories (ELHs)* and *data flow diagrams (DFDs)*, both of which introduce the concept of sequence, which is impossible to impose on either a function hierarchy or an entity relationship model. Indeed, trying to show life history on an entity model is a common cause of error. Where ELHs are not being used, business rules may be used to supply the missing information—for example:

- Only a vehicle that has been checked and certified by a service attendant since last being driven on the public highway can be allocated to a rental contract. (This definition carefully includes vehicles that have been used or transferred between locations by company employees or contractors.)

As a final step in the analysis phase, the team draws up a plan for system testing. Figure 1-4 shows an entity life history diagram for a rental car.

Design

The designer (or design team) takes the output of the analysis and produces:

- A database definition (or *schema*)—based on the entity model developed during the analysis phase

- A set of module specifications—built from the function models

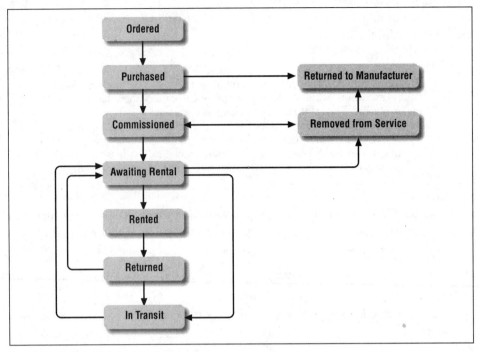

Figure 1-4. Entity life history for a rental car

This section gives a quick overview of the design phase. The later sections called "Planning the Design Phase" and "Design Tasks" provide more detail about what goes on during this phase.

NOTE   On the subject of the handover of deliverables note that in a very small project, it is possible that the analysts, designers, and builders are the same people (or person). If so, then you should aim to be disciplined about the transition and hand over the deliverable to yourself (wearing a different hat). Treat the process as if you were handing over the deliverables to someone else who has little knowledge of the system.

The database schema will contain all the database objects: tables, views, columns, indexes, clusters, constraints, triggers, etc. The design will not only produce the definition of the objects, but also the physical objects themselves that the developers will build against.

The specifications must be detailed enough that a developer can take them and turn them into a working program that meets the requirements. Much as we may all hate to think this far in advance, we must also turn our thoughts to testing and implementation. This means that we must deliver plans that ensure a thorough test of the application and a smooth transition into the production environment.

Many projects package most of their design deliverables into a single definitive document, called something akin to a *technical specification*. This document also outlines the approach taken to any complex technical issues.

The designers need to ensure that the database schema and the modules are mutually consistent in addition to being consistent with the analysis. For instance, the RENTAL_CARS table that is derived from the RENTAL CAR entity must have a module somewhere that allows the insertion of new cars. One of the key elements of design is to ensure that the system will perform well when built, given whatever constraints are imposed by the target system architecture. For this reason, the designers need to scrutinize the architecture itself. For example, the required throughput on the database server may lead us to consider using some form of parallel processing. Or we may look at alternative approaches to dividing the processing between the client and the server. We look at these architectures in detail in Chapter 14, *Designing for Parallel Processing*, and Chapter 11, *Designing for Client/Server*.

As we've said, performance is critical to any system. To get the best possible performance out of this system, we may need to make some compromises and tradeoffs. To our Car Rental Corporation, the most critical area is the ability to find the lowest price for a contract quickly and accurately. We may have several thousand possible combinations of price plan and discount plan for a single hire; the SQL to find the best combination is starting to look both tricky and potentially expensive in terms of CPU time. So we decide that, although we are going to hold all the price and discount plans in the database for maintenance and reporting purposes, for pricing we will load them into memory once at start of day (into an application-managed cache). We also decide that the pricing algorithm will be completely written in C against the cache (we won't use SQL).

During the design process, we seek out common or similar functionality in the functional definitions and design it as a single module. We decide if it makes sense to implement common modules and modules which enforce our business rules as *database-resident code* (triggers and stored functions, procedures, and packages). Where the processing is highly database-intensive, this makes good sense. This part of the code is best produced and tested during design and put in place before the rest of the modules are built. In our case, we create a trigger on the RENTAL_CARS table to prevent the creation of an agreement with a special billing rate on a car that was registered less than a year ago. This implements one of the business rules we mentioned earlier.

In our case study, we are replacing a legacy system and we therefore have to deal with the issue of *data migration*. Much as we would like to start with a blank database, this is not an option; the existing system has lots of useful data, both current and historic, that we need to retain. We decide that the most sensible option is for the old system to produce a set of flat data files that are brought across to the new system and loaded in. We draw up specifications of these file formats in agreement with the system programmers on the mainframe who will have to produce them. Chapter 8, *Loading and Unloading Data*, has much more to say about data migration.

There are many deliverables from design; these will vary from project to project. However, every Oracle project will have to deliver a database schema (or schemas if the data is to be distributed) and almost all will deliver some formal module specifications. Samples are illustrated in Table 1-1 and Figure 1-5. The deliverables to and from design are summarized in Figure 1-6.

Table 1-1. Sample Module Specifications

MODULE SPECIFICATION

TITLE	Volume Discount Calculation (B23478)
LANGUAGE	Pro*C
COMPLEXITY	Medium
CALLING INTERFACE	Command Line : B23478 [Invoice Number]
TABLES USED	CUSTOMERS, INVOICES
DESCRIPTION	Compute the total gross invoice amount for the customer over the last six months. If it is a parent company, then include all subsidiaries.

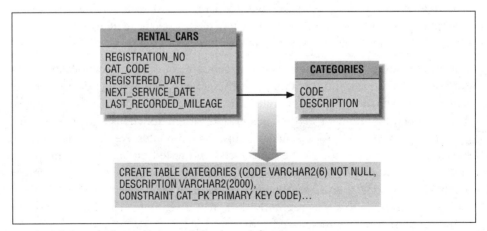

Figure 1-5. Sample data schema and database definition

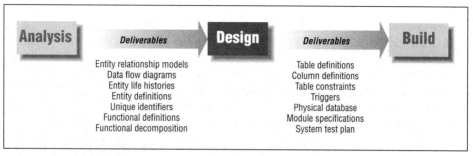

Figure 1-6. Deliverables to and from design

Build and Beyond

After the initial design is complete, we begin the build phase. During this phase, the program modules specified during design are coded and tested. The major deliverables from the build phase are the source and object modules and the unit tests. After the build phase, the project moves into system test and finally into implementation when the new system is commissioned. We won't discuss these phases in any detail here because they are beyond the scope of our emphasis on design. It is, however, important to realize that we should expect issues to be referred back to design (and to analysis) right up to production. If the testing is anything other than perfect (and it rarely is anything like perfect), then we must also expect design-related issues to crop up frequently during early production running.

Successful Project Completion?

It is a sad fact of life that not every project gets to the implementation stage. One especially common cause of failure, simple failure to provide what was expected, is discussed in the next section. Figures vary depending on who you ask, but some believe that as many as 40% of projects are either abandoned completely or are severely reduced in scope along the way. An essential facet of design that we have mentioned only briefly above is risk identification and management. Every project has risks; as designers, we must focus in on technical risks and confront them as early as possible. Once we have identified the risks, we need to articulate them, along with a plan to eradicate or minimize them.

Returning to our case study, we note that the accounts system with which we have to integrate is an aging system written by a third party who has unfortunately gone out of business. There is no documentation for the interface and all

Keeping a Design Log

It is important that you record all of the issues that crop up during your design of a system. You need to record (somewhere…it doesn't matter where) all options that were discussed (even casually), options considered, and final decisions made. You may hold this information in a CASE repository, in a series of well-indexed word processing documents or text files, or even on paper. The important thing is to make absolutely certain that you keep it *somewhere*.

Why are we so emphatic? Because both of us have been burnt in the past when our project teams changed design decisions—in part, because nobody on the project could justify the current state and because all of the arguments were long forgotten. In more than one case, the reason for the original design decision became all too clear a few months later when a serious problem was found with our new improved approach.

The design log also makes excellent background reading for new project members when they join the team; whether they are designers, developers, testers or management, the log will give them an insight into the technical background of the project.

Here is a small extract from the design log for the car rental system:

Design Log

Section: Data Distribution

Initial Thoughts (02/07/95): There is a general feeling that the corporation should move away from the heavy reliance on a central mainframe and go distributed. The main reasons are performance and resilience. These could be addressed by upgrading the mainframe hardware and providing a hot standby machine. The introduction of distributed architecture will not completely remove the reliance on the central server, and the design team remains unconvinced by the theory that in the event of failure of the central host, one of the other servers could temporarily assume its role. We are also concerned that the regional offices do not have the necessary skilled staff to manage a server so all maintenance and administration will have to be done remotely.

⋮

Meeting with Operations (09/07/95): The operations staff are happy that remote maintenance will not be a problem. However, they are concerned about the effect of a distributed database on the lines between offices; they may have to provide more bandwidth. A benchmark is to be set up ASAP.

⋮

Meeting with Oracle (09/27/95): We discussed all the replication options that Oracle can supply and determined that we will predominantly be using read-only snapshot. Oracle has arranged a visit to a reference site so we can see it in operation.

we have to go on is what we can observe from the system we are replacing. We document this risk and consider certain alternative strategies:

1. Buy a new accounts package. Unfortunately other in-house systems use it as well, so this would be a major project in itself.

2. Take the accounts interface modules directly from the old system and use them as much as possible.

3. Develop a layer of software ("middleware") that lies between the application and the accounts package. The application software make simple and well-defined calls to this generic software layer, such as "PostDebit <account> <amount>." The middleware turns this into a call to the current accounting system. The middleware can be developed in isolation of the main application and, when a new accounts package is acquired, we only have to rewrite the middle layer; the application programs are nicely isolated from the internals of the accounting software.

We decide that option 3 is the best alternative and start designing the middleware approach.

Looking at Alternative Methods and Approaches

What we've presented in the preceding sections is a rather traditional approach to database design. That is, even though we've previously said that design usually isn't done all at once, in fact we have shown it happening that way in the car rental example. But when does analysis actually end and design actually begin? Likewise, when does design end and build begin? In most projects, these transitions are not "all or nothing" issues. As parts of the analysis become stable, the designers are already at work familiarizing themselves with the analysis and starting the early design tasks. The periods of overlap are often quite significant. Similarly, as parts of the design stabilize, the programmers can start building modules; this makes particular sense when there are common modules that must be widely called within the application.

During design, there is often an end user and management perception that nothing is being achieved because there are no finished applications components for them to run. Although education may help, this reaction may have serious implications for an overall project. Let's take a brief look at a few alternative methods that may help to allay this perception.

What About RAD/JAD?

One reason that so many projects fail is that they simply don't deliver what the users want or what the business requires. Often what the users want is not exactly what the business requires, and the project guarantees failure by delivering neither. Somewhere along the path through the analysis, design, and build phases, communication has broken down and the requirements have been lost or misinterpreted.

There may be pressure from project sponsors or budget holders to build early to get a subset of the project built and able to be demonstrated as being "on the shelf" as soon as possible. Often when analysis and design are skimped it is mistakenly done so in the name of *rapid application development* (*RAD*) or *joint application development* (*JAD*) methods. We are skeptical about these methods. Would you start building a bridge or manufacturing a car before you had done a full design? Probably not. So why are such methods deemed acceptable in an information technology (IT) development? The answer is that they should not be.

With RAD and JAD methods, the designer/builders of the system sit down with users to develop the system in an iterative process. The designer develops a working prototype and demonstrates it to the users in a workshop session. The users provide input about what they like and what they don't like. The designer takes the input under consideration; he or she goes away and enhances the prototype for a second workshop. The process may go through several iterations until finally the users like what they see and the prototype "becomes" the live application. Usually, there is a time limit or a restricted number of iterations built into the process; otherwise, the users could go on enhancing it forever!

In theory, the RAD/JAD approach should deliver to users exactly the system they want to see. However, there are some extreme dangers in this approach:

- Everyone becomes very focused on the content of screens because they are so visible. Unfortunately, the processing behind the screens and the database or schema design are often neglected.

- There is often a misconception that once the final prototype is agreed upon, the module is complete. The truth is often quite different: the module has not necessarily had to interact with other modules or even the database; it may be nothing more than a pretty screen with a few dummy routines behind it.

- Designing modules in complete isolation of each other leads to inconsistencies and conflicts when they eventually have to be put together for a system test.

—Continued—

- As functionality is evolving on several different fronts simultaneously, someone needs to keep a firm hand on the database structure that is supposed to support the functionality. RAD can become a free for all where tables are "knocked up" and columns are "slapped on" with no regard to the overall effect. The consequence will often be a database that holds redundant or inconsistent data and that performs very badly.

- It is easy to forget to produce documentation when developing in RAD.

RAD or JAD can work, but in our opinion should only be used in cases where all of the following criteria apply:

- The scope of the project and the requirements in business terms are very well defined.

- The project is relatively small and self-contained. By this, we mean that it does not have a lot of external interfaces to deal with.

- The system is very screen-oriented and the usability of the screens is among the top five critical success factors of the project.

- The users are already computer literate, have an understanding of IT development, and are very positive about the idea of the new system.

Where these conditions do not all apply, it may still be possible to use a RAD approach, but to restrict it to a subset of the application.

Moscow Analysis

Whatever methodology you employ on a project, it is always good to have some kind of contingency to fall back on when you are up against the wire. As part of the analysis and design phases, you should always grade the intended functions of the system by importance. One format we like to use is *MoSCoW,* a term borrowed from Clegg and Barker.[*] This acronym is derived as follows:

<u>M</u>ust have
<u>S</u>hould have
<u>C</u>ould have
<u>W</u>on't have

The final category is perhaps the most important: It is essential that we be honest and up front about what we are *not* going to deliver.

---

[*] Clegg, Dai and Richard Barker, *Case Method Fast-Track. A RAD Approach,* Addison Wesley, 1994.

The items in *must have* are the critical deliverables and success factors of the system (must process rentals, must respond to price inquiry in under 5 seconds in 95% of cases, must run 20 hours a day, and so on).

The middle categories (*should have* and *could have*) fit into a *timeboxed* or *cashboxed* structure—in other words, the life of the project is restricted by timescales or budget. According to this scheme, we will develop the *must have* items and as many of the *should have* and *could have* items as we can, in order of priority, until we run out of either money (cashboxed) or time (timeboxed).

Let's apply Moscow to our hypothetical car rental example. The sample list is deliberately controversial.

Must have:
>   Price inquiries take less than 5 seconds in 95% of cases
>   Seamless integration with our third-party accounting software
>   Support for a fourth category of rental car
>   Support for loyalty and volume discounting
>   Screens to support all data entry
>   Take-on of all reference and transactional data from legacy system
>   Complete audit trail of all transactions

Should have:
>   Management reports
>   Support for varying levels of user and security access
>   Support for dial-in home-based users
>   Inquiry screens

Could have:
>   Ability to introduce new discounting schemes in the future
>   Support for ad hoc invoice runs for a single customer
>   Invoices customized to customer requirements

Won't have:
>   Support for archive of old data
>   Ad hoc reporting capabilities

Planning the Design Phase

Earlier in this chapter we provided a quick summary of what goes on during the strategy, analysis, design, and build phases. In this section we provide additional detail about the design phase.

Careful planning is essential to any project or project stage. The planning of the design phase is usually the joint responsibility of the project management and the chief or lead designer (if you have one). The benefits of planning should be obvious to everyone, but we'll examine them anyway. Planning:

- Breaks down a momentous task into small, self-contained, manageable and (above all) achievable steps.

- Provides short- and medium-term goals and milestones, which can act as a yardstick for measuring "actuals" against the plan. This provides early warning of any likely slippage in the plan.

- Identifies the dependencies between tasks (i.e., which tasks must be complete before other tasks can start).

- Determines the *critical path*, those resources (usually an individual person or a team) on whom the plan depends most heavily.

- Allows management to forecast staffing requirements over the life of the project.

- Gives project management a good indication of when the build stage can start.

The last two points are inextricably linked. If you add staff during the design stage, you may possibly be able to move the build date forward. In practice, you can rarely juggle these two parameters since at least one is a "given." For instance, the budget may determine the staffing or, alternatively, the delivery date for the project might dictate the latest date that the build stage must commence. If budget/staffing and delivery are both constrained, then the planning at this stage is essential to ensure that the project can be achieved within the given constraints.

Replanning

Although project sponsors always want plans to be set in stone, experience tells us that such plans simply will not work. As design progresses, ideas and techniques mature and we learn more about the system. Periodic review and re-planning sessions are essential to any planning process. Working to an out-of-date and now unachievable plan is much worse than working to no plan at all. At least when there is no plan, everybody knows the position!

In the hypothetical car rental system, the project manager has an outline plan for a year's project. The design phase is scheduled to take three months using three full-time designers. One designer will concentrate primarily on the database; the second will assume responsibility for screens, reports, and processes; the third will tackle interfaces. The plan currently shows that the person responsible for code (screens, reports, and processes) is on the critical path and may share the work on processes with the interface designer because there is a strong synergy between the two.

Two Phases of Design

In the more traditional models of project development, design is sometimes broken down into two phases *high-level design* and *low-level or detailed design*. This is more relevant for a large project, where an intermediate stage breaks up what would otherwise be an onerous task. High-level design is geared toward solving generic issues and providing a framework and may be replaced by the technical architecture component of a strategy study. Detailed design is where the first physical database cuts are made and individual module specifications are written. In this book, we generally treat design as a single phase for the purpose of semantics. The techniques outlined in this book will apply equally whatever the underlying methodology.

Splitting the work in this way is one sensible staffing option. Another is to section it up by (business) functional areas. Both approaches have their pros and cons. However the work is divided, it is essential that strong communication be maintained between the designers. To this end, our project manager arranges short weekly design reviews where any issues can be brainstormed and resolved.

Design Tasks

Let's now draw up a draft list of design tasks that will collectively produce the deliverables that we have identified for that mythical animal, the "typical Oracle-based project." In this section, we present them in roughly chronological order, although it is impossible to specify a strict order since not all tasks assume that others are complete. Some of the material in the section is expanded later in the book, but we feel it is useful to present it here to provide the "big picture" of design that can be used as a checklist.

Obviously, the time spent on each task will vary from project to project, and some tasks may not be relevant at all on very small-scale projects. Most of these tasks will appear as separate items in the project plan and will warrant at least a small section in the technical specification (which should set out the decisions that you have made). Again, we'll refer to our sample car rental application for meaningful examples.

Design: The Early Days

There are certain decisions and tasks that we must confront at the very start of the design phase. Doing so is very important because deferring them could impact some of the design that has already been completed. These tasks are largely about agreeing upon a strategy and an approach to design, as well as making sure that the necessary infrastructure is in place.

Review and accept the analysis deliverables

This is a hand-over process. Here, we make sure that the analysis is complete and in a fit state from which to design. In practice, this is often an iterative process with the designers questioning the analysis as they begin to understand the requirements. The key check to make here is that the analysis output tells the design team what the application is supposed to achieve and not how to achieve it (otherwise they are stepping on our toes as designers!).

As designers, it is impossible for us to verify that the analysts have covered the entire business areas for the system. We just have to assume that this is so. What we can check are some common-sense concepts and axioms. Here are some examples:

- Does every entity have a unique identifier and at least one non-key attribute?

- Does every entity have at least one function that creates occurrences of it, and at least one function that references it?

- Does every attribute have both a creator and a reader?

If the analysis is held in a CASE repository, there are usually automated checks of this nature that we can run.

In our sample application, we have captured the analysis in Designer/2000. We run some of the completion reports and find that there is no function to create new instances of the RENTAL CAR entity. We notify the analyst, and he creates a new function for us. We also note that some of the functions come with screen designs already sketched out. We do not reject these, since there might well be some useful information captured on them, but we make it clear that we can't guarantee that the screens we'll ultimately design will bear much resemblance to the originals.

Walk through and test designers' understanding of analysis

To put it very bluntly—if you jump in and start designing before you fully understand the requirements, then you will fail, and you will fail badly.

Reading through reams of paperwork or paging through screens of definitions in a CASE product can be a boring and unproductive way to understand the requirements of the system. There is a limit to the amount of information that can be absorbed in this way. Walkthroughs conducted by the analysts are a much better way of getting the designers up to speed with the requirements. It is much more interesting to hear someone present an overview of some area of the business and describe orally how the analysis represents the requirement. These walk-throughs should describe one area of the system, should not be more than an hour's duration, and should be spread out with at least a day between each one. Walkthroughs are a very effective means of gaining a rapid understanding of what the system is (or will be) all about, and they often provoke very informative discussions.

The early days of design are invariably a hard slog. Reading documentation, even broken up with some walkthroughs, will still leave us unsure about many aspects of the required functionality. As designers, we will tend to prematurely start to form pictures of how the system will all be put together. This can lead to misconceptions that are hard to put right.

We need to stop, take a step back, and test our understanding. One good way of doing this is to take a small number of scenarios that we believe are common to the business and to run them through our current understanding of the system. This can take the form of a simple data flow diagram (DFD), flow chart, or a basic writeup of the steps. We should indicate manual procedures and working practices as well as system functions. Take at least one common scenario from conception to completion.

Let's look again at the car rental scenario. We hold a series of mini-workshops with our analysts on the complex discounting process that is a part of the system. We are led through several examples of varying complexity. We test these scenarios against our entity model and function definitions.

Here is a simple scenario that we use to test our understanding:

Customer comes to the desk and asks if we have any stick shift cars for rent.
> The clerk uses CRTS0310—Query cars in stock, using a simple query by example to specify "stick shift." The query is against the RENTAL CAR entity, restricted to our SITE.

The search reveals that there are none currently at this site. Customer indicates a willingness to wait up to 30 minutes if we can get a stick-shift car delivered.
> The search is widened by selecting a nearby site in CRTS0310 and rerunning the query. This has to be run for a single site in turn; there is no "proximity" searching.

The search identifies a stick-shift car at a nearby site and the customer decides to take it.
> A car may not be reserved unless it is either at the site of origin of the reservation or in transit to that site. The clerk presses the "Request Transit" button on the screen. This removes the "currently at" link between the RENTAL CAR and the old SITE and replaces it with an "in transit" link to our site. An alert

(in the form of an urgent email) is sent to the dispatch office at the other site so they know to send the car.

Having reserved the car and requested the transit, the clerk can now process the rental and payment details.

This is an existing customer so the clerk checks the driver's license details against those held in the system, using CTRS0430; this also verifies that this customer is entitled to a loyalty discount.

Identify critical areas

What are the *critical success factors* (CSFs) for the project. For example, is good performance essential? (And if so, is it defined in functional terms such as the length of time that it takes a user to create an order, rather than as the response time at the workstation?)

Let's look particularly at what we mean by "critical." It is quite common for the critical areas to be covered in the initial strategy study, but the emphasis tends to be lost in the detail of the analysis. The term "critical" can mean either vital to the acceptance and success of the project or critical in business or functional terms. Areas of the system that have been identified as critical are good candidates for prototyping. Prototypes can help the designer gain a better understanding; they may also help prove that the demands of the critical area can be met. It is often helpful to prototype more than one approach to the problem, and compare the outcomes.

It is fairly common for new areas to emerge as critical during the design phase. Some functions or areas of the model that are easy to specify in logical terms during analysis can become frighteningly difficult to support when they're viewed from a more physical perspective during the design.

There is a strong affinity between a project's CSFs and its risks. Obviously, if we fail to meet a CSF, then we run the risk that the project will be a failure. We also need to identify other risks which aren't necessarily directly connected to CSFs. Risks can be anything from pushing the leading edge of technology (developing on beta software, for example) to staffing and human risks (such as the risk of not being able to recruit a sufficient number of people with the required skills).

One of the CSFs of the car rental system is that our users embrace the GUI technology that will be new to many of them. We plan to minimize the risk of acceptance by holding a series of workshops at which we demonstrate screens with a series of GUI controls (drop down list boxes, radio buttons, tabbed dialogue boxes, etc.) and a series of color schemes and navigational methods (icons, function keys, menus, etc.) We will ask users for their opinions and preferences and will aim to get the users to sign off on a document of common look-and-feel standards that we'll use throughout development.

Another area of risk is the short(ish) time window for the billing/invoice run. We tackle this by developing the run early in the project to allow plenty of time for testing, optimization, and tuning. We know that online application response time is crucial—usually a customer is waiting, and quite often there is a queue. We agree with the users that a subsecond response is required on 80% of all screen transactions. Throughput is also an issue since the invoice production run has to complete in a 6-hour window, and it may be processing up to 500,000 billing items per run. We decide that using Oracle's parallel option in conjunction with a symmetric multiprocessing system is appropriate. We will also evaluate the feasibility of a distributed database covering our remote locations.

Evaluate system constraints

All systems being developed are constrained in some way—there is no such thing as a bottomless pit! We have already mentioned that the budget and/or implementation date may be fixed. There may be further business constraints, such as the need to check security clearances on staff before they are allowed to start work on a sensitive military project. Other decisions that may have been made (and are irreversible) include hardware platform, software choice, and compatibility with legacy systems, to name but a few. If the project is not completely new, but is an add-on to an existing system, then the number of inherited constraints is potentially quite large. You must check the feasibility of analysis requirements in the light of all of these constraints to see if you are about to attempt Mission Impossible!

In the car rental system, we are constrained by tight timescales for the project. We also have constraints on the response times of the screens and on the throughput that must be achieved by the invoice and billing run. We consider that all of these are achievable and will address them individually during the design.

Determine the target architecture

What do we mean by architecture? Of course, we have to decide on the hardware platform or platforms. But there is something even more fundamental: note that we said "platforms." More than one computer may be involved; in fact, the chances are good this will be the case. We have some additional questions to ask:

- Is the system to be client/server?

- Is the database to be distributed or replicated and, if so, is every participating database Oracle or is it a heterogeneous network?

- Might we need the Oracle Parallel Server to handle the required load or throughput?

We often find that these decisions have been made prior to the design stage. If so, during design it pays to review the basis on which they were made. Quite often there are implications that have not been anticipated. For instance, suppose that you are brought in to design a user-friendly GUI client/server system. Then you learn that access is required to the system by another group of users who have only VT100 character-mode terminals. Clearly, you have to consider your options. You may need to come up with a compromise between, on the one hand, having common applications and ignoring some of the GUI and client/server features and, on the other hand, developing two sets of application software.

If a network is involved in the target environment, you'll have to incorporate some additional tasks into the plan. You will need to define the required service levels of the network and to review or design the network topology. This is the time to formulate contingency procedures and make plans in anticipation of network down time and reduced service. If you plan to utilize an existing network, then you should monitor it to ensure that it has sufficient spare bandwidth to support the new application.

The car rental system will be employing client/server technology. The front-end will run on Microsoft Windows 95 and the back-end will be large UNIX servers. The servers will be symmetric multiprocessors so that throughput of large batch jobs can be optimized. We will be using a distributed database, with each rental site having a local database.

Identify potential bottlenecks in the proposed system

If you are ever told that performance doesn't matter in a computer system, take it with a pinch of salt, or temper the remark to mean that response time is not a critical success factor of the system. Better yet, ask for an explanation as to exactly what the remark means and why response time is not important. Quantify it if possible: Is a response time to an inquiry of an hour acceptable?

As we all know, the bottom line is that performance is always an important factor in any system. Every system will have a bottleneck somewhere. It is a fact of life that once you remove one bottleneck, you will just hit the next one. If you keep removing them, you will—with luck—eventually hit one that is acceptable.

Bottlenecks come in many forms. They can range from unacceptable load on a server due to too many online users running complex inquiries to a limit on a number of batch threads restricting the nightly throughput of jobs. The process of identifying potential bottlenecks can be made easier by drawing a graph of loads during a given time period—a day, a week, or a month.

In the car rental system, early indications are that transactions which need to be distributed across databases will be a major source of bottlenecks for us. We aim to partition and fragment our data across the network in such a way as to keep the number of distributed transactions to a minimum.

Review third-party products

Sometimes, developers and designers jump into the design and build stages of a system with both feet because they are so keen to get on and deliver something. We don't always pay enough attention to code that is already out there. There is an increasingly large number of third-party products on the market that run on an Oracle database. These range from entire suites of applications such as Oracle Financials and SAP, to small utilities such as DBA tools, batch schedulers, security add-ons, etc.

Always take the time to objectively evaluate off-the-shelf products against each other and against a home-grown solution. Appendix A, *Off-the-Shelf Packages*, examines in detail the types of challenges and problems that you may encounter with a purchased solution. If timescales and budget are tight, then a purchased solution may alleviate some of our worries. (Of course, it may also introduce new ones.)

In our car rental system, we decide to evaluate batch scheduling packages which provide more flexibility than the standard UNIX utilities *cron* and *at*. We look specifically at products which record the jobs and runs in Oracle tables. These will allow us to write our own reports against them and programmatically submit requests by simply inserting into a table.

Agree on design and build standards

You will need a set of standards covering such things as naming conventions for database objects, design documentation standards, mechanisms for raising change requests, and so on. You will also need standards that govern how you set out your SQL and PL/SQL and a specific standard for each tool or product you are using for development.

Before you take the time to invent your own standards, find out if your organization has its own set of standards and ask what standards previous projects have used. Many wheels are being reinvented in the world of standards. If you do adopt a set of preexisting standards, be sure to review them and adapt them to the specific needs of your project. You are allowed to reinvent (or at least to refine) a small part of the wheel!

In our scenario, Oracle is new to the organization so we have to develop standards from scratch. However, we find some standards on the Internet that are shareware, and using these as a starting point eliminates a lot of the hard work.

Consider use of CASE tools

You may consider the installation of a CASE tool at this stage. However, if the analysis of the system is not already in a CASE tool, then you will need to weigh the advantages of using CASE against the odious task of retrofitting the current analysis into the CASE product. Some CASE products will allow you to jump straight into design and "reverse engineer" back into analysis.

Despite the popularity of CASE, both of us have severe practical and theoretical reservations about the benefits of reverse engineering a physical database definition. It creates the unfortunate illusion that analysis has been recorded when in reality it almost certainly has not since the information contained within a design is different from that contained within an analysis. It is a little bit like claiming to be able to describe someone's personality by inspecting their wardrobe; you'll get some useful pointers but are unlikely to uncover the whole story.

In our example system, the analysis was captured in Oracle Designer/2000, and we will continue to use this product for the design.

Provide an infrastructure for design and a complete build environment

The design and build processes need hardware and software resources. They also need a mechanism to control all the documentation and code that is produced. We recommend that you deal with these issues in an early stage of the project so the facilities will be available as soon as they are required. Source code control is examined in Chapter 15, *Introduction to Code Design*.

Perform Database Design

The tasks described in this section focus on the actual database design. This is where we design the physical table and column definitions and indexes or clusters to support them, the constraints and triggers that enforce certain rules and integrity controls, and some of the database-resident code.

Ensure a consistent, implementable, and normalized information model

As database designers, we rely heavily on a good information model. The model produced in analysis should not contain any abstruse constructs that cannot be implemented in an Oracle7 database (more on this in Chapter 3). The model should be fully normalized to third normal form (3NF) or to Boyce-Codd normal form (BCNF). You should not need fourth or fifth normal forms (also covered in Chapter 3).

Produce a logical and physical data model

This is the major part of the database side of design. The conceptual model from analysis is translated into a logical design, then into a physical one. Next, a first-cut database is created for development purposes. The logical model will evolve throughout the entire duration of the design as decisions are reached and changes are made. As design progresses into build, the data model should become more stable as physical aspects such as file placement, indexes, and sizing are resolved.

Remember that database design cannot take place in isolation of application or module design. This is particularly true of Oracle7 where business rules may be created as constraints or other database-resident objects such as stored procedures.

The following list identifies the main tasks that need to be accomplished to deliver the working database; for each item in the list, we indicate the chapter in this book where the subject is discussed in detail:

- Identify unimplementable and unusual data constructs in the entity relationship model (ERD) or the entity definitions. (Chapter 3).

- Resolve all arcs and supertypes/subtypes (Chapter 3).

- Review all primary and foreign keys (Chapters 3 and 6).

- Design and implement database denormalizations to speed up query processing of any time-critical applications (Chapter 4).

- Determine which application processes are to be implemented within the database schema as stored procedures (Chapter 16).

- Identify and implement constraints to enforce referential integrity and selected data rules (Chapters 15 and 16).

- Design and build triggers to implement any centrally defined data rules or referential integrity rules that could not be specified as constraints (Chapter 15).

- Develop an indexing and clustering strategy (Chapter 6).

- Perform sizing estimates on all tables, clusters, and indexes (Chapter 9).

- Determine levels of users, and compose and implement a policy for security and audit. Create roles and synonyms to facilitate multiuser access with agreed-upon levels of access privilege (Chapter 10).

- Design the network topology of the database and a mechanism for allowing seamless access to remotely stored data (replicated or distributed database) (Chapter 12).

Create a development database

This is often the job of the development DBA, if you have one. If not, it usually falls into the designer's lap. The developers must have a physical database to develop against; designers need one to test out their ideas and theories. There will normally be several iterations of this database throughout the project and it needs to be strictly controlled. Chapter 15 looks at the issues surrounding source and version control.

For the car rental example, we create instances called DEV1, DEV2, and DEV3. These will be used on a circular basis for development database releases. This round-robin effect ensures that the developers who are in the middle of developing a module are not unduly disrupted by a new database release. We create a further instance called SYS_TEST.

Perform Process/Code Design

In parallel with the data model design, you will need to perform the process design (and ultimately develop your module specifications.) The two are heavily intertwined. The dividing line is especially thin with Oracle7, since this version of Oracle allows processing logic to be contained in the database.

The primary goal of the process design is to take the function definitions from the analysis and map them into modules that will be implemented as a single unit of source code (possibly including shared files such as C header files). These module definitions are then expanded into program specifications. This section describes the main tasks that we have to perform to achieve this goal.

Before you look at the list of tasks, recognize that some of the atomic functions from analysis will not map to a module at all. These will simply be translated into *manual procedures* or *working practices*, in other words, something outside of the computer system. Such procedures will have to be documented in user guides and it is important that you don't lose or overlook them during design. In most cases, these procedures are tasks that couldn't be implemented by a computer system. In some cases, however, we will decide during design to utilize a working practice to implement something that could be achieved on the system. This may be for convenience or simply to save development time.

Determine which build tools to use

You may come into design with no idea of what build tools are to be used. If so, draw up a short list of possible products, and put each one through evaluation. Delaying this decision can have a serious impact on module design and even data model design. Chapter 19, *Selecting the Toolset*, examines some of the currently popular tools for GUIs, screens, reporting, and ad hoc query.

Map functions to modules

We have to develop a list of functions that we will implement from the modules. This is by no means a one-to-one correspondence since the functions are organized by business functionality and we reorganize for ease of development. This means merging some functions that have common or similar functionality and in some cases splitting up a function which is overly complex or turns out to have areas in common with another function when we start designing it. Chapter 15 examines the mapping process in some detail.

In our ubiquitous car rental system, we have a function for working out an ad hoc bill and invoice for a single customer and a function for monthly billing. There is a lot of commonality between these tasks, so we will create a module named "Calculate bill for Customer" that can be called directly from a screen or from the monthly invoicing run. It is passed a customer ID and a pair of dates, and it passes back the amount that the customer is liable for over the given period.

We also have several interface functions that take on data from external systems by reading flat files. Each function has a requirement to open, manage, and read data files and to log errors. We decide to write generic modules to handle these common parts.

Determine program navigation

As part of module design, we map out menus, together with any other "hot key" mechanisms for navigating directly from one application to another. There are two basic types of direct navigation: *with context* and *without context*. Navigation with context means that the target screen is automatically populated with data related to that on the source screen. Navigating without context means that the target screen may not contain any data or may contain unrelated data.

In our car rental system, we devise a flexible navigation system mechanism. For instance, we allow the user to search for a customer record in one window and an available rental car in another; both can be copied into a "context area." With one approach, when the user brings up the "Rent Car" screen, the car and customer details are automatically populated from the context area. Alternatively, the user can go directly to the "Rent Car" screen with no context and perform searches to pull the details in.

Produce module definitions or specification

This is the major part of the functional side of design. During this step, you:

- Loosely translate the functional definitions of the analysis into implementable modules.

- Write a specification which articulates the functionality in physical terms.

- Identify the toolset for coding the applications, and map tools to individual functions.

For each module or code unit, you must develop a specification from which it can be built. These vary considerably in their detail and content from project to project, and even within a project. A module specification for a database-oriented program should, at the very least, list the tables that are accessed, indicating the type(s) of access (insert, delete, query, update, reference). Chapter 15 discusses what should and should not be in a module specification.

For the car rental example, we elect to use a combination of Pro*C, PL/SQL, Oracle Forms, and Oracle Reports as the comprehensive set of tools. We map the business functions into modules. For instance, "Check for cars requiring service" becomes the module "CRB0110: Produce a report of cars requiring service," which is classified as a simple Oracle Report. Because this module is so simple, it has a minimal specification and we estimate that it can be designed, built, and unit tested in four days.

Develop metrics for design and build

Metrics are simply templates for estimating how long a module of code will take to produce. They are covered in detail in Chapter 17, *Metrics, Prototypes, and Specifications.*

Examine the use of generators

Code generators can save us time and enforce a level of consistency in the code modules. If you have a large number of relatively straightforward modules to develop, then a code generator could significantly reduce your timescales. This somewhat controversial subject is covered in Chapter 15.

Develop template code

Template code is another technique for cutting out some of the tedious donkey work from module development. We use a prebuilt module as a starting basis for all new code that comes with some of the common functionality already built in. This technique is also described in Chapter 15.

Later Design Tasks

In this section we identify some of the tasks that can often be legitimately deferred until the later stages of the design phase of the project. In particular, we turn our thought to the planning of system test, taking on of external data, and some of the housekeeping tasks that we may need to specify.

Design for testing

Formulate an overall test strategy that lays out what types of tests you will run and when you will run them. Typically a *unit test* will be run when a single module is completed, related modules will be subjected to *link tests*, and the entire suite of applications will undergo a rigorous *system test* followed by a *user acceptance test*. However, there are many variations on this theme.

In short, it is the designer's responsibility to ensure that the acceptance test criteria set during analysis are met and that the system undergoes sufficient testing so that it is robust and suitable for production environment. Chapter 15 expands on testing methods.

In our sample car rental system, we plan our system testing around some real-life scenarios. These range from the very simple (customer rents a car) to the very complex (customer with loyalty discount wants to rent two compact cars, but we have only intermediate and sports cars in stock at this site).

We are developing our screens in Oracle Forms and we develop a skeleton unit test plan with a list of standard check points that ensure consistency. For instance:

- Go to the last field in each block and press the next-field key. The cursor should navigate to the first field of the next block or (if this is the last block) to the first field of the first block.

- Press the help key (F1) from any enterable field on the screen to ensure that the appropriate context-sensitive help is invoked.

Examine external and legacy systems and data feeds

How many new Oracle databases start off with a completely clean sheet of data, and begin with data entry on day one of their implementation? The answer is almost certainly very close to zero. Most organizations have existing data that is vital to their business and that they want the new application either to reference in place or to take on. Data take-on may be a one-off process, that is, one in which the data is taken from a legacy system that is being decommissioned and loaded into the new one. Alternatively, it may be an ongoing feed with periodic data transfer taking place. Data feeds are one of the major components of a data warehouse application. Chapter 8, *Loading and Unloading Data*, looks carefully at this entire subject.

The car rental system is replacing a legacy mainframe system and has a large once-off take-on of data. This is to be achieved with a series of flat file data loads. There is also an ongoing requirement to interface with the accounts system. The accounts interface will be achieved via a set of interface tables which are loaded from and unloaded to external files for transfer between the system. This interface needs to be as automated as possible.

Specify security, access, and housekeeping requirements

Every system has its own special requirements for security, audit, backup and recovery, event logging, archival, and so on. These requirements are very often not captured during analysis since they are often considered to be "physical" attributes of a system. During design, you must clarify these requirements and identify the mechanisms needed to implement them. Requirements of these kinds (those that are general across the entire system) are ideal candidates for implementation as objects within the Oracle7 database (triggers, stored procedures, etc.).

As part of the definition of security for the system, you must be sure to identify classes of end users at this time.

These topics are examined in detail in Chapter 10, *Safeguarding Your Data.*

The car rental system has a requirement that every financial transaction is logged. We will achieve this by recording details into an audit table using triggers on the tables which hold financial data. Some transactions, such as the issuing of refunds, will have to be approved by a suitably authorized employee before they can be released to the accounting system. We will implement a policy that requires users to change their passwords every four weeks. This will be made part of the login process.

Backup represents a problem for us since we have servers at many of our sites, but no operational staff to operate them. We decide to invest in some backup software that will automate the process so the only human intervention required will be the daily replacing of the tape.

Write functional specification and technical specification

You will package together many of the deliverables from design into a document called a *functional specification*. This document essentially gives the designers the interpretation of the requirements and the proposal of what the system will do. The main purpose of the document is to obtain a user sign-off on the design. For this reason, don't include in this document volumes of technical detail that the user cannot digest or even understand. Rather, make sure that this spec documents all the major design decisions and provides an overview of the database and modules.

Whereas the functional specification is for user consumption, the *technical specification* of the system provides an equivalent document for developers. This document is also a bundle of design deliverables, but it contains more detail.

When CASE technology is employed, the technical specification may consist of a series of reports from the repository.

Ensure completeness of design

Before we begin the build operation, we need to make sure that the design is complete and of the quality required by the project. There are various checks that should be run at this point. A matrix of table usage against module is a useful starting point.

Into build and beyond

As soon as the build starts, the designers can tidy their desks, log off the system, and head off into the sunset confident in the knowledge of a job well done. No, unfortunately, they cannot. The role of the designer usually extends into build and often beyond. What do the designers do during these later stages?

Earlier in this book we pointed out that design is about making the best use of the technology. For this reason, designers need hands-on experience with current hardware and software. Most good designers like to keep their hands in as developers, and they will often form a part of the build team. This may frequently be in a more senior role, such as a team leader.

The following are some of the important ongoing input that the designers can have to a project during the build phase.

- When a module is handed over to a developer for coding, it is useful for the designer who wrote the specification to give a "paper" walk-through of the module and demonstrate any relevant prototypes.

- After the code is written, the designer can participate in code reviews, acting as the *standards police* and the *design decision enforcement agency!*

- Most projects are split into phases to make them more manageable, so large projects don't run for years without delivering anything. As development of one phase begins, there are likely to be further phases of analysis coming along and the cycle begins again. Now there are new constraints to ensure integration with the current phase and you will need to provide additional planning for migration from this phase to the next....Oh well, one day you might be out of there!

2

Why Is Design So Important for Oracle?

This chapter examines why a comprehensive design is vital to the success of an application that uses Oracle as its underlying database technology. The main thing that sets Oracle apart from many other relational database management systems is its ability to support a wealth of different architectures and operating environments. The same application may run on a standalone PC and on a mainframe that supports over a thousand users—whether it can operate efficiently at both ends of the scale depends, of course, on the design. Oracle also offers a rich set of functionality in its products, meaning that there is invariably more than one way of achieving the same result. As designers, we are called upon to decide the most appropriate method for a given requirement.

In this chapter we'll introduce the significant architectures that Oracle supports, including client/server, distributed database, data warehousing, and parallel processing. We'll expand on this discussion in Part III of this book. We'll also present an overview of how to design for a system that will perform optimally. Finally, we'll give an brief list of the features of Oracle7 that are significant to us as designers and a very quick introduction to what's coming in Oracle8 that will have an impact on design.

Designing for Specific Architectures

Sometimes the architecture of the target system must be regarded as a "given." For example, the fact that the users at a particular site already have PCs on their desks and are using them to run other applications may lead us down the road to client/server architecture. Often the constraints documented in analysis force us into a particular option. For example, throughput may be critical for a particular system, and benchmarks may lead us to conclude that the only way of achieving the required throughput is by using Oracle's Parallel Query Option. Whatever the reason, we should always consider the alternatives. Much as many of us would like to use a technology because it is exciting (and looks good on our resumes), we have to be realistic and understand fully the implications of going down a particular technological path.

Let's look at a number of specific architectures that we could target in our design.

Client/Server

In the way that the term, *client/server*, has come to be used, client/server systems are characterized by the fact that the screen, or *client*, is generally on a separate computer from the database engine, or *server*. The client and server may be separated by a *local area network* (LAN) operating at high speeds with a high bandwidth, or possibly by a *wide area network* (WAN) which potentially operates much more slowly and with a lesser bandwidth.

The key to good client/server design is to separate the processing between the client computer and the server computer such that round trips (sometimes referred to as *message pairs*) are minimized. A secondary goal is to keep the size of the messages down. If you follow these design criteria, you will usually find that both the client and the server are doing what they do best. The client is presenting data in an intuitive and user-friendly manner and is gently guiding the user through the transactions. The server is responding to requests for data in a timely fashion and is safeguarding the integrity of the data.

As we design our procedures, we need to consider whether they should reside on the client or the server or both. In exceptional cases, some may be best served by being split between client and server, while others may be implemented in duplicate on both client and server. However, in general, we should place only the management of the user interface at the client and perform all of the application and data logic at the server. Wrong decisions about the location of the processing can have a serious impact on the performance and usability of the system.

As we move towards three-tier architectures, we expect to find the presentation logic in the client, the application logic in the middle tier, and the data logic in the data server. Oracle's Network Computing Architecture (NCA) makes three-tier, and indeed n-tier, applications much more readily accessible to designers. (For more information, see the discussion of the NCA in the later section called "Version 7.3.")

Let's go back to our car rental example. Our users will be running a client/server PC application. What is important for our users is that they be able to process a car return quickly; they need to do this because often the customer is in a hurry, for instance, with a plane to catch. We decide to design the check-in procedure in such a way that when the rental number is keyed, all the information required to complete the transaction is downloaded from the server to the PC and is held locally. It won't necessarily appear on the screen all at once (thereby cluttering it up), but it will be held in the memory or local disk of the PC. When the transaction is complete, only new and modified data is sent back to the server. In Oracle terms, we would have a package of stored procedures on the server that handles requests from the client; the client would never need to directly reference Oracle tables in the server.

For a more detailed discussion of designing for client/server, see Chapter 11. *Designing for Client/Server.*

Distributed Databases

Distributed database systems are characterized by the fact that data management, and the associated data storage, are handled by more than one server. The key to designing a distributed database is to establish the optimal way of splitting the data between the servers. Valid reasons for splitting the data are to improve performance by putting the data closer to its principal user, and to increase resilience by removing the total dependence on a central server. The choices of technology are many.

Some data may be so difficult to partition sensibly that the only solution is to maintain it all at a single server. Other data may be naturally partitioned so that identifiable subsets can each reside on a separate server—for example, data that is based on a geographical location such as country or region may be maintained at the server for that region. Data that is partitioned in this way could be accessed from a remote site with a distributed query, or even updated remotely with a distributed transaction that can update data on multiple nodes simultaneously. An alternative implementation of partitioned data is to have read-only copies of the partition on some or all other servers. These copies, known as *snapshots*, are updated periodically but are never guaranteed to be 100% up to date.

For data that does not necessarily "live" on any particular server, a *multi-master* solution may be more appropriate. This technology allows several nodes to own the same table and update it just like any other local table. However, changes to the table are propagated to all other copies, either synchronously (within the commit unit) or asynchronously (at a later time).

Oracle with SQL*Net supports all of these features via facilities such as *database links, two-phase commits, snapshots, read-only snapshots*, and *replication*.

In our example application, we decide to locate a server in each of our larger sites (which are major airports). The local database contains the details of cars that are currently sitting in the parking lot at that site, waiting to be rented. As soon as the car is rented, the details of the car and the rental agreement are sent to the central server (since we don't know where the car will be returned). All of the billing information comes from the central server, but we elect to keep read-only copies on the local machine for performance purposes. Local taxation information is held on the local servers. We will design a distributed schema based on read-only snapshots (for pricing and reference data) and asynchronous replication (for the database of cars). This schema design enables local offices to continue renting and taking car returns when the central server is down.

For detailed information about designing for distributed databases, see Chapter 12, *Designing for Distributed Databases*.

Data Warehouses

Some applications include requirements for potentially complex management reports. But we stated in our Moscow analysis of the car rental system (see Chapter 1) that management reports definitely do not fall in the scope of this particular project. Why? Developing management reports as part of the project and planning to run them against the operational database is not usually a good idea for the following reasons:

- We can't anticipate all of the reports that users will want. Even the decision makers themselves can't anticipate this. Decision making is a heuristic and iterative discipline; seeing the results of one report often makes us hungry for another.

- The operational database is optimized for transaction-based processing. Complex reports that span many tables are likely to be extremely slow and to drag the performance of the operational system down with them.

The concept behind a data warehouse is that we extract the data from our operational systems, and convert it into a format more suited for complex ad hoc queries. This data is stored in a separate database that is capable of growing very large and retaining historic information that is not necessarily kept on the "live" systems. We add to this database a set of custom-made ad hoc query tools that allow the users to drill down into data of interest, and we let the users loose with the tools. Designing the data warehouse database and data feeds is a radical departure from designing a traditional *online transaction processing* (OLTP) system. There are many new skills to be learned in such designs—for example, *dimensional analysis*.

The management at the car rental company in our example application want to understand regional and seasonal variations and trends in the car rental market. Sometimes a particular location will run out of cars of a particular category on a busy day. On really busy days, locations have been known to run out of cars completely. It is essential for the business to anticipate these surges in demands and to make provisions by transporting cars from one location to another.

For detailed information about designing for data warehouses, see Chapter 13, *Designing for Data Warehouses.*

Parallel Processing

Parallel processing techniques are all about using as much as possible of the available hardware resources by initiating enough activities to keep the machine busy. The most obvious resources are the *central processing units* (*CPUs*) and storage devices, typically disks. The Oracle Server has been specifically engineered to take advantage of multiprocessor machines. Using the Parallel Query Option certain queries can be split up into component parts and each part sent to a different CPU for execution. Parallelism can equally well be applied to disk technology via *striping* techniques that spread the I/O load across disks. We have to assess where we think the bottlenecks will be in our system and whether we think that throughput and server load will really be more of a problem than the limitations of networks, for example.

There are some disciplines and common sense rules that we can follow even if we decide not to use any of Oracle's parallel options. Let's look at one these in the context of our hypothetical car rental system.

The target platform for the car rental system is a UNIX server with four CPUs and 128 megabytes of memory. When the monthly billing run is in operation there will be no other activity on the server; therefore, in the normal course of events three of the CPUs will be mostly idle. In our design, we decide to increase throughput by splitting the run into four chunks of similar size and submitting them concurrently. Of course, we have to make sure that there is no contention between the processes or our clever design might start working against us!

We decide to use RAID 1 technology to provide resilience to single device failure on the database disk volumes since any downtime will cost us money, noting that this also gives us some parallelism in disk I/O.

For detailed information about designing for parallel processing, see Chapter 14, *Designing for Parallel Processing.*

Designing for Performance

Ensuring adequate performance of a system is one of the main objectives of database design. In general, poorly designed Oracle databases will perform badly, and you can't make performance problems go away by simply throwing more powerful hardware at them. The cost of fixing bad design is to redesign, which means discarding a lot of work and starting over. These days, users tend to be less forgiving of systems with poor response time. Their expectations have been raised by the benchmark of their everyday desktop software (e.g., word processing), their perception is that as hardware specifications increase, so too should performance improve in a linear fashion.

Oracle Corporation has recognized the need for high levels of performance and, as a consequence of the trend in hardware technology, has produced the Oracle Parallel Server to allow us to take advantage of clustered and massively parallel systems. Some of the benefits of this architecture are implicit, while others need careful design.

One major cost of not fixing bad design is that the system will be poorly received by the user community and will get a bad reputation. Many users are hardened skeptics because in the past they have been delivered poor systems with unacceptable performance or restrictions.

Almost every aspect of design touches on performance in some way, but the following sections focus on some of the key ones (no pun intended!).[*]

Keys and Indexes

We must select the keys and indexes for our tables with the greatest care. This selection can't be done in isolation from the application code that needs to access them; we must examine the modules and question the users to determine what search or access paths are commonly used to query data. We have to strike a careful balance between query and insert/update operations—the more indexes we put on a table, the more housekeeping Oracle has to do when creating, deleting, or updating rows. We may consider dropping indexes prior to running a heavy-duty batch process that does lots of inserts, updates of keys, or deletes.

In certain cases the placement of the data is crucial for performance. We might consider *clustering* data around a key value so that data with the same key value is physically close. In other cases where we have a fairly static table which is usually accessed by a fully specified unique key, we would probably use a *hash cluster*.

For our sample application, we don't think that any form of clustering is appropriate; however, we do want to define some additional indexes on our tables to improve query response. For instance, we put an index on the REGISTRATION_NUMBER column of the RENTAL_CARS table (the primary key of RENTAL_CARS is CAR_ID) so that cars can be easily found in the system using the unique key

---

[*] OK, we admit it, the pun was intentional.

that the state insists be displayed on the rear of every car (and in most places in the world, on the front as well).

Chapter 6, *Choosing Keys and Indexes*, covers this subject in depth.

Denormalization

Denormalization is the art of selectively storing redundant information within the database. This information is *redundant* if it can be derived from other items in the database. By far the most common form of denormalization is the holding of aggregates and totals on a parent record that could otherwise be computed by working our way through the child records. As with choosing keys, deciding when to denormalize is a balancing act between speeding up query and slowing down data manipulation.

There are sometimes viable alternatives to denormalization. If we have a report that is likely to be extremely slow without extensive denormalization, we may prefer to write a pre-report extract routine that copies the relevant data into a set of temporary holding tables that are structured to make the report run much more quickly.

In our example application, we create a column on the CUSTOMERS table called OUTSTANDING_INVOICE_AMOUNT that is the total of the INVOICE_AMOUNT column in all rows of INVOICES for that customer where the STATUS is not 'PAID.' This enables us to do quick credit checks for any customer without having to read through their invoices. We define triggers on the INVOICES table that maintain this value. For instance, when the STATUS column is updated to 'PAID'. the INVOICE_AMOUNT is subtracted from the OUTSTANDING_INVOICE_ AMOUNT on the CUSTOMERS table for that customer.

More information is available in Chapter 4, *Deciding When to Denormalize.*

Choosing the Optimizer

Oracle7 offers us the choice of two optimizers, each providing a different approach to making your SQL queries optimal. The traditional *rules-based* approach uses a series of well-defined rules to determine which access paths to the data are preferable to others. The *cost-based* approach attempts to be more intelligent and to make informed decisions based on its knowledge of the relative size and distribution of the data.

Perhaps it ought to be the case that you can freely switch between the two modes of optimization without having to worry about how you designed and wrote the system. The truth is that you really need to design with a method of optimization in mind; there will almost certainly be times when you know the optimal path to your data better than the optimizer does, and you will need to influence the optimizer to select this path.

Since the car rental system is a brand new project and is not using any older code, we decide to opt for the cost-based optimizer. We feel comfortable knowing that if the distribution of our data changes radically, the optimizer of our choice should be able to adapt automatically.

Deciding on an optimizer is heavily linked to an indexing strategy and is covered in Chapter 6.

Coding Techniques

Most of the performance techniques we have looked at have focused on the database. We also need to focus some attention on the methods we employ when developing our code. We have already mentioned some of these methods in the discussion of client/server. For example, we write common and database-intensive code in stored packages and procedure. We have also decided to cache nonvolatile data locally to speed up pricing.

We might look at other ways of reducing the number of calls between the application and the Oracle server. For instance, most Oracle-supplied tools allow you to use the *array interface* which processes a set (array) of database rows in a single *fetch* operation for queries, or a single insert, update, or delete for data maintenance operations.

Other Design Considerations

This section discusses some additional features of relational databases that we need to consider in making database design decisions.

Very Large Databases (VLDBs)

Most modern databases are expected to be able to cope with gigabytes, if not terabytes, of data. The data is likely to be growing year after year at some phenomenal rate, and the rapid expansion of the data must not have an adverse effect on performance. The database and the data within it must remain manageable and controllable. DBAs will not be able to cover up the cracks of a poor design that did not anticipate high data volume, no matter how skilled they are.

Fortunately, the Oracle Server is able to cope with large volumes of data, usually without any adverse effects on performance. The main role that the designer has to play is in sizing the various database objects and schemas and in performing the best possible capacity planning so that the anticipated growth will not cause any problems.

Time Series (Temporal) Data

Since relational systems view data in tables, the data is two-dimensional by its very nature. When you try to add dimensions (thus making it multidimensional), you have to make some adjustments. If you fail to adapt, you'll end up with a system that produces unexpected results or a system that produces expected results, but takes an eternity to do so. Many projects have managed to produce code that takes forever to give the wrong answer, which is the worst of both worlds.

The most common dimension that you are likely to add to a table is that of time; when you update a row, you need to keep the old values so you have a complete history of the data. This may be required either for audit purposes or to enable you to do transactions as if you were at some date in the past (for example, apply last month's prices to an invoice run). Typically, you will add columns to each row in the table (such as DATE_TO and DATE_FROM). Don't be deceived by how easy this may appear at first glance; there are many complications lying beneath the surface, and discussed more fully in Chapter 7, *Dealing with Temporal Data.*

In our car rental example, we add the column pair (DATE_TO, DATE_FROM) onto our BILLING_RATES table. This allows us to recalculate invoices from the past, if we ever need to do so.

Interfacing with Other Systems

Unfortunately, very few projects start from scratch. When you commission an application, there is invariably a batch of initial data to take on from legacy systems. This may be reference data, transactional data, or both. Similarly, very few computer systems run in blissful isolation of the world around them—they will usually need to exchange data with other applications on other systems.

There are many ways of exchanging data. The flat file interface is still quite common because of its simplicity. The "data providing" system dumps data out in a predefined format to a file. The file is transferred to the "data receiving" system where a utility reads the file and updates the database. However, with modern network technology, it is possible for an interface to read directly out of one system and write to the other in a single step. Each interface needs to be evaluated to determine the most appropriate transportation mechanism for the data. One important factor, of course, is how "current" the system that receives the data needs to be. Loading data overnight means that by the end of the day the data is 24 hours out of date. For volatile data, this might not be acceptable.

Chapter 8, *Loading and Unloading Data,* explores the various options and their implications.

Let's go back to the car rental system. We plan several data loads from the legacy system that we are replacing. Each is a flat file with fixed-length records since that is the easiest format for the developers on the legacy system to produce. Once the new system is live, we will have an outbound interface to the accounts software through a set of intermediate tables which we write to and the accounting software reads. We also plan an inbound interface. There is a "quick returns" facility for customers who are returning cars in a hurry. They simply complete some details on the original rental agreement and post it into a box when returning the car. Using bar code readers and Optical Character Recognition (OCR) devices, we capture the data into a file that is loaded overnight.

Designing for Oracle7

As we said earlier, design is about making the best possible use of the material and technology available. When you are designing for Oracle, you'll find that the specific release of Oracle to be used for the build is a major factor in making design decisions. The later the version, the more features it is likely to contain.

We assume in this book that you already has a good deal of experience of Oracle. In this section, we do not attempt to give a complete description of Oracle7, but simply to cover some of the features that have a major impact on design and to explain briefly why they are important.

NOTE   If you know Oracle7 well, you may want to skip this section. How-
               ever, make sure that you have a good knowledge of these features:

- Triggers and stored procedures
- Shared pool
- Buffer pool
- Declarative constraints
- Read-only tablespaces
- Symmetric replication
- Manual partitioning

Be aware that many Oracle customers today are running multiple instances on multiple servers and are extremely unlikely to be able to keep all of their instances in step. In other words, at any given point in time, they may be running different instances under different versions of Oracle—even if all of the instances are operating on the same server. There are a number of reasons why this might occur; the simplest (and perhaps the most common) is that it allows a new release to be tested before being put into production.

More complex situations arise when a site has multiple hardware platform types because Oracle does not release versions at the same time for every platform that they support. Indeed some versions never appear on certain platforms.

One of the great features of Oracle over the years has been that code which runs successfully against one release of Oracle will (in general) run against the next version. Oracle Corporation has gone to considerable lengths to ensure that the versions remain compatible in this way. Exceptions to this rule have occurred mainly in the transition from Oracle Version 5 to Oracle Version 6. For most readers, this fact is now of purely historical interest, although rumors abound of sites around the world which are still running production systems using Oracle Version 5. We do know of one multinational which in June 1996 had several Oracle Version 5 sites in Europe; part of their justification has been that the application was still meeting its performance goals and that there was therefore no reason to disturb it.

Note, though, that when or if a change is made to a version of Oracle, such as adding new reserved words to Oracle's implementation of the SQL language, you will have a choice to make: You can either run in compatibility mode (which makes at least some new features unavailable) or ensure that the reserved word has not been used anywhere in the application as an object or column name.

In the sections that follow, we don't consider software licensing issues. Note, though, that many of the features described are only available as extra-cost options. Since Oracle's charging policies on these options are subject to change, we recommend that you check the status of your own licenses with Oracle before assuming that a particular feature will be available to you on all of the relevant platforms.

Version 7.0

This section summarizes the key features of Oracle Version 7.0 that have a significant impact on design.

Triggers, procedures, and functions

The original releases of Oracle7 introduced the concept of being able to store and execute code within the database engine either in the form of triggers that could be applied to tables, or as procedures and functions that could be called from the client application through PL/SQL anonymous blocks.

PL/SQL, Oracle's portable and proprietary 3GL, underwent a major upgrade between Version 6 and Version 7.0, but it still remains somewhat limited in its scope. Although the language has a number of features which make it both attractive and effective for implementing data rules and business rules within the data schema, we think that it lacks sufficient power and flexibility to be a realistic option for writing a complete application.[*]

From an architectural viewpoint it is important to realize that the PL/SQL engine is essentially independent of the SQL engine and is made available by Oracle in other environments such as Oracle Forms and Oracle Reports.

A key element of design for Oracle7 involves creating an effective distribution of functionality between application code and database-resident code.

Cost-based optimizer

Version 7.0 also introduced Oracle's cost-based optimizer (which we mentioned above in the section called "Choosing the Optimizer"), along with the new SQL statement ANALYZE for collecting statistics. Although the new optimizer brought a number of benefits, the performance of cost-based optimization failed to meet the expectations of many of Oracle's customers who continued to use the (old) rules-based optimizer for their existing applications (and, in some cases, for new applications). The Version 7.0 cost-based optimizer fails to take account of the distribution of key values, and also has no cost model for the execution of query predicates.

One major feature of the cost-based optimizer is that it allows the code writer to instruct the optimizer how to execute the query by using a hint rather than having to use obscure side effects, as in previous versions of Oracle. The traditional way of insisting on a full table scan, even if a suitable index was available, used a construct such as:

```
SELECT  e.employee_name
FROM    employees e
WHERE   NVL(e.division, NULL) = 'SALES'.
```

whereas with the cost-based optimizer, the same effect can be achieved with the rather more rational form:

```
SELECT /*+ FULL E */ e.employee_name
FROM    employees e
WHERE   e.division = 'SALES'.
```

---

* However, Steven Feuerstein has done some amazing things with the language. See *Oracle PL/SQL Programming* (O'Reilly & Associates, 1995) and *Advanced Oracle PL/SQL Programming with Packages* (1996).

This second form has the considerable performance advantage of not applying a totally redundant function to every row in the table. SQL functions are not especially inefficient, but the language is executed interpretively and the cost of function execution is an overhead best avoided.

NOTE   As an aside, most books and courses on Oracle advise the use of concatenation or addition to suppress the use of an index. For example:

```
WHERE e.division || '' = 'SALES'
```

or

```
WHERE e.deptno + 0 = 30
```

It may be helpful to note that in every Oracle version that we've tested, the NVL function was measurably faster than both concatenation and addition.

The ability to control optimization of queries is of benefit to the designer, giving more flexibility in the database design by removing some of the obstacles caused by the need to avoid certain programming constructs which are likely to perform poorly. However, as we discuss later, you have to wait for Version 7.3 to get the advantage of an optimizer that takes into account the actual distribution of data values.

In Oracle Version 7.0, significant changes were also made in the optimization of distributed joins, removing some major performance problems.

Declarative constraints

In addition to the ability to define triggers against tables, Version 7.0 also implemented declarative constraints beyond the previously available NOT NULL constraint. This extension had originally been planned for Oracle Version 6, which supported the syntax but not the enforcement. One of the things that has never ceased to amaze technical auditors since the introduction of Oracle7 has been the apparent unwillingness of designers and DBAs to use declarative constraints—a feature that has been found to be both effective and efficient.

Use of declarative constraints has a major impact on design. In particular, using FOREIGN KEY constraints will influence the design of look-up or reference tables. Although declarative constraints provide significant data integrity benefits, they operate at the command level rather than at the transaction level. This means that so-called "interim violations" are trapped.

Distributed database

Version 7.0 also added DML (INSERT, UPDATE, DELETE, LOCK, SELECT FOR UPDATE) to SQL*Net's existing support for distributed database operations by implementing a completely transparent form of *two-phase commit (2PC)*. This was extremely effective but not widely used for a number of reasons discussed in Chapter 12, *Designing for Distributed Databases*. Designing a network topology and distributing data between the nodes opens up a whole new discipline in Oracle design.

A new database object type, the *snapshot*, was introduced and a mechanism provided which allowed changes to a table at one site to be moved to other sites (the snapshots) at stated intervals. This mechanism contained a number of design and implementation defects which have been addressed in later versions.

Server performance

Version 7.0 also set out to address a number of the performance issues which had been apparent in Version 6, and made major changes to the way that the SQL engine managed its caches.

Oracle has always used dynamic rather than static SQL; that is, the execution plans used for individual SQL statements are determined at runtime rather than during an earlier program preparation stage. Thus, every time a process wanted to execute a SQL statement, it had to present it to the database engine where it was parsed and optimized before being executed.

An area called the *shared pool* was introduced in Version 7.0. Among other benefits, the shared pool allowed one user to take advantage of the execution plan built by another. A series of steps can be taken within client applications to maximize the effectiveness of this feature.

Earlier versions of Oracle had tended to suffer from excessive network message rates when used in client/server configurations, and Version 7.0 formally introduced the concept of compound calls. (These had been present in varying forms in a number of earlier versions.) The significance of this support is discussed in Chapter 11, *Designing for Client/Server*.

Other significant features

Of the many other features that arrived with Oracle7, we will single out two that have some impact on design.

The first is the extended support for *binary long objects (BLOBs)* that enables us to hold up to two gigabytes of data in a single column. BLOBs let us hold data items such as graphics or word processing documents without having to artificially span rows. However, although piecewise retrieval was supported in Version

7.0, the entire BLOB had to be inserted at once, making for an effective size limit of perhaps one megabyte. The database space management routines were not tuned to handle BLOBs, introducing some further inefficiencies.

The second enhancement is in the area of security, where the addition of *roles* and *profiles* eased some of the problems of designing the security subsystem of less demanding applications. Data-sensitive security (for example, this user can only see the salaries of employees in divisions 21, 22, and 25) remains an application responsibility.

Version 7.1

Based on Oracle's experience with Version 7.0, Version 7.1 introduced new features aimed at both administrators and developers. Both sets of features turned out to be highly relevant to effective design.

Dynamic SQL within PL/SQL

One of the uses of stored PL/SQL procedures in Version 7.0 was the encapsulation of application functions—that is, inviting the client application to call a single procedure to achieve a result, rather than expecting it to issue all the required SQL. It transpired that this worked well for updates but poorly for queries since the caller would invariably need to supply the selection criteria. This left the PL/SQL procedure with a very high number of possible SQL queries that might have to be issued; to resolve this situation, Version 7.1 provides a mechanism to allow stored PL/SQL procedures (and functions) to issue true dynamic SQL. The procedure can build up its own SQL query in a VARCHAR and then execute it.

This facility gives the designer freedom to specify a middle layer between the application and the database that removes the dependency on database structure within the application. By doing so, it also frees the application from Oracle-specific code and makes it easier to port to other database management systems, although it is probable that this benefit was not sought by Oracle itself.

Multiple triggers

As more and more use was made of table-level triggers for complex validation and cross-posting between applications, users found that install scripts were liable to fail when creating the required trigger on a particular object because a trigger already existed with the same trigger timing. In Version 7.1, therefore, tables are allowed to have multiple triggers on the same event with the same timing. Using this feature, any number of install scripts can place independent mechanisms on the same table to ensure that they are each informed independently of changes to the table.

The implication for design is that we can map each business or data validation rule to a separate trigger, rather than having to combine several nonrelated business rules into one functional trigger specification.

PL/SQL functions within SQL

As discussed earlier, the PL/SQL engine is essentially independent of the SQL engine. In Version 7.1 it is possible to call a PL/SQL function from within SQL. For example:

```
CREATE OR REPLACE FUNCTION cube (x IN NUMBER)
RETURN NUMBER IS
BEGIN
  RETURN x ** 3;
END;
```

Such a call makes the SQL language extensible with queries like the following:

```
SELECT e.emp_name
     , e.basic
     , t.gross
  FROM employees e
      ,emp_year_totals t
 WHERE e.emp#   = t.emp#
   AND t.year   = 1995
   AND t.gross >= CUBE(e.basic)
 ORDER BY t.gross/e.basic DESC;
```

This causes a number of potential problems since PL/SQL has persistent package variables and is also capable of issuing DML commands. Oracle has provided mechanisms to declare the *purity level* of a PL/SQL function, that is, the extent of its possible side effects, such as making database changes.

If you are going to use PL/SQL functions within SQL you should test them during design for use during the build. We advise against using PL/SQL functions within SQL statements unless the functions were designed especially to be called from SQL.

Read-only tablespaces

Oracle maintains header blocks in its data files that tell the database engine, among other things, which is the oldest redo log that must be available for a valid start-up to take place against file. Before Version 7.1 this meant that all data files had to be regularly backed up, even if the administrator knew that they had not been changed, because otherwise at recovery time Oracle would insist on processing all of the recovery logs from the date of the oldest file forwards.

In order to reduce backup (and recovery) times for databases containing a high percentage of static data, Version 7.1 also introduced the ability to change the status of a tablespace to read-only. Once such a tablespace has been backed up, it does not need to be included in any subsequent backup because the recovery code is aware that the data within it cannot have changed since the original backup, and will not ask for recovery logs to process against the files within the tablespace. This is ideal for large tables of archive data, and has reduced the routine backup volume by more than 90% at some sites. The penalty is that some data partitioning may be required in order to establish a section of the data which can be declared as read only.

When you are designing the physical database placements, you may wish to separate volatile and nonvolatile data and place the nonvolatile in a read-only tablespace. Take this placement into account when you plan the backup strategy with the DBA.

Parallel Query Option (PQO)

Oracle always had a reasonably scalable architecture by virtue of the fact that every user had a dedicated Oracle server process in addition to the background processes that perform Oracle housekeeping and database writing. The user processes allow processing for different users to be distributed among all of the available CPUs in a symmetric multiprocessing (SMP) environment. This architecture, however, has little effect on a single process running a large and complex SQL query. The Parallel Query Option in Version 7.1 enables a single full table scan query to be split up and distributed to multiple CPUs. The Parallel Query Option should be capable, for any given full table scan query, of driving either CPU utilization or (more often) disk I/O to 100% of capacity.

When you are designing batch processes and complex reports, you must identify modules that could take advantage of this feature and determine the optimum number of processes that it should use on the target production platform(s). Also, be sure to discuss with the DBA how the target table can be "striped" across multiple disks.

PQO can also have a dramatic effect on index build time.

See Chapter 14, *Designing for Parallel Processing*, for additional information about parallel processing.

Version 7.1.6

Version 7.1.6 introduced a few additional features that have an impact on design.

Symmetric replication

The 7.1.6 sub-version saw the first production release of Oracle's symmetric replication support, which allows multiple copies of the same data to be held at different sites and updated independently with asynchronous or deferred change propagation and conflict detection and resolution.

In order to specify the replication actions which are required within a distributed environment, Oracle has implemented a series of packaged procedures called *RepCat* (replication catalogue) to perform the maintenance of all the data dictionary objects required o support replication.

The data change propagation mechanism uses *asynchronous RPCs* (remote procedure calls). These, in turn, use two-phase commits to ensure the integrity of tracking the passing of actions from one database instance to another. The asynchronous RPC facility is also available to user application code within PL/SQL running on a database server.

Chapter 12 goes into some detail about the considerations that you need to take into account when you contemplate using asynchronous updates. We hope that it is obvious why an asynchronous operation cannot be a query: the reason is that it has no way of returning any result to the original caller who has long since moved on to performing some other operation.

Shared pool

Earlier versions of Oracle7 suffered from a number of problems with the management of the shared pool. A full analysis of these problems is outside the scope of this design book, but the key difficulties have been with the way in which triggers were cached, and the tendency of the pool to become highly fragmented.

As mentioned earlier, a major use of triggers is to take ancillary action when changes are made to a database table. As might be expected, Oracle's symmetric replication support makes considerable use of triggers, and a number of steps were taken in this version to reduce the problems occurring with the shared pool.

Version 7.2

This section describes the Version 7.2 features you'll need to pay special attention to during your design.

Manual partitioning

Version 7.2 introduced limited support for data partitioning in the form of "manual partitioning." Put simply, under certain restrictive conditions, the query optimizer in Version 7.2 can push join predicates down into a UNION ALL view.

Imagine that we have two tables, ORDERS and OLD_ORDERS, with identical columns and indexes, and that we declare a view ALL_ORDERS as:

```
SELECT * from ORDERS
UNION ALL
SELECT * from OLD_ORDERS;
```

The query:

```
SELECT c.cust_name , o.order_date , o.order_value
   FROM customers  c
       , all_orders o
  WHERE c.zip   = 12345 AND c.cust# = o.cust#;
```

will now be executed as:

```
    SELECT c.cust_name , o.order_date , o.order_value
       FROM customers c
           , orders o
      WHERE c.zip   = 12345 AND c.cust# = o.cust#
UNION ALL
    SELECT c.cust_name , o.order_date , o.order_value
       FROM customers c
           , old_orders o
      WHERE c.zip   = 12345 AND c.cust# = o.cust#;
```

In contrast, in earlier versions the view would have been instantiated before the join took place. View instantiation involves building the temporary table described by the view and then applying any join conditions and predicates against it; for highly selective queries against large tables, the performance implications are disastrous.

This feature has special significance when designing multidimensional tables such as temporal or spatial data where use of this technique is commonplace. It can also be useful when designing archive strategies where you may need to periodically process archived data and current data together.

PL/SQL scheduler

Version 7.2 also contains a PL/SQL scheduler, which allows the user or developer to set up PL/SQL tasks to run at specific dates and times, and to repeat at specified intervals. This goes some way towards addressing the lack of a bundled batch scheduling subsystem with Oracle7.

Nonblocking calls

Another feature long sought by designers using Oracle had been the ability to ask Oracle to do something without having to wait for a response. This was introduced in Version 7.2 in the form of nonblocking calls available from the **Oracle Call Interface** (OCI), which is typically used from either C or C++.

Many years ago, after Oracle Corporation released its Version 1 precompilers, which allow SQL calls to be coded directly into 3GLs such as C and COBOL, the company announced its intention to drop support for OCI. For a number of technical reasons, this move was strongly resisted by the software vendors who sell software to work with Oracle; most importantly OCI allows a cursor to be freely passed by reference from one routine to another, making it possible to write general-purpose code that will handle any number of cursors. Since Oracle made some internal changes to bring OCI up to date in Version 7.0, the availability of nonblocking calls in Version 7.2 means that there is now another important piece of functionality which can be obtained only through the call interface.

Nonblocking calls are especially attractive in situations where the application may be connected to several instances at once and may wish to initiate actions in parallel across each of the instances. The feature also allows the GUI designer to attempt to retain the user's interest by displaying some form of animation on the screen while awaiting server response.

Using OCI comes at a development cost, as it generally takes longer to develop than equivalent code written using the Oracle precompilers. You will have to weigh the benefits against the costs and maybe investigate the feasibility of using a combination of the two technologies. In older versions of Oracle, using OCI could result in programs which ran many times slower than the equivalent Pro*C or Pro*COBOL program. This penalty has been removed in Oracle7, but users are still most unlikely to see any performance improvement resulting from the use of OCI.

Version 7.3

The release of Version 7.3 presents a large number of major new features. In fact, as a number of Oracle speakers have already observed at conferences and briefing sessions, the only reason that Version 7.3 is not called Oracle8 is that the name was reserved many years ago for an object-oriented extension to Oracle.

Shared pool

Under Version 7.3, Oracle has reimplemented the way in which triggers are managed within the data dictionary, in addition to making improvements in the cache management of stored procedures. This should remove a number of the performance-related concerns that currently surround the use of stored procedures in general, and triggers in particular.

Value histograms

The cost-based optimizer for Version 7.3 has access to the distribution of column values for each indexed column, and even for nonindexed columns. Although this feature is definitely good news, it raises at least three cautions:

First, the value histograms are of *column* values rather than *key* values. Of course, these are exactly the same thing for single-column indexes, but they are very different things for concatenated indexes. As a result, there are still a number of cases in which the cost-based optimizer still has no good data on which to base the decision about whether or not to use a concatenated index. This is an issue in the common case where the leading columns are not particularly selective and have a low number of distinct values but the combinations of these values are highly selective.

Second, the query optimizer in Version 7.3 still does not have a model which takes into account the CPU load of executing predicate clauses. Earlier versions of the cost-based optimizer were found to have a strong tendency to use full table scans for predicate clauses that would execute faster using index range scans. A series of tests on Version 7.3.2 found that, although in some cases the optimizer adopted a full table scan in situations where an index range scan would have been faster, in other cases it chose an index range scan where a full table scan would be faster.

Third, Oracle has not extended the use of value distributions to optimizing queries that use bind variables. A query such as:

```
SELECT COUNT(*) FROM trades WHERE currency = 'NOK'.
```

is relatively simple to optimize if there is an index on currency and we have a histogram which tells us that the value NOK occurs in less than 1.25% of cases. However, if the same histogram also tells us that the value USD occurs in just over 85% of cases, then there is no single correct optimization for:

```
SELECT COUNT(*) FROM trades WHERE currency = :curr;
```

and we must know the value of the bind variable before we can pick a good access strategy. This is a particular issue since over the years programmers working on high performance applications have had it drummed into them that bind variables, like *:curr* above, are the preferred approach in order to leverage the shared pool and save parse time. The problem arises because Oracle has maintained its traditional approach of optimizing each parse tree before its first execution and then using the same query plan for subsequent executions.

Unlimited extents

In Version 7.3, objects (tables, indexes, clusters, rollback segments, temporary segments) can each have an unlimited number of extents within the database. This feature is very helpful to DBAs. For the designer, this feature reduces the potential penalty of errors in space planning.

Bitmap indexes

Prior to Version 7.0, Oracle supported only B-Tree indexes. Hash clusters were added in Version 7.0 but have not proved to be particularly attractive to designers and implementers. Hash clusters appear to be relatively little used, and there are reports that those who have used them have not seen the expected performance gains.

In Version 7.3.3, Oracle supports bitmap indexes in the server (they have been used for some years in the SQL*TextRetrieval product); these can be highly effective for less selective keys such as foreign keys to code tables, especially when such conditions are ANDed together in the WHERE clause.

New join strategies

Oracle's traditional join strategies for equijoins have been nested loop joins and sort merge joins. These approaches are both highly effective, but they yield poor performance under certain types of conditions commonly found within data warehousing and OLAP applications.

In Version 7.3 Oracle offers both "star joins" and "hash joins." The query optimizer can deploy these separately or together.

The *star join* seeks to make sense of queries where a central fact table is joined to a number of lookup tables, each of which may have predicates against it but none of which are joined to each other. It is this lack of interrelationship that the star join seeks to exploit by first forming the Cartesian product of all of the qualifying rows from the lookup tables, and then joining this to the fact table. Star joins are particularly pertinent for data warehouse applications.

The join operation, depending on the volumes, may be best conducted as a *hash join* in which the engine tries to use hashing techniques as an alternative to performing a full sort of each of the relations followed by a merge stage.

Star joins have been implemented "by hand" in a number of applications by building the Cartesian product in a user-defined table, and have been shown to provide very significant performance benefits over the clumsy approach traditionally taken by Oracle's optimizers in this special case.

Network Computing Architecture (NCA)

As Oracle's networking products have developed from the original SQL*Net, the communication capabilities have been expanded to include not only the execution by a client of SQL statements at a server, but also the passing of remote procedure calls.

In the new Network Computing Architecture (shown in Figure 2-1), Oracle has published a series of standard interfaces to allow *cartridges* or named services to make and respond to requests from other cartridges. These cartridges, which can include relatively traditional clients and servers, are not formally arranged in a hierarchy, but each interacts with a common connectivity layer. There are clear analogies here with the use of the World Wide Web and, indeed, Java is specifically supported as one of the languages in which cartridges may be written. We must also expect that Oracle will promote its own Network Computer (the NC) as a prime user interface device for running cartridges written in Java.

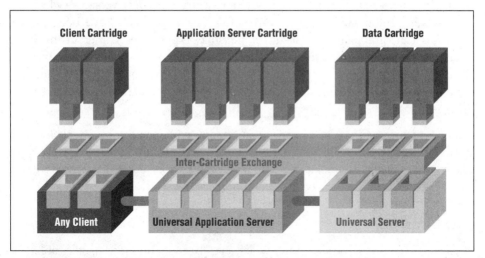

© Copyright Oracle Corporation. Reprinted with permission.

Figure 2-1. Oracle Network Computing Architecture (NCA)

Of perhaps even more interest to designers (who are looking at how to meet complex server requirements in an Oracle environment) is the ability to use PL/SQL calls to make requests of another cartridge. This facility is very new at the time of writing, and neither of us has had the opportunity to build anything using it. However, it seems to offer a flexible method of "calling out" from inside Oracle to any cartridge service. Traditionally, the design options have been limited to calling out to other Oracle instances using SQL or PL/SQL, and calling out to other database engines through Oracle's transparent gateway services.

A large number of third-party vendors have signed up as Oracle partners to supply cartridges of various types, and we are watching this development with great interest. When we write the second edition of this book, we confidently expect to have a great deal to say about the approaches which need to be taken to make effective use of data cartridges, as well as on the costs and benefits of using the features that are going to arrive in Oracle8.

Introducing Oracle8

Many Oracle watchers expected that Oracle would announce Oracle8 at the joint Oracle Open World and International Oracle User Group meeting in San Francisco in November 1996, but the conference passed with very few formal statements from Oracle staff about the content or timing of Oracle8. It is acknowledged by Oracle that a number of customers and partners have beta copies, but one of the major lessons we've learned over the years is that the production code of any given version can be markedly different from the beta versions (which can themselves exhibit quite marked variations). Features which have been already included can disappear as a result of negative experiences earlier in the cycle, although this is unusual. More often, features undergo substantial changes in the light of user experience during the beta program. For this reason, we normally recommend against basing design decisions on beta code whenever it can be avoided.

These comments may be especially important with respect to Oracle8, which contains new functionality primarily targeted at supporting substantially larger databases than at present. It has also been long expected that the new version will have some support for *object orientation (OO)* within SQL.

Partitioning

The most important new feature which has been announced is the ability to declare a *key-partitioned table*. A key-partitioned table is one where the logical table is defined as a series of columns and constraints, and then a series of physical partitions are defined in which to store the rows, with each partition being assigned to a particular range of values for the partition key. In this book we make a number of references to the steps that designers can take within Oracle7 to achieve many of the benefits of partitioned tables, but clearly it is preferable for them to be directly supported by the data server. A major goal is to make the partition, rather than the table itself, the unit of recovery and also to permit partition indexes with the optimizer enhanced to take full advantage of the indexing structure.

We caution that there is a major issue here with respect to unique keys which need to be enforced at table level rather than at partition level. If the partition key (the field that determines into which partition a row is stored) is part of both the primary key and all other unique keys, then there is little problem,. However, if this is not the case, then a table-level index is needed to enforce uniqueness.

Not for the first time, designers must expect to be confronted with the need to compromise. In this case, they must choose between the penalties of a table-level index (create time, space usage, single point of failure for all partitions) and the data integrity risk of not applying the constraint.

Forward Compatibility from Oracle7

The only major potential compatibility problem that we're currently aware of is that the format of the rowid has been changed so much that there are now actually two forms of rowid. The shorter form is all you need to reference a row of a named table, and there is a longer form that uniquely identifies any row within the database.

Although these changes will almost certainly invalidate a large number of scripts that DBAs have written over the years to survey tables, there should be very few applications which rely on the internal structure of the rowid. The shorter form (which is all that is required for SELECT ROWID...FOR UPDATE) will fit into the 18 bytes which should have been allocated for the old form. We are tempted to observe that any application suites that are currently using the internal format of the rowid do not deserve to be able to migrate to Oracle8.

But...

To repeat the message at the start of this short section on Oracle8, although these features and many others appear highly attractive at first glance, you'll have to take a number of steps before you decide to deploy them within a project. At a minimum, before you use them within a production application, Oracle should have placed them into a production release. And before their effects can be adequately predicted, the industry must have a body of experience using them under realistic production conditions.

What about the Oracle7 material contained in this book? Will it be outdated by Oracle8? Our current feeling is that Oracle8 will invalidate very little of the material presented here. It's our hope, though, that new features will help provide more alternative solutions to your design problems.

3

Data Modeling

What is data modeling? It is simply a means of formally capturing the data that is of relevance to an organization in conducting its business. It is one of the fundamental analysis techniques in use today, the foundation on which we build relational databases.

This chapter builds on the introduction in Chapter 1. It describes what deliverables we can expect to receive from the analysis phase, and what these deliverables are all about. We'll introduce the concept of semantic data models and *entity relationship diagrams* (*ERDs*). We'll define such terms as entities, attributes, keys, relationships, supertypes, subtypes, and normalization. We'll pay particular attention to those obscure and difficult data structures that can't be directly implemented in a relational database without some intervention from the designer. We'll consider the value that can be added to the analysis deliverables by both entity life history and data flow diagrams.

You may be asking why, in a book on design, do we devote almost a whole chapter to data modeling techniques—techniques which are often considered to be a part of analysis? The answer is that it is vital to designers to have a thorough understanding of the concepts behind the data model and the constructs that make up the model. Even more importantly, we rarely (if ever) leave the model exactly as it was when we began our design. We need to be able to recognize which constructs will cause problems if we implement them as they are, and we need to understand the implications of changing these constructs. We need to do this early in the design phase so we can produce a physical data model towards the end of design. This is all about taking a concept and turning it into a practical and workable physical database.

Types of Models

There are two distinct types of models that we need to take a look at. The analysis stage produces the *information model*, and the design phase produces the *data model*. Although, as we will see, the data model must take detailed account of Oracle7's technical characteristics, the information model should assume nothing about the technology which is going to be used to implement the application. Its job is to clarify the real-world situation that the application is going to attempt to model. Put another way, a good information model is usable as a design input for any data manager, regardless of whether the environment is networked, hierarchical, object-oriented, or relational. Here is a list of what you should expect to see in a model:

- Entity relationship diagrams (ERDs)
- Data flow diagrams (DFDs)
- Entity life history (ELH) or state transition diagrams (STDs)
- Entity definitions
- Entity unique identifiers (UIDs)
- Attribute definitions
- Relationships between entities

This list covers the characteristics of the data. We will also need to generate a function hierarchy and descriptions of most functions in terms of the entities and attributes they use and the business rules they implement. (The topic of functional modeling is covered in Chapter 15, *Introduction to Code Design.*)

Surely, implementing this list is as simple as falling off a log, you say. Entities become tables; UIDs become primary keys; attributes become columns; relationships become foreign keys; we convert functions into module definitions; and we're home in time for tea! Indeed, Figure 3-1 *is* quite simple, and does show, in rough terms, what we do in design, but unfortunately it isn't quite as simple as we'd like it to be!

The first task is to verify that the analysts have indeed delivered most (if not all) of the items on our list. We can probably live without data flow diagrams and entity life histories, but the others really are essential.

The next step is to perform some type of quality assurance check on the deliverables; the purpose of this check is to ensure both completeness and correctness. Some CASE products have utilities that perform some of these mundane tasks for you. For example, a CASE tool can check that every entity has a UID and also has at least one function that creates instances of it (not much use in an entity that

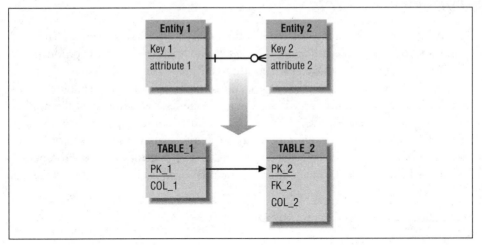

Figure 3-1. The data design process made simple

never gets populated) and at least one function that references it (not much point creating something that can never be accessed).

In this chapter, we will run through the main deliverables and provide some generic guidelines on checking them. We can only help you to check the formal correctness of these analysis deliverables, that is, whether they are valid in their own right. A C compiler can only tell you that a program is legal C, not whether the program will generate the correct results. Similarly, we can only tell you how to find out whether an entity relationship model is a valid model, not whether it accurately reflects the real world situation on which it claims to be based. You will have to make that assessment for yourself; you'll do this by reading the documentation and asking questions of both the analysts and the user community.

To return to the formal checks, we'll start by looking at the basic objects of the analysis: the entities and their keys, attributes, and relationships between entities. Next we'll look at entity relationship diagrams, which are arguably the most powerful tool in traditional analysis methods.

What Is Data Modeling?

In this section, we aim to provide a very basic introduction to semantic data models, and we introduce such topics as entities, attributes, primary keys, relationships, supertypes, and subtypes. (Don't worry if these terms mean nothing to you now—all will be revealed.) If you are already familiar with these concepts, you may wish to skip or browse this section (although we advise you to read it since you may not be familiar with the diagramming conventions we're using). This section is mostly theoretical; as such, it doesn't cover Oracle specifics.

Entities, Attributes, and Keys

An *entity* is a distinct class of real world things, such as cars, trains, and ships, about which something is known. An entity can also be something purely conceptual, such as goodwill, provided that when a "goodwill" occurs, we will know some facts about it. An *entity occurrence* is a particular instance (object-oriented people call it an *instantiation*) of the entity class. For instance, the "Titanic" is an entity occurrence of the entity "Ship." In information modeling, it is important to distinguish between types and instances of things.

Any property of an entity that is of interest is referred to as either an *attribute* or a *relationship*. Every entity must have properties that describe it, things which are known about it; otherwise, it cannot exist. Some attributes of an entity not only describe it but uniquely identify it. These may be a single attribute property or a combination of properties. These properties are referred to as the *primary key*, or sometimes as the *unique identifier* of the entity. When the primary key is composed of more than a single property, it is referred to as a *composite primary key*. When a choice of primary keys is available, each choice is referred to as a *candidate key*.

As with entities, it is important to distinguish between attributes and attribute occurrences. An attribute of car is "Registration Number", and an occurrence of this attributes is "180 EOD". Whether this attribute can be used as a primary key is doubtful: registration numbers can be swapped between cars, and a number may be unique only within the country of registration. "Chassis Serial Number" may be a better bet, but if several cars are dismantled and the pieces jumbled up and reassembled, what defines the car? Let's not get any deeper into this argument, but it does serve to illustrate the fact that finding candidate keys is not always as straightforward as you might think it is.

Relationships

We've seen that entities can be described in an information model in terms of their primary key and other non-key attributes. However, we don't have the complete picture yet, because entities are not viewed in isolation. Real world relationships occur between them. For instance, you are related to your car as its owner. You, and possibly your spouse and children, are related to the car as its drivers. If you took out a loan to buy the car, then your bank may be related to it as financier of it. And so on...

Once again, we need to distinguish between the relationship and the relationship occurrences. If we define a relationship between "Cars" and "People" and call it "Is Owner Of", then an occurrence of this relationship links "Batman" to the "Batmobile" (if the Batmobile can be classified as a car, and Batman as a person!).

When we try to implement the information model as an Oracle schema, we find that although Oracle has table columns which can directly implement the attributes, the only mechanism that it has to implement a relationship is the *foreign key constraint.* Since relational databases do not support "pointers" from one record to another, what we have to do is to store in one record a unique identifier from the other.

The only relationships we can implement in this way are one-to-one (1:1) and one-to-many (1:many). (We'll explain these later in this chapter.) If we need to implement a many:many relationship, then we must add what is called an *intersection entity* (more about this later as well). The key point here is that if the "one" end of the relationship has more than one unique identifier (candidate primary keys), any one of them may be used to support the relationship. This is our first example of a design decision which has to be made during the transition from information model to data model, and it is one that may have a profound effect on performance.

Relationships can relate an entity to itself; such relationships are termed *reflexive.* A common example is a relationship on employees used to determine the management reporting structure. Reflexive relationships are often indicative of an underlying hierarchy within the data structure. Because of the way that they are drawn on entity relationship models, reflexive relationships are sometime colloquially referred to as *pig's ears.*

Subtypes and Supertypes

Sometimes an attribute has a special significance to an entity: it categorizes it into distinct types, and the entity is split to reflect this importance. The new entities are known as *subtypes,* with the original entity becoming a *supertype.* For example, "Cars" could be broken down into "Two Wheel Drive" and "Four Wheel Drive". "Car" itself may be a subtype of a wider group called "Motor Vehicles." It is essential that all entity occurrences of the supertype belong to exactly one of the subtypes. Some cars can be switched between two- and four-wheel drive, so perhaps we need to introduce a new subtype called "Selectable Drive." The acid test for whether a supertype is required is to establish the extent to which the different subtypes have the same properties. The less similar they are, while still sharing a primary key, the better the case for using supertypes.

Overuse of subtypes and supertypes is a common problem, and this problem is most easily identified by finding an entity occurrence that can be validly included in more than one subtype. Since doing so is illegal, the subtyping must be invalid.

Entity Relationship Diagrams

As we've often been told, a picture is worth a thousand words! A data model that is presented as a listing of entities, attributes, relationships, supertypes, and subtypes may be complete and correct, but is not easy to understand and is extremely boring to peruse. So, enter the *entity relationship diagram (ERD)*. The ERD supports a graphical representation of all of these objects, although often attributes are omitted or only primary key attributes are shown. Generally, the reason for this is to not to clutter the diagram up with too much detail.

The idea of the ERD is as a conceptualization of the requirements. The task of the designer is to take the concept forward into reality. Often, the information model is too complex and has too many objects to be represented on a single diagram, so several diagrams are produced, categorized by a subject. For example, there may be a Manufacturing ERD, a Billing ERD, an Orders ERD, etc., all of them separate. If you are using a CASE product that can produce the wider picture, it is worth doing so and putting it on the wall in a communal place. Such a diagram may resemble the motherboard of your PC, or a road map of Europe, but it serves two useful purposes:

1. It can be used as reference when considering the impact of a decision that affects the system as a whole.

2. It serves as a useful reminder that each area is not an isolated system, but a subsystem of a wider and complex beast.

Drawing Entities and Attributes

There are several conventions for ERDs, each depicting the various objects in a somewhat different way. We will use the *Information Engineering Methodology (IEM)* conventions. These differ slightly from the conventions used in the Oracle CASE Tools and related subject matter. Using our conventions, an entity is depicted as a box with its name at the top, as shown in Figure 3-2.

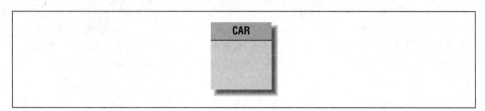

Figure 3-2. A single entity

An entity may have its attributes listed inside the box, as shown in Figure 3-3. Notice that the unique identifier or primary key attributes are underlined.

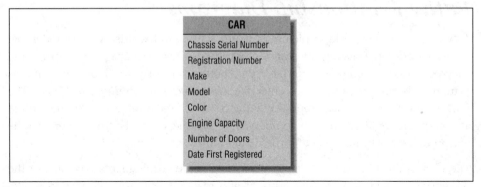

Figure 3-3. An entity with attributes and a unique identifier

Drawing Relationships

Relationships are represented as a line between two entities, as illustrated in Figure 3-4. The relationship expressed here states that every car must be registered to a person and that a person may have one or more cars registered in his or her name.

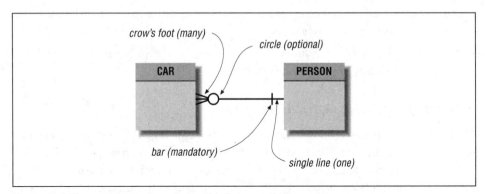

Figure 3-4. Two entities and a relationship between them

Here we have introduced the key concepts of *cardinality* and *optionality* of relationships. The "crow's foot" symbol on the left indicates "many"; the straight line on the right indicates "one." The relationship is read along the line; thus, a car can only be registered to *one* person, but a person can have *many* cars registered in his or her name.

The other symbols on the line, which appear as a circle and a bar, indicate the optionality of the relationship at either end. A circle indicates optional and a bar mandatory. Thus a car *must* have an owner, and a person *may* have a car registered in his name.

It often helps to clarify the relationships on the diagram by adding names to the relationships. A relationship can have a single name, but again to aid understanding it is best if both ends are labeled, as shown in Figure 3-5.

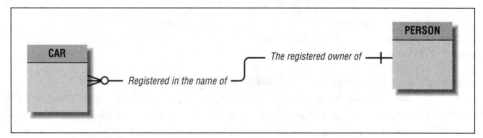

Figure 3-5. Two related entities, with labeled relationship

Drawing Subtypes and Supertypes

Is it true that every car is owned by a person? What about a taxi or a company car? We need to introduce a supertype entity called "Car Owner" and subtypes called "Private Owner" and "Corporate Owner" (see Figure 3-6). This is sometimes referred to as *inheritance*, since the subtype entities inherit the characteristics of the supertype. Attributes can be defined at both levels, with common attributes occurring on the supertype.

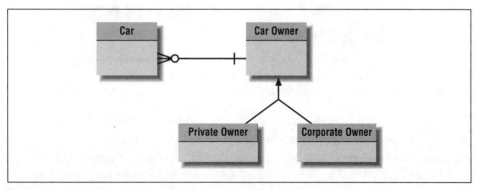

Figure 3-6. Depicting a supertype (Car Owner) with two subtypes

Drawing Many-to-Many Relationships

Some relationships are many-to-many. In such a relationship, each occurrence of one entity may be related to more than a single occurrence of the other entity. For instance, a car can be insured to be driven by many drivers, and a driver can be insured to drive many cars (illustrated in Figure 3-7).

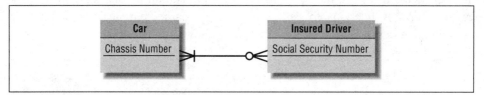

Figure 3-7. A many-to-many relationship

Many-to-many relationships cannot be directly implemented in the relational model. So we introduce an *intersection entity* (sometimes referred to as a *link entity* or *synthetic entity*) to resolve this. This new entity derives its primary key from both related *cardinal entities* (this is the term used to describe the real world entities that it joins), but it has no attributes, only relationships. The relationship is said to be *dependent* and is depicted in Figure 3-8. The primary key of "Car Insured Driver" is Chassis Number (inherited from "Car") and "Social Security Number" (inherited from "Insured Driver").

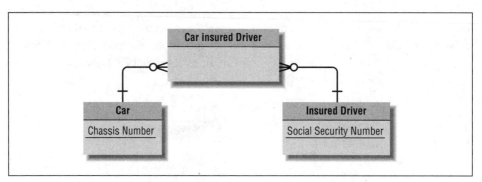

Figure 3-8. A link entity (Car Insured Driver) to resolve the many-to-many relationship

Some analysts feel that they must resolve each many-to-many relationship by introducing associative entities. This should really be left for design. The conceptual information model produced in analysis should represent business entities and should not be cluttered up with physical structures introduced for implementation purposes.

Drawing Pig's Ears

Finally, in our quick tour of entity relationship diagrams, let's look at relationships that are *reflexive*, sometimes referred to as *recursive relationships, self relationships* or *pig's ears* (because that is what they resemble when drawn—well, perhaps you have to use your imagination a bit!). Figure 3-9 shows an example of a pig's ear. Notice that the relationship is always optional; otherwise, it would be, by definition, an infinite hierarchy. This rule will be covered later in this chapter when we examine data structures that are illegal or unimplementable.

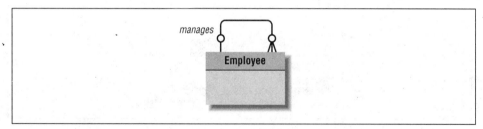

Figure 3-9. A pig's ear

Quality-Assuring the Conceptual Information Model

Three important models are produced during the life cycle of a project:

*   The conceptual information model
*   The logical data model
*   The physical data model

As we've said, one of the most important deliverables from the analysis phase is the conceptual information model. That model should represent the entities of the business or enterprise and nothing more. Anything that smacks of an implementation or physical issue should be introduced during design, when the logical and physical data models are created, and not before. A very important goal of the design phase is to verify the quality of the information model produced during analysis.

The conceptual information model should not contain associative entities; many-to-many relationships should be modeled as such. The model should be fully normalized. In the early part of the design phase, the conceptual information model is translated into a logical data model. Objects are added to support physical and implementation matters (such as a print queue entity, for instance). Many-to-many relationships are resolved, and selective denormalizations are undertaken. In the later phases of design, the physical data model is produced from the logical model. During this transition, structures such as arcs and supertypes are resolved, and physical properties and objects such as indexes are defined.

Many projects operate with only two models: logical and physical. The reason may be that some CASE tools don't support a three-tier model. But we believe that it is advisable to maintain the three tiers of model (as illustrated in Figure 3-10).

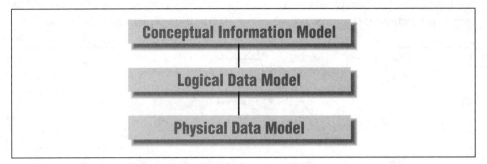

Figure 3-10. Three-tier model used in systems development

In this section, we'll look at the important subject of *normalization* of the model, followed by some insight into unusual and unimplementable structures within the data model. By checking that the model is in at least third normal form and has suitable justification for any unorthodox-looking relationships, we'll go a long way towards verifying the quality of the conceptual information model.

Normalized Data Model

One of the key requirements of the information model that is handed over from analysis to design is that it be delivered in at least third normal form (3NF). If you are not sure what 3NF is, then read on. The design team must verify that third normal form has been achieved before they accept the model. They may, at some later point, selectively denormalize the data for reasons which are almost invariably performance-related. However, denormalization is very much a part of the design process; it shouldn't be in evidence at all in the conceptual information model.

What is this process called normalization? It was first defined by Dr. E.F. Codd at the same time he defined the relational model (in 1970). Normalization is the basis for removing unwanted *functional dependencies (FDs)* from our entities. An FD is implied if we can determine the value of an attribute by simply knowing the value of some other attribute. For instance, if we know the name of a country, we can determine the name of its capital city; therefore there is a functional dependency between a country and its capital city.

A slight variation of an FD is known as a *multivalued dependency (MVD)*, which means that if we know the value of one attribute, we can determine a set of values of another attribute. For instance, if we know the name of a country, we can determine the name of all its airports; therefore, there is a multivalued dependency between country and airports. You may see the following notation to express FDs and MVDs:

FD: A◆B (A determines B)

MVD: A◆◆B (A determines set of B)

Why is a normalized information model so important in relational design? It has been proven through years of testing that the process of normalization gives us the best shot at modeling the world using two-dimensional objects (tables) without imposing too many constraints or compromising the facts (data) that we are using the database to capture. In practical terms, normal forms help us to design databases that don't have unnecessary redundant data or inconsistencies that may lead to performance problems or loss of information when we later perform database inserts, updates, and deletes. In summary, normal forms ensure that we do not compromise the integrity of our data by either creating false data or destroying true data.

How do we check if the information model (delivered as entity and attribute definitions) is normalized to the requisite level (for example, 3NF)? We will need to examine each of the normal forms individually. To illustrate this process, we will keep the theory short and provide practical examples that contravene the rule and then go on to show the corrected form.

First normal form (1NF). For an entity to be in first normal form, only atomic attribute values are allowed. All repeating groups must be removed and placed in a new (related) entity. An example is shown in Figure 3-11. In the first case, all the attributes on a consignment (Consignee, Insured Value, and Declared Value) would be repeated four times, for each of the four Consignments allowed in a Shipment. Notice that this enforces a rule that a Shipment can never have more than four Consignments, because we have nowhere to enter the fifth and subsequent ones. So if you use this model, remind your boss never to buy any bigger container ships!

Many problems would occur if you tried to implement a data structure that does not conform to first normal form. For instance:

- If a Shipment is canceled and the row is deleted, all traces of the consignments that were supposed to be on board sink with it (so to speak).

- If a new Consignment arrives at our port depot, but we have not assigned it yet to an outward-bound shipment, we have nowhere to store details of the consignment.

- There is the restriction mentioned above of never allowing more than a fixed number of occurrences of the repeating group (four consignments in our case).

Clearly, we will encounter some major operational problems if our model is not in first normal form! To normalize the structure to 1NF, we simply take out the Consignment information from the Shipment and put it in a separate data structure. The new data structure becomes a child of the Shipment. This is illustrated in Figure 3-11.

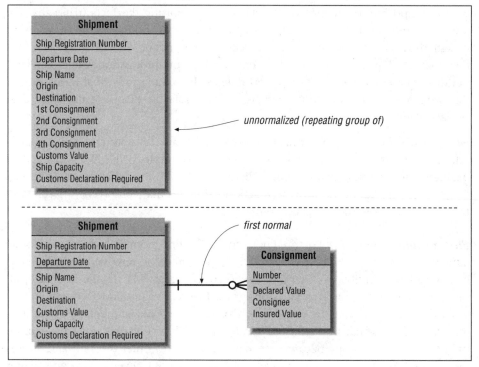

Figure 3-11. First normal form

Second normal form (2NF). For an entity to be in second normal form, it must first be in first normal form; in addition, it must have all non-key attributes be fully dependent on every key component in the primary key. This only applies to entities with compound keys (made up of two or more attributes). Second normal form specifies that there must be no non-key attributes that depend on only part of the primary key.

Let's continue with the same example from Figure 3-11. Clearly, the Capacity of a ship is not dependent on the Departure Date, only upon the ship itself—except in the highly unlikely event that each ship is refitted between every sailing!

In Figure 3-12 we fix this anomaly and transform our model into 2NF. As with the transformation to 1NF, the action involves taking dependent attributes out of Shipment and creating a related child entity (called Ship in this case).

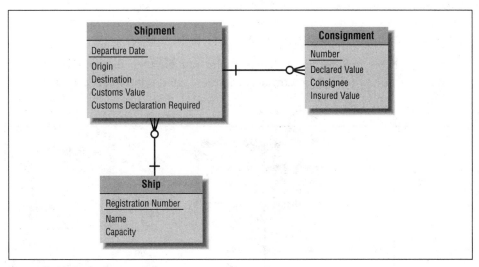

Figure 3-12. Second normal form

Again, let's consider some of the implications if we had tried to implement the model that did not conform to 2NF:

- We could not record the Name and Capacity of a Ship that had not yet made any Shipments, for instance, when it is being built or on order. The only way we could overcome this is to define a "dummy" Shipment for it—a horrible kludge!

- Similarly, if we delete a Shipment record once the Shipment is completed, we would lose all records of any of our fleet of Ships that had no current or planned (future) Shipments.

If a Ship *is* refitted and has a new Capacity, how do we record this simple fact? Do we update all Shipment records, including those that were completed before refitting? If so, it would appear that the Ship had been sailing under capacity when in fact it was full. If we choose to update only Shipments that occur after the refit is complete, again we may have problems since the Ship is out of service and probably doesn't have any current or planned Shipments.

There are many more potential holes for us to fall down if we do not conform to 2NF. Clearly 2NF is a desirable place to be, but is it enough?

Third normal form (3NF). For an entity to be in 3NF, it must first be in second normal form; in addition, all non-key attributes must be *only* dependent on the primary key. That is, they may not also depend on some other non-key attributes.

In our example from Figures 3-11 and 3-12, the "Customs Declaration Required" is really a property of the Origin and Destination. If the sailing is between two ports in the same country, or two countries that have completely free trade between them, then we shouldn't need customs clearance for our Shipment. Our example in Figure 3-12 clearly violates 3NF, so let's put it right.

Figure 3-13 shows the resolution. Once more, our entities "divide and conquer" and we relocate the offending attributes to a new child entity (called Route in our example).

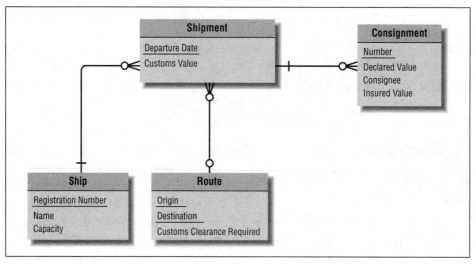

Figure 3-13. Third normal form

Normalizing to 3NF. In actual fact, normalizing the information model to third normal form is mostly a matter of applying common sense, using intuition, and remembering the old adage "All attributes of an entity must depend on the key, the whole key, and nothing but the key (so help me Codd")."[*]

Some experienced people who have a background in non-relational database systems (such as hierarchical or networked DBMS) view the normalization process with some skepticism. They observe that we are proliferating tables. (It's true that in moving from Figure 3-11 to Figure 3-13 we have jumped from a single entity to four.) These critics also perceive poor runtime performance as a result of having to join tables in order to regroup the data back into its original form.

In one sense (and in one sense only), they are correct: if we have a unique key through which we can retrieve the single unnormalized record, then having the data all in one indigestible bundle will give us the fastest retrieval time. On the other hand, Oracle7 is not exactly slow at performing a four-table join when

---

[*] A reference to Dr. E. Codd, the father of the relational database.

required to do so. Even this rather misses the point that most of the queries that we will need to write against the normalized data structures will not be trying to reconstruct the whole of the original flat model that we started with in Figure 3-11, and they won't start with the unique identifier conveniently available. Many will join a subset of the four normalized tables, using keys such as the "Origin" and "Departure Date." Such ad hoc queries are notoriously expensive against unnormalized structures, in addition to all of the other disadvantages that we have already discussed.

Third normal form is not a panacea for all applications. In particular, it is not the best technique to use for designing a data warehouse. See Chapter 13, *Designing for Data Warehouses*, for more detail.

Beyond third normal form. Most of us who have had some exposure to relational systems will have heard of 3NF. However, we don't necessarily stop counting when we reach third normal form. The progression beyond 3NF is as follows:

- Boyce-Codd normal form (BCNF)

- Fourth normal form (4NF)

- Fifth normal form (5NF)

We'll cover these briefly, but for more information see the excellent book by Chris Date on the subject.[*]

In practice, Boyce-Codd is a slightly better version of 3NF. Analysts and programmers should not need to bother with fourth or fifth normal form, but designers should be aware of the problems which they resolve. These difficulties are invariably the result of using compound primary keys where only part of the key contains information in its own right. Indeed, any structure which is in 3NF and has no compound keys must also be in 5NF.

Boyce-Codd normal form. BCNF imposes the additional rule that all transitive dependencies must be removed. Formally, a table R is in Boyce-Codd normal form if, for every nontrivial FD $X \rightarrow A$, X is a superkey. What does this theory mean in practice?

Staying with the nautical theme, let's assume that our crew are divided into teams for various activities. A crew member may be on many teams, but within any one team there is only one team leader. However the team itself may have several leaders. In addition, a crew member can lead only a single team. This is quite a

---

[*] Date, C.J., *An Introduction to Database Systems*, sixth edition, Addison-Wesley, 1995.

complex scenario. The table represented in Table 3-1 is in third normal form, but contravenes BCNF.

Table 3-1. Crew Assignments: A Table in 3NF that Contravenes BCNF

Crew Member	Team Name	Leader Name
Jawor	Lookout	Webb
Jawor	Catering	Cowie
Wells	Lookout	Ramewal
Cooper	Lookout	Webb
Derham	Catering	Hardisty
Derham	Maintenance	Cowlard
Poad	Maintenance	Cowlard

The problem here is that although the table is in third normal form, we still have a deletion anomaly. If Wells is removed from the Lookout team, then we lose an additional piece of nonrelated knowledge, namely that Ramewal is a team leader of the Lookout team. When a new member is assigned to the Lookout team and we pull up a list of team leaders to whom we can assign the new member, Ramewal will not appear on the list.

Unlike previous normal forms, where we were able to break up the table without creating any redundancy, we are forced to hold some redundant information to solve the conundrum. The original Crew Assignments table from Table 3-1 stays as is, but it is supplemented by a table of Team Leaders, as illustrated in Table 3-2.

Table 3-2. Team Leaders: A New Table Introduced to Satisfy BCNF

Team Name	Leader Name
Lookout	Webb
Catering	Cowie
Lookout	Ramewal
Catering	Hardisty
Maintenance	Cowlard

Now, when Wells walks the plank, we still have knowledge that Ramewal leads the Lookout team (even though the team now consists of zero team members). A new team member can now be assigned to Ramewal.

Fourth normal form (4NF). This form has to do with multivalued dependencies (MVDs). It solves the problem of a table having more than one MVD in it. Consider a table of Ships, the Voyages they make, and the Captains that can skipper the Ships on those Voyages. This is illustrated in the ERD shown in Figure 3-14.

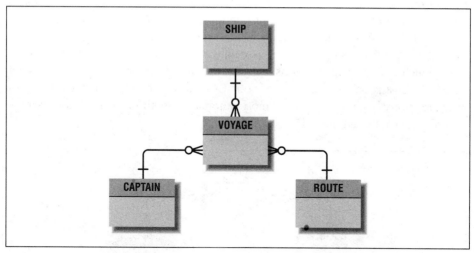

Figure 3-14. An example used to illustrate contravention of fourth normal form

What is wrong here? The Voyage entity is recording too many details for a single structure. The table that is derived from this is shown in Table 3-3. It has no FDs, so it is in BCNF. However, again we have a deletion anomaly. If Ehren decides to leave and we delete his records, we thereby lose all record of the fact that Flute sails between Zebrugge and Boston. Moreover, if we add a new Voyage, we may need to add more than one row in Table 3-3.

Table 3-3. Crossings: A Table Example of Data in Fourth Normal Form

Ship	Crew	Voyage
Dark Horse	Gall	Southampton—New York
Dark Horse	Ehren	Southampton—New York
Dark Horse	Falconer	Southampton—New York
Dark Horse	Stone	Southampton—New York
Dark Horse	La Spina	Portsmouth—Le Havre
Dark Horse	Stone	Portsmouth—Le Havre
Flute	Ehren	Zebrugge—Boston
Flute	Danforth	New Haven—Dieppe
Flute	Falconer	New Haven—Dieppe

Just in case you hadn't already guessed it by now, we will solve this problem by splitting the table up into two tables, one with (Ship, Voyage) in it and the other with (Captain, Voyage).

Fifth normal form (5NF). Fifth normal form is sometimes referred to a *join-projec-tion normal form (JPNF)*. It can occur when resolving three (or more) entities, all related with a many-to-many relationship to one another. In some cases, resolving each of these relationships with an associative entity can lead to a flawed model from which nonexistent relations can be inferred (known as a join-projection anomaly). This problem can occur if your CASE tool attempts to resolve many-to-many relationships for you, since most automated methods would not spot the dependencies here. Figure 3-15 shows an example.

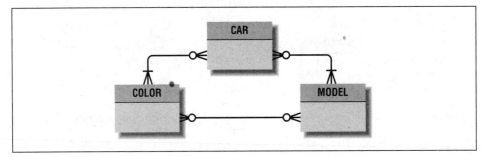

Figure 3-15. A three-way many-to-many structure

Each car is available in a selection of colors, and each car is available in certain models. Some colors are only available on certain models (e.g., metallic paint only on the higher specification models).

If we choose to break the problem down and view it as three isolated many-to-many relationships, we would solve it by introducing three associative entities which we will call "CAR COLOR LINK," "CAR MODEL LINK," and "COLOR MODEL LINK." Figure 3-16 shows the resulting Oracle tables, with some represen-tative data.

Suppose that a customer comes into our dealership to order a car. Her preference is for a blue Ghia but she does not mind which model. So we issue a query against the database to see what cars she can choose from. The code here shows the SQL used by our fictitious application against our Oracle7 database to achieve this:

```
SELECT car.name
FROM    cars car
,       car_color_links ccl
,       car_model_links  cml
WHERE   car.name = ccl.name
AND     car.name = cml.name
AND     ccl.color = 'Blue'
AND     cml.model = 'Ghia'
```

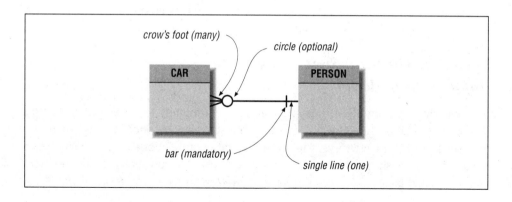

Figure 3-16. Table definitions which contravene 5NF

The query returns:

Name
Escort
Probe

The result is surprising, because we see from MODEL_COLOR_LINKS that Ghia models are not available in blue. A spurious record has therefore been returned. This spurious row is our join-projection anomaly and is an example of a violation of fifth normal form.

Fortunately, the correct solution is much simpler than the flawed one. Simply introduce a single associative entity linking the other three, namely CAR_COLOR_MODEL_LINK. Table 3-4 illustrates the correct form of the single table implementation.

Table 3-4. CAR_COLOR_MODEL_LINKS: A Three-Way Associative Table, Illustrating 5NF

CAR	COLOR	MODEL
Escort	Red	GL
Escort	Red	Ghia
Escort	Metallic Green	GL
Escort	Metallic Green	Ghia
Probe	Blue	L
Probe	Blue	GL

We should stress that information models that exhibit violations of fourth and fifth normal form are relatively uncommon.

Illegal or Unusual Structures in the Information Model

If we study any Entity Relationship Diagram, we are likely to observe that the vast majority of relationships are one-to-many, most with the "one" side optional and the "many" side mandatory. This common type of relationship is illustrated in Figure 3-17 and should be read as "Each *department* may *employ* one or more *employees* and each *employee* must be *employed* by exactly one *department*."

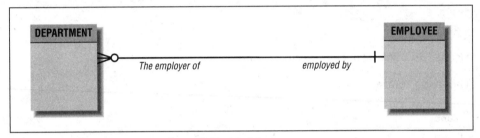

Figure 3-17. The most common form of relationship

Any relationship that is not of this type is worthy of some investigation. In particular, look out for those presented in the following sections which are either illegal or illogical. Some constructs discussed below are not illegal, but are rare or unusual. Some can be explained. Others require nontrivial design decisions to be made on the implementation of these constructs as Oracle database tables.

Mandatory pig's ears

As we have already noted, a pig's ear is a relationship of an entity to another instance of itself. If either end of the relationship is mandatory, then the effect is an infinite hierarchy. For instance, the relationship depicted in Figure 3-18 implies that an employee *must* have exactly one manager. If this is true, who is the manager of the CEO of the company or whoever is in ultimate charge? It is equally invalid to make the other end of the relationship mandatory; in that case, everybody must manage somebody, giving rise to problems at the bottom of the hierarchy where most of us reside! Mandatory pig's ears are always errant.

Nonexclusive or noninclusive subtypes

As we have seen, some entities are broken down into subtypes during analysis. It is easy to confuse subtypes with class membership. The atomic entities are called subtypes of the compound one (which is called the supertype). These subtypes

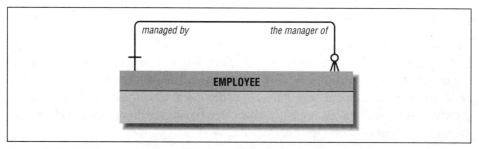

Figure 3-18. Mandatory pig's ear—illegal construct

must be disjoint and collectively make up the entire supertype. In other words, the subtypes must be mutually exclusive, and there cannot be any occurrences of the subtype which do not belong to a subtype. Figure 3-19 is an example taken from the agrochemical industry which violates both these rules.

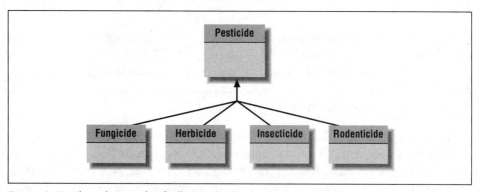

Figure 3-19. Flawed example of subtypes and supertypes

It is certainly true that the vast majority of Pesticides in the agrochemical market are either Fungicides (for treating disease), Herbicides (for controlling weeds), Insecticides (for deterring or killing off insects) or Rodenticides (ditto for the hapless rats). However, there are some Pesticide products that can serve a dual purpose—for example, as both a Fungicide and a Herbicide. Furthermore, there are some Pesticides that are not a Fungicide, Herbicide, Insecticide, or Rodenticide; an example is a Plant Growth Regulator.

The model is flawed by failing to comply with either of our rules since the subtypes are not exclusive and the supertype is not inclusive.

What is clear is that some understanding of the business is required to complete the check. If in doubt, seek out an analyst or user (preferably solicit opinions from both camps). Ask them pertinent questions such as, "Are there currently, or could there conceivably ever be, any Pesticide on the market that treat two or more categories of pest? For instance, are products ever marketed as twin-packs with dissimilar components?"

Beware of attempting to group an entity into more than one unrelated category. Let's look at a model of patients in a hospital. We may categorize our patients as inpatients or outpatients; our medical staff are particularly interested in this distinction! On the other hand, our finance department has a different view of the patients and see them as either private (fee-paying) patients or health service (non fee-paying) patients. See Figure 3-20.

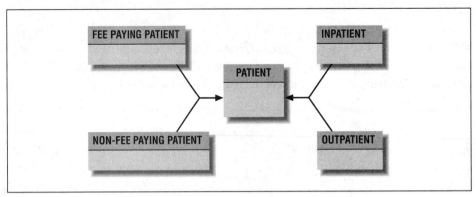

Figure 3-20. A supertype with two categories of subtype

This double grouping gives rise to some interesting problems if you attempt to implement either or both of the categories as separate tables. Attempting to combine the nonrelated categories, as shown in Figure 3-21, will only exacerbate your problems, again especially if you attempt to implement these entities as separate tables. Suffice it to say that you probably need to decide which of the categorizations is least important and make it an attribute instead. So who wins, our medical staff or our financial staff? Let the battle commence!

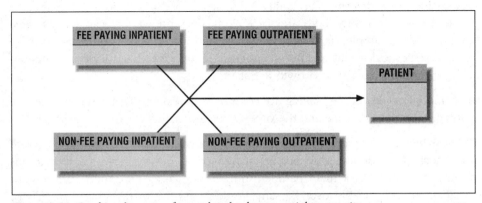

Figure 3-21. Combined groups of nonrelated subtypes—nightmare city

Resolving a subtype

We alluded to implementation options for subtypes in the previous section. It basically comes down to a choice between combining the subtypes into a single table or making them individual tables in our Oracle database. The choice is usually fairly obvious by doing the following:

- Observing if the subtypes all have the same primary key

- Checking the number of common attributes and the number of uncommon ones

- Checking the number of relationships to the subtypes against the number of the supertype

Let's take the case of Patients from Figure 3-21, considering the Inpatient/Outpatient types. It is highly likely that most attributes for a patient will be recorded regardless of whether they are an Inpatient or an Outpatient. There may be some relationships that only apply to Inpatients, such as Bed Allocation. We will assume that a single table is the decision. What more needs to be done?

We will add a Patient Type column to the table to indicate Inpatient or Outpatient. We will use a constraint to restrict this column to one of these two values. Any mandatory columns or foreign keys that only apply to one of the subtypes will be constrained to be not null for the subtype for which they are mandatory. Conversely, we must add constraints to ensure that columns that are only applicable to certain subtypes are always null for the other subtypes. Finally, we may choose to create views to mimic what the tables would be like had we opted for separate tables. These views may be used in applications that are only interested in one of the subtypes.

TIP   Notice the inclusion of the WITH CHECK OPTION constraint. This prevents users from using the view to insert into table rows that do not satisfy the WHERE clause of the query used in the view creation. Thus, the view definition ensures that we can only create valid subtypes.

The following DDL script creates all this in simplified form.

```
CREATE TABLE mc_patients
(id NUMBER(9)           NOT NULL
,ptype VARCHAR2(10)     NOT NULL
  CONSTRAINT mc_pat_cc1 CHECK (ptype IN ('INPATIENT'
                                        ,'OUTPATIENT'))
,surname VARCHAR2(30)   NOT NULL
,forename VARCHAR2(30)  NOT NULL
,date_of_birth DATE
```

```
,f_bal_bed NUMBER(9)
,CONSTRAINT mc_pat_pk PRIMARY KEY (id)
,CONSTRAINT mc_pat_bal_fk FOREIGN KEY
  REFERENCES mc_bed_allocations
,CONSTRAINT mc_pat_cc2 CHECK(ptype = 'INPATIENT' OR
                             f_bal_bed IS NULL));

CREATE VIEW mc_outpatients_v AS
SELECT pat.id
      ,pat.surname
      ,pat.forename
      ,date_of_birth
FROM   mc_patients pat
WHERE  pat.ptype = 'OUTPATIENT'
WITH CHECK OPTION CONSTRAINT mc_opt_cc1;

CREATE VIEW mc_inpatients_v  ...
```

Many-to-many relationships

The conceptual information model should be delivered with many-to-many relationships intact, and we should process and resolve each one in our logical model. First, check that the relationship really is many-to-many. Sometimes, a many-to-many relationship is used to represent a temporal relationship. Figure 3-22 illustrates this point. There is a one-to-one correspondence between a car and its engine. Over time, however, a car may be fitted with replacement engines and an engine may be reconditioned and fitted to another car. Of course, neither model is correct or incorrect; it depends on whether the system is required to maintain historic details.

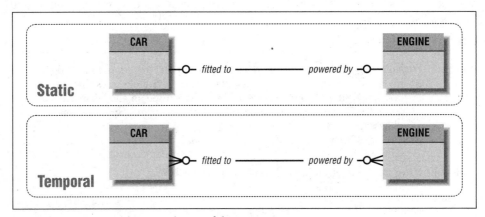

Figure 3-22. Static and temporal view of the same construct

Since a many-to-many relationship cannot be directly implemented within a relational database, it is resolved by putting a new "entity" in the middle. Thus, the example shown in Figure 3-23 is resolved by creating a new entity, as shown in

Figure 3-24. This new "entity" is known variously as a *link, associative,* or *intersection* entity. If you cannot think of a meaningful name for this new entity, then you can call it "Entity1 Entity2 Link", or similar. You may discover at some point that the link entity has attributes of its own. In the example, the new entity JOB TASK LINK may have an important attribute called Task Order that determines the order in which the Tasks are undertaken within the Job. If you find new attributes, check with the analysts. You don't want to be stepping on their toes! Generally, if what you've found is required, they haven't fully done their job.

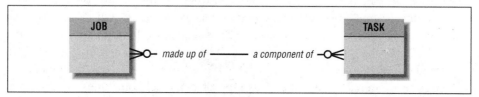

Figure 3-23. A many-to-many relationship between jobs and tasks

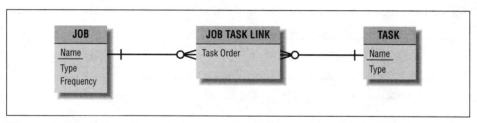

Figure 3-24. Resolution of a many-to-many relationship using a link entity

The primary key of the link entity is nearly always composed of a combination of the foreign keys of the entities that it links (which are often to referred to as the *cardinal* entities). When we come to implement this entity as a table, the order in which the key components are defined is significant. Oracle can only use an index if the leading edge (i.e., the first component) is known. If we always "navigate" the database from Job to Task (as seems quite likely in this case) then it is important to define the primary key of JOB TASK LINK to be (Job Name, Task Name). If the relationship can be traversed in either direction, Job to Task and Task to Job; then an additional index should be defined on (Task Name) or (Task Name, Job Name). For additional information about this subject and about indexes in general, see Chapter 6, *Choosing Keys and Indexes.*

The associative entity has no life of its own. In fact, it loses its raison d'être if either side is deleted. You need to define rules such as these: if a user attempts to delete a TASK, they are prevented if the TASK has any JOB TASK LINKs or if the delete is cascaded to all JOB TASK LINKs. This tends to be a business decision rather than a technical decision (ask the analyst or, better still, a qualified user).

Identical considerations will apply when deleting a job. Once you have the decision, you must decide how to implement it. In fact, both options in this case are
best implemented by Oracle's foreign key constraints. Simply enabling a foreign
key constraint will prevent deletion if children exist; adding the qualifier
CASCADE DELETE will cause the children to be deleted with their parent.

One-to-one relationships

Figure 3-25 shows two derivations of one-to-one relationships. The first one,
between A and B, is not really a valid construct. A and B are, by definition a
single entity (formed by merging the two sets of attributes.) If A and B have
different primary keys, then we must choose one as the primary key of the
merged entity; the other becomes a candidate key (supported by a UNIQUE
constraint on the column(s) within the table. There is no good argument for
keeping the two entities separate. This type of construct sometimes occurs when
models are developed to consolidate two separate systems that name the same
thing differently. Since we are presenting a logical model, not a physical one, they
should be merged and given a common name.

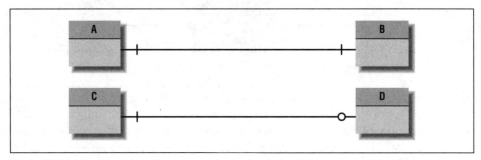

Figure 3-25. Two examples of one-to-one (unary) relationships

The relationship between C and D in Figure 3-25 is a valid construct. An example
is a personal computer and a mouse. A PC can operate with or without a mouse,
but the mouse can only operate with a computer. There is a design decision to be
made here. Do we implement the PC and the mouse as separate tables, or do we
merge them? Table 3-5 lists some of the advantages and disadvantages of each
case.

The attributes of the mouse become attributes of the PC in the merged solution.
Any attributes of the mouse that were mandatory become optional attributes of
the new PC-mouse entity, to cover the case in which the PC has no mouse. It is
possible to implement the rules through triggers and an additional attribute that
tells us if the PC currently sports a mouse. This solution is a bit cumbersome,
though.

Table 3-5. Pros and Cons of Single-Table and Two-Table Solution to a One-to-One Relationship

	One-Table Solution	Two-Table Solution
Maintenance programs	(+) Only one maintenance program to write to maintain PCs and mice	(–) Two maintenance programs to write
Data integrity	(–) Cannot use NOT NULL constraints to enforce mandatory columns of the mouse	(+) Can enforce mandatory columns using NOT NULL constraints
Isolated entities	(–) If we make the mouse an extension to a PC, how do we maintain information about a mouse not currently attached to a PC?	(+) Objects can exist in isolation.
Altering relationships	(–) If a mouse is taken from one PC and attached to another, the updates involved are complex	(+) Relocating a mouse is simply a matter of updating two foreign keys

A relationship that is mandatory at both ends (see Figure 3-26) is fairly unconventional, but certainly valid. A common example is order and order line. An order line cannot exist on its own without an order to be placed on. An order with no order line is not really an order at all; we would be wasting our time delivering or invoicing for nothing!

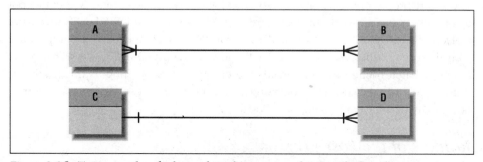

Figure 3-26. Two examples of relationships that are mandatory at both ends

The problem here is that we have a "chicken and egg" situation. An order cannot be created without an order line; an order line must have an order to be placed upon; so which do we create first? The answer appears to be that it probably doesn't really matter as long as they are both created within a single transaction and that whenever a line is deleted, a check is made to determine if the order is now empty; if so, we delete the order too. However, things aren't always as they appear...

Let's now think about this in Oracle table design terms. We will have a foreign key on ORDER_LINES to ORDERS that we can make mandatory using a NOT

NULL constraint. This will ensure that all ORDER_LINES have ORDERS. How do we enforce the rule that an ORDER must have ORDER_LINES? The obvious choice would seem to be to use triggers. We would use a "before insert" row trigger on ORDERS to check for a related ORDER_LINE and fail the insert if none were found. An "after delete" row trigger on ORDER_LINES would check for other ORDER_LINES in the same ORDER and, if none are found, would delete the ORDER. *Unfortunately, neither of these triggers will work.*

TIP   With the insert scenario, we still have our chicken and egg situation. If the ORDER is created first, the trigger will not find any ORDER_LINES since the insert for ORDER_LINES has not yet occurred. If the ORDER_LINES are inserted first, the foreign key constraint will fail since the parent has not been inserted yet.

The delete trigger will fail because we are attempting to select from the table from which the delete originated (ORDER_LINES). Because the table is regarded as being "mutating" during row-level triggers, an error will occur. For the deletion problem, there is a solution. We use the row trigger to simply tag the event (insert or delete) in a PL/SQL package persistent variable and defer the check until an "after row" trigger. There is a comprehensive example of this technique in Appendix B, *Tricks of the Trade*.

The insert problem is a harder nut to crack! We have two options. We could put the check in the application(s) that create ORDERS and ORDER_LINES to ensure that empty ORDERS are not created. Alternatively, we could reach a compromise with the user or the analyst. If they will allow an empty ORDER, we will provide a nightly batch routine that eliminates the empty orders. As long as this routine is run before any other critical processing or reports, then these ghost ORDERS may not do any harm. Neither solution is ideal.

Raiders of the Lost Arc

When an entity has a set of relationships to other entities that are mutually exclusive, the relationships are said to be in an *arc*. Consider the trivial example from a banking application illustrated in Figure 3-27; this should be read as "Each *account* must be either *for* one and only one *person*, or *for* one and only one *corporation*."

Resolving arcs

Arcs can often be transformed into subtype/supertype constructs. Figure 3-28 illustrates two ways of making such a transformation.

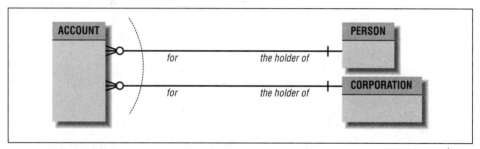

Figure 3-27. An arc

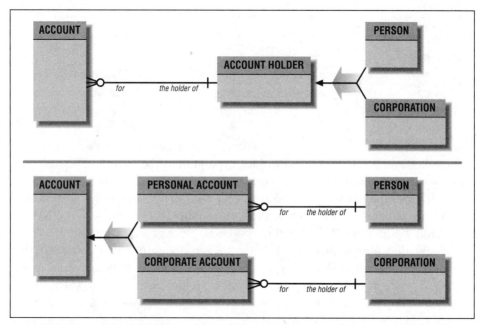

Figure 3-28. Translation of an arc into a subtype/supertype

The fact that arcs can be resolved into supertype/subtypes hints at some options for implementation. In this section, we'll look at various methods of solving the problem of the arc.

TIP   *It only matters how an arc is implemented if you intend to navigate outwards on it.* In our example, this means that we intend to go from Account to Corporation or Person (or both). If we don't intend to do this, then the arguments we describe in this section are irrelevant!

Method 1. In cases where a supertype solution would not be appropriate, we could implement the relationship as either one or two foreign keys in Accounts. Let's consider these two alternative solutions by looking at the simple table definitions shown in Table 3-6.

Table 3-6. An Arc as a Single (Generic) Foreign Key and a Pair of Foreign Keys

Solution 1a:

Accounts

No	Credit Limit	Person	Corporation
01623907	100.00	195	
01694295	150.00		297

Solution 1b:

Accounts

No	Credit Limit	Holder	Holder Type
01623907	100.00	195	P
01694295	150.00	297	C

The solution shown in 1b is often referred to as a generic arc; there is a single foreign key and a column (called Holder Type in this case) which effectively indicates which table the foreign key refers to. In Oracle7, 1a is usually the preferred solution, since foreign key constraints can be used to implement the relationships. In 1b, the "Holder" could either reference the PERSONS or the CORPORATIONS table, and it is not possible to define conditional foreign key constraints. Solution 1b would therefore require us to code triggers to ensure that on insert (and possibly update), if the Holder Type is "P", then Holder references a valid row in PERSONS and, if Holder Type is "C", then Holder references a valid row in CORPORATIONS.

Another advantage of 1a over 1b is that the SQL used when joining the tables is slightly easier to read and understand (also to code!). The following two SELECT statements demonstrate the differences.

```
/* 1a */
SELECT acc.credit_limit
      ,acc.no
FROM   accounts acc
      ,persons per
WHERE  per.id = acc.f_per_id
AND    per.name = 'HEANEY';

/* 1b */
SELECT acc.credit_limit
      ,acc.no
```

```
FROM    accounts acc
        ,persons   per
WHERE   per.id = acc.f_hld_id
AND     acc.holder_type = 'P'
AND     per.name = 'HEANEY';
```

Method 2. In this solution, we must implement PERSONS and CORPORATIONS in a single table, as demonstrated in the first diagram within Table 3-6. This would normally be possible only if PERSONS and CORPORATIONS have similar attributes. We could, however, hold only common details in the merged table and have optional (conditional) one-to-one relationships with the PERSONS and CORPORATIONS tables that contain the uncommon attributes. In Table 3-7 we present a trivial (and somewhat artificial) example in which there seems to be a one-to-one correspondence between the attributes of PERSONS and CORPORA-TIONS that are collectively implemented as a table called ACCOUNT_HOLDERS. Notice in this example that the foreign key from ACCOUNTS to ACCOUNT HOLDERS can be implemented with a foreign key constraint on ACCOUNTS.

Table 3-7. An Arc as a Subtype Where Attributes Are a Close Match

Accounts

No	Credit Limit	Holder
01623907	100.00	195
01694295	150.00	297

Account_Holders

ID	Type	Name	Credit Rating
195	P	MONKOU	GOOD
297	C	HALL HOLDINGS	FAIR

Method 3. In the case shown in Table 3-8, we have a foreign key from PERSONAL_ACCOUNTS to PERSONS and another from CORPORATE_ACCOUNTS to CORPORATIONS. In both cases, the foreign key column will be mandatory; it enforces the rule that an account *must* be for a person or a corporation.

Table 3-8. Separate Tables for Personal and Corporate Accounts

Personal_Accounts

No	Credit Limit	Holder
01623907	100.00	195

Corporate_Accounts

No	Credit Limit	Holder
01694295	150.00	297

This solution has disadvantages when processing all accounts (personal and corporate) collectively.

Which solution?

What conclusion have we reached about arcs? Well, none yet. We have looked at some alternatives, but have we established which one is best? It is virtually impossible to answer this question from the data model alone. We have to look at the function definitions of all the functions that will use (and even maintain) this data; only then do we get the full picture. Our main recommendation here is that you design in favor of the critical or online functions of your business. If this approach doesn't yield a clear preference, then simply take a majority decision and document it as such. Or perhaps all functions could carry a predetermined weighting so a mathematical formula could be used to determine the decision; this would at least avoid subjectivity and personal preference. At least Noah only had a single ark to deal with (as far as we know!).

Entity Life Histories and Data Flow Diagrams

In Chapter 1, in the discussion of the deliverables from analysis to design, we noted that the entity life history diagrams and data flow diagrams were not necessarily mandatory items. Although that is true, these diagrams are extremely useful input to the designer. How do these diagrams relate to the deliverables we've already looked at?

- The entity relationship diagrams and the entity definitions describe the data.

- The functional hierarchies and descriptions describe the processes.

- The entity life history and data flow diagrams serve to pull the data and the process together to give a more complete specification of how the system should work.

Entity Life Histories (ELHs)

Entity life history diagrams are a specific instance of a class of diagrams known as state transition diagrams (STDs). Their main purpose in life is to illustrate the life cycle of an entity as it passes through the phases from its original inception to a final "resting" state.

Inclusion of entity life histories makes the analysis more comprehensive and gives an insight into the meaning of an entity. If these histories are included as deliverables in your project, make sure to specify a separate one for each of the major entities within the system. There may be one for every cardinal entity in the model. Remember that a cardinal entity is one that represents a real world thing, as opposed to one that is introduced to resolve a many-to-many relationship. Of course, not every entity in the systems will be subject to a change of state other than the two implicit states of "created" and "deleted," sometimes with the additional state "archived." However, if an entity has a column named *status* or something similar, then it should have a life history specified—whether in diagrammatic form or simply written.

There are many conventions for drawing this type of diagram. Figure 3-29 borrows the fence diagram convention used by James Martin[*] and shows the life history of an Order in a simplified fictitious Order Entry System.

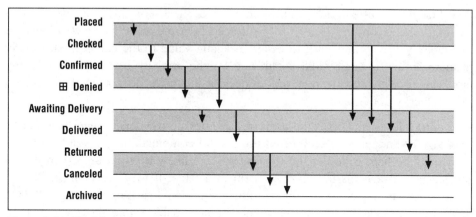

Figure 3-29. The life and times of an order

The arrows in the fence indicate valid transitions of state. For example, it is valid for an Order to progress from "Checked" to "Confirmed" or from "Checked" to "Denied", but not from "Checked" directly to "Delivered."

The symbol against the status "Denied" indicates a state that can be decomposed into further statuses—for instance, "Denied due to poor credit rating", "Denied due to unobtainable stock items", etc.

What is not obvious from this diagram is which states are valid start points in the life of an Order and which are valid terminal states. In the example case (Figure 3-29), the state at the top of the diagram is the only valid initial state of an Order ("Placed") and the bottom is the only valid final state ("Archived"). However, most analysts don't concern themselves with archiving, since the process is a physical, system type of thing. If we remove the "Archived" state, then there are four viable terminal states ("Denied", "Delivered", "Returned", "Canceled").

What do we, as designers, do with these entity life history diagrams (other than admire how neat they look)? Most of our work has to do with an attribute (which exists for most of the entities) called something like "STATUS." When we implement STATUS as a column in a table, we will need to enforce three rules:

1. The column should be constrained to only take those values listed as valid statuses.

---

[*] Based on Marth, James and James Odell, *Object-Oriented Analysis and Design*, Prentice-Hall, 1992.

2. The initial value of the column in a new row must be a valid initial value.

3. When an update of this column occurs, we must ensure that it is a valid state transition.

The first rule is usually best implemented as a check constraint on the STATUS column. The second rule is typically enforced by a pre-insert row-level trigger on the table; you may also wish to assign a default value to the column, particularly if there is only a single valid initial state for the row. By using the default, any applications which create new occurrences of this table do not need to concern themselves with the status.

The third rule usually takes the form of a pre-update row-level trigger that checks *:old.STATUS* and *:new.STATUS* to ensure a valid combination. The valid combinations may be hard-coded in the trigger (or more likely a procedure called by the trigger); even better is to soft-code them in a table. If they are being held in a table, then we may consider (for performance reasons) caching them in a PL/SQL table that is declared as a package persistent variable. Note, however, that in current production releases of Oracle7 this approach is likely to prove resource-hungry. As usual, the best answer lies in encapsulation; we write the trigger to call a packaged procedure and then test which approach is fastest for this data, this platform, and these software versions. If we ever want to change our approach, then we need to change only the packaged procedure; the trigger code is unaware of the mechanism used to supply the result.

To illustrate some of the points we made earlier in this section, let's take another example and use another diagramming convention. Figure 3-30 shows the life of a check, as issued by your friendly bank.

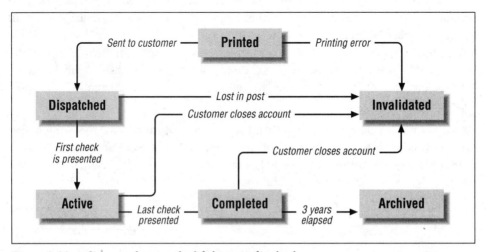

Figure 3-30. A diagram showing the life history of a check

This style of diagram has the advantage that it shows the events which trigger the changes of status to the entity. As with the previous approach, it is not obvious at first glance which of the statuses may be an initial status of a check and which are valid terminal statuses. In this case, a Check comes into being as "Printed" and departs as either "Invalidated" or "Archived." One major clue to a check's particular status this is that "Printed" has no inbound arrows, and "Archived" and "Invalidated" have no outbound ones. However, this is not a 100% proof method of determining initial and final statuses; you need to document it separately.

Data Flow Diagrams (DFDs)

Data flow diagrams are used to model the passage of data through the system by showing a networked structure of the data. DFDs do not show the processes that control this flow of data, nor do they make any attempt to distinguish between valid and invalid paths through the data. However, DFDs have many useful features; they:

- Provide a way to document the system from the point of view of the data itself.

- Illustrate external data feeds that will require an interface of some kind.

- Document the manual processes of the system, as well as computer-based ones.

- Perform a data-centric partitioning of the overall system.

Figure 3-31 shows a simple data flow diagram that demonstrates many of the typical constructs. The box marked "Customer" represents a *repeating external entity*. Notice that this entity appears twice in the diagram. This repetition is a common feature of DFD; it is better to show the flow from left to right, rather than attempting to loop it back to the first construct. Loops are a bit alien to the concept of DFDs since they smack of processing rather than data flow.

The boxes with rounded corners marked "P1" and "P2" are our *data processes*. It is likely that these are high-level data processes which would eventually be broken down into more detailed DFDs. For instance, the "Take Order" process (P1) would probably determine the payment method and would check on the credit rating of the Customer.

The open-ended rectangles marked D4, D7, and D8 are our data stores.

There is much more that can be said about data flow diagrams, and we've only touched on the topic here. But because DFDs are an analysis tool, they're outside the scope of this book.

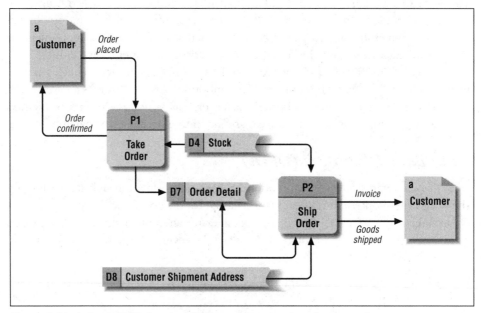

Figure 3-31. A simple DFD showing the flow of data in an order processing system

Data-Driven Design and Meta Models

Most applications are designed to be code-driven. What does this mean? Although their action may well depend in any given case on the values of the data items held (such as whether there is enough money in a bank account to allow a check to be drawn), the rules to be applied in a particular case are specified in the code of the application—or perhaps in declarative constraints applied to tables. This means that any change to the rules can only be implemented by making a change to the code and (if the site has any sense) incurring the cost of retesting the application. If the application is highly distributed, then issues of code and version control may have to be addressed.

Clearly, if we can remove rules from the application code and place them instead in the database, we add flexibility to the actions that the application is able to take. The analysis output for most projects will include a number of reference tables. Some of these will often be used simply to store textual expansions of code values (such as mapping "FR" to "France" and "DE" to "Germany"), but we would expect that others will contain values required within the code (such as tax rates and authorization limits). We do not classify these as data-driven design and, in general, regard it as extremely poor practice to code as a literal any value which is liable to change.

In some projects, however, it is clear that the users require (or may require, which is not quite the same thing) the ability to change how the application works, possibly on a per-record basis. A frequent request is the ability to be able to assign an arbitrary property to a record, the computerized equivalent of writing a comment across the bottom of a contact card. Figure 3-32 shows an example:

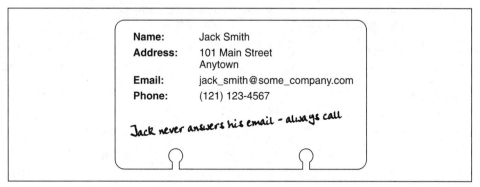

Name:	Jack Smith
Address:	101 Main Street
	Anytown
Email:	jack_smith@some_company.com
Phone:	(121) 123-4567

Jack never answers his email - always call

Figure 3-32. Assigning an arbitrary property to a record

The analysts should have been able to detect this requirement, and should have introduced an attribute with a name like COMMENT or, more rigorously, a new entity CONTACT_COMMENT to allow any number such comments to be held for a given contact. The problems start when we also want to add an entity CONTACT_PROCEDURE, which contains the details of not just the procedures to be followed clerically by the user on reading the record, but also the procedure to be followed by the application when it reads the record. We are now introducing into the data the ability to specify *application rules*.

In Appendix B, *Tricks of the Trade*, we discuss some of the techniques which can be used to cope with this type of requirement. For the moment, we will simply observe that to support this type of requirement, your entity model will need to take the form of a *meta model* and that this raises the risk profile of your project.

A *meta model* is simply a model of another model. Every data dictionary is a meta model because its structures are defined as a set of tables which are used to store the definition of a set of tables. With Oracle, as with most relational database managers, this meta model also describes itself, so the Oracle table SYS.OBJ$, which has information about all of the objects in an Oracle database, must itself contain an entry for the table SYS.OBJ$.

We refer to such a model as having two *levels of abstraction*. There is an entry in a dictionary that defines an entry in a dictionary that defines a table.

If you need to employ a meta model, then the discussion at the end of Appendix B should help you, but please be quite sure that you really do need this level of complexity.

WARNING   Few people can cope with operations spanning more than one level
             of abstraction, and almost nobody can cope easily with operations
             spanning more than two levels of abstraction.

II

Designing the Database

This part of the book describes the design of Oracle databases:

- Chapter 4, *Deciding When to Denormalize*, examines specific techniques for denormalizing the data in the database to improve performance.

- Chapter 5, *Choosing Datatypes and Nulls*, defines the various Oracle datatypes and explores the thorny issues of what null means and how nulls should be treated.

- Chapter 6, *Choosing Keys and Indexes*, discusses how to choose the best keys for your particular database.

- Chapter 7, *Dealing with Temporal Data*, explores a specific problem with Oracle and other relational databases—they don't adequately support time-series (temporal) data. It suggests a number of Oracle-specific techniques that you can use to overcome restrictions on this type of data.

- Chapter 8, *Loading and Unloading Data*, explores the various ways that you can populate your Oracle7 database from external data sources. It also discusses how to extract data from the Oracle7 database.

- Chapter 9, *Deciding on Object Placement and Storage*, looks at some of the most important physical aspects of database design, such as sizing and file placement.

- Chapter 10, *Safeguarding Your Data*, covers the topics of backup, archiving auditing, and security

4

Deciding When to Denormalize

In the previous chapter, we took a look at some of the decisions the designer needs to take when mapping entities to tables. Once we've achieved this mapping and we are happy with it, is the data element of our design complete? Unfortunately, no: we still have some important issues to deal with. One of those is the art of denormalization. After all the trouble we went to in the previous chapter to ensure that the information model is in third normal form (or Boyce-Codd normal form), we are now going to start breaking it! But, as we will see, we "break" the model only in a very controlled manner and only where it will improve performance.

This chapter examines the various types of denormalization and the methods of implementing this process. We also look at the use of triggers to support denormalization without having to rely on the application code to maintain the integrity of the data.

Denormalization: What, Why, and When?

Denormalization is a process of making compromises to the normalized tables by introducing intentional redundancy for performance reasons.

You'll often realize that denormalization is required only when you are in the middle of designing a module. In other words, you can't normally make decisions about denormalization from the data model alone. Remember that one man's meat is another man's poison, and a denormalization decision that benefits one module (by increasing its efficiency and simplicity) is likely to have a detrimental effect on one or more other modules (typically by making updates more complex or introducing the potential for lock conflicts). Sanity has to reign here. You will certainly be rational enough to realize that making the code that generates an annual report more efficient at the expense of an online application would not be a sound decision. Make sure to select the critical processes in your application and, in general, make your denormalization decisions in favor of these processes. The critical processes are usually determined on the basis of high frequency (they are run a lot), high volume (they process a lot of data), high volatility (the data is changed frequently) or explicit priority (the users say they are important).

Of course, if a radically different data model would reduce 200 hours of annual report processing to 20 minutes, then there may be a strong case for creating the required tables once a year. But even this will be a sound option only if you have the required disk space and if the table creation takes markedly less than 200 hours. See Chapter 8, *Loading and Unloading Data*, for some of the techniques that may help you to achieve this goal.

TIP   We have both seen denormalization employed purely to simplify the SQL when accessing the database. If you need to simplify the SQL at the generator or user level, then you should probably be using views rather than introducing redundancy. Remember, however, that views do *not* simplify the SQL as seen by the Oracle7 SQL engine, which has to expand the view definition within the context of the query.

Typically, a denormalization will improve query time at the expense of DML (insert, update, and delete) (see Figure 4-1). Think of denormalization as an extension to the normalized data model that will improve query performance. Consider what is important to your application, and make sure that you record all decisions (with justifications) somewhere in your design log. Always bear in mind that there may be other ways of achieving high performance without denormalizing. For example, these may include changes to indexing and run unit design.

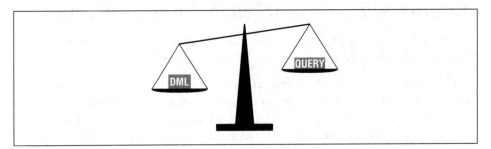

Figure 4-1. The delicate balance of denormalization

Let's go on to consider the various common types of denormalization. Some of these we recommend, and others we don't (or we recommend them only in exceptional circumstances).

Downward Denormalization

Downward denormalization involves pulling down an attribute from a parent. In Figure 4-2, you can see in the denormalized logical model that we have pulled the customer name amount down from the CUSTOMER entity into the ORDER entity. Why would we do this? Actually, in general our advice is: *don't do this!!* The only advantage is that by doing this we avoid a join when we want to see a customer name with an order.

Eliminating joins via downward denormalization rarely justifies the expense of having to maintain the denormalized column in ORDER. These joins are not usually a major problem, and performing a downward denormalization to eliminate them tends to result in lots of expensive update cascades for little or no real benefit. For example, if a CUSTOMER changes name, then we have to update all ORDERS to reflect the name. Or should we? We may be in a quandary about whether old orders that have been fulfilled and closed should be updated. If we didn't denormalize, then we wouldn't have this quandary.

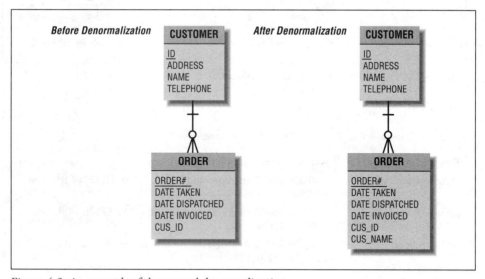

Figure 4-2. An example of downward denormalization

In our experience, only data warehouse applications really justify a downward denormalization to eliminate a join. Why? Because in data warehouses the data is historic, so update cascades cannot occur. Without downward denormalization, many queries may need to join a billion-row table to several other tables of significant size, which can be time consuming, to say the least. Data warehouses are discussed in detail in Chapter 13, *Designing for Data Warehouses.*

Upward Denormalization

In the case shown in Figure 4-3, we are storing information from the child in the parent, in summary or aggregated form.

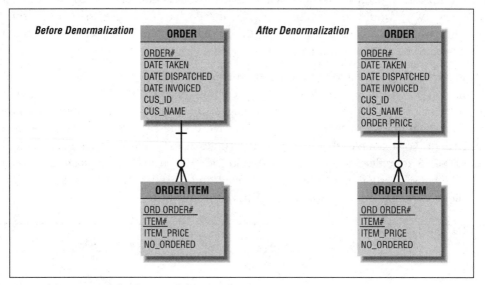

Figure 4-3. An example of upward denormalization

Consider the simple, but classic, example shown in Table 4-1.

Table 4-1. Housekeeping Tasks to Maintain Denormalized Values

Event on ORDER_ITEM	Actions on Related ORDER
New row added	ORDER_PRICE incremented by the ITEM_PRICE of the new ORDER_ITEM
Row deleted	ORDER_PRICE decremented by the ITEM_PRICE of the old ORDER_ITEM
Price updated	ORDER_PRICE adjusted by the difference between the old and the new ITEM_PRICE of the ORDER_ITEM

If some of the critical functions in this order processing system process ORDER, and require the value of the ORDER (the sum of ITEM_PRICE on their ORDER_ITEM entities), then we can improve the performance of these important functions by storing this derived order total as a redundant column (called ORDER_PRICE in our example) on ORDER. Table 4-1 illustrates the additional housekeeping tasks that are required to maintain the denormalized values. This puts an extra load on processes that perform heavy DML on ORDER_ITEM. This is the cost we have to bear for better query performance. Notice in our example that we are holding a total value, but the techniques apply equally to maximum, minimum, average, or any other type of aggregate.

Methods of Implementing Denormalization

In the example in the previous section, we highlighted some tasks that need to be carried out to maintain the denormalized data within our database. How, specifically, will we perform this task? In the dark ages (Oracle Version 6 and before), every application that issued DML on ORDER_ITEM was responsible for ensuring the integrity of any denormalized columns by performing the appropriate action(s). This led to inevitable inconsistencies in the data. Even if you were careful to check your applications, someone would come along with an ad hoc tool such as SQL*Plus and "make a quick fix" to the data (such as delete an invalid ORDER_ITEM), but forget to make the appropriate adjustment to the denormalized or derived columns.

The scenario described here led to the endless development of scripts for Version 6 databases that had to be run periodically by the DBA to check the integrity of the denormalized data and to report violations. The following SQL is an example of such a script, written for the tables derived from our ORDER and ORDER_ITEM entities (after denormalization).

```
SELECT ord.order#
  FROM orders ord
 WHERE ord.order_price <> (SELECT SUM(oit.item_price)
                             FROM   order_items oit
                             WHERE  oit.ord_order# = ord.order#);
```

Now those days are gone and the integrity script writers can hang up their keyboards, turn off the lights and go home; in Oracle7 we can implement the denormalizations with *database triggers*. Well, hold on a minute before the last script writer locks the door—triggers can be disabled, and so we have no way of checking any data that slipped through while they were sleeping. We may still need those diagnostic scripts! The following trigger illustrates how simple it is to implement as database triggers the rules that were listed in the table.

```
CREATE OR REPLACE TRIGGER oit_bir BEFORE INSERT ON order_items
FOR EACH ROW

l_item_price ORDER_ITEMS.ITEM_PRICE%TYPE;
l_ord_order ORDER_ITEMS.ORD_ORDER#%TYPE;
```

```
begin
  l_item_price := :new.item_price;
  l_ord_order := :new.ord_order#;

  UPDATE orders ord
  SET    ord.order_price = ord.order_price + l_item_price
  WHERE  ord.order# = l_ord_order;
END;

CREATE OR REPLACE TRIGGER oit_bdr BEFORE DELETE ON order_items
FOR EACH ROW

l_item_price ORDER_ITEMS.ITEM_PRICE%TYPE;
l_ord_order ORDER_ITEMS.ORD_ORDER#%TYPE;

BEGIN
  l_item_price := :old.item_price;
  l_ord_order := :old.ord_order#;

  UPDATE orders ord
  SET    ord.order_price = ord.order_price - l_item_price
  WHERE  ord.order# = l_ord_order;
END;

CREATE OR REPLACE TRIGGER oit_bur BEFORE UPDATE OF tot_price ON order_
items
FOR EACH ROW

l_old_item_price ORDER_ITEMS.ITEM_PRICE%TYPE;
l_new_item_price ORDER_ITEMS.ITEM_PRICE%TYPE;
l_ord_order ORDER_ITEMS.ORD_ORDER#%TYPE;

BEGIN
  l_new_item_price := :new.item_price;
  l_old_item_price := :old.item_price;
  l_ord_order := :new.ord_order;

  UPDATE orders ord
  SET    ord.order_price = ord.order_price - l_old_item_price + l_new_
item_price
  WHERE  ord.order# = l_ord_order;
END;
```

Implementation of the denormalized columns via triggers seems like a robust and elegant solution—but is there a down side to this approach? There is an obscure problem that can impede performance under certain conditions. Assume that our orders have a lot of items on average (say, 1,000). We periodically delete orders and, because of our referential integrity constraints, we must delete the order items first. Consider the seemingly innocuous statement:.

```
DELETE order_items oit
WHERE oit.ord_id = :x;
```

A simple delete like this will incur a high level of database activity. If you look back at our trigger definition, you can see that our triggers are "for each row," meaning that the OIT_BDR triggers will fire 1,000 times if the order being deleted has 1,000 items attached to it. To add to our frustration, we know that the end result will be ORDER_PRICE = 0, and we are going to subsequently delete the order anyway!

Now that we've revealed this flaw, don't be put off using triggers to support denormalization just because of it; there are ways around the problem, and it's just something you have to watch out for. To overcome this potential problem, we signal the trigger not to do anything by setting a package persistent variable to indicate our intention prior to the delete. This could actually be set in a delete trigger on ORDERS in conjunction with a cascade constraint, which will cause automatic deletion of related ORDER_ITEMS. Even with our prevention mechanism in place, the trigger will fire 1,000 times but won't perform an update each time. In fact, it won't really do any processing at all other than checking the variable and terminating.

To find out more about using package persistent variables to influence the behavior of triggers, see the example in Appendix B, *Tricks of the Trade*.

Other Types of Denormalization

This section looks at some additional types of denormalization: intra-table, "divide-and-conquer," and table merging.

Intra-Table Denormalization

Another form of denormalization occurs within a single table. What is the benefit of holding a value that is derivable from other data in the row? The only valid reason would be if there is a requirement for the row to be queried on the derived value. For instance, if a row has two numeric columns, X and Y, then the value Z defined as the product of X and Y ($Z = X \times Y$) can easily be computed at runtime with negligible overhead. However let's assume that there are queries which need to search on Z (for example, where Z is between 10 and 20). By storing the redundant Z values in a column, an index can be built on Z and the queries can use this index. If no index were going to be built on Z, then the decision about whether to hold it as a derived column would depend on the perceived load of having to continually recompute it versus the increased scan time resulting from holding it and making the rows longer.

A more common example is to hold a text column in mixed-case for display and data entry, and in uppercase with an index to allow speedy case-insensitive query. See the example in Figure 4-4.

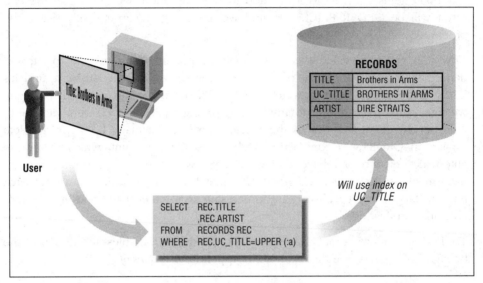

Figure 4-4. Using a derived column to optimize a query

NOTE   Oracle has announced its intention of supporting indexes on expressions in a future version. This will be especially useful for supporting case-independent searches.

You can avoid this type of denormalization by using a technique that we've found gives decent performance on moderate size tables, with no effect on the table size or DML performance. The trick is to preprocess the query, as shown in the following listing. This technique works well on data which is not highly skewed, but it is not so hot for attributes like titles of abstracts or papers, many of which start with "An " or "The ." You can enable this mechanism in Oracle Forms Versions 4.0 and 4.5 (case insensitive query option).

The query:

```
SELECT rec_title
     , rec_artist
  FROM records r
 WHERE r.title = 'Brothers in Arms'.
```

is transformed to:

```
SELECT rec_title
     , rec_artist
  FROM records r
 WHERE (   r.title LIKE 'Br%'
        OR r.title LIKE 'br%'
        OR r.title LIKE 'BR%'
        OR r.title LIKE 'bR%' )
   AND UPPER(r.title) = UPPER('.rothers in Arms'.;
```

Divide and Conquer Denormalization

Splitting a normalized table into two or more tables, and creating a one-to-one relationship between them, can just possibly be categorized as a form of denormalization—but why would you want to do this? Well, it may be for practical reasons (you have no choice). There is a restriction in Oracle that a table cannot have more than one LONG or LONG RAW column. Suppose that you have a table called PROGRAMS and we need to store both the source code (LONG) and the object code (LONG RAW). Because of the restriction, you can't achieve this in a single table, so you have to move one of them out. The Oracle restriction of allowing only one LONG or LONG RAW column per table is expected to be relaxed in Oracle8. For the moment, however, this restriction may cause a designer to split a table into two.

It is sometimes a good practical decision to move a LONG column into a separate table even when the restriction does not apply. Consider the table whose row contents are illustrated in Figure 4-5. If the LONG column is usually populated with data, and we are likely to perform non-indexed queries on any of the non-key columns, Oracle will use a full table scan to evaluate these queries; this will involve additional I/O because of the presence of the LONG column in the table.

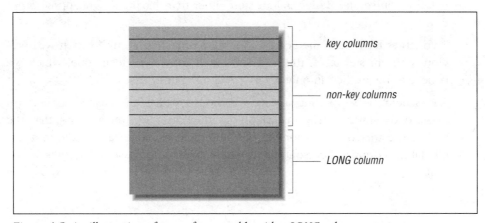

Figure 4-5. An illustration of a row from a table with a LONG column

To eradicate this problem (if it is going to be a problem—really, we would like to avoid full table scans completely), separate the table as shown in Figure 4-6. Chapter 5, *Choosing Datatypes and Nulls,* contains some further advice about the use of LONG and LONG RAW columns.

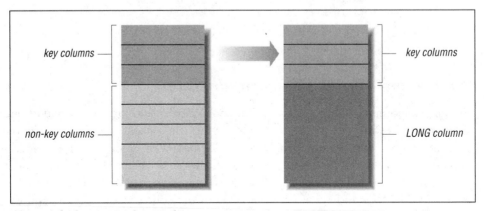

Figure 4-6. The LONG column split out

Again, we have some reason to expect that Oracle8 will remove the need for such an artificial solution, in this case by not storing the LONG value in-line but instead holding it in a "side table" reserved for the purpose.

Oracle7 has a limit of 254 columns per table, and if a table were proposed with more than 254 columns, this would also present a reason for having to divide the table into two. We seriously question whether any well-designed schema would need tables with anything like 254 columns except in three specific cases:

- The application is being directly converted from a legacy system and each table is constructed in the precise image of a file in the legacy system; in this case, of course, the design is inherited rather than having any relational properties.

- Two tables have been merged by forming a repeating group in what was previously the master table; the next section discusses this technique, which we believe to be justified in only a very small number of cases.

- The schema is supporting a data warehouse which has elected to perform massive downward denormalization: in this case, we recommend that the table be restricted to the number of columns that Oracle can handle in a single table as any other solution is likely to cause massive 1:1 joins to be required.

In fact, a good pragmatic measure of the degree of normalization is the number of columns per table. As a rule of thumb, very few primary keys have more than 20 truly dependent attributes.

Table Merging Denormalization

After all the hard work that we put into normalizing data structures and splitting entities, are we really going to start merging tables together? What about all the dangers of anomalies in the data that we warned you about? In fact, there are only a few cases where a merger can be justified. Remember that we shouldn't normally be considering this to avoid a join—outside data warehouses joins aren't bad.

One example of a valid case for a merger is a repeating group that is guaranteed to have a fixed number of members. Good candidates for this are tables with a row for each month of a year or each day of a week. The example shown below, however, is a simplified system for recording golf scores. Working under the assumption that a round is never more than 18 holes (which may be flawed), we could implement our SCORE table as a single row per round, rather than 19 rows per round (a header plus 18 detail records). Figures 4-7 and 4-8 show such an implementation when we merge SCORE and HOLE.

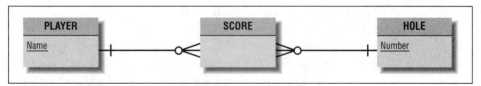

Figure 4-7. A simple model for golf scores

Figure 4-8. A score table illustrating a repeating group with a fixed member count

What is the advantage of this implementation? In our trivial case, there may not be an appreciable advantage, but notice that we can calculate the total for the round (or the first nine or the last nine) by referencing only a single row. This might be significant if we were holding details of a vast number of golf rounds in our database and often performing aggregate queries such as "Best round for Arnold Palmer," "Best first nine holes for Cory Pavin at St. Andrews," etc. With our denormalized design, these types of queries will perform well.

What will perform very badly indeed, and will also be less than elegant to write, will be any requirement to access holes as a set. Consider the query to find all the holes-in-one or, worse still, the query to find all the albatrosses by joining to a table which has a single row per course which gives all 18 pars for the course. It's the old, old story—our approach to denormalization must be guided by the processing requirements that we have for the data. One of the great features of the table above illustrating the repeating group is that we can insert it very quickly. It takes only one INSERT statement, whereas the normalized version will use 19.

We mentioned that our assumption of a round always having 18 holes was suspect. Some rounds never reach 18 holes, and in match-play events the game can go beyond 18 holes if the match is tied after 18. However, we might not need to record playoff holes and we can leave unplayed holes null, so maybe our assumption is OK. However, this situation is indicative of the kind of trouble we can run into with such a design. The only cases where fixed groups are safe are when they are for truly invariant things such as days of the week. In particular, it is dangerous to use this technique to reflect a current trend and allow contingency in the future. For example, we would be playing a dangerous game if we were to denormalize seats onto aircraft and allow for up to 1,000 passengers per flight. You can bet that whatever figure we use, both Boeing and Airbus Industries will one day build a plane that is bigger!

An alternative to this method of denormalization is to physically cluster the tables together using Oracle's table clusters. This enables us to keep the tables logically separate, but to store related rows in close physical proximity. We discuss clusters further when we start to get more physical in Chapter 6, *Choosing Keys and Indexes*.

5

Choosing Datatypes and Nulls

Every table column in a database has a number of properties that dictate what can and what cannot be stored in it. These properties are the *type,* the *size* (or length), and any *constraints* that may further restrict the valid set of values that can occupy it. For instance, a column may be described as follows:

```
amount NUMBER(8,2) NOT NULL CONSTRAINT cc_limit_amnt CHECK (amount > 0)
```

This column can take only numeric data; it must be populated for every row of the table; it must be a positive value; and it will be held to two significant decimal places. The maximum value it can hold is 999999.99. In this simple definition of the column, we have actually defined a number of implicit rules that Oracle will enforce when data is entered into it.

In the conceptual model, produced during the analysis phase, no consideration is given to the implementation medium. The analyst simply defines attributes as being string, number, or date; ideally, he or she also assigns a *domain* to the attribute. A domain is simply an attribute type, such as *money* or *working day,* and may include a series of validation checks or data rules such as a requirement that the value be positive, nonzero, and have a maximum of two decimal places (useful for the amount of a dollar banker's draft). The use of domains makes it easier to enforce consistency. Unfortunately, Oracle does not (yet) support abstract datatypes (ADTs) (loosely, these are user-defined column types). Thus, during design we must translate both the attribute and domain descriptions into the column definitions. For example, we could define a domain called MONEY that is defined as NUMBER(8,2), and a domain called CHASSIS_NO that is NUMBER(11). Oracle8 is expected to support ADTS, and many CASE tools support them.

This chapter is all about helping you decide what datatypes are applicable for your columns. For instance, when you are storing numeric data that is used for reference only (it is never used in calculations), should it be held as a NUMBER, as CHAR, or as VARCHAR2? There are sometimes subtle implications to a particular choice of datatype, and there may be undesirable side effects. In this chapter, we focus particularly on the use of null. Nulls seem so innocent until you start to delve more deeply into them and ask such philosophical questions as "What exactly does a null value mean here?" Nulls are very prevalent in most databases that we have encountered; here we ask the question: "Should they be?"

Available Datatypes

There are actually remarkably few column types in Oracle7. If you exclude those that are used exclusively for Trusted Oracle, there are only eight types:

> VARCHAR2 (aka VARCHAR)
> NUMBER
> LONG
> DATE
> RAW
> LONG RAW
> ROWID
> CHAR

Of these types, three cover the vast majority of columns. These are VARCHAR2, NUMBER, and DATE. Having such a small set of datatypes may seem restrictive, but if you think about it, this is not the case. Types that are popular in other database products and languages can be derived. For instance, MONEY is simply a NUMBER with two decimal places, POSITIVE INTEGER is a NUMBER with no decimal places and a constraint to ensure that negative values are rejected. At least you don't have to worry about internal storage constraints to decide, for instance, whether a real number should be a FLOAT or a DOUBLE.

When you are choosing from the available datatypes, the most important thing is that you be consistent. If you define a vehicle chassis number as NUMBER(11) in one table and VARCHAR(15) in another, you will find yourself in all kinds of difficulty when you come to join them. Try writing the SQL to match 918273645 with "918-27-36/4/5". Did you say "easy" to yourself? Now write it so that it will be efficient in a join clause!

Numeric Data

There are two types of numeric data:

1. Integer or real values. These are the subject of arithmetic processing—for example, a bank account balance or an interest rate.

2. String data, such as bank account numbers, in which the only valid characters are digits.

Integer or Real Values

You must be sure to evaluate integers and real values during design to ensure that the column is defined large enough to hold the highest (and lowest) allowable number in the domain. You also need to enforce the maximum and minimum by defining a check constraint on the column. Picking a suitable precision for a number column is likely to be a problem only if the value is a real number—that is, one with digits after the decimal point.

Many designers simply ignore these requirements, and implement the column without specifying either scale or precision as follows:

```
, length  NUMBER CHECK (length BETWEEN 0 AND 100)
, height  NUMBER CHECK (height BETWEEN 0 AND 50)
, width   NUMBER CHECK (width  BETWEEN 0 AND 100)
```

This will work, but may use unexpectedly high amounts of storage. Oracle stores numbers in *decimal* floating point rather than *binary* floating point, and it also stores them as variable length. Although any whole number (e.g., 123,226,334) can be translated exactly from binary to decimal and back again, very few real numbers can. So if, in a C program, we have the binary floating-point representation of 10.2, it will be inserted into an Oracle number as a 38-digit string that will be very, very close to 10.2 but not exactly equal. This effect is very difficult to demonstrate without using a 3GL program, because all of Oracle's tools very wisely use Oracle's own decimal floating-point format. The following SQL*Plus dialogue demonstrates this problem:

```
SQL> set numwidth 40
SQL> select 1/8 fraction from dual;
FRACTION
----------------------------------------
                                    .125
SQL> select 1/7 fraction from dual;
FRACTION
----------------------------------------
 .1428571428571428571428571428571428571143
```

Fortunately there is a solution, introduced some time ago but rarely used, which allows the precision of an Oracle number to be constrained to be just enough to hold accurately a floating-point number of a certain number of bits, typically 32 or 64 bits. The syntax is:

```
, length  FLOAT(64) CHECK (length BETWEEN 0 AND 100)
, height  FLOAT(32) CHECK (height BETWEEN 0 AND 50)
, width   FLOAT(64) CHECK (width  BETWEEN 0 AND 100)
```

Wherever a number is supposed to be an integer, we recommend that you constrain it to be an integer using NUMBER(nn) and that you also constrain all floating-point numbers to the required precision using FLOAT(nn). Now you may ask whether this is worth it just "to save a few bytes" when disk is so cheap. Our answers:

- It is very easy to do.

- The shorter your data, the less I/O you will consume scanning it; if you have a table which is mainly composed of floating-point data, you can often save 75% of the space using FLOAT and therefore 75% of the block visits in a full table scan.

- You really do not want real numbers in columns that are supposed to contain integers; the logic is likely to assume that they really are integers, and may start failing if fractions turn up.

NOTE   We recommend against using the datatypes INTEGER, SMALLINT and REAL because, although Oracle supports these keywords in DDL, it does not support them in the data dictionary. They are interpreted as NUMBER(38), NUMBER(38), and FLOAT(63) respectively. Like us, you may feel that a 38-digit number cannot really be defined as a SMALLINT!

Strings of Digits

The preceding section talked about numbers that really are numbers. But how about the second type of numeric data—items like a social security number on which no sensible system would be performing numeric functions? What about surrogate keys that are generated from a sequence? Should you use NUMBER columns or VARCHAR2? There are several points to consider.

Leading zeroes that are entered into NUMBER columns are not recorded. If the domain of account numbers contains a number such as "0321234", the database will accept it but will be unable to distinguish it internally from "321234", even though it will find it when queried for "0321234". Serious problems occur if it is possible that "321234" and "031234" are both valid, yet separate, account numbers.

If you use an ORDER BY clause on a VARCHAR, then Oracle will use a character sort collating sequence and the values will be returned in the sequence 1, 10, 11, 12, 13, 14, 15, 16, 17, 18, 19, 2, 20... We have all seen this one! Putting a TO_NUMBER function around the column in the ORDER BY clause will rectify the problem, but will preclude the use of an index to perform the sort. Of course if we left-pad the values with zeroes on INSERT, then the sort sequence will be correct and an index can still be used. However, this approach is performed at the expense of disk space, and we have to decide if it is acceptable for the data to be displayed with leading zeroes. Does it look right, or (worse) does it change the meaning?

When we have to compare the values in a range check, it is safer and more efficient to do so with pure numbers. For instance, putting a cap or ceiling on a column with a constraint like this:

```
ss_no NUMBER(9) CONSTRAINT cc_valid_ss CHECK (ss_no < 711111111)
```

is more efficient and less prone to error than

```
ss_no VARCHAR2(9) CONSTRAINT cc_valid_ss CHECK (ss_no < '711111111'.
```

which relies on the ASCI collating sequence (so the value 9 will fail). If you insist on using a VARCHAR in this case, the preferred form is

```
ss_no VARCHAR2(9) CONSTRAINT cc_valid_ss CHECK (to_number(ss_no) <
711111111)
```

Our preference is to use NUMBER for strings of digits in most cases. The main exception is where leading zeroes are significant in distinguishing values.

Date and Time (Temporal) Data

Storing dates is straightforward, isn't it? We simply use a DATE column, since Oracle does not offer any choice. No, that isn't quite right. In reality, there are a series of choices, and the results of these choices can materially affect both the reliability and the performance of the application.

Oracle dates have a granularity of a second, meaning that all times are recorded to the nearest second. If you need to store dates with time to a higher precision, several options are available to you.

1. You can hold the date in a fixed format in a character field (such as "1995 02 19 21 40 57.223456"). This approach holds the time to the nearest millisecond and also collates correctly, but it requires a rather tedious function to perform date difference.

2. You can solve the date difference problem by holding the date and time as a number representing the milliseconds, microseconds, or nanoseconds since a

fixed point in time. This has the disadvantage that it requires a function to convert it to and from a meaningful format for display and reporting, but with 38-digit numbers you are most unlikely to have any problem with precision.

3. A good compromise may be to hold the date truncated to the nearest second in an Oracle DATE column and to hold the residual amount in nanoseconds (or your chosen unit) in a separate NUMBER column. But be sure that the "date" is truncated and not rounded!

In passing, it is worth noting that Oracle7 Version 7.1 and higher, with the ability to call user PL/SQL functions from SQL, makes it somewhat easier to handle ad hoc reporting from tables which have used essentially artificial techniques to record dates. If we have a table that contains sensor readings whose time is recorded to the nearest millisecond, we can create (non-updatable) views which report the data however we wish. An example of such a view definition is:

```
CREATE VIEW sensor_readings_v1
       ( sensor_id
       , sensor_name
       , reading_taken
       , reading_value
       ) AS
    SELECT r.sensor_id
         , s.sensor_name
         , readings.point_in_time_text(r.read_date, r.read_msec)
         , reading_value
      FROM sensor_readings r
         , sensors          s
       WHERE s.sensor_id = r.sensor_id;
```

Unlike some other RDBMS products, Oracle has only one datatype for recording date and time information, and many would argue that Oracle currently falls a bit short of the ANSI-92 SQL standard in this respect. With Oracle's DATE datatype, every date has a time component—whether you want it or not, and whether or not you regard it as significant. If the time has not been specified, or if the value has been truncated using the TRUNC function, then the time will be recorded as midnight.

We suggest that you adopt a naming convention to distinguish date-only columns from DATE and TIME columns. For instance, APPOINTMENT_DT is a date and time column, whereas APPOINTMENT_D is a date-only column.

In addition to adopting a naming convention, we recommend that you also actively prevent columns that are date-only from having a time component. The next example shows both a prevention (which rejects violations using a constraint) and a cure (which truncates the time using a trigger). The choice is yours. It is advisable to have at least one of these in place since comparisons will yield both unexpected and undesirable results if the table has a mixture of dates with and without time in a single column. You might choose to have both prevention and cure in place if you are concerned about the consequences of triggers being disabled—for example, during bulk loading.

```
CREATE TABLE events
    ( event_code  VARCHAR2(10) CONSTRAINT event_code_exist
            FOREIGN KEY REFERENCES event_types
    , event_date  DATE         CONSTRAINT event_date_no_time
            CHECK (event_date = TRUNC(event_date)) — prevention
    );

CREATE TRIGGER event_date BEFORE INSERT OR UPDATE ON events FOR EACH
ROW
BEGIN :new.event_date := TRUNC(:new.event_date);
END;                         — cure
```

A common problem with dates is that a developer incorrectly specifies a format mask in a program somewhere. Typical examples are the use of MM instead of MI for minutes (MM is the month as a numeric) or the use of HH for hour rather than HH24 (for a 24-hour clock). Unfortunately, there is nothing that we, as designers, can do to prevent these problems from occurring, other than inspect code closely during reviews! However, if you have code-checking programs, then these can look for suspect date masks; for example, a mask like "DD-MON-YYYY HH:MM" is doubly suspect because:

- It contains the month twice, and

- It contains the hour according to the 12-hour clock, with no a.m./p.m. indicator.

With the year 2000 looming, there is likely to be a host of date-related problems on the horizon. Stories are already emerging of entire legacy systems being rewritten because the anticipated impact is so severe. Any defensive coding or validation techniques that can be employed now will serve to minimize these problems in years to come. This subject is covered in some detail in Appendix B, *Tricks of the Trade*.

Chapter 7, *Dealing with Temporal Data*, describes the handling of dates in greater detail.

String Data

Most character or string data is stored in Oracle CHAR or VARCHAR2 columns. The essential difference between these two datatypes is that CHAR data is fixed length and can hold a maximum of 255 characters, whereas VARCHAR2 data is true variable length and can hold a maximum of 2000 characters. Unless the data is genuinely fixed size, such as a one-character flag value, we recommend that you use VARCHAR2; it is much the safer option.

What if the column could potentially hold more than 2000 characters? We have several choices:

- We could assign the column the type LONG (although we will deal with reservations about the use of LONG later in this chapter).

- We could split the data over several columns in the table (not really recommended!).

- We could put it in a detail table (thereby giving it virtually unlimited size since it can occupy many rows).

The last option is generally the favored one, and in Oracle7 is essential if we are to be able to refer to the data in predicate clauses—that is, to reference it in WHERE and HAVING clauses.

String Comparison Semantics

There are a series of nasty traps built into SQL's comparison semantics, such as the problems that can arise when comparing truncated date values with date values which also contain the time, and comparing numbers of varying degrees of precision. In addition, there can be problems when comparing character strings of different lengths. It may also be worth bearing in mind that in SQL all string literals are (quite reasonably) deemed to be fixed length (i.e., they have the datatype CHAR).

With strings of equal length there is no problem, they are simply matched character for character and they are either equal or they are not equal. However, if the two strings are of different length and either is fixed-length, then inside the comparison logic the shorter is padded with spaces to bring it up to the length of the longer. Thus, if we have two VARCHAR2 columns, A and B, which contain 'ab' and 'ab,' then we will find that SQL will tell us that A is not equal to B. However, if we compare 'ab' and 'ab' directly, as literals, then SQL will tell us that they are equal.

Whether or not you agree with this behavior is unfortunately irrelevant because that is how it works. The only sensible action is to ensure that your application does not insert insignificant trailing spaces in VARCHAR columns. (Oracle tools other than SQL*Plus usually remove them for you whether they are insignificant or not.)

Free Text

What about "Comments" or "Description" domains? It is a common feature for tables to include a descriptive column in their definition. What size should you make this column? This is a far from trivial decision; you must consider:

- What percentage of the records will have a comment or description

- Whether even 2000 characters (the maximum for a VARCHAR2) will really be sufficient in every case

- Whether we will always need to fetch the text, or whether (for example) your batch processing will completely ignore it

- What tools the user will have available for editing the text

- What kinds of inquiries will be made against the text

In Oracle Version 5, most projects simply opted for a 240-character field, upping this to 255 in Version 6 when the maximum size of a character string was increased. The simplest choice with Oracle7 is to use a VARCHAR2(2000); this will allow fairly extensive comments.[*] Your screen handler may have a feature that allows the user to maintain this field as though it were a simple document, giving users the ability to add lines, join lines, move lines, and so on.

However, if you now want to create a piece of logic that needs to know how many lines are in the field, or the length of the longest line, or the number of blank lines, you will again need to start writing functions. If the lines are held as rows in a detail table, then these values can be returned by trivial SQL queries.

Also, if we assume that the comments on any given record are likely to grow over time, we have the real risk that we will start to suffer from "migrated rows," as the original physical row grows too large for the database block in which it was originally inserted. This will begin to impact our performance when the rows are queried.

One technique has proved highly successful in cases where comments or case notes are added over time: use a detail table to hold one row per line of comment or description, and place this table in a single table cluster with a cluster key of the primary key of the master table, as shown in the following example:

```
CREATE CLUSTER case_notes_c ( case# varchar2(12) );

CREATE INDEX ON CLUSTER case_notes;
```

---

[*] There is a known problem with VARCHAR2(2000) in some versions of Oracle; populating it fully on a single occurrence can lead to an *ORA-1467: Sort key too long* condition when sorting the table by any nonindexed column.

```
CREATE TABLE case_notes
     ( case#     varchar2(12)
     , line#     number(3)     not null
     , made_at   date          not null
     , text      varchar2(80)
     ) CLUSTER case_notes_c ( case# );
```

This technique has some useful characteristics:

- The CUSTS table does not consume any space for customer comments that are irrelevant during batch processing; this has the effect of reducing I/O.

- Because of the clustering, all of the comments by/for a given customer will tend to be physically adjacent on disk even if they have been created at different times.

- As additional comments are added, dates and times can be formally recorded rather than being embedded in the text.

However, this technique also raises some issues:

- Clusters take time to load, so any reorganization or EXPort/IMPort operation will take considerably longer (several times longer, in fact).

- Any requirements to edit the comments as a single stream require some utility or function to query them, concatenate them, pass them to an editor, and then, on return, delete the entire set and insert them.

Unstructured Data and BLOBs

Data does not always fit neatly into tables with a number of relatively short and well-formatted columns. A database may be required to store text, sound, graphic, multimedia, or other types of what are known as *BLOB* (Binary Large OBject) data. Storing these items in the database has benefits in terms of encapsulation, but has disadvantages in terms of the restrictions that Oracle places on columns that are defined as LONG or LONG RAW—the type of columns that we typically use to store this type of data in. These restrictions are as follows:

- Their use prevents rows from being moved or copied using the SQL format

  `INSERT INTO a SELECT * FROM B;`

  which is the quickest way of moving data inside an Oracle database.

- It is not possible to reference LONG columns in a predicate clause.

- Whenever any reference is made to part of the row, the entire row has to be assembled within Oracle's buffer pool. If the LONG value itself is not always required, then it would be better if it were in a separate table, either using the

1:1 relationship or by dividing the value into an arbitrary number of pieces and holding these in a detail table.

- If we wish to avoid using a LONG column for any of the reasons stated above, we could consider storing the BLOB outside the database (probably in a file on the host computer). The row would simply contain the full name of the external file. Depending on the application, this may or may not be a viable option. If you do consider this method then you must remember the following points:

  — The contents of the file can be changed without touching the database. This may have awkward audit or security implications, or it may be highly desirable.

  — There will be no mechanism to ensure that if the file is moved or renamed, the file name will be updated to reflect the new location. Similarly, if the file is deleted externally. the table will be unaware of the data loss.

  — Amendments made to the file cannot participate in a database commit unit; therefore, the contents of the file and the row in the table cannot be guaranteed to be in sync.

  — You will have to come up with a suitable naming convention for the files to contain the BLOBs or a means of partitioning them into different directories. This is particularly important if there is a potentially large number of rows in the table, and therefore a large number of files.

Before you reject this approach because of its very real difficulties, you should also consider the performance issues inherent in using current versions of Oracle to record (say) 10 megabytes of full motion video. In addition to very heavy traffic through Oracle's space allocation logic, you will also generate more than 10 megabytes of redo log. Should you ever delete the BLOB, you will find that it is recorded in a rollback segment just in case you decide to roll back the delete, or in case some other user needs a read-consistent view from a point before you issued the delete.

We have been led to expect that future releases of Oracle will address all of these issues, but for the present we must urge caution when considering the RDBMS as a store for BLOBs.

Other Datatypes

There are five other Oracle datatypes which we haven't yet mentioned, and there are some additional comments that need to be made about CHAR. Of the missing datatypes MLSLABEL and RAW MLSLABEL are used only in Trusted Oracle, and are outside the scope of this book. We do briefly discuss CHAR, RAW, ROWID and VARCHAR below.

CHAR

As we've already discussed, CHAR data is fixed length. We really mean this— the length is absolute. *Any* CHAR(255) column which is not null will consume 255 bytes of disk space in each row of the table where it appears (which is bad news) and will also take up 255 bytes in the index leaf set of any index in which it appears (which is worse news).

There is very rarely any advantage to using CHAR, rather than VARCHAR2, except where the string is fixed length and you wish to document it as such. Oracle does not currently support zero-length strings, and the empty string '' is (incorrectly) regarded as a null value. For this reason, VARCHAR2(1) is not completely meaningful since the length can only be one. It cannot be zero because of the implementation restriction, and it cannot be greater than one because of the definition. Thus, we recommend that single-character strings such as true/false flags be coded as CHAR(1).

RAW

The key difference between RAW and VARCHAR2 is that RAW data will never be translated from one character set to another. In addition, Oracle's tools by and large refuse to handle RAW data, so by using this datatype you are in effect taking full responsibility for all operations concerning that data.

There are very few valid applications for this datatype, though there are uses for LONG RAW in handling BLOBs, as we discussed earlier.

ROWID

This datatype allows a rowid to be stored in its internal six-byte form which contains the kernel block number, the row number, and the file number. Although the datatype rowid is used by Oracle for a few data dictionary operations, such as storing references to rows that are in violation of constraints, its use is only *required* to synthesize a foreign key to a table which has no candidate primary key.

Because (unlike DB/2) Oracle does not require a table to have a primary key, the Oracle kernel development team was forced to use the internal pointer, the rowid, in the case described above in which a database table holds a row for each row in another table which violates a constraint.

We cannot recommend the use of the ROWID datatype within a table. There may be exceptional cases where its use in a view definition can be supported to allow a view to hand the rowid to the query process for later use in an UPDATE or DELETE statement. You should be aware that such an operation should be protected by an exclusive table-level lock taken before the view query is issued.

VARCHAR

This datatype currently has exactly the same definition as VARCHAR2, but there is an important difference. Oracle Corporation has stated that if a future SQL standard (rather than a proposed standard) provides a definition of the action of VARCHAR, the company will conform to that standard. They will not, however, change the definition of VARCHAR2 (unless that also is named by the standard, which appears extremely unlikely).

We recommend, therefore, that you do not use VARCHAR in current versions of Oracle, but that you use VARCHAR2 instead, since its definition is more likely to be stable.

In the earlier discussion under CHAR, we stated that Oracle is incorrect in treating zero-length strings as nulls. This is a topic of some debate, but we regard the zero-length string as analogous to the number zero. In any event, Oracle has announced an intention to support the storage of zero-length strings, as distinct from nulls, in Oracle8. We don't know yet whether this will require the use of a new datatype or whether the support will be a change to VARCHAR; it presumably cannot be applied to VARCHAR2 since that would imply a major change of behavior and spoil the whole intent of having VARCHAR2 in the first place.

Null Values

The topic of null values is one that really fires people up. The debates about nulls have been raging for many years. There have been heated discussions on the subject of null in the magazine *Database Programming and Design* for more than a year, involving key figures in database circles such as Chris Date. Even the two authors of this book have some differences of opinion. We won't delve too deeply in this book into the philosophy of nulls; we'll simply examine some of the issues and present the cases for various design decisions.

The Meaning of Null

What sets a null apart from any other value? Here are some reasons:

- If a null is used in a function or expression, the result is always null— although concatenating a null to a string leaves the string unchanged.

- A null value is not considered to be equal to any other value, including another null value.

- Completely null keys are never stored in an Oracle index; partially null keys are, but there are a series of restrictions on how they are used (we'll discuss this later).

- Null can have many different interpretations.

- Most 3GL or host languages cannot represent a null value.

Let's pick up on the point about interpretation. A null value can mean at least any of the following items in the list and probably a whole lot of other things not listed here:

- Not applicable

- Unknown

- Unspecified

- Currently unknown (to be added later)

- Was specified, now obsolete (updated to null)

- Unavailable (maybe for security reasons)

A null value can represent a specific meaning under certain circumstances. For instance, a null in the upper bound of a range may specifically mean unbounded or infinity. It may equally mean that there is an upper bound but we don't know what it is. What we do know, of course is that it must be greater than or equal to the value specified for the lower bound of the range, so we do have some knowledge about it. It is our job as designers to spot these types of ambiguity in the use of null and to decide whether it is important enough to do something about it.

Some self-appointed experts say that a relational database should support more than a single type of null; others warn you against using null at all because of unpredictable behavior based on the use of many-valued logic (MVL) against two-valued logic (2VL). What does this mean to us practitioners? The basis of the arguments are that a Boolean statement that would normally return a simple True or False response can return a third value when any of the conditions can return a null. This third value (Unspecified) can lead to a very obscure fourth value when combined with a NOT.

Some Coding Issues for Nulls

This section summarizes some issues you'll come across when your code includes references to nulls.

When is null equal to null?

Let's briefly pick up on another of the points—the fact that one null value is not equal to another. First, note an exception that Oracle makes to this rule, concerning the use of null in a unique constraint: if we define that a combination of columns must be unique, and if one of them allows null, then for the purposes of the unique constraint, null is considered to be equal to null. For example, suppose that table X has a unique constraint on columns A and B, where B allows null. If you try to insert a row with A=1 and B null twice, the second insertion will fail with a unique constraint violation. So, in this specific and unusual case, one null must be deemed to be equal to another!

Consequences of null != null

Let's look at one consequence of null not being equal to null (noting our exception). Examine the following two SQL statements:

```
/* 1. */
SELECT *
FROM    t
WHERE   t.a = 'X'
UNION
SELECT *
FROM    t
WHERE   t.a <> 'X'

/* 2. */
SELECT *
FROM    t
WHERE   t.a = t.a
```

Both of these statements, on the face of it, look as though they should return all the rows of table T. However, neither will return rows where A is null. This becomes significant when you are developing a report or application which accepts a parameter that will be used as a predicate in a WHERE clause. If the parameter is null, then the SQL should return only rows where our predicate column is null. Otherwise, it should return those matching the parameter. This leads to our having to write the following ugly and potentially dangerous piece of SQL:

```
SELECT *
FROM    t
WHERE   NVL(:p, NVL(x.a,'.NULL'.) = NVL(x.a,'.NULL'.
```

Why is it ugly? Because it doesn't read particularly easily, and because it doesn't make it clear what we are trying to achieve. Why is it dangerous? Because we are using '$NULL' as a "magic value" and making the serious assumption that column A will never legitimately be equal to this value. If it ever is, our logic fails!

Implications for coders

What about 3GL languages? If we are using the Oracle precompilers, then we can use indicator variables as per the ANSI standard for embedded SQL. This means that for every host variable in our program that is mapped to a column which allows null, we supply a second variable that is used by the program and by Oracle to indicate whether the corresponding variable is null. In Pro*C, these variables are declared as short. Here is an example using indicator variables in an embedded SQL statement:

```
EXEC SQL
UPDATE t
SET    t.a = :a:a_ind
WHERE  t.b = :b:b_ind;
```

What if we are not using a precompiler, but we are using Visual Basic and an ODBC driver? We may have problems because Visual Basic does not have the equivalent of a null. With character strings you can generally get away with an empty string as null, but numbers and dates present problems. Often there is encoding and decoding of nulls between the database and the host language. Again, this is dangerous because in a language like Visual Basic, it is not always possible to choose a number to represent a null that cannot occur in the column in the database. In such cases, it may be better (and sometimes necessary) to hold an indicator column within the table which contains a flag to show whether the column in question contains a real value.

Using encoded values instead of null

As designers, we need to look through all nullable attributes in the logical model, or columns in the physical model. We should regard nullable columns with suspicion and use them sparingly, because of the somewhat quirky behavior that we have described. We should ask ourselves questions such as, "Is there more than one possible meaning of null in this column and, if so, is it important to distinguish the various cases?"

Suppose that we are recording details about people and that one column in our PERSONS table is SOCIAL_SECURITY_NO. This column allows null, but why? First of all, if the person is a minor, they may not yet have been given a social security number (Not Applicable). Second, not everyone knows his or her number when asked initially to supply it; if this is the case, we don't want this to hold up the process of registering the person (Currently Unspecified). If we register a vagrant, they will undoubtedly have a number, they but may not know it or may not have any means of determining it (Unknown).

If we need to distinguish between these various meanings (Not Applicable, Currently Unspecified, Unknown), we should consider using an encoded value rather than using null. In fact, we could still use null for one of our various meanings and encode the others. Of course, when you choose an encoded value, you must be sure to choose a value that won't occur in reality. For example, if a

SOCIAL_SECURITY_NO is numeric, we could use negative values for the encoded items. This has the added benefit of making it simple to check for any of the encoded values in places where we don't need to differentiate them—for example, where SOCIAL_SECURITY_NO < 0. However, we would be on dangerous ground using a negative number to encode a null that would be used in an aggregate set operation, such as the average or minimum social security number. An advantage of nulls is that they are passed over in such aggregates. Fortunately, it is rarely necessary to perform set arithmetic on social security numbers.

ISO provides us with some standard encoding conventions. For instance, the ISO standard for encoding of Sex or Gender is as follows:

0 = Unknown

1 = Male

2 = Female

9 = Not Applicable

Notice the separate values for "Unknown" and for "Not Applicable."[*] When using an encoding scheme such as this, it is good practice to keep the codes and their meanings in the database.

When null is used to mean "currently unknown, to be supplied later," we could consider using a default qualifier to initialize the column to an encoded value with this meaning.

What if we can't be sure that any value we choose to represent a null type will not occur in reality. We are left with little choice but to define a new column that is only populated if our main column is null and holds a value to indicate which type of null is meant in this particular row. We can use table constraints to ensure that if the column is null, the reason column is populated, and vice versa:

```
CREATE TABLE persons
(per_id NUMBER(8) NOT NULL
.
.
.
,social_security_no CHAR(10)
,ss_null_reason char(1)
   CONSTRAINT per_cc1 CHECK (ss_null_reason IN ('.'.'.'.'.'.)
.
.
.
```

---

[*] It also appears that the ISO committee has either not heard of hermaphrodites or chooses to ignore them!

```
    ,CONSTRAINT per_cc2 CHECK ((social_security_no IS NULL OR
ss_null_reason IS NULL)
AND social_security_no || ss_null_reason IS NOT NULL)
    .
    .
    .
```

Dominant value null

One pragmatic use of nullable columns is for exception indicators. We may have a table of orders with 100,000 rows, but only 50 or 60 of these may be the subject of disputes. We want to be able to find these quickly, so we implement an IN_ DISPUTE indicator and build an index on it. If we make this nullable, and constrain the values to "Y" and null, then the index will contain entries only for the few rows for those orders which are in dispute. This technique is sometimes referred to as *dominant value null*.

Recommendations for Using Nulls

Let's summarize our conclusions about nulls. Be sure to:

- Examine their meaning in all cases and determine whether there is an ambiguity.
- Use them sparingly because of their quirky behavior and the potential for ambiguous meaning.
- Consider an encoding system as an alternative, but be wary of using an encoded value that could also occur as an actual value, no matter how unlikely it seems.
- If encoding is deemed to be too dangerous, introduce a new column whose sole purpose in life is to describe how the null value of its sister column should be interpreted.
- Remember that nulls can be very useful in exception indicators.

6

Choosing Keys and Indexes

This chapter looks at the special design issues you'll encounter when you choose the keys and indexes for tables in your database. Indexes are extremely important and are the cornerstone of a good performance strategy. Just imagine searching for all references to "normalization" in this book without using the index! Indexes are often not given due consideration during design because "We can easily add them during system test or production when it becomes apparent that we have performance problems." This statement has some truth in it, and we do not recommend that the design team attempt to specify the full index strategy. In our experience, this leads inevitably to overindexing the largest tables with considerable costs in both storage and update performance. But we certainly don't advocate just leaving the developers to add indexes as they see fit.

The design team is responsible for mandating any indexing techniques they wish to see employed (such as the use of a hash cluster for a specific purpose or the indexing of a foreign key to avoid locking problems). The team is also absolutely responsible for specifying constraints. *Indexes* and *key constraints* are inextricably linked, and key constraints are as important to the integrity of your database as indexes are to the performance. Without key constraints, your data can become logically corrupt. For instance, it might contain ORDER_LINES for a nonexistent or deleted ORDER, giving rise to surprising anomalies in your application reports and screens.

Within a database, every table should have a *primary key* that is used to uniquely identify any row. Some tables don't have a natural candidate for this, so a new column might be specifically introduced for this purpose—a *surrogate key*. Other tables have several *candidate keys* and you will have to choose among them. All candidate primary keys should have a *unique constraint* on them to enforce the fact that they must be unique within the table. A table that is the child in a rela-tionship will have a *foreign key* for each relationship that maps on to the primary key in the parent record.

Columns and group of columns that are regularly used as search criteria when querying a table may be given an index to improve the performance of the lookup. There is more than one type of index in Oracle, and we will examine each of them.

Primary Keys

Being able to uniquely identify a row in a table is fundamental to relational design. The way we do this is to assign a primary key. No two occurrences in the same table are allowed to have the same primary key. This is not as easy as it sounds! In life, everything is distinct in some way. In a computer model, because it is only a model, we might not be able to capture distinguishing features; never-theless, relational theory dictates that every table must have a primary key. Sometimes we have to introduce an artificial identifier in the form of a surrogate key. This may be simply a number sequence starting at one for the first row to be created and incremented by one for each subsequent row. Other times there will be a series of numbers and/or letters that are meaningless to most people (have a look at the serial numbers on paper money, for instance).

Occasionally, what we thought would be a primary key for a table turns out to be not fully unique when we take into account the practicalities of implementing it in a relational database. Take an event. The date and time at which an event occurs is guaranteed to be unique as long as you take it to a fine enough granu-larity. However, in an Oracle database the finest grain of time is a second, and of course it is common for two events to occur within a second.

Sometimes, even when a table has a natural primary key, we choose to replace it with a surrogate. This is purely a design decision made for practical purposes and is usually implemented when the natural key is very long or has a large number of component columns.

Examining Synthetic or Surrogate Keys

During the analysis stage, every entity defined in the conceptual model should have been given a *unique identifier (UID)*—assuming that the conceptual model has been properly normalized. At the start of design, we need to study these UIDs in detail to make sure they are truly unique. In the great majority of cases, during design we'll simply map our primary keys from the unique identifiers assigned during analysis. However, in some cases, you may find that there are problems in definition.

In particular we should verify any *synthetic UIDs* (often referred to as surrogate keys) on an entity. You'll recognize such keys because they will have an attribute called "ID" (or something similar); the ID is usually a number that is meaningless outside of the computer system. We should verify that the analyst has not just created these surrogate keys for convenience or even applied a blanket approach to the UIDs of all entities. There may be some real UIDs lurking in there that have been missed or overlooked.

Let's look at an example. How do we identify a person unless we can capture that person's fingerprints or genetic makeup? Arguments about unique identification, and how to accomplish this by social means, have raged for years. Many countries require that every citizen obtain an identification number, such as a social security number. But many other countries do not have the equivalent of a social security number for all its citizens, and in some countries that do (such as Canada), it is illegal to store the number unless it is of direct relevance to the system. If we can't use a social security number, how about using a person's full name together with his or her date of birth. Is this combination unique? Unless we also know that person's time of birth to the actual nanosecond, then probably not!

If you are going to accept a surrogate key from analysis, ask yourself the following questions:

- Are there, or could there be, two instances of this entity that will have identical attributes and relationships (apart from the ID)?

- If so, then what, in business terms, distinguishes them?

- In such cases, will the user be required to write down or memorize these IDs?

- Would it actually matter if the IDs were mixed up?

In fact, better than asking yourself, ask the analyst! (But try, as an exercise, to answer these questions for yourself with respect to the money in your pocket. It's useful to know how much money you have with you, but there seems little point in tracking each individual bill or coin.)

It is important to draw a distinction between a surrogate key and a generated key. Surrogate keys are always generated (usually from an Oracle sequence), but *generated keys* are not necessarily surrogate. If you go to your bank and open a new account, you will be given an account number that is probably the next available number generated from a sequence of some kind. However, once it has been generated, this number assumes a significance for both you and your bank. It will be used in all correspondence between the two parties. Surrogate keys, on the other hand, have no significance other than to the database itself.

Nonunique (or Nearly Unique) Keys

This section looks at cases where we choose to alter the unique identifier of an entity from the identifier defined during analysis. In particular, we are going to look at keys that don't guarantee uniqueness when implemented in an Oracle7 database. The next section suggests a replacement: the use of long cascading keys with a surrogate key.

After all we've said about the importance of unique keys in the normalization of the information model, how can we possibly end up with a nonunique key? The answer is simple. The key may have been unique in the conceptual model, but when we translate it into a logical model that we intend to implement as an Oracle table, it is no longer unique. If the key had a date and a time stamp as a component of the key, then we may have a problem. The time in Oracle7 is rounded to the nearest second; therefore, if we create two rows with identical keys within a second, the time stamp won't help us.

Consider the example illustrated in Figure 6-1. Let's assume that we can create multiple versions of source code with the same directory and file name. Including the column INSERTDATETIME in the key may help make each version unique, since it would be difficult to create two versions of the same source code by hand within a single second. However, if we have a code generator that creates two derivatives in very quick succession, we could be in trouble! In such cases, we will start to get occasional runtime error messages telling us that a unique constraint has been violated. To correct this, we could take the data and time stamp out of the key and put in a simple integer version number into the key, as shown in Figure 6-2.

SOURCE_CODE

FILENAME
DIRECTORY
INSERTDATETIME
...

Figure 6-1. A table with a primary key which is "nearly" unique

Now, even if the system date and time are moved back for some reason (for example, the end of daylight savings time), the VERSION# column will tell us the true sequence of the versions, whereas the INSERTDATETIME may not. Bugs of this kind—where a record very occasionally appears in the wrong order—are

Figure 6-2. A table with a primary key which is now fully unique

both easy to prevent and notoriously difficult to fix once the system is in production.

The approach we've described does appear to make the primary key unique. However, there are still a number of potential pitfalls which many applications encounter. In fact, assigning a new version number using this structure is not as easy as you might think, especially if you want the version numbers for each file to be guaranteed to run in an ascending sequence, with no gaps. Most people try to determine the next version number using a query such as the following:

```
SELECT MAX(version#) + 1
FROM    source_code
WHERE   directory = :d
AND   filename = :f;
```

This code issues a read without a lock, so more than one user can get the same answer. Even if you've already performed a SELECT FOR UPDATE on what you believe to be the latest version, that will not prevent another user from issuing a SELECT MAX()... and again getting a duplicate number. The result is that two users will potentially attempt to create the same version at the same time, and one will fail with a violation of a unique constraint.

You may also run into the situation in which many modules need to extract (only) the latest version. To find it, they will have to use a statement something like the following:

```
SELECT ...
FROM    source_code
WHERE   directory = :d
AND     filename = :f
AND     version# = (SELECT MAX(s2.version#)
                    FROM    source_code s2
                    WHERE   s2.directory = :d
                    AND     s2.filename = :f);
```

Let's get back to our examination of the query. The first pitfall is that the query is not very efficient. Even though its execution has been improved in recent versions, it will still make two lookups on the primary key index. If you have read the previous chapter, then surely you'll realize that the table SOURCE_CODE should actually be called SOURCE_CODE_VERSIONS and that a new table SOURCE_CODE should be introduced to record any attributes of a file that are true for every version. We can now add a *derived column* to this master table to record the version number of the latest version of this unit of source code.

NOTE   Take a look at the "scope" *s2* in this query. Because of the way that Oracle resolves names, it is a good idea to always use a scope in a subquery. Also note that the subquery must reuse the bind variables; if you make it a correlated subquery, then you will incur a full table scan, at least in Version 7.2.

Once this table has been introduced (and it is almost certain to be required in any event) and the derived column added, then our query becomes:

```
SELECT ...
FROM    source_code s
     ,  source_code_versions v
WHERE   s.directory = :d
AND     s.filename = :f
AND     v.directory = s.directory
AND     v.filename = s.filename
AND     v.version# = s.latest_version#;
```

Now we also have a fully effective way of maintaining the version number. If we perform a SELECT FOR UPDATE on the appropriate row in SOURCE_CODE, then we can perform an insert into SOURCE_CODE_VERSIONS and an update on SOURCE_CODE and can maintain both integrity and efficiency of action. Just in case you think that this is an inefficient solution, try writing the query to retrieve the latest version number for each file using both the single table implementation and the master-detail solution.

Replacing Long Cascading Keys with Surrogate Keys

We said earlier that we ought to question any synthetic or surrogate primary keys that were introduced during analysis. Let's now look at the opposite situation. Sometimes, we are justified in replacing the real primary key from analysis with a surrogate one during design (no, we're not just being contrary...).

Why would we do this? In relational systems, a primary key serves a dual purpose. It is used to force uniqueness of the rows so that two occurrences in the same table are not allowed to have the same primary key. It also serves as a means of referencing the row—in particular, as a foreign key (kind of a legal alien) in another table. In this respect, it serves the same purpose as a pointer in a network database.

When a primary key is based on more than one column, it is referred to as a *compound key*, and every key component of it has to be represented in the foreign key.* When a key is used as a foreign key (the table is the parent or master in a relationship) and it has more than (say) four components, the key starts to become unwieldy in terms of both the amount of foreign key data stored in child records and the SQL necessary to join the tables.

In such a case, it is worth considering introducing a surrogate primary key onto the table. By convention, this key is normally called *<table_short_name>_*ID or simply ID, and it will usually take its values from an Oracle sequence.

Tables with large compound primary keys can often arise from a long hierarchy of entities where the keys are inherited. In other words, for several generations the foreign key of the parent forms part of the primary key of the child. This is illustrated in Figure 6-3 (follow the progression from COUNTRY to BUILDING CONTRACTOR)."

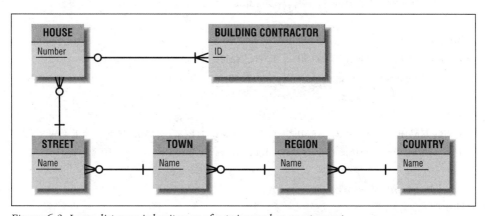

Figure 6-3. Long-distance inheritance of a primary key component

In this example, COUNTRY has a simple atomic key of just the country name. A REGION within a COUNTRY is uniquely identified by its relationship to the COUNTRY (foreign key column F_CO_NAME) and the name of the REGION. This is necessary since two countries could have regions with the same names. By the time we get to TOWN, which is identified by a combination of the REGION (within the COUNTRY) and the name of the TOWN, the key has three components. STREET will have four components, HOUSE five, and so on. To reference a particular HOUSE in the BUILDING CONTRACTOR table, we have to hold five foreign key components. This seems a bit excessive, or does it? Table 6-1 shows

---

* With certain obscure exceptions, as we describe in Chapter 7, *Dealing with Temporal Data.*

the tables based on the entity relationship diagram (ERD) in Figure 6-3 with a small amount of data (one row each) included.

Table 6-1. Table Definitions Demonstrating the Long Cascading Key

Countries

NAME	POPULATION	Area	GNP
United Kingdom	57,121,000	94,247	$758 billion

Regions

F_CO_NAME	NAME	METROPOLITAN_F
United Kingdom	Surrey	N

Towns

F_CO_NAME	F_REG_NAME	NAME
United Kingdom	Surrey	Guildford

Streets

F_CO_NAME	F_REG_NAME	F_TN_NAME	NAME
United Kingdom	Surrey	Guildford	The Rise

Houses

F_CO_NAME	F_REG_NAME	F_TN_NAME	F_ST_NAME	NO	F_OWN_ID
United Kingdom	Surrey	Guildford	The Rise	10	2061

(*Building Contractors* table not shown.)

Every column of the HOUSES table is now a primary key component. How can we simplify this situation? We could give HOUSES a surrogate key, but suppose a requirement of the system states that, given an owner, we are required to locate the other highest house number on that owner's street (for some obscure reason). Given the table structure from Table 6-1, the required SQL would be:

```
SELECT MAX(hs1.no)
FROM    houses hs1
WHERE   EXISTS
        (SELECT NULL
         FROM    houses hs2
         WHERE   hs2.f_own_id = 2061
            AND  hs1.f_st_name = hs2.f_st_name
            AND  hs1.f_tn_name = hs2.f_tn_name
            AND  hs1.f_reg_name = hs2.f_reg_name
            AND  hs1.f_co_name = hs2.f_co_name);
```

Suppose that we give STREET a surrogate key and observe the difference. Table 6-2 shows the changed table definitions; note that those definitions which are still the same as those in Table 6-1 are not shown here.

Table 6-2. New Table Definitions with a Surrogate Key Introduced in the STREETS Table

Streets

ID	F_CO_NAME	F_REG_NAME	F_TN_NAME	NAME
41	United Kingdom	Surrey	Guildford	The Rise

Houses

ID	NO	F_OWN_ID
41	10	2061

The SQL needed to find the maximum house number on our owner's street is quite a bit simpler:

```
SELECT MAX(hs1.no)
FROM   houses hs1
WHERE  EXISTS
       (SELECT NULL
        FROM   houses hs2
        WHERE  hs2.f_own_id = 2061
        AND    hs1.street_id = hs2. street_id);
```

Has the introduction of the surrogate key actually bought us anything, other than simplifying the SQL? Don't always dismiss the benefits of simplified SQL—the statement is terse and therefore easy to read and understand; it will be shorter to parse and less prone to errors when you have to type it.

One effect of using long keys as foreign keys within rows is that it causes the child rows to be longer than they would be if surrogate keys were used. "So what, when I can buy disk so cheaply?" you might ask. Well, whatever the cost of disk, it still takes time to read from disk into memory. The longer your rows, the more blocks you will have to visit in any type of scan, The same is true of indexes, and index range scans are an important part of any join operation that uses a foreign key or partial key. Also, with shorter keys, some indexes will lose a level from their B*-trees, which will result in a further performance improvement.

The simple message: shorter keys mean faster applications.

There is always another side to any design decision we may choose. Surrogate foreign keys make it impossible to perform certain types of queries without navigating the entire join chain. If we take the unlikely example of wanting to know the highest house number anywhere in the UK, then with the original data model we would simply write:

```
SELECT  MAX(hs1.no)
FROM    houses hs1
WHERE   hs1.f_co_name = 'United Kingdom'.
```

We can reduce the impact of the cascading keys by using "short names," so in the previous example, we might choose to always use "UK" rather than "United Kingdom", as our foreign key value. The equivalent query using surrogate keys is left as an exercise for you, but we can assure you that it is not nice!

There is another problem with the long cascading keys when key columns need updating somewhere within the chain. Clearly, the higher up the hierarchy the change occurs, the further down it has to cascade. In these times in which we live you can't depend on anything being static any more! Even countries change—as witnessed by the breakup of the Soviet Union! Let's look at a simple example of a country changing its name, rather than the more complex example of a split or merger. Persia became Iran, Rhodesia became Zimbabwe, and so on. Remember: in our data model, we can't get away with merely updating the COUNTRIES table; we have to cascade the update to REGIONS, TOWNS, STREETS, HOMES, etc.

Relational purists would tell us that we cannot go updating primary key columns, so we would actually have to delete all of the addresses within Rhodesia and rein-sert them in Zimbabwe. We will leave it up to you to decide whether primary key updates should be allowed or not. There are actually some strong arguments on both sides of the debate. Suffice it to say that Oracle7 tolerates primary key updates without providing support for cascading the changes to the foreign keys. Some other relational database management systems simply will not allow an update of a primary key. Where there are candidate primary keys (i.e., more than one mandatory unique key), we certainly suggest that if one of these candidates will not change, there is a strong case for selecting that as the primary key.

Of course, it is not only countries which may split, merge, and change their names. Regions, towns, and streets can change too! So, should we give them all surrogate keys, or just some of them, and if only some of them, how do we choose which ones? Clearly, the higher up the hierarchy the change occurs, the further down it has to cascade. Use of a surrogate key means that we are free from relational constraints when we want to change the original unique identifier.

When we are dealing with a long hierarchy such as the one we've described here, the decision of where to introduce the surrogate key may seem rather arbitrary. Remember, though, database design cannot be done in isolation from functional requirements. Some functions may require a walk up the hierarchy. If the cascaded keys are maintained, this walk can be transformed into a "jump", cutting out the middle men and allowing a more optimal query to be performed. We can demonstrate this point by joining HOUSES directly to REGIONS (shortcutting both STREETS and TOWNS).

```
SELECT  MAX(hs.no)
FROM    houses hs
        ,regions reg
WHERE   hs.f_reg_name = reg.name
AND     hs.metropolitan_f = 'N'.
```

The purpose of this query is to find the highest house number in a non-metropolitan region (another inquiry from the archives of "Pointless Queries Inc.")!

WARNING   Beware when designing or developing SQL like this. This query could potentially perform much worse than its complex counterpart (which involved joining in all of the intermediate tables). This join will not use the primary or foreign key indexes on the tables concerned since the region name is not the leading edge of a key in either table. You will need to define additional indexes to support optimization of queries such as this one. In many cases, the cost of these additional indexes will *not* outweigh the savings derived from shortening the join chain. In any specific case, you will have to make a decision based on careful consideration of the index maintenance load against the query load.

Another note of caution. If you do elect to use surrogate keys, make sure that they are well hidden. Don't start slipping them onto any screens or reports; they will only confuse your users.

Are there any lessons to be learned here? How do we decide when and where to introduce a surrogate key in a long chain of concatenated keys? We have to make a balanced decision based on the length and the type of inquiries that are anticipated in the system. Examine each case on its own merits, but be aware of these general rules of thumb:

- If a table has more than four primary key components and has related child tables, it is a good candidate for a surrogate key.

- If a key is long due to the cascading effect we've described, some time-critical functions may benefit from skipping generations in their queries. In such a case, there is a strong case for retaining the long key.

Other Keys

We have looked in detail at primary keys. In this short section, we look at two other types of keys: candidate keys and foreign keys.

Candidate Keys

Candidate keys occur when an entity has more than one unique identifier. For instance, it may be valid to uniquely identify a car by its license plate number or by its chassis serial number. License plate number and chassis serial number are said to be candidate keys since they are both candidates for the mantle of the primary key. There is no physical construct within Oracle that directly supports a candidate key.

The questions that we need to address in design are:

- Which one do we choose as the primary key?

- What do we do with the one that is not the primary key?

We may find that the analyst has already selected one as the primary key, but we should not just take his decision as binding; we should make our own judgment. We may opt for one because it is significantly shorter than the other—therefore, we can get more in a block and potentially reduce our search times. However, we prefer as usual to look at the applications that use the table. The primary key will generally be used as a foreign key in related child tables. If the key itself has significance to the application, then we may be able to avoid having to join to evaluate it. In our car example, we might want to look up traffic violations for a particular vehicle. It is highly unlikely that we would know the chassis number when performing this lookup, so if chassis number were the primary key it would be necessary to join to the CARS table to search by license plate number (which is a far more likely search criterion).

Suppose we choose "license plate number" as the primary key; what about the loser? We should certainly put a unique constraint on chassis serial number to prevent us from allowing duplicates. In some cases we may even make it the foreign key in child tables—although we personally are not very keen on this practice, since it can lead to confusion.

Foreign Keys

Foreign keys occur in tables that participate as a child in a relationship to another table (or the same table). There are not really a lot of design issues with foreign keys, other than those concerning arcs (that we covered in Chapter 3, *Data Modeling*) and issues when both the parent and child table are *date effective* (that will be dealt with in Chapter 7, *Dealing with Temporal Data*).

In Oracle7, foreign keys should be implemented using FOREIGN KEY constraints. Within these constraints you can specify what should happen if the parent row is deleted—should the deletion be cascaded to the child table or restricted so that it is only permitted if no related children exist? The cascade option seems attractive since the process is then automated and the application doesn't have to worry about it. However, beware of users being frustrated in their attempts at a deletion because of locks on a child row or because some parent rows have a huge number of children, which slows the process down significantly. Beware also of data being deleted without the users being made aware of their actions.

Indexes: An Overview

Why create an index on a column or group of columns? Before Oracle7 there were three possible reasons:

- To speed up lookups on the columns
- To enforce uniqueness on the columns (unique indexes only)
- To retrieve rows in a specific order based on the columns indexed

---

NOTE   This third reason for creating an index is rarely justified if it is the *only* reason for creating the index. However, it may justify the addition of an extra column to an index key.

With Oracle7, uniqueness should be enforced by primary key and unique key constraints. We know, of course, that in fact these keys work by creating a unique index when we enable the constraint. However, it is still important to note the distinction: what we explicitly create with Oracle7 is the constraint, not the index.

Before Version 7.3, Oracle7 offered only two ways of locating records other than by using a full table scan:

- B*-tree (balanced tree) indexes on tables and clusters
- Hash clusters

Version 7.3 adds bitmapped indexes (on tables only) to this list.

There are some important choices here about what to index and how to index it, as well as whether to use cost-based or rules-based optimization. Given all of these choices, you can see that it is important to establish a well-conceived indexing policy during the design stage (see the sidebar). If you are using a CASE tool to generate your database creation scripts, chances are that it will generate primary and unique key constraints on all unique identifiers and will also generate nonunique B*-tree indexes on all foreign keys that it finds in its repository. The rest will normally be up to you. You may elect to suppress some of the foreign key indexes either to save disk space or to save the CPU time spent maintaining the index.

Why an Index Policy?

Every project needs to have a written policy on indexes for Oracle tables. (At some sites, the policy on indexes may be part of a wider policy on performance issues.) If you don't have a stated policy on indexes, then the likelihood is that you will end up with an arbitrary set of indexes that are optimal for some programs and processes, and less than optimal for others. Worse, the programs for which the indexes are optimized may not be the ones that are critical from an overall systems or business perspective.

How Does an Index Work?

For review, let's quickly explain how an index works in relatively simple terms. Consider this simple query statement:

```
SELECT emp.empno
     , emp.ename
  FROM EMPLOYEES emp
 WHERE emp.ename = 'SMITH'.
```

The way the query will retrieve the data depends heavily upon whether (and how) the column *ename* in the table *emp* is indexed, which Oracle7 version you are running, and which optimizer mode is in use. Here are some of the possible scenarios:

1. *Table not indexed.* Oracle reads every data block of the EMPLOYEES table and searches each row of each block occurrence of "SMITH". This is known as a *full table scan* and uses much more CPU cycles than most people would suspect. A known limitation of Oracle's cost-based optimizer is that it fails to give enough weight to this CPU usage when comparing costs and as a result is over-fond of employing full table scans.

2. *B*-tree index on ename column.* Oracle reads down through successive levels of the index until it reaches a *leaf block* in which the key "SMITH" is either present or not present. If one or more instances of the key "SMITH" is found, these instances will be followed by the rowid, which enables the query processor to locate the data blocks that contain "SMITH" and to go directly to the rows. With this information, the query processor can access the data directly (assuming that the row has not been migrated; we'll discuss row migration in Chapter 9, *Deciding on Object Placement and Storage*). Of course, if you are using the cost-based optimizer and if the statistics show that the column is not highly selective, the optimizer may opt for a full table scan. In Version 7.3, which has column value histograms, a full table scan is much

more likely to be invoked for "SMITH" than it is for "ENSOR" or "STEVENSON". Version 7.2 and below will take the same action for each value; if the index is selective, it will be used and otherwise it will not. What makes an index selective? A fairly reliable rule of thumb is that the index will be classified as selective if it has more than 20 distinct key values.

3. *Concatenated index on B*-tree index on ename column followed by other column(s).* This case is the same as the one described in #2, except that indexed retrieval will use only the leading edge of the index key. An attractive feature of Oracle's nonunique indexes is that where there are rows with equal keys (for example, there may be many SMITHs) the rowids are held in rowid order. This has one significant benefit: If two of the SMITHs have their rows in the same physical database block, we will access these two rows one after the other; in almost all cases, this will minimize disk head movement between blocks (if the required data is not already in the System Global Area, or SGA). Unfortunately, if we are using the leading edge of a concatenated index, the basic sequence will be that of the full key. As a result, we can expect this operation to be less efficient than using a single column index. The index will also be longer, and we will have to scan more of it. These effects are normally minor, and would not justify creating an index on (*ename*) if we already had, and needed, one on (*ename, initial*).

4. *Concatenated index on B*-tree index on other column(s), then on ename.* The index is not used, so a full table scan is employed (same as #1).

5. *Hash key on ENAME (table is in a hash cluster on ename).* The hashing algorithm is applied to "SMITH", and the hashed value is used to read a cluster data block. If the algorithm used is good, and if you sized the cluster correctly, then this block should contain the rows we are seeking. If not, we might have to read one or more chained blocks to find our data, or to find out that there are no employees called "SMITH". In any event, we must search the entire hash chain for that hash value, which can be several blocks (or, in pathological cases, several thousand blocks).

6. *ename is an indexed cluster key.* The index will be used in a manner similar to #2. The difference is that the index will contain either zero or one entry for "SMITH". If there is an entry, it will point to the head block of a cluster chain which we must search to find the rows we want. With good cluster design and a measure of luck, the chain will be only one block long.

7. *Table is clustered but ename is not the cluster key and is not at the leading edge of any other index.* The cluster will be scanned much as it is in #1, except that the row directory in the cluster block header will be used to

locate the rows in that cluster block which are part of the EMPLOYEES table. Each of these rows will be tested to see if it contains the name "SMITH".

8. *ename is the subject of a bitmapped index.* The bitmap, if any, for the value "SMITH" is retrieved and expanded to form a list of rowids of the rows which match the predicate clause. These rows can then be retrieved to satisfy the query. If there are only a few key values, then having a bitmap for every key (each with one bit for every row in the table) is efficient of storage and also provides quite efficient retrieval. However, for an index on name, there are likely to be a high number of such bitmaps and the bitmaps for most names are likely to be highly sparse (i.e., almost all of the bits will be "off").

So which of the eight methods of access described do we prefer? The answer, as you might guess, is "it all depends."

A full table scan is the best solution if the EMPLOYEES table contains hardly any rows, or if a large proportion of our employees are called "SMITH", though it is just barely possible that a bitmapped index might win in the second case. On the other hand, if we had a large number of employees with a fairly even distribution of names, then a hash key might be the best option, particularly if no one name occurs more than a handful of times. Clearly, this is unlikely for employee names.

Suppose that our queries aren't all simple equality criteria (such as in our example), and that we also have to issue queries such as:

```
SELECT emp.empno
     , emp.sal
  FROM employees emp
 WHERE emp.ename LIKE 'SM%'.
```

In this case, we would probably choose a B*-tree index or a full table scan. By the time the search expression is reduced to "S%", then a full table scan starts to look quite desirable. The Version 7.3 cost-based optimizer should be capable of optimizing this correctly, but as a designer be aware of the bind variable trap, discussed in the section in this chapter entitled "The Bind Variable Problem".

Why Not Index Everything?

Why don't we simply index every column that is likely to be searched upon in every table on our system? Three reasons spring immediately to mind:

1. When there are several nonunique indexes which could be used, the rules-based optimizer has no sensible algorithm for deciding which one to use. The

cost-based optimizer has such an algorithm, but in versions prior to 7.3 it is unable to use the value, only the selectivity of the index.[*]

NOTE   Oracle addicts waste large quantities of computer time trying to work out which index the optimizer will pick. In case you ever need to know the answer to this question, the answer is "the first one it finds." Of course, this answer is completely useless because it is so difficult to tell which index it is going to find first. The optimizer is extremely bad at picking which nonunique indexes can slow down a query in some circumstances, particularly on columns that aren't very selective (they don't have very many distinct values).

---

2. The more indexes there are, the higher the overhead of maintaining them when DML statements are issued. As a general rule of thumb, if it takes one unit of work to insert a row in a table, then it takes three units of work to make an index entry. So an insert into a table with three indexes is ten times more work than an insert into an unindexed table. Food for thought!

3. Indexes occupy valuable database space, and the leaf blocks which usually comprise well over 90% of the index space are never compressed. In addition, repeating keys are held as many times as they occur (except in cluster indexes).

Index Types and Indexing Techniques

This section will look in more detail at some of the subjects we've raised in this introduction to indexes.

B-tree Indexes*

B*-tree (balanced tree) indexes are the traditional index format for Oracle databases. They are structured like an inverted tree (hence the name) with a *root block, branch blocks,* and *leaf blocks.* Together, these are known as the *sequence set.* Oracle's implementation of this index format has a number of interesting features, including an optimization that allows for true one-level indexes in which the root block is also the only leaf block. (At this point, the tree analogy does break down somewhat.)

---

[*] This is a deliberate oversimplification of the index statistics built by Oracle7 Versions 7.0 to 7.2. The algorithm used takes into account both the number of distinct values and their clustering factor or the tendency of equal keys to be physically adjacent within the table. (Be honest, did you really need to know that?)

Figure 6-4 illustrates a B*-tree index for our EMPLOYEE example from the previous section. For a given key value, Oracle first reads the root block. By comparing the values in the root block with our search value, Oracle determines the appropriate branch block for the range of values containing the one we are seeking. The branch block is read, and a similar exercise is performed to determine the appropriate leaf block (or the next level of branch, depending on the depth of the index). When the appropriate entry is located in the leaf block, it gives us the rowid of the corresponding data item in the data block, which can then be accessed with a single *block visit*. Unless the block is already in Oracle's buffer cache, this block visit will require a disk I/O operation.

NOTE   For completeness we should point out there are two circumstances under which more than one block visit will be required after the rowid has been retrieved from the index. The first is when the block being retrieved is more than one block long (a *chained row*) and the second is when the row has expanded during its life and has had to be moved from its original block to another block (a *migrated row*). It is possible, though rare, for a row to be first migrated and then to expand again and become chained.

Let's consider some of the properties of B*-tree indexes.

1. The number of I/Os required to acquire the rowid of a data row depends on how many levels of branch we have. As the index grows in size, Oracle may add another level to the index as part of the balancing mechanism. However, in reality it is almost impossible to have more than four levels. For instance, with two-kilobyte database blocks, an index on a six-byte column value will grow to four levels when the number of index entries exceeds about 2,000,000 and (depending on how well the branch blocks compress) will stay at four levels into billions of rows. In terms of physical I/O (disk reads), we should not normally have to read more than the two lowest levels since the first two levels are likely to be cached in the SGA for frequently used indexes.

2. The root and branch nodes of the index are compressed, so they only contain enough leading bytes of the value to distinguish it from other values in the index. The leaf nodes contain the full index value. This enables the index to be used to fully resolve some queries without recourse to the data block at all. An example is:

```
SELECT COUNT(*)
FROM    employees emp
wHERE   emp.ename LIKE 'S%'.
```

Note that this example will only work if *ename* is defined as NOT NULL (since nulls aren't indexed).

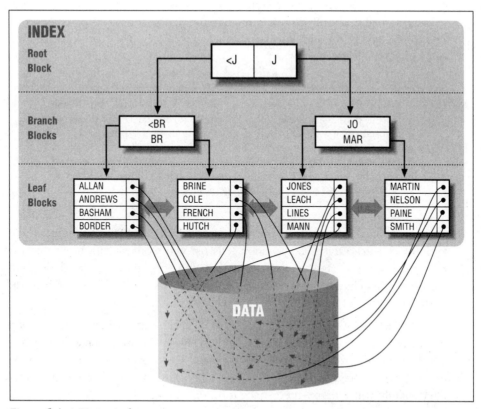

Figure 6-4. A B*-tree index

3. The values in the index are ordered by key value, and the blocks of the indexes are linked together in a doubly-linked list. This allows sequential access through the index and enables the index to be used to resolve an ORDER BY clause in a query.

4. B*-tree indexes can be used for finding an exact match or a range of values. For instance, it can be used to resolve predicates such as:

```
ename < 'JONES', ename BETWEEN 'JONES' AND 'SMITH'
```

5. B*-tree indexes can cover multiple columns from a table (known as compound indexes). The optimizer can use compound indexes only where the leading column of the index is specified. For example, if there is an index on (ename, job) then a query such as:

```
SELECT * from employee emp WHERE emp.job = 'SALES'.
```

cannot use the index since the leading edge (*ename*) is not specified.

6. The Oracle optimizer will make the choice as to whether or not to use an index unless we decide to influence it using a hint or by altering the SQL.

7. Nulls are not indexed. If the column you are considering indexing allows null values, then the optimizer will refuse to use it for certain operations which you might expect the index to be able to support; the most obvious example of this is ORDER BY.

NOTE　　　Oracle does not store completely null keys in indexes, but it will store a partially null concatenated key in an index. Under these circumstances it will class null as equal to null for the purpose of enforcing primary and unique key constraints. It will even accept a null value as the leading edge of a concatenated index key and store this key in the index, but it will also refuse to use the index to find those rows whose leading edge is null.

---

8. Branch blocks are never removed (except by a TRUNCATE on the underlying table or cluster). Oracle Corporation tells us, with some justification, that this restriction greatly assists its implementation of true row-level locking. However, this characteristic was also present in Oracle Version 5, which did not have row-level locking!

9. Leaf blocks (sequence set blocks) are reused only when they become completely empty (and even this is a relatively recent improvement; traditionally leaf block space was *never* recovered). Thus, even in current versions, indexes which have suffered high rates of insertion and deletion are often filled mainly with unrecovered space from deleted entries.

Disabling Indexes

Good designers are pragmatic. What do we do when we are designing two modules with very different requirements for indexes on the same table? Instead of favoring one module over another, we usually aim to satisfy both!

One of the simplest conflicts to resolve is that of an overnight batch program that performs heavy updates of a table (and wants as few indexes as possible to keep the housekeeping overhead down) versus an online program that requires lots of indexes to support flexible searching. We simply get the batch program to drop the indexes before it starts and recreate them when it finishes. If the batch program runs during online connection time, then it may just have to suffer the indexes.

What about disabling an index within a query? We briefly mentioned that indexes are not always beneficial to the performance of queries. Let's take an extreme case. Imagine reading the entire EMPLOYEE table shown in Figure 6-4 in index order.

Reading the index blocks is easy enough since they are chained together and the index entries are ordered. However, as we see from the pointers to the data block in Figure 6-4, the data rows are all over the place. If we read the table in index order, we will be reading the data in random order and rereading the same data block many times for different rows. It is much more efficient to perform a full table scan in this instance and to read the data blocks one at a time. With the read-ahead feature of Oracle7, when we do a full table scan, we are actually reading several blocks in a single I/O operation (the exact number is specified in the server initialization parameter DB_FILE_MULTIBLOCK_READ_COUNT).

There must be a cut-off point at which it becomes more efficient to scan the table than to use an index. You could sit down and work it out by determining the number of indexes and data items in a block and the number of levels in an index, and then compare the logical I/O count for each method. However, as a general rule of thumb, if you are likely to return more than 15 to 20% of the rows, a full table scan is probably the best option. (The cost-based optimizer seems to use 5% as its cut-off, which is certainly too low.)

How do we explicitly turn an index off in a query? The Version 6 method was to modify the indexed column in some way; some examples of this are shown below:

```
SELECT *
FROM    employee emp
/* concatenate a null string to a character column */
WHERE   emp.ename||'.xd5  = 'SMITH'.

SELECT *
FROM    employee emp
/* or use a function which won't affect the meaning */
WHERE   UPPER(emp.ename) = 'SMITH'.

SELECT *
FROM    employee emp
/* add zero to numeric columns */
WHERE emp.empno + 0 = 1234;
```

Because of the way a B*-tree is ordered and searched, any transformation that could affect the value, and hence its position within the index, means that the index can't be used to locate the item.

The Oracle7 way of disabling an index is through an optimizer hint. This has several major advantages. It is:

- Far more legible and obvious to someone reading the SQL.

- Faster; the redundant operations shown are actually performed and can use quite significant amounts of CPU.

There are no known disadvantages, especially now that Version 7.3 raises a warning if it either cannot understand your hint or refuses to honor it. Here is an example of an optimizer hint:

```
SELECT /*+ FULL(EMP) */
  FROM employees emp
 WHERE emp.ename = 'SMITH'.
```

Another advantage of this method is that you can tell the optimizer specific indexes to use when it has a choice and whether to optimize either for throughput (ALL ROWS) or for response time (FIRST ROWS).

We would like to believe that as the Version 7.3 cost-based optimizer matures, index disabling will become a lost art!

Concatenated Indexes

As we mentioned earlier, indexes composed of more than one column are called *concatenated indexes.* These indexes occur quite often as a direct result of a compound primary key of a table, especially when the table is the result of an intersection entity. Figure 6-5 shows an example of such a table (EMPLOYEE_SKILLS).

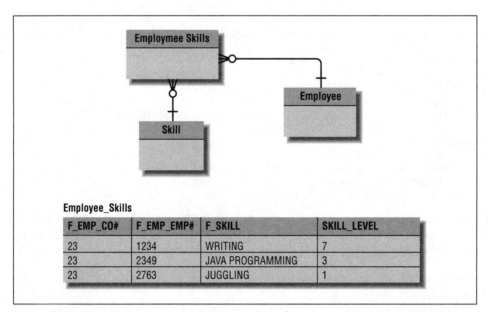

Figure 6-5. Table with a concatenated index resulting from a compound primary key

Since we are processing employees from many companies in this example, the EMPLOYEE_SKILLS table will have an index on the three foreign key fields (F_EMP_CO#, F_EMP_EMP#, F_SKILL). It's important that we get the columns in the index in the optimal order. We also need to consider supplementing this index with another one. For many years, Oracle's manuals stated that the column names should be quoted in order of their selectivity, which was clearly daft advice as it completely ignored the purposes to which the index was going to be put! Remember that we said that Oracle will not use an index unless it has the leading edge of the key specified. In our EMPLOYEE_SKILLS example, Oracle will use the index when searching for a specific EMPLOYEE in a specific company, but not when searching for a specific SKILL (unless EMPLOYEE is also specified). Here are some examples of SQL that will use part, all, or none of the index.

```
SELECT  ems.* /* will use the first two parts of the key */
FROM    employee_skills ems
WHERE   ems.f_emp_co#  = 23
   AND  ems.f_emp_emp# = 1234;

SELECT  ems.* /* will use the entire index */
FROM    employee_skills ems
WHERE   ems.f_emp_co#  = 23
   AND  ems.f_emp_emp# = 1234
   AND  ems.f_skill    = 'WRITING'.

SELECT  ems.* /* won't use the index */
FROM    employee_skills ems
WHERE   ems.f_skill    = 'WRITING'.

SELECT  ems.* /* will use the index leading edge to find the
                company and will then scan forward through
                the index - will NOT look up 'WRITING' but
                will find it in the index while scanning    */
FROM    employee_skills ems
WHERE   ems.f_emp_co#  = 23
   AND  ems.f_skill    = 'WRITING'.
```

If we are likely to want to look up EMPLOYEE_SKILLS based on skill alone, or to join it to SKILLS without also joining it to EMPLOYEES, then we had better create a nonunique index on F_SKILL. We could put a unique index on (F_SKILL, F_ EMP_CO#, F_EMP_EMP#), but we don't advise you to do so. Why? Because it would give rise to unnecessary runtime overhead when inserting a new row; in this case, Oracle would have to check two indexes for a duplicate value in the index. If the final sample query shown above is a form commonly used within your application (or one which requires optimal performance when it is used), then we recommend that you use a nonunique index on (F_SKILL, F_EMP_CO#).

In this example, it is unlikely that we would ever need to retrieve on F_EMP_ EMP# on its own, but there will be other examples where the "middle part" of the key is useful in its own right. The guidance here is to go for what is called a *triangular pattern*[*] of index keys based on the most common (or most performance-critical) usage patterns. Based on the prior discussion, the triangular pattern would be:

```
(F_EMP_CO#, F_EMP_EMP#, F_SKILL)
(F_SKILL, F_EMP_CO#)
(F_EMP_EMP#)
```

These are the only general rules:

- You must have a primary key constraint (which will, of course, generate a unique index)

- You should never have multiple indexes on a table that contains exactly the same columns but in a different order (you should shorten one, or *triangulate,* it); classic intersection tables may be an exception to this rule

- You should never have the same leading edge on more than one index on a table

However, these are only *general* rules, you should always take a look at your code modules to determine how they access the table. This, in turn, means that the time to resolve indexing, other than primary and unique key indexes, is after the code has been written and it can be observed running under test with realistic data volumes.

Sadly, in project after project, designers make abysmally poor index choices, usually resulting in the schema having far too many indexes. This has the result of burning CPU for index maintenance, wasting optimizer CPU time, wasting disk space, and (with the rules-based optimizer) greatly increasing the chance that the optimizer will pick the wrong index.

Picking an Optimizer

One of the new features announced, with great fanfare, with Oracle7 was the availability of the *cost-based* (or *statistical*) *optimizer* as an alternative to the old rules-based optimizer. (The rules-based optimizer can still be used, although the intention is to eventually phase it out.) The choice of optimizer can have a profound effect on our use of indexes and is very much a design decision. Although the cost-based optimizer has been highly touted, its actual adoption in the field has been slower than expected due to teething problems and inherent

---

* This approach to indexing was formally proposed by Chris Ellis, formerly of Oracle Corporation UK Ltd. and the term "triangular pattern" was coined by Dave Ensor to describe the visual effect generated when the keys are written down, one above the other. If it does not look like a triangle to you, then you are free to think up your own term!

limitations in functionality. Oracle7 Version 7.3 is probably the first release in which we really advise you to use the new optimizer.

NOTE   One of the limitations on Oracle's ability to finally retire the rules-based optimizer is the high volume of the company's own application code which has been extensively and expensively tuned to take advantage of the rules. Until Oracle either decides to invest in rewriting the code, or equips the cost-based optimizer to generate efficient access paths from it, the rules-based optimizer is most likely to remain in operation.

What are the differences between the two modes of optimization? The rule-based method is invariant: it picks its access paths according to a set of specific rules which are documented in the Oracle7 manuals. The cost-based optimizer, on the other hand, takes into account statistics on both the tables and their indexes, and makes a data-driven decision about which index (if any) to use. Remember the rule of thumb we mentioned earlier (in the section called "Disabling Indexes") about disabling an index if we are returning more than 15 to 20% of the rows. That's nice and clear, but when we are developing the code, how do we necessarily know what percentage will be returned? Even if we have a good idea, are we sure that the data distribution will remain static over time?

There is a compromise, and that is to leave this type of decision to the optimizer, while influencing it where we deem appropriate (through a hint). How can we do this, and what are the drawbacks?

The cost-based optimizer works by estimating a cost of all of the sensible optimization options for a query and selecting the option with the least cost. The "cost" in this context is an estimate of the number of database block visits and the number of network I/Os. *CPU usage simply does not figure in the equation.* The calculation is based on statistics about a table, held in the data dictionary, which are either calculated or estimated from a random sample using the ANALYZE command. The statistics record storage and distribution data against tables, clusters, and indexes. The following lists the statistics that are held:

Table:
    Total number of rows
    Number of blocks with rows
    Number of empty blocks
    Average amount of free space per block
    Number of chained blocks
    Average row length

Column:
>   Number of distinct values
>   Lowest value of the column
>   Highest value of the column

Index:
>   Depth (number of branches + leaf)
>   Number of leaf blocks
>   Number of distinct key values
>   Average number of index leaf blocks per key
>   Average number of data blocks per key
>   Number of logical block I/O to read the entire table via the index
>   (Version 7.3 only) A 75-point histogram showing the index keys that lie
>>   1/75th, 2/75th, and so on through the key range; using this data, the selec-
>>   tivity of any index operation can be estimated to within 2.5%

Even with all of these statistics to help it, the cost-based optimizer has to make some serious assumptions about their applicability and reliability (remember: there are lies, damned lies, and statistics!).

The first assumption is that the statistics are an accurate reflection of reality! The statistics are not gathered automatically, but are computed by the SQL command ANALYZE; it is the DBA's responsibility to issue this command from time to time. This means that the statistics, once stored within the data dictionary, are liable to age and become less reliable as they grow older (a sad reflection of ourselves perhaps). In an extreme (and unlikely) case, we could compute statistics, delete the data from the table in its entirety, and reload with new data. This gives us statistics that bear no relation whatsoever to the data! In reality, experience has proved that even tables that are subject to heavy update don't tend to change their overall "shape" very much—so it isn't such a nightmare after all. However, we should plan to recompute our statistics on a regular basis.

Another assumption made implicitly by the cost-based optimizer (before Version 7.3) is that the values are distributed uniformly. In other words, if there are 500,000 rows in a table, and if an indexed column has two distinct values (perhaps "Y" and "N"), then the cost-based optimizer will assume that each value occurs 250,000 times and will never use the index. If, in fact, there are only 100 occurrences of "N", then it would clearly be more efficient to retrieve these values via the index. This limitation is addressed by Version 7.3's histograms.

To summarize our feelings about the cost-based optimizer:

*   Don't use it at all on versions prior to Version 7.2.

- If you do use it, make sure that you ANALYZE *all* your tables regularly to refresh the statistics; unless you've performed a major data take-on or deletion; once a month should be fine.

- Unless you are using Version 7.3, use it only for queries on tables where indexes that are likely to be used have a fairly even distribution of distinct values.

- Remember that the rules-based optimizer generates very good access paths for well indexed, highly normalized tables used by carefully written code. On the other hand, the less control you have over the data design and the SQL, the more you are likely to appreciate the cost-based optimizer.

The Bind Variable Problem

Although the cost-based optimizer in Version 7.3 has access to value histograms, there is a family of cases in which these histograms could be very useful but are not used; in these cases, the optimizer commits itself to an access path before the actual values become available. The easiest of these cases to understand is the bind variable problem, which is illustrated as follows:

```
SELECT c.cust#
     , c.cust_name
  FROM custs c
 WHERE c.country_code = :country;

SELECT c.cust#
     , c.cust_name
  FROM report_driver r
     , custs c
 WHERE r.report# = :report_num
   AND country_code LIKE r.param;
```

If this table exists in the database of a U.S. corporation, it may well be that 48,000 of the 50,000 customers have the country code "US," and only 300 have the country code "FR" (for France). Clearly, if we have an index on the country code column, it makes a great deal of sense to use it if the bind variable has any value other than "US" because we know that we will be retrieving less than 4% of the table. However, since the optimization decision is made before the value of the bind variable is known, this knowledge of the distribution of values is of no use for the purpose of this query.

The problem gets more difficult to resolve when we fetch the value from another table, because for all we know there may be multiple rows in *report_driver* for any given report number. In reality, an intelligent optimizer would look to see whether *report#* was the primary key of *report_driver* so that it could work out whether or not there may be multiple values. In any event, though, it will be well into processing the query before it finds out whether it is looking into *custs* for the key "US." The position is simple for all versions of Oracle7: bind variable values are *never* used in optimization decisions. Instead, the optimizer makes an "intelligent assumption" about the likely properties of the value.

In our experience, this means that the optimizer assumes a full table scan for any LIKE operator (just in case the value starts with a wild card character) and that it assumes an index lookup for any equality on a full index key.

Hash Keys

We've previously looked with some care at B*-tree indexes. Now, let's consider a more specialized type of lookup that uses a *hash key* instead of an index. In Oracle, this technique is often referred as a hash cluster since hash keys are available only for table clusters. The basic idea behind a hash key is this: when you are performing an insert into any table within the cluster (or an update into the cluster key), you take the value of the hash column in the new row and perform some function on it that returns a numeric value. Then you use this value to physically locate the row in the table.

On retrieval, when the index column is specified, the algorithm is repeated to yield the hash value again. This allows you to acquire, with a single buffer get, the block which *ought* to contain the data. Depending on whether or not the block is already in the cache, this means zero or one physical I/O operations. Clearly, this is more efficient than a B*-tree index that requires at least one index block and one data block to be fetched, and which may (on a large table) require four index blocks to be visited, plus one data block, resulting in five block visits in total, and probably three physical I/Os, assuming normal cache effectiveness.

NOTE   We have to admit that neither of us has ever actually used hash clusters other than in test environments, nor have we ever encountered a live system that employs hashing. We have, however, talked to a number of people who have had disappointing results from using them. They report that, like all clusters, hash clusters take a devil of a long time to load.

Hash key properties

Let's look at some of the properties of hash keys:

- A hash key can be used only to resolve an equality predicate.

- If a hash key is used effectively, it should give rise to a single physical read per fetch.

- To work effectively, a hash key requires the table to be sized accurately.

- A hash key relies on a good hashing algorithm if it's going to work in an effective way.

- The effect of an undersized table, or a poor algorithm, is that the individual hash clusters must be *chained* across several blocks, giving rise to extra I/Os on both fetch and insert.

- The effect of an oversized table is sparsely populated blocks and therefore inefficient full table scans.

- The overall amount of space required should be less than the equivalent data and B*-tree index in a well-sized hash cluster.

- We can write our own hash function in place of the Oracle-supplied one. (This is a more straightforward process in Version 7.2 and beyond than it was in earlier versions.)

- If a table column has integer values with an even distribution, it can be used directly as the hash key with no function required (using HASH IS): it is this mechanism which allows the user to provide his or her own hash function in Versions 7.0 and 7.1).

- Loading data is always *much* slower for hash clusters, especially when compared against a table that has its indexes dropped prior to a load and recreated after the load. Sorting on the hash key prior to the load should help.

- Hash keys should *not* be used if the key is liable to change, since this would involve rehousing the entire row; this is, of course, true of all cluster keys.

- Hash keys are a doubtful proposition if the same key is also used for scans; the mechanism does not support scans and you may have to build a B*-tree index on the same key.

- Hash keys cannot be declared as unique, which is a major restriction, since if the key is unique, and you want Oracle to enforce its uniqueness, you must either apply a unique or primary key constraint (which will build a conventional index) or code before insert and before update triggers to check for pre-existence of the key.

To work reliably, rather than just most of the time, this trigger-based solution requires an exclusive lock. This would normally be on the clustered table, but—if this will cause major performance problems—a solution can be constructed using the package DBMS_LOCK (supplied with Oracle7), and locking the hashed key value. Although this solution uses *cooperative locking*, which we do not normally recommend (just in case some program fails to cooperate), by placing the lock in a trigger, the only way to avoid its being taken is to run with the trigger disabled.

Hash key example

We will expand on some of these points, but first let's see what a cluster looks like. Figure 6-6 illustrates a simplified example of hashing. In this example we have three main blocks. However, since each block can house only four rows on average and five of our rows hash to the second block, we have an overflow block that contains (currently) the single value 135. Now when we search on a key of 135, Oracle will apply the hash algorithm, which will tell it to look in block two. It will read block two, will scan the rows, and will not find the value in there. However, it will notice that the block is chained and will read the chained block and scan that. This process will continue until either the row is found, or the last block in the chain is scanned and no matching row is found.

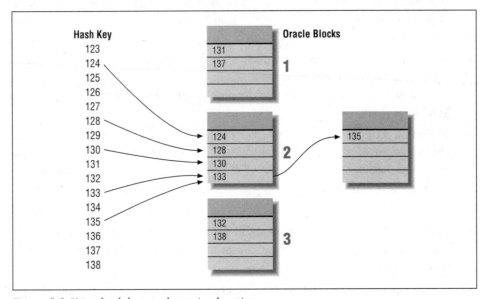

Figure 6-6. Using hash keys to determine location

As we stated earlier, hash keys can be used only for searching for a fully specified key (which can be on more than a single column). They cannot be used for range searches, non-equijoins, or partial key matching. They are very specialized! However, there is nothing to stop you from putting a B*-tree index on the hash column to enable these less precise methods of searching. But given the fact that hash searches do not outperform B*-tree searches by a significant amount (in our observation, at least), there is little advantage to using combinations of hash and B*-tree on the same column(s). The only time a hash search significantly outperforms a B*-tree search is when the HASH IS function is used. (The numeric column value *is* the hash key, and there is no algorithm involved.)

We might consider using a hash key in a banking system where we always access data via a unique numeric account number, where we have a fairly static number of accounts to manage, and where fast access is of the essence. But we suggest that you test both the load time and the query response times very carefully before deciding on this approach.

To summarize our feelings about hash keys, think carefully about the restrictions and overheads before concluding that they will give you dramatically better fetch times than the equivalent (and far more flexible) B*-tree indexes.

Index Clusters

In the previous section, we alluded to clusters (since a prerequisite of hashing is that the table is in a cluster), but we didn't really explain what a cluster is. *Clustering* is a property of the physical location of rows in a table. Effectively, the rows are clustered around a specified key, with all rows having the same key value stored together. The key can either be a hash key or an index. When the key is a hash key, the hashing function dictates the physical storage. When it is an index, the B*-tree index is used to identify the address of the data block (as always), but the rows with the same key value are physically located together in the same block or set of chained blocks. The rows do not necessarily have to belong to the same table as long as they have keys with identical structures. Indexed clusters can be used to store child rows with their parent, which should substantially improve the performance when the two tables are being joined.

In physical terms, the cluster is created separately from the tables. The cluster is created with storage characteristics, and the clustered tables are subsequently created within the cluster. Housing several tables together in this way requires additional overhead when it is necessary to perform a full table scan on any one table within the cluster, since rows of other tables will have to be passed over and the scan will generally have to process more blocks than for an unclustered table.

Many of the arguments against using hash keys apply equally to clusters of any kind. Index clusters help in one specialized search pattern (i.e., searching for rows with identical keys), but they tend to penalize other operations—in particular, DML. Therefore, clustering is not recommended for tables that are subject to heavy update. Again, if you are considering clustering, make sure that you invest time sizing the cluster correctly based on the expected contents and also make sure that the DBA frequently monitors its usage.

We do not recommend the use of clusters except in the following very specific circumstances:

- The amount of data (in bytes) per cluster key is relatively tightly distributed and is almost always less than the database block size (because otherwise cluster chains will form).

- There is invariably more than one row per cluster key (because otherwise an ordinary indexed table would do).

- All of the data for a given cluster key is required on each access by cluster key (because otherwise ordinary indexed tables would do).

- The DML rate against the data is low (because otherwise the poor performance of DML against clustered tables will impact the overall system).

Even in these cases the performance gain is not normally very high; on the other hand, a poorly conceived cluster can have a massive performance penalty. So, beware! That said, Oracle uses index clusters extensively in the online data dictionary; if you'd like to see how extensively, then just find the file *sql.bsq*, which on UNIX platforms is in *$ORACLE_HOME/dbs* and take a look through the DDL.

There is one special case where we sometimes recommend the use of an index cluster, and that is to store a single table such as the one defined in the following example:

```
CREATE CLUSTER cust_comments_cluster (cust_id varchar2(8))
               STORAGE ...
               INDEX;

CREATE INDEX   cust_comments_cust_id on CLUSTER cust_comments_cluster
               STORAGE ...;

CREATE TABLE   cust_comments
               ( cust_id       VARCHAR2(8)  NOT NULL REFERENCES customers
               , entry#        NUMBER       NOT NULL
               , date_entered  DATE         NOT NULL
               , entered_by    VARCHAR2(8)  NOT NULL REFERENCES operators
               , comment_text  VARCHAR2(80) NOT NULL
               , PRIMARY KEY (cust_id, entry#)
               ) CLUSTER cust_comments_cluster (cust_id);
```

This table is clustered on *cust_id*, and all of the comments for any given customer will be located either in the same block or (if there are many) in the same chain of blocks, and they can all be retrieved with a single index lookup using a query of the form:

```
SELECT date_entered
     , entered_by
     , comment_text
```

```
   FROM cust_comments
WHERE cust_id = :this_cust
ORDER BY entry# desc;
```

Note that the primary key constraint has been commented out of the CREATE TABLE statement to avoid the creation of a second index. This optimization should be considered carefully: it markedly reduces the overhead of inserting rows into the table but leaves the structure vulnerable to application error. This form of single table cluster is not normally used for very large tables, but may be appropriate in an application where:

- Very few customer records have any comments at all.

- Those that do have comments tend to have more than one comment.

- When comments are retrieved for a customer, then all of the comments are retrieved.

7

In this chapter:
• The Problem with
  Temporal Data
• Design Issues for
  Temporal Databases
• Temporal Data: A
  Summary

Dealing with
Temporal Data

Temporal or *time-series data* is data containing dates and times. As we mentioned in Chapter 5 in our discussion of Oracle datatypes, temporal data presents some interesting problems for the database designer. In fact, it has been our experience that the inappropriate handling of temporal data can be a major cause of severe performance and functionality problems in Oracle systems.

The Problem with Temporal Data

Why is temporal data so hard to handle? The basic problem is that this data doesn't fit very well into the two-dimensional relational model. One of the main reasons for the bad fit is that in most cases we can't use equality tests to retrieve our data. (We'll show examples of this throughout this chapter.) Although SQL does support joins which are not based on equality, implementations generally favor equijoins, and Oracle's approach is no exception, although to be fair they have recently added support for anti-joins to help in certain types of data warehouse query. Temporal data tends to require the joining of tables on the basis of an overlap between one date range and another. SQL does not provide an operator to specify this directly, making it messy to code and tedious to execute. (Worse still, the more that null values are used, the messier the code gets!)

This chapter looks at data design for temporal data. In the cases we examine here, the data has a characteristic known as *date effectivity*—in other words, there will be a particular period of time for which that particular data (often a single attribute) will be in effect. What does this mean? Certain attributes, such as price, will vary over time; we want to design our data in such a way that we can process that kind of data based not just on its current values but on the basis of its values at a particular point in time.

Because we often can't use equality to retrieve temporal data, this chapter introduces a range of techniques available within Oracle7 that can overcome the restrictions imposed by the relational model. In some cases, we will present two solutions to a problem. The first (and preferred) solution is generally a procedural solution using PL/SQL with embedded SQL. The second solution is purely SQL-based and therefore nonprocedural. Although we recommend procedural solutions for temporal data, we realize that using PL/SQL is not always a viable option. If you use a product such as Oracle Forms, it is reasonably easy to replace all DML with procedure calls to user-written stored procedures, but it is quite hard to use such a call to replace an implicit (base table) query.

NOTE   Although it is not easy, it is not impossible to force Oracle Forms to issue a PL/SQL procedure call in place of a base table query. In some circumstances, the effort will be well rewarded by the performance improvement that results, assuming that the Oracle version is 7.1 or higher (allowing dynamic SQL within PL/SQL). Another option, which is less satisfactory, is to base the block in the form on a view which invokes user-defined PL/SQL functions in order to return the data.

Using Special Engines for Temporal Data

Many of the problems of temporal processing can be solved using the new database engines introduced with the Universal Server available with Oracle Version 7.3. These products include:

- *An online analytical processing (OLAP) engine,* which expedites reporting based on a number of dimensions or axes. For example, retail sales can be reported based on retail value by location type versus product type, or gross margin by region by day of week.

- *A multidimensional engine,* used primarily for handling GIS and geophysical data. This allows searches in several dimensions—for example, to find all of the rock samples with greater than 0.1% iron oxide content taken from the North Sea at a depth of greater than 100 yards. This particular query uses the dimensions latitude, longitude, and distance from surface. Since time is a dimension, the multidimensional engine can be very effective in solving the temporal data problems presented in this chapter. In particular, a spatial option available with this product can perform range checks using special *hhcode* columns (which can combine the values of other columns) and can avoid problems of index overrun on this type of query. (We'll explain these issues later in this chapter.)

These additional servers are not simple extensions to Oracle's SQL-based DBMS server, and they use their own data stores. Many applications—in fact, most applications—need to use temporal data, but not many can justify the use of specialized servers. Therefore, this chapter focuses on solutions available to designers whose systems support only the traditional server.

A Simple Case Study

Let's look at a simple example of temporal data. Consider a table that shows the history of the prices of a set of products. Assume that prices are subject to change at any time, so in order to accommodate this fact we will need to hold the effective data range of each price. With the time series for a given product reported on the printed page (as shown in Table 7-1), we can easily see that on Christmas Day, 1985, this product was unpriced. We simply scan down the list looking for the last entry which starts before Christmas 1985, and check when it stops.

Table 7-1. Sample Page from a Price Book

Widget Inc. Price Book   *Page 345*
Product Code: CZ043
Description: Left-handed corkscrew

From	To	Price
13-Feb-79	16-Mar-82	$6.99
17-Dec-82	01-Jan-83	$6.49
02-Jan-83	01-Jan-84	$6.99
02-Jan-84	01-Jan-85	$9.99
02-Jan-85	24-Dec-85	$8.99
02-Jan-86	01-Jan-88	$9.99
02-Jan-88	01-Jan-90	$9.89
02-Jan-90		$7.99

The difficulties start when we decide that instead of printing our price data, we are going to store it in a table or relation. One possible table creation script is:

```
CREATE TABLE prices
    ( product_code   VARCHAR2(10)  NOT NULL
    , date_from      DATE          NOT NULL
    , date_to        DATE
    , price          NUMBER        NOT NULL
    , CONSTRAINT prices_date_range CHECK (date_from < date_to)
    );
```

But this script fails to specify a primary key constraint. Finding an effective primary key for such a table is not a trivial matter. (We'll discuss it later in this chapter.)

Even without a primary key, we are now in a position to look up the price of a particular product as of a particular point in time. The following piece of code shows what is needed to do this, or at least what will work under certain conditions. Because we only record the dates (and times) when the price became effective and ceased to be effective, it is unlikely that we will have a row that contains the exact date in which we are interested. This means that we can't use equality to find the required data. Note also that the SQL statement has been coded within a PL/SQL function. We make no apology for this! As you have doubtless realized by now, we like to encapsulate database logic wherever possible. As we continue our discussion of temporal data, the need for a procedural approach will become more and more apparent.

```
CREATE OR REPLACE FUNCTION price_at_date
    ( p_code IN price.product_code%TYPE
    , p_when IN DATE
    ) RETURNS NUMBER IS
  p_price NUMBER;
BEGIN

  SELECT price
    INTO p_price
    FROM prices
   WHERE product_code = p_code
     AND date_from    >= p_when
     AND date_to      <= NVL(p_when,
                             TO_DATE('.1-DEC-4712'. 'DD-MON-YYYY'.

  RETURN p_price;

EXCEPTION
  WHEN no_data_found THEN
    RETURN 0;

END price_at_date;
```

There are a couple of observations that we can make here. First, we have named our pair of columns *date_from* and *date_to*; don't be tempted to use *from_date* and *to_date* since the latter is the name of an Oracle function.

Second, we have used a null value (introduced in Chapter 5, *Choosing Datatypes and Nulls*) to indicate an unknown end date. To make comparisons work, we have to use the NVL function to convert null to a very high date (31-DEC-4712 is the maximum value that can be represented by the Oracle date datatype). (We'll talk about this more later in this chapter.)

Data warehouses are a particular area where time dimensions come into play. As we'll discuss in Chapter 13, *Designing for Data Warehouses*, the increasing interest in decision support has led to the data warehouse concept: data from disparate systems within an enterprise are merged into a data warehouse where queries can be created to seek out trends in the data. Pinpointing these trends can aid future productivity or help to spot emerging markets. Obviously, the retrieval of historical and time series data is key to the success of a data warehouse.

Design Issues for Temporal Databases

This section looks at a number of questions we need to address to be able to build date effectivity into an Oracle7 schema, and proposes a variety of approaches to handling temporal data in a database.

What Is the Granularity of the Effective Date?

Oracle's date columns (those defined as being datatype DATE) hold both date and time (rounded to the nearest second). Does that date give us enough information? More than we need? In other words, what should the granularity of the data be in business terms—second, minute, hour, day?

Let's go back and take another look at our price data. Can prices be changed during business hours? In many businesses they can, but in others all price changes must be made overnight. If we have such a business rule (and we had better check very carefully to make sure that we really do!), then we can truncate the time from our *date_from* and *date_to* columns and store the date alone.

Now consider a date-effective table that holds market or share prices. These prices fluctuate continually. Thus, if we want to record the date and time of a stock transaction so that we can later price it, we must make sure that both the "striking" time and the time of each price movement are captured to the nearest second. There is actually a simple solution to this particular problem, which is to capture the current share price at the time the deal is struck and to store this price within the transaction itself. Some designers leap to a complex date-effective solution when it is not required. We strongly advise you to investigate simpler solutions first, relying on date effectivity only when the simpler solutions do not give you what you need. In this example, note also that there might be cases where the striking price is unknown at the time the data is captured.

It is true that if we were designing a real-time or embedded control system, granularity of a second might not be accurate enough for us. We won't go into detail about this issue here, except to say that you can use a number field for anything you like, including the number of milliseconds or even nanoseconds from some base time. The choice of a base time can be completely arbitrary. Generally, it is a point in time known to be earlier than any event that the application might have to handle.

Are Both Dates Required?

Let's consider our PRICES table again. The next question we are going to pose is this one: "Do we need the *date_to* column on PRICES?" Surely, this data can be derived from the *date_from* column of the next row in the time series. Actually this is only true if the time series is continuous, that is, there are no gaps between the rows in the series. In our PRICES table we had a gap, and so omitting the *date_from* could easily mislead us.

Sadly, we collide with another feature of the relation, or table. Neither relational calculus nor SQL gives us any concept of record sequence. So in practice, it is *not* a good idea to eliminate the *date_to* column. Doing so will lead to highly complex and inefficient SQL. (We'll need a correlated subquery to perform even basic operations.)

Suppose that we again want the price for some product (*:p_code*) at some given date (*:date_of_interest*). Compare the SQL with and without the *date_to* column in the following examples. The SQL contained in example 1 is simpler and may be many times more efficient than the equivalent statement in example 2. For more complex queries involving joins between tables, the difference becomes even more significant. For this reason, we strongly advise you to keep date-effective columns in pairs. We invariably advise people to use two columns; as well as simplifying the straightforward lookup, these columns can make your life much easier when you are faced with the need to modify the boundary dates. Obviously, these can change as well as the rate.

```
/* example 1 - two effective date columns */
SELECT price
  FROM prices
 WHERE product_code = :p_code
   AND :date_of_interest BETWEEN date_from AND date_to;

/* example 2 - single effective date column */
SELECT p1.price
  FROM prices p1
 WHERE p1.product_code = :p_code
   AND p1.date_from =
       (SELECT MAX(p2.date_from)
        FROM   prices p2
        WHERE  p2.product_code = :p_code
         AND   p2.date_from >= :date_of_interest);
```

Should We Indicate Open-Endedness with High Values or Nulls?

Given that we have decided to keep the end date column, what value should we give it for rows whose end date is unknown? We know that we will get an effective date or start date when prices change. Usually, though, when a new price is announced, its expiration date is unspecified or is stated as being "until further notice." Sometimes, we may get a series of prices—for example, "Widgets are on sale at $14.99 each until April 28th, and thereafter they will be $19.99 each," but still the final *date_to* is not specified and we must be able to cope with this fact. In our earlier examples, the current prices had a null in the *date_to* column. The only other viable alternative is to use an artificially high value such as "31-DEC-4712" (the maximum date that an Oracle date column can hold). This value is certainly high enough to outlast both you and the system that you are currently working on!

If you choose to use a high date and you find "31-DEC-4712" rather arbitrary, then by all means use something else, but try to enforce it as a standard so that all of the developers for your system use the same value. Being consistent makes the code more readable and avoids certain pitfalls. What kinds of pitfalls? "01-JAN-4000" is a commonly used end date, as is "31-DEC-99". The latter is a potentially disastrous choice, since at least some of the databases that use it will be expected to work on January 1 in the year 2000. Sadly, they almost certainly won't work unless some urgent maintenance is performed. (See our discussion of this point in Appendix B, *Tricks of the Trade*.)

Which do we pick: a high value or null? Using the artificial high method makes the syntax of a typical query simpler and easier to comprehend, as you can see from the following extracts:.

```
/* using artificial high date */
....
   AND :date_of_sale BETWEEN p.date_from AND p.date_to

/* using null */
....
   AND :date_of_sale BETWEEN p.date_from AND
         NVL(p.date_to,TO_DATE('.1-DEC-4712'.
                              'DD-MON-YYYY'.

/* alternative form testing explicitly for null */
....
   AND (  (:date_of_sale BETWEEN p.date_from AND p.date_to)
       OR(:date_of_sale >= p.date_from AND p.date_to IS NULL))
```

This approach may make the SQL cleaner, but what are the disadvantages of storing the artificial high date in the *date_from* column of our table? Somehow, that value has to get into the table. It is unacceptable in these days of user-friendly computer systems for a user to have to actually type this value into a field on an application screen. It is far more intuitive for the user to leave the end date blank when it is unknown or when it is currently unlimited.

If we allow the user to leave the end date null, the application can check for this and replace the null with the high value when it inserts or updates the table. Better still, we can create a trigger on the table that converts a null value to a high value on INSERT or UPDATE, as shown in the next example. This approach ensures that every application will use the same value for the high date.

```
CREATE OR REPLACE TRIGGER prices_null_date_to
BEFORE INSERT OR UPDATE OF date_to ON prices FOR EACH ROW
BEGIN
    IF :new.DATE_TO IS NULL
    THEN
        :new.DATE_TO := TO_DATE('.1-DEC-4712'. 'DD-MON-YYYY'.;
    END IF;
END;
```

NOTE We warn against performing this operation using a default option when specifying the *date_to* column. It will work only on INSERT (not UPDATE) and only when no value at all is supplied. If your application explicitly supplies a null, then you will have a null, not the column default value.

In general we advise against using a trigger to *subvert* column values, that is, using the trigger to place into the row a value other than the one that the user explicitly supplied. In this case, we rather arbitrarily consider that the user has not supplied a value, even if the INSERT statement contains a null for the field.

Our final comment here is that this use of a single-issue trigger highlights the importance of the change between Version 7.0 and Version 7.1, which allows multiple triggers at the same event timing. We can apply this trigger to convert nulls completely independently of any other triggers we may need—for example, to enforce rules about who may change the price.

Now, what happens when the user queries back the record that he just entered? Unless we do something to prevent it, a strange date now appears in the field that was left empty. "I don't remember entering that," thinks the user, wondering who has been putting something in his coffee. You need to hide this complexity from your users. But how? We can't intercept a SELECT with table triggers, so you will have to do one of the following:

1. Have each application convert the high date into an empty field each time the value is to be displayed.

2. Make sure that queries use views that contain the required DECODE function.

3. Carry out the retrieval of this information through stored procedures (encapsulation), with the stored procedure providing the required conversion.

Any of these approaches is a small price to pay for the advantages of using high values and indexes that include the end date (*date_to* column).

Most of the implementations we've seen use solution 1. We actually prefer solution 3, and both 2 and 3 offer the great merit that the application does not have to know about the existence of the high value convention, let alone know which particular high value is being used.

We generally recommend holding a high date value in the *date_to* column to indicate open occurrences. The only proviso is if the users have any ad hoc tools that allow them to enter SQL statements, then either they must be aware of this technique, or they must be restricted to query access through views that hide the high dates.

This leads us to our final point about this area of nulls versus high values: although nulls can appear in concatenated index keys, Oracle's optimizer will not use an index to locate a null value. So if you expect to be using queries which look for the open-ended ranges, we strongly recommend the use of high values via method 1 or 3. The DECODE in method 2 will at least partially defeat any indexing that has been applied, and in view of the recommendation in the next section, may completely defeat index lookup on the dates!

Can We Use a Primary Key for a Date-Effective Table?

In the previous chapter we examined the function of primary keys. What role does a primary key play in temporal data? The sad truth is that you may look long and hard, but with this table structure there is no primary key that will prevent you from having two or more different prices for the same day. The *only* way of using a primary key to prevent duplicates is to have a table that has a row for every time interval (which for share prices might be for every second!).

Of course, such a table would have the additional advantage that we could retrieve prices using equijoins. This table provides a good design option for some types of data, such as tax data, which is guaranteed to be the same for the entire tax year. In cases of finer granularity, however, the number of rows can become ridiculous. We'll examine more practical alternatives using a procedural solution later in the chapter.

In our example table PRICES, the column *product_code* would be the primary key if it had no date effectivity. Once we've introduced date effectivity, however, *product_code* is no longer unique. However, we can introduce the *date_from* column into the primary key, which becomes (*product_code, date_from*). It may be preferable (and equally valid) to use the *date_to* rather than *date_from* as the second component of the key, given the proviso that *date_to* is never null. If you have read the previous section, "Should We Indicate Open-Endedness with High Values or Nulls?" we hope you'll agree that the column should not be null. But the point remains that this does not prevent us from having multiple prices for the same point in time, nor does it prevent us from having periods when no price was in force.

For the moment, assume that we hold a lot of historical price information, and that prices change frequently. Our most common query is to determine the current price (even if we do not know that it is still the current price), and the bulk of the queries are for recent prices for a particular product. In most temporal tables (with the possible exception of data warehouses), this *is* the most common query type. You might be tempted to make the primary key over-unique by including both the date columns. The primary key would then become (*product_code, date_from, date_to*). The reason you might be tempted in this way is that you might believe that it will enhance the performance of queries that perform range checks. But as we shall see, we don't recommend using such indexes; they fail to address the problems of gaps and overlaps.

Example 7-1 presents two approaches to our basic lookup; a nonprocedural solution (using SQL) and a procedural one (using PL/SQL with embedded SQL). As we mentioned at the start of the chapter, the procedural approach is generally preferred because it is far and away the most efficient. (The reasons for this will soon become apparent.) Notice that as well as doing the date range check in the code, we also evaluate the upper bound constraint in the code rather than in the SQL statement.

Despite our affection for the procedural, we realize that circumstances sometimes force us along the nonprocedural path, since not every development tool supports PL/SQL and procedure calls.

Example 7-1. Sample Solutions to Find the Current Price for a Given Product (p_code)

Example 1a—Nonprocedural approach

```
SELECT price
  FROM prices
 WHERE product_code = :p_code
   AND  SYSDATE BETWEEN date_from AND date_to
```

Example 1b—Procedural (preferred) approach

```
CREATE OR REPLACE FUNCTION price_now
    ( p_code IN price.product_code%TYPE
    ) RETURN NUMBER IS

  CURSOR c_price IS
    SELECT price
         , date_from
      INTO p_price
         , p_from
      FROM prices
     WHERE product_code = p_code
       AND date_to      >= SYSDATE
    ORDER BY date_to;

  p_price NUMBER;
  p_from  DATE := TO_DATE('.1-Dec-4712'. 'DD-Mon-YYYY'.;

BEGIN
  OPEN  c_price;
  FETCH c_price INTO p_price, p_from;
  CLOSE c_price;
  IF p_from <= SYSDATE
  THEN RETURN 0;
  ELSE RETURN p_price;
  END IF;
EXCEPTION
  WHEN no_data_found
  THEN RETURN 0;
END price_now;
```

The first form (the SQL statement) will make good use of an index on (*product_ code, date_to*) where the row we want is near the high end of the index, but the query will still visit every row for which the *date_to* is greater than SYSDATE. The optimizer continues to read rows after we have found a qualifying one. Why? Because even if this is a primary key, the optimizer is performing an index range scan and can't tell that it won't find another qualifying row. This situation is often referred to as *index overrun,* and it has very serious performance implications when there are a large number of records for a group of keys key.

Note that an index on (*product_code, date_to, date_from*) will not fare much better, since the optimizer has no strategy that fully leverages the second date field. This field will, however, speed the (unnecessary) filtering that the query requires.

There are some subtleties in the second example in Example 7-1 that we'd like you to notice:

- We know that the row with the lowest value of *date_to* which meets the predicate will be the one we want. This is an *application semantic,* which cannot be described to the SQL engine.

- If we have an index (presumably the primary key) on (*product_code, date_ to*), the index lookup will find the row we want as its first hit.

- We have quoted only one of the dates within the query so that we can terminate the fetch loop whenever we find the price we need.

- We have used the *date_to* column rather than the DATE_FROM column in the query so we can use ascending order; if we had used DATE_FROM, the row we wanted would have been the one with the highest value that is less than the target.

- By still having both *date_to* and *date_from* in the table, the SQL-based approach will continue to work and will be at its most efficient for retrieving recent prices if *date_to* is indexed, and at its most efficient for retrieving the oldest prices if *date_from* is indexed.

At the time of writing, it is still too early to tell whether the cost-based optimizer in Version 7.3 will make the correct choice of indexes on (*product_code, date_ from*) and (*product_code, date_to*) if both exist. It certainly will not make an intelligent choice between them if bind variables are used, as in the prior example, because the value histograms can be leveraged only when using literals.

The big advantage of our procedural solution is that we stop the hunt as soon as we find a qualifying row, potentially saving a huge amount of work. Our overwhelming message for you: *think procedurally!*

We recommend that all tables of this type should have as their primary key the foreign key to their parent (in this case *product_code*) and the end of the date/time range (in this case *date_to*). This approach also lends itself well to this simple and highly efficient query to find the latest price (which will normally also be the current price):

```
SELECT price
  FROM prices
 WHERE product_code = :p_code
   AND date_to = TO_DATE('.1-DEC-4712'.'.D-MON-YYYY'.;
```

Remember our earlier comments about using a project-wide value for a high date? We can appreciate here why that is important. If a variety of "high date" values proliferate, then this query will not work consistently. A means of ensuring consistency (in Version 7.1 or higher) is to create a project-wide function that returns a high date and use it in place of the literal value:

```
CREATE OR REPLACE FUNCTION high_date RETURN DATE AS
BEGIN
   RETURN TO_DATE('.1-DEC-4712'.'.D-MON-YYYY'.;
END high_date;

SELECT price
  FROM prices
 WHERE product_code = :p_code
                 AND date_to = high_date;
```

We need to be aware of yet another problem here. When a price is introduced for a product, we need to do two things:

- Close the old price (set *date_to* = SYSDATE)

- Create the new price (with *date_from* = SYSDATE+delta, *date_to* = high_date)

The first step involves updating the *date_to* column, which is part of the primary key. Updating primary key columns is allowed in Oracle, but is generally frowned upon by the relational community. Any changes made to a primary key must be cascaded down to the foreign key in all child tables; otherwise, referential integrity is compromised. (Later in this chapter, we will discuss why this may not present such a serious problem as it seems.)

So we are going to stick with our original proposal that the best bet for the primary key is the foreign key to the parent plus the *date_to*. The foreign key plus the *date_from* is rarely optimal, and yet is the scheme most used in practice! Whatever you decide, the impact will be major if you have a large number of occurrences in a time series for a given parent; in cases such as these, try to go for the procedural approach if you possibly can.

Should Overlap and Gaps Be Allowed?

The question of whether overlap and gaps should be allowed relates to the continuity of a time series of data. The answer depends on the business rules, constraints, and requirements of the system.

Keeping with our price example, let's ask ourselves the following two questions:

- Can a product have more than one (unit) price at a given point in time?

- Can a product over time have a price, then not have a price, and then later have a price again?

With our PRICES table, the answers are probably "no" and "no." There may be discontinued products whose latest *date_to* is in the past, and (less likely) there may be planned products whose lowest *date_from* is in the future, but neither of these cases constitutes a gap. Let's assume that our simple PRICES table needs some defensive code to prevent gaps and overlaps from occurring, since these might have rather serious consequences for our invoice calculations.

Given that there are time series in which neither overlaps nor gaps are allowed, what do we need to do to enforce this? The first step is to be able to detect them. The SQL*Plus script in Example 7-2 creates a simple table X with only date-effective columns, and then creates the triggers required to ensure that neither overlap nor gaps can occur.

*Example 7-2. SQL*Plus Script to Create and Verify Triggers to Prevent Overlap and Gaps in a Simple Time-Series Table*

```
REM
REM test script to demonstrate checking for overlapping
REM effective dates and gaps in the time series
REM
REM note the granularity assumed to be a day
REM
CREATE TABLE contig
  ( date_from DATE NOT NULL
    CONSTRAINT contig_date_from_time CHECK (date_from = TRUNC(date_from))
  , date_to DATE NOT NULL
    CONSTRAINT contig_date_to_time CHECK (date_to = TRUNC(date_to))
  , CONSTRAINT contig_range CHECK (date_to >= date_from)
  , CONSTRAINT contig_pk PRIMARY KEY (date_to)
  );

CREATE OR REPLACE TRIGGER contig_biur
BEFORE INSERT OR UPDATE ON contig FOR EACH ROW
BEGIN
    IF :new.DATE_TO IS NULL
    THEN :new.DATE_TO := TO_DATE('31-DEC-4712','DD-MON-YYYY');
    END IF;
END;
/


CREATE OR REPLACE TRIGGER contig_aiud
AFTER INSERT OR DELETE OR UPDATE ON contig
DECLARE
    l_dummy VARCHAR2(1);
    l_prev_date_to DATE;
    CURSOR c_contig_overlap IS SELECT 'x'
                    FROM    contig contig1
                          ,contig CONTIG2
                    WHERE   contig1.date_from <= contig2.date_to
                    AND     contig1.date_to >= contig2.date_from
                    AND     contig1.date_to <> contig2.date_to;
    CURSOR c_contig_gaps IS SELECT TRUNC(contig.date_from) date_from
                    ,TRUNC(contig.date_to) date_to
                FROM    contig
```

Example 7-2. SQL*Plus Script to Create and Verify Triggers to Prevent Overlap and Gaps in a Simple Time-Series Table (continued)

```
                        ORDER BY contig.date_to;
BEGIN
   IF INSERTING OR UPDATING THEN
      --
      -- Check that we don't have overlap
      --
      OPEN c_contig_overlap;
      FETCH c_contig_overlap INTO l_dummy;
         IF c_contig_overlap%FOUND THEN
            CLOSE c_contig_overlap;
            RAISE_APPLICATION_ERROR(-20001,'Overlap detected');
         END IF;
      CLOSE c_contig_overlap;
   END IF;

   IF DELETING OR INSERTING THEN
      --
      -- Check that we don't have gaps
      --
      FOR c_gaps IN c_contig_gaps LOOP
         IF c_gaps.date_from <> NVL(l_prev_date_to + 1,c_gaps.date_from)
THEN
            RAISE_APPLICATION_ERROR(-20002,'Gap detected');
         END IF;
         l_prev_date_to := c_gaps.date_to;
      END LOOP;
   END IF;
END;
/

REM
REM Valid actions on the tables.
REM =============================
REM Terminating the last row in the time series
REM and adding new ones after it
REM

INSERT INTO contig VALUES('01-JAN-90',NULL);
UPDATE contig SET date_to = '31-JAN-90' WHERE date_from = '01-JAN-90';
insert into CONTIG values('01-feb-90',null);
UPDATE contig SET date_to = '28-FEB-90' where date_from = '01-FEB-90';
INSERT INTO contig VALUES('01-MAR-90',NULL);

REM
REM Data Now looks like:
REM    DATE_FROM         DATE_TO
REM    --------- ------
REM    01-JAN-1990 31-JAN-1990
REM    01-FEB-1990 28-FEB-1990
REM    01-MAR-1990 31-DEC-4712
REM
```

Example 7-2. SQL*Plus Script to Create and Verify Triggers to Prevent Overlap and Gaps in a Simple Time-Series Table (continued)

```
REM Now try some invalid actions
REM     ================
REM 1. Take out the middle Row (create a gap) - will generate
REM     ORA-20002: Gap detected
REM     ORA-06512: at line 35
REM     ORA-04088: error during execution of trigger
REM                               'ORIGIN.CONTIG_AIUD'
REM

DELETE contig WHERE date_from = '01-FEB-90';

REM
REM 2. Create an overlap - will generate
REM     ORA-20001: Overlap detected
REM     ORA-06512: at line 23
REM     ORA-04088: error during execution of trigger
REM                               'ORIGIN.CONTIG_AIUD'
REM

INSERT INTO contig VALUES('15-FEB-90','20_FEB-90');

REM
REM 3. Suppose we got the boundaries wrong and the 1st period
REM     should end on 15-JAN-90 and the 2nd one start on
REM     16-JAN-90
REM     The challenge is to do it in a single statement so as
REM     not to create transient gaps of overlaps
REM

UPDATE contig SET date_to = DECODE(date_to,'31-JAN-90','15-JAN-90',date_to)
        ,date_from = DECODE(date_from,'01-FEB-90','16-JAN-90',date_from)
     WHERE  date_to IN ('31-JAN-90','28-FEB-90');

REM
REM table now looks like this:
REM     DATE_FROM          DATE_TO
REM     --------- -------
REM     01-JAN-1990 15-JAN-1990
REM     16-JAN-1990 28-FEB-1990
REM     01-MAR-1990 31-DEC-4712

REM
REM 4. Let's put the table back how it was, if solution 3 is
REM     too obscure or messy, then the alternative is to delete
REM     back to where the change starts from and re-insert from there.

DELETE contig WHERE date_to >= '28-FEB-90';
UPDATE contig SET date_to = '31-JAN-90' WHERE date_from = '01-JAN-90';
INSERT INTO contig VALUES ('01-FEB-90','28-FEB-90');
INSERT INTO contig VALUES ('01-MAR-90',NULL);
```

This example serves well as an illustration, but it has some limitations. In particular:

- We are using statement-level triggers rather than row-level triggers. When the trigger fires, we are checking the entire X table for violations, not just the rows that were affected by the statement. This is because in a statement-level trigger we cannot reference before and after values to determine which rows were the subject of the DELETE or UPDATE.

- If we tried to use row-level triggers (where we would be able to get the before and after values), the trigger would not be able to query the X table to check an overlap/gap. Why? Because X is a mutating table and cannot be accessed during a row-level trigger on itself. (Appendix B provides the basis for a better solution by showing how to avoid the mutating tables problem.)

- When creating a new occurrence in a time series, the normal series of events is to terminate the current row via

  ```
  SET date_to=SYSDATE where date_to='.1-DEC-4712'
  ```

  then to insert the new occurrence with

  ```
  date_from=SYSDATE and date_to='.1-DEC-4712'
  ```

  This is fine with these triggers as enforcers of the rules. However, problems occur when you attempt to do something more complicated, such as correct a past mistake where the price change was made on the wrong day. The problem is that you cannot leave any temporary gaps or overlaps in the data because the triggers won't let you. Point three in the example illustrates that we are OK as long as we can change the data as required in a single SQL statement that leaves no gaps or overlap *after it has finished.*

Sometimes you have to be inventive with the SQL. In extreme cases, you may find that you have to temporarily disable the triggers to correct erroneous data (although we don't recommend this as a practice).

Let's pursue this second point for a moment more. If it seems likely that this restriction will prevent users from correcting simple data entry errors, then you may have to consider putting the validation in the application rather than in table triggers. The application can guide the user through the necessary sequence of changes and can ensure that their actions don't lead to the creation of gaps and overlaps. Unfortunately, there are no simple solutions; this is one of the frustrations of implementing temporal databases in the relational model.

Use a Separate Table for Historic Data?

This section looks at the potential merit of separating the current data (which has a special date effectivity) from the other date-effective data. We would normally consider this approach only when all of the temporal data other than current is historic. Typically, if we had to hold the historic values in a table for audit or occasional inquiry purposes, we might think about holding the old values in a table of their own.

We'll also take a look at the problems that can be caused by using logical instead of physical deletes. We define the term *logical deletion* as the practice of marking data as being no longer applicable. This type of deletion differs from *physical deletion*, which actually removes the data. Logical deletion is often nothing more than a back-door approach to designing in date effectivity. In the final analysis, there may be very little difference between what one designer calls logical deletion and what another refers to as an active flag—that is, an additional column that defines whether or not a row is active or inactive. If you do choose to have such a flag, it's essential to use triggers to ensure that only one row per group (in this case, one row per product) is marked as the current or active row.

So far, we have been looking at means of optimizing queries that were interested only in the current occurrence of data. This is a common requirement, since quite often historical data is kept purely as an aid to audit or the very occasional ad hoc inquiry. In cases where the current data is of primary interest, we could consider splitting the table into two, with one table holding only the current row and the other holding all of the historic versions. The table that holds only current rows is like an ordinary (nontemporal) table, and as a result will suffer none of the performance or usability problems we've observed with temporal data. Indeed, for a simple example like a product price, the current price can simply be held on the product master record, removing the need for a separate table; this is a relatively simple example of a derived value.

TIP   If we decide to hold the current data separately from the historic data, we will need to consider those occasions when we need to query current and historic together. If the tables are separate, querying them together will require a UNION ALL of the two relations (tables). If we then need to join this union to other tables, then we will have to create a real or virtual view based on the union. At this point, we'll start to pay a heavy price for splitting the data because there are a number of severe performance issues that arise when joining to union views. Although the manual partitioning support in Version 7.2 can help us here, it only handles tables with identical column definitions. In this type of partitioning, it is likely that the two tables will have somewhat different attributes.

But there is a solution which we hinted at earlier. We can have the history table include the current row as well or, to put it another way, we can regard the current data as derived or summary data from the temporal table. At the cost of a little bit of redundancy, we can have fast query of current data and reasonable query of current and history together.

The next question, of course, is which way around should we be performing this data derivation? Should we allow the users to directly maintain the current price and use a trigger to create a date-effective record from the old value, or should we allow the user only to change the temporal records, using a trigger to update the current price when required?

We recommend that if the current value is exactly that by definition (i.e., it has no date effectivity stored with it), then we should perform its maintenance on it directly, and cascade this to the history table using triggers. The history table itself should be protected as far as is possible from direct DML and there is a delightfully sneaky way of doing this. We mentioned in the earlier section, "Should We Indicate Open-Endedness with High Values or Nulls?," that there are difficulties with using triggers to prevent gaps and overlaps in date-effective tables because the trigger has to query the table that fired it, and the table is considered to be mutating. (See Appendix B for a solution.) However, in this special case, we can use the mutating table restriction to our advantage: specifically, we can put a trigger on the history table to update the current price. If this succeeds, then we give an error, but if it fails because the current table is a mutating table, we can allow the DML to proceed because we know that it must have been invoked by a trigger on the DML that invoked our trigger.

We have to be a little careful in this king of processing with dates and times to make sure that we create neither gaps or overlaps. To be absolutely rigorous, we need to use a persistent package variable so that each stage of the processing sees the same value of SYSDATE. We can simplify the problem considerably by defining *date_from* to be the second before the price became effective, and *date_to* to be the second at which the price will cease to be effective. With this less intuitive convention, the *date_to* in one record will be equal to the *date_from* in the next record in the sequence if there are no gaps.

We (modestly) commend the logic in the previous paragraph as a classic example of design—that is, making decisions in such a way that it is easier to create code that achieves the right result.

When logical deletion is used, the rows that users may regard as deleted are not actually lost without a trace. They may be deleted from the "live" table, but data will still exist for them in history tables. When a delete is actioned, the current (open-ended) historic row is terminated by setting *date_to* to SYSDATE. This begs the question, "How do we obliterate all reference to a row from a date-effective table?"

Suppose that a user enters a new product in error, realizes his or her mistake the next day, and deletes it. Our trigger-based logic intervenes and creates an epitaph of the mistake for all to see in the history table! Even worse, there is potential for real confusion in the sales reports since the product now appears to have existed, with a price, for one day. Anyone with experience using financial systems knows that erroneous entries must always be reversed out, rather than removed, but this logic may be lost on a marketing department that points out (with some justification) that they do not want nonexistent products appearing on their reports.

Clearly, in such cases we may need a separate set of functions to perform "physical" operations that can be used to rectify mistakes in data entry (or elsewhere). After all, we all make mistakes! These functions can be implemented as a set of stored procedures, encapsulated in a package that will act directly on the historic data table in our case.

NOTE   We must also recognize the possibility of allowing physical operations on date-effective tables to correct data entry errors. If we exert too firm a control over user operations, we will end up constraining, rather than empowering, our users. However polite and friendly you and the operations support staff are, users rarely like systems where they have to grovel to the DBA to apply a "quick fix" every time they key something in error.

Application design can play an important part here. It sometimes helps to show the user the actual mechanism of date effectivity. The start and end dates of applicability of the rows can be shown on the screen so the consequences of an action are clear to the user. Systems that attempt to "simplify" the task for the user by completely hiding the effective dates behind the scenes can end up being more mystifying for that user.

What have we learned here? We've seen that splitting a date-effective table into separate tables for current and historic data can be a useful technique for uncluttering the current data so that it is simpler and performs more optimally. But we have to be cautious about relationships when we do this. We need to investigate the implications of deletes, in particular, since the children will actually reference a different table once the parent is (logically) deleted and the current row disappears. Remember, though, that most of these problems will pale into insignificance if we take the advice of the next section and leave the date component out of foreign keys.

What About Foreign Keys?

Throughout the example used in this chapter, we have assumed a simple model in which our product records each have a time series of prices. In Figure 7-1 we see an extension to this model, intended to support volume discounts. The issue here is that both the PRICES and the DISCOUNTS tables are date-effective. Remember that the primary key of PRICE was defined as (*product_code, date_to*). So, the foreign key in DISCOUNTS should be defined as the column pair *f_price_product_code* and *f_price_date_to*. This is fine, but discounts themselves are date effective and so we now have three columns describing date effectivity (*f_price_date_to, date_to* and *date_from.*) This starts to become very confusing, especially if taken to a further level where we would have even more *date_to* columns in each row. Not only is it confusing, but it becomes very cumbersome and error prone writing the SQL around this kind of structure.

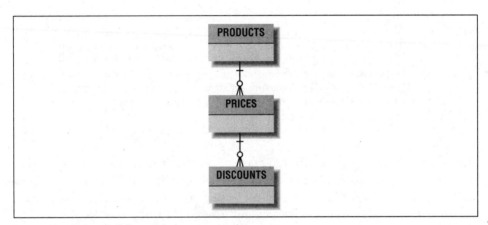

Figure 7-1. Data model extended to support discounts

We can make an assertion here that the date range of the DISCOUNTS must be contained within the date ranges of the associated PRICE. If a price runs from 01-JAN-97, it does not make sense to discount it from 20-DEC-96. This assertion always holds when a date-effective table is the child of another date-effective table.

One solution is to omit the date column of the parent in the child, so that the child record only holds a partial "foreign key." Given our assertion that the child is contained within the parent, we can derive the parent from (in our case) *f_price_product_code* and knowing the date range of the discount. We have seen this approach adopted, but we have strong reservations, namely:

- We cannot use foreign key constraints to enforce the relationship; we would have to use triggers.

- Relational purists would throw their hands up in horror—we are breaking one of the fundamental rules of the relational model, as evidenced by the difficulty of trying to represent the resulting structure using our modeling convention.

- Performance is adequate when seeking the price net of discount for a given date but becomes very much a problem when seeking aggregate values such as the average net price over a year.

There are a number of questions raised by this model. The most important are:

- Can we modify the FROM and TO of a single discount range for a given product?

- Can a product's price change when one of its discounts changes?

- Must the discounts change when the price changes?

If we answer "Yes" to the first question, we are likely to be demanding the right to create gaps. If we have the discount ranges shown in Table 7-2, any attempt to change the upper limit of the first range must be accompanied by a change to the lower limit of the second range to avoid either leaving a gap or creating an overlap.

Table 7-2. Sample Discount Rates

Product	From	To	Range	Discount
CZ043	01-Jun-97	31-Dec-97	10 - 49	5%
CZ043	01-Jun-97	31-Dec-97	50 - 99	10%
CZ043	01-Jun-97	31-Dec-97	100 or over	15%

We suggest that, under any normal circumstances, the answers to all three questions are going to be "No" or, at the very least "Not necessarily." Therefore, the model is almost certainly wrong and we should allow both PRICES and DISCOUNTS to be children of PRODUCTS. This is a common feature of time series data; time series which appear at first sight to be children of another time series often turn out to be siblings (children of the same parent). Recognizing this fact can greatly simplify the handling of the resulting data structures.

Furthermore, ensuring that all of the discount ranges for a given product have the same effective dates will further simplify processing. The resulting data model is shown in Figure 7-2 and the table definitions follow.

```
CREATE TABLE prices
  ( product_code  VARCHAR2(10) NOT NULL
  , date_from     DATE         NOT NULL
    CONSTRAINT prices_df CHECK (date_from = TRUNC(date_from)
  , date_to       DATE         NOT NULL
```

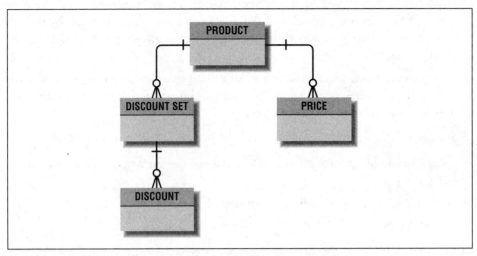

Figure 7-2. Remodeled approach to discounts

```
          CONSTRAINT prices_dt CHECK (date_to    = TRUNC(date_to))
        , price          NUMBER        NOT NULL
        , CONSTRAINT prices_date_range CHECK (date_from <= date_to)
        , CONSTRAINT prices_pk PRIMARY KEY (product_code, date_to)
        , CONSTRAINT prices_fk FOREIGN KEY (product_code)
                                      REFERENCES (products)
        );


CREATE TABLE discount_sets
   ( product_code  VARCHAR2(10) NOT NULL
   , date_to       DATE         NOT NULL
   , CONSTRAINT disc_set_pk
         PRIMARY KEY (product_code, date_to)
   , CONSTRAINT disc_fk FOREIGN KEY (product_code)
                             REFERENCES (products)
   );


CREATE TABLE discounts
   ( product_code  VARCHAR2(10) NOT NULL
   , date_to       DATE         NOT NULL
   , qty_from      NUMBER(8,0)  NOT NULL
   , qty_to        NUMBER(8,0)  NOT NULL
   , discount_pct  NUMBER(2,2)  NOT NULL
   , CONSTRAINT disc_pk
         PRIMARY KEY (product_code, date_to, qty_to)
   , CONSTRAINT disc_fk FOREIGN KEY (product_code, date_to)
                             REFERENCES (discount_sets)
   , CONSTRAINT disc_qty_range CHECK (qty_from <= qty_to)
   );
```

This structure is also going to mean that we avoid the double range problem,
since, in order to find out what discount applies to a particular order line we must

first find the discount set that applies, and then look for the appropriate discount record. Assuming that we have triggers in place to prevent gaps and overlaps, we can use a modified form of the earlier query to locate the required discount record with moderate efficiency. Consider the following example:

```
/* sample query to get discount which applies to
   :qty of :pcode sold on :sdate */

SELECT discount_pct
FROM   discount_sets s
     , discounts     d
 WHERE s.product_code = :pcode
 AND   s.date_to        >= :sdate
 AND   d.product_code = s.product_code
 AND   d.date_to        = s.date_to
 AND   d.qty_to        >= :qty;
```

In reality, this is dangerous without an ORDER BY clause. Why? Because in order to ensure that the first row returned is the one we want, we are relying both on the existence of certain indexes and on the query optimizer's choosing to use those indexes. A more reliable approach would be to perform the join within the application (whether in PL/SQL or using a 3GL with embedded SQL) to ensure that only one row is fetched for each of the two queries.

How Can You Deal with Double Range Checks?

Let's now imagine that we have a product record that contains the date the product was first released, and (for discontinued products) the date that the product was discontinued. The market analysts want to see which of the products were launched between 01-FEB-1970 and 31-MAR-1972 and which were discontinued between 01-JAN-1980 and 15-FEB-1981. No problem, you say, and you write the simple SQL as follows:

```
SELECT p.product_code
     , p.date_released
     , p.date_dropped
FROM   products p
WHERE  p.date_released BETWEEN '01-FEB-70' AND '31-MAR-72'
AND    p.date_dropped  BETWEEN '01-JAN-80' AND '15-FEB-81'
```

You assume that the problem is solved. Unfortunately, if the data volumes are high, then Oracle has no good way of optimizing such a query.

This is one of the classes of problems that multidimensional engines are very good at addressing. In a purely relational database, the high performance solutions are both artificial and awkward, but they are worth knowing if you expect to meet this type of query against your time-dependent data. The problem also arises with spatial data; the classic example is the situation in which you are looking for all the records in a given range of both latitude and longitude.

The solution is to hold a derived field for each dimension; this field gives a value that you can search for on equality. In our example, we might decide to use the calendar month and to supply this value using a trigger. Then we build an index on (*month_released, month_dropped*). When we are building the query, we give it a query number (:QUERY) and insert into a driving table (QUERY_DRIVER) all of the month pairs we might be interested in. In the example, there are 42 of these pairs. Then we execute a query such as the following:[*]

```
SELECT p.product_code
     , p.date_released
     , p.date_dropped
  FROM query_driver q
     , products p
 WHERE q.query# = :QUERY
   AND q.month_released = p.month_released
   AND q.month_dropped  = p.month_dropped
   AND p.date_released BETWEEN '01-FEB-70' AND '31-MAR-72'
   AND p.date_dropped  BETWEEN '01-JAN-80' AND '15-FEB-81'
```

This is not at all natural, and cannot reasonably be performed ad hoc, so many research users will require a query builder to analyze their "primitive" SQL and to build the required form for them. However, correctly indexed, the revised form can give quite good performance.

We are often asked why we use a driving table in this example (a driving table is both an overhead and a considerable complication), rather than simply generating IN predicates which can be looked up in an index. The required form is shown in the following SELECT statement, but it has the problem that many versions of the query optimizer contain the heuristic that long lists of IN arguments are best processed using a full table scan. Do not use this form unless you are sure that your optimizer release will always generate index lookups. After all, if you are happy to use a full table scan, then the previous query will work just fine (assuming either no indexes or a /* +FULL */ hint).

```
/* base month is JAN 70, value 1 */

SELECT p.product_code
     , p.date_released
     , p.date_dropped
  FROM  products p
 WHERE q.query# = :query
   AND (p.month_released, p.month_dropped) IN
       ((1,121), (1,122), (1,123), .... (3,134))
   AND p.date_released BETWEEN '01-FEB-70' AND '31-MAR-72'
   AND p.date_dropped  BETWEEN '01-JAN-80' AND '15-FEB-81'
```

---

[*] The fact that this example yielded 42 has nothing whatsoever to do with *The Hitchhiker's Guide to the Galaxy.*

The key to the double range check problem is the fact that with the natural data it's impossible to get to the point where we can either use equality or use a range check (where the key values we want will be closely clustered within the index). If we hadn't invented the *month* columns, our attempts to find the target products would have had to do one of the following:

- Inspect the *date_dropped* for every product that was in our *date_released* range

- Inspect the *date_released* for every product that was in our *date_dropped* range.

Whether this is a problem depends on the data volumes, the selectivity of the ranges, and how long your users are prepared to wait. The effects can be disastrous when each range describes a significant percentage of the data, but not when only a handful of records lie at their intersection.

Temporal Data: A Summary

Here is a quick summary of the guidelines for using temporal data that we described in this chapter:

- Most effective dates do not require a time component, since the granularity is a day.

- Using only a single date column rather than a start/end pair is not a good idea.

- Use of a high value such as "31-DEC-4712" in the end date column is recommended when the effective end date is unknown.

- In most cases, the primary key of a date-effective table should be the "real" or business key concatenated with the end date column (rather than the start date).

- Procedural solutions to retrieval may yield many times better performance than pure SQL solutions, even if the procedural solutions are relationally invalid.

- Triggers can be used to prevent overlaps or gaps occurring in a time series if this is a business requirement.

- Keeping historic data in a separate table from current data may be beneficial, depending on how often historic data is likely to be accessed. It is advisable to hold the current record in both tables.

- We have to allow users to correct mistakes by letting them perform physical delete and update operations on the data.

- It is worth going to quite extreme solutions to get around the double range check problem; if these solutions are too onerous, you are probably justified in moving to an OLAP or multidimensional engine.

Even if you follow all of these guidelines, dealing with temporal data is not going to be a breeze. However, it should be possible to handle it within Oracle's relational model with good performance and at a reasonable implementation cost.

8

Loading and Unloading Data

This chapter examines the problems of loading "foreign" data (data from an external source) into our Oracle database, and of unloading data from our database for subsequent loading into other databases. We will discuss the initial data loads that populate our tables from so-called *legacy* systems, as well as the ongoing periodic loads that occasionally bring our data up to date or in sync with another data source. The chapter also takes a look at the issues that arise when the incoming data is incomplete or invalid in some way. We will examine data conversion issues and the various approaches to the timing of data conversion and transformation. Finally, we'll look at the file formats and programming tools that are used for loading data.

Dealing with External Systems

These days, few computer systems can operate in a vacuum. There is almost always a need to interact with other systems, if only to load initial data from a legacy system. In fact, much of the success of a system depends on its ability to exchange data with other computer systems.

Despite the widespread need for interfaces with external systems (often called *data feeds*), few analysts and designers spend sufficient time on the problems of loading and unloading data. Because many analysts regard these problems as "physical" problems, they feel that they are beyond the scope of analysis. The database designer ends up assuming total responsibility for the design work in this area. Often, external interface issues are treated as separate projects or subsystems, outside the realm of the typical database project.

Types of Interfaces

External interfaces can be broken into two distinct categories:

- The initial data take-on that will only be performed once (apart from test runs, of course).

- The periodic exchange of data both to and from other live systems that share an interest in some of our data.

If an exchange of data must be achieved in something close to real time and cannot be made periodic, the problems that arise should actually be considered a part of the overall distributed database strategy for the system, not simply a data feed issue. Those issues are beyond the scope of this chapter; they are described in detail in Chapter 12, *Designing for Distributed Databases*. For the moment, we'll simply note that the use of a real-time link to legacy data may remove the need to take on a particular group of entities if it can be shown that the required access rates are within the capability of distributed technology.

Note that the issues raised by the need to translate from legacy data structures to current data structures are also of critical importance to the success of data warehouse projects. These are described in detail in Chapter 13, *Designing for Data Warehouses*.

Issues to Consider

As a database designer, what data load and unload issues do you need to worry about? They can be categorized roughly as follows:

- Determine which systems need an interface.

- Determine the periodicity and volume of the interface (e.g., 1,000 records per day).

- Establish how closely synchronized the two systems need to be.

- Investigate means of data transport (file, communication, etc.).

- Agree on a data format for exchange with designers from the other systems. This includes the type of file and specific field formats for dates, integers, real numbers, etc.

- Draw up a list of dependencies between the various interfaces, such as the fact that some interfaces must be run in a particular order.

- Establish a policy for handling incoming *dirty data*—that is, data that has somehow become corrupt or lost integrity

- For each load, set out fallback and recovery plans for failed and partially complete take-ons.

- Formulate a policy for rejecting errant or invalid input records.

- Create a common policy for logging data transfers (in and out).

- Begin to map out a plan for nightly batch operations for periodic exchanges. This can only be completed when viewed in context with other batch operations within the system where dependencies are resolved.

- Agree on a development timetable and test strategy and plan with designers from the other system.

- For once-off data loads, agree a cutover strategy and plan.

As we've mentioned, as investigation progresses, some interfaces may evolve to use distributed databases, communicating in real time rather than using data feeds.

Working Together with the "Other Side"

It is essential to build relationships with your counterparts who are working on the other systems. Sometimes, you may run up against a certain level of hostility. You may be working on the brand new Oracle system that is to replace the beloved mainframe application which they earn their living by maintaining. In the ideal world, such obstructive behavior can often be overcome by remaining friendly, showing understanding, gently persuading people that they should be professional, and selling the advantages of the new system.

If that approach fails (and it often does) and you cannot get active cooperation from the guys who think that they will lose their jobs the day your project completes, you will almost certainly have to take the alternative approach of working around them. This may sound difficult to achieve, but the sad reality is that almost all of the data transformation code will have to be written for the new environment rather than the old. In other words, data will be converted and transposed on the way in, rather than on the way out. There are a number of reasons why it almost always works out this way; the most important are usually these:

- The development backlog on the legacy system is often so long that management will not permit anything to be added to it; even if they did allow a new extract routine to be added to the list of outstanding requirements, you'd probably never see it.

- The legacy system may not have adequate spare processing time for testing and running the new data extract.

- There may already be a data extract facility available and the legacy people say "If you really want our data, why don't you just use what we've already got." The smart move in this case is to do just that. Regard it as yet another design constraint.

Data Compatibility Issues

Speaking of constraints, when data is to be carried forward from an older system to a newer one, there is usually another effect which poses a major additional challenge. Most older systems (which includes Oracle Version 6 in addition to nonrelational technologies) are not fully normalized, nor have they been operating with the protection of database-level constraints. The older the technology, the less normalized the data is likely to be.[*]

Handling Dirty Data

The lack of database constraints, plus the inevitable application errors and late night data patches, means that over the years these applications are likely to have accumulated a healthy amount of "dirty" data (or do we mean an unhealthy amount?). If you have fully implemented declarative constraints and also checked for more complex conditions in trigger logic in the "new" database, then the legacy data will probably not load. There may (will, to be quite honest) be pressure to relax some of the constraints to let the dirty data in. In many cases, you will find that you have to relax almost all of them in order to achieve loading of any reasonable percentage of the data—unless you either take steps to repair or clean the data, or alter your data model.

If you do yield to pressure, you might find yourself on a slippery slope. Constraints cannot be enabled when a table contains data that violates them. Given other pressures, performing a cleansing operation on the data may end up being viewed as a time-consuming activity that doesn't have a high enough priority. The longer constraints remain disabled, the larger the potential for proliferating more dirty or nonconforming data.

Our advice in this situation is to fight for a cleaner database. A few days' slippage in the project timescales pales into insignificance when compared to the consequences of storing data that lacks basic integrity. One of the authors worked at a site where year-end figures spanning several years were later found to be many millions of dollars adrift because of a lack of integrity in the data.

---

[*] Though one of the authors of this book went to his first project pep talk on the importance of 3NF in 1973 while working on a IBM System/370 assembler project using ISAM files.

Loading Obsolete Codes

You may also find that in some of the legacy datasets there is data which was once valid, but which is no longer strictly valid. For example, there may be coded values using codes which have long since been retired; sometimes, these can reliably be mapped to current values, but in many cases an algorithm will be required to turn the old status into something that your new integrity rules can recognize.

One approach that has proved successful under these circumstances is to address the problem head-on and to implement the old codes in the reference tables in your new schema. You may also decide to add a further column to the reference tables that dictates whether or not the code can be applied to new records. This can work well, but increases the implementation cost as a result of the need to use different sets of data for validation and display.

A table that used to be defined as follows:

```
CREATE TABLE cancellation_reasons
       ( reason_code CHAR(1)        PRIMARY KEY
       , reason_text VARCHAR2(30) NOT NULL
       );
```

can be transformed into one that supports obsolete and current codes by adding a column and a constraint:

```
CREATE TABLE cancellation_reasons
       ( reason_code CHAR(1)        PRIMARY KEY
       , reason_text VARCHAR2(30) NOT NULL
       , current     CHAR(1)        NOT NULL
          CONSTRAINT canc_reason_current
          CHECK (current IN ('.'.'.'.) DEFAULT 'N'
       );
```

It may prove useful to implement a view for use in data entry and data maintenance screens. This view hides the codes which can no longer be assigned; however, this view is not updatable, so any maintenance must be performed against the underlying table. Here is the view definition for our example:

```
CREATE OR REPLACE VIEW current_cancellation_reasons
       ( reason_code
       , reason_text
       ) AS
   SELECT reason_code
        , reason_text
     FROM cancellation_reasons
    WHERE current = 'Y'.
```

Unless you either map all of the old codes in the legacy data to valid current code, or continue to support the old codes, it will prove impossible to load the data with foreign key constraints satisfied. In any event, these constraints must reference the table (which contains all the values) rather than the view (which contains only current values). For this reason, you should consider defining a trigger on any table with a foreign key to *cancellation_reasons* to ensure that only current reasons are entered on the system. Such triggers would obviously have to be disabled for the duration of any load from the legacy system.

Loading Referentially Invalid Data

In almost all legacy data there will be cases where something does not connect up the way it should; there may be order lines with no corresponding order, or orders with no identifiable customer, or orders with no order lines. In some cases, the data really will be missing, and in others the foreign key or pointer will have been corrupted by application error, hardware, or software fault, or by some hand-applied data adjustment. In any event, the design must identify a way forward.

Each case has to be determined on its merits, but we strongly recommend that your design allow you to load all of the data with all of your constraints satisfied. This may require you to use such design techniques as these:

- Dropping data that fails to meet the referential integrity requirements; although this is the easiest option to implement, it may be unacceptable, particularly for any data that might be required as part of an audit.

- "Inventing" the missing entity; for example, order lines with no order header can be linked to a synthetic order which contains a combination of default data and data inferred from the order lines. If you use this technique, then you should have a unambiguous means of identifying the synthetic rows. This makes it possible to write SQL which excludes these rows from selected batch processes and reports. Such exclusions are vital if we are to avoid such situations as reserving stock for orders which cannot be shipped because the customer is unknown. Some designers use special primary key ranges for this purpose, but a separate attribute (column) is preferred.

- Posting all of the referentially invalid data to separate tables and then attempting to match up the data. This data matching is typically done by a combination of rules-based processing and input from skilled users, and its application support is a full-fledged system component (even if it is planned to have a relatively short life). As such, it must be included in the development plan. It may be as simple as a single screen or it may be a series of screens and reports.

A Case Study: Loading Corrupt Data

One of the authors was responsible, many years ago, for the conversion of more than 1.5 million records from a combination of metal addressograph plates, paper payment records, and bank transaction tapes. Although the primary key (a membership number) and the member's name should have been on every record, both were routinely mistyped. In many cases one was missing, and in some cases both were missing. The data take-on was performed as a rolling process and was originally planned to take twelve months.

Unmatched data was held as "pending" and listed using a set of rules for identifying possible matches. Once a month we held a meeting with the team of clerical staff who were using online transactions to assign membership records to payment records, and there we refined the rules applied by the reporting programs in the light of the feedback from the end users. The result was an almost perfect take-on completed in just under nine months.

We had to give up on the conversion of something fewer than 1,000 records, but that does not include around a thousand members who were discovered to have slipped through the net on the manual system and had never either paid or been chased for payment.

The cost was the need to write a major subsystem to perform the reporting and online reassignments. This subsystem was decommissioned once the data take-on was complete, though a small part of it was carried over into the handling of payments that did not carry a valid membership number.

One of the keys to this type of detective work is to find some data which *is* reliable. We found that banks and credit card companies almost always quote their own reference numbers correctly. So if we had a payment but did not know what it was for, our reports would look for an member whose account had already received payments from that bank account or credit card. If we found only one such account, we would report it as a "possible match"; if the account had owed us the same amount as the payment, we would report it as a "probable match."

You must *expect* to find both dirty data and real-world situations which are unacceptable to the business. These will include cases such as payments made for nonexistent goods, safety checks that were not performed, reconciliation errors, and so on. If the analysis does not tell you how to handle these conditions, it is dangerous to simply use your initiative; you need to share the problem with both the analysts and the end users.

Loading Data That Fails Entity Constraints

An entity constraint is one that can be applied in the context of a single entity, and the term is also used to describe constraints that apply to a single row. Two examples of entity constraints are as follows:

```
user_name VARCHAR2(30)
          CONSTRAINT secu_user_case
          CHECK (user_name = UPPER(user_name))

discount   NUMBER NOT NULL,
          CONSTRAINT ordr_discount
          CHECK ((discount = 0) OR
                ((discount_approval IS NOT NULL)
                   AND
                (discount < ordr_value)))
```

In some of the data being loaded, there will be inevitably be invalid values; some of these can be trivially corrected (such as enforcing uppercase on strings) whereas others will require detective work similar to that required for data which fails to meet the referential integrity requirements (described in the previous section).

Loading Null Values

In many data conversions there is a problem in deriving null values; because traditional systems (including serial files) do not support null values, they can be present in a data feed only by convention such as an empty string, a very low or very high date value, or in some cases the number zero. As you may have spotted in Chapter 5, *Choosing Datatypes and Nulls*, we are no great lovers of null values, but we recognize that they are part of the Oracle environment and that it is essential to be able to load them correctly.

As we discussed in Chapter 5, Oracle does not currently support empty strings, and so any empty strings which are present in the input data will be implicitly converted to nulls unless some application processing makes them nonempty (usually a single space).

A larger problem is generally encountered with numeric fields. Where a numeric value may validly have the value zero or be null, the data feed should supply it as zero in the first case and as an empty string in the second case. When the data feed is in text format, this may be relatively simple to arrange. Where the data is supplied as a binary value, the decision about whether to record it as zero or null has to be made on the basis of the context (i.e., the values of other fields in the same record or even by lookup of foreign keys). The best plan is to design the schema so that everything that may arrive as numeric zero can be loaded as a zero value.

Selling the Sound Approach

The management and end user reaction to all of this will be to ask you if you can't just load the data complete with the errors and let them sort it out later when they have time. Aside from the fact that they never will have the time, the problem with this is that all of your code will be designed and written against the belief that the data is valid. The resulting application simply won't work if the data does not agree with the rules. Moreover, because the code is most unlikely to have been tested with a comprehensive cross section of bad data, it won't just fall over—it will fall over in unpredictable and often misleading ways. So you appear to have two choices:

* *Either* change the data

* *Or* change the rules

Most projects find that they have to do a bit of each.

Triggers Versus Declarative Constraints

There is a very important difference here between declarative constraints and data rules enforced through triggers. You can enable and disable the triggers whenever you like, and the "only" effect is that their checking will not be performed while they are disabled. Of course, you can also disable a constraint whenever it suits you to do so, but when you try to enable it again you pay two penalties:

* The constraint is reapplied against every row in the entire table, or at least until a row fails to pass. This will take a substantial amount of time for tables with significant amounts of data.

* The constraint will only be enabled if every row in the table meets the constraint. So if you want to load dirty data then you just have to say goodbye to your declarative constraints!

At first glance, it may look as though there is a big advantage to triggers in that they can be disabled to allow some processing to occur, and then can be re-enabled at very little processing cost, whereas declarative constraints have the disadvantage of heavy processing cost to re-enable them with no guarantee of success. Our strong recommendation to you is that you should use declarative constraints despite this "disadvantage." It is an advantage really, because it prevents you from corrupting your database. What you have to do is to clean the incoming data as well as you possibly can, and to operate with constraints that are achievable.

Using Nullable Values to Defeat Foreign Key Constraints

If you do have to weaken the data rules (constraints), then you must go back around the application design and ensure that every component can cope with the new rules. For example, you may be tempted to make certain foreign key columns optional (nullable), but remember the discussion of some of the less welcome effects of null values.

If we were loading a CUSTOMERS table, we might make the column *sales_id* nullable so that we can load customers whose designated account manager is unknown. However, the effect of this is that a query such as:

```
SELECT  e.emp_name
      , c.cust_name
   FROM customers c
      , employees e
  WHERE c.country  = 'USA'
    AND c.sales_id = e.employee_id
```

will fail to return any customers who have a null value for *sales_id* even if the customer is in the USA. To give the answer that most end users would expect, the query has to be re-coded as:

```
SELECT  NVL(e.emp_name, 'Not assigned'.
      , c.cust_name
   FROM customers c
      , employees e
  WHERE c.country  = 'USA'
    AND c.sales_id = e.employee_id(+)
```

With a little bit of care, we should be able to ensure that this change is made everywhere that it is required in the code that is being developed within projects under our control, but it is very difficult to enforce the use of outer joins in ad hoc SQL. A better solution might be to ensure that a salesman at least appears to be assigned to every single customer, even if the "salesman" sometimes turns out to be a dummy record. (With some salesmen you would be hard pressed to notice the difference!)

So we try to introduce an employee called "Not assigned" who has no social security number, no address, and no salary, but this may cause problems with the payroll processing. The "correct" solution is to recognize that our original, intuitive model was wrong. We have a new entity that we may call "customer list," and by introducing a list which is not assigned to any salesman, we can rewrite the original query to operate without an outer join. Figure 8-1 shows the change to the data model. We can now issue a query such as:

```
SELECT  l.list_responsibility
      , c.cust_name
```

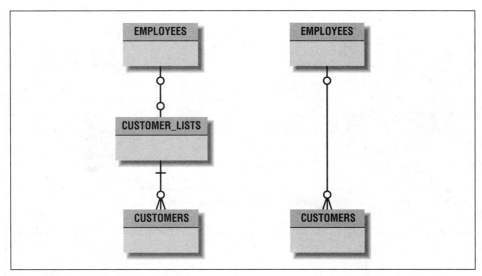

Figure 8-1. Refining the data model

```
FROM customers  c
   , cust_lists l
WHERE c.country = 'USA'
  AND c.list_id = l.list_id
```

Note, however, that what we do now have is a 1:1 relationship between the entities CUSTOMER_LISTS and EMPLOYEES which is optional at both ends. As with every facet of design, you should expect detailed work on data take-on to cause you to question parts of your data model.

Data Migration Steps

The key activities in any data migration are:

Extract
Reading the required data from its current store

Transform
Making any adjustments that are required

Move
Handing the data from one physical system to another

Load
Inserting the data into the destination database

As shown in Figure 8-2, Figure 8-3, and Figure 8-4, there are various ways in which we can organize these four stages by moving the point in the sequence at which we perform any transformation which is required. In some cases, we may

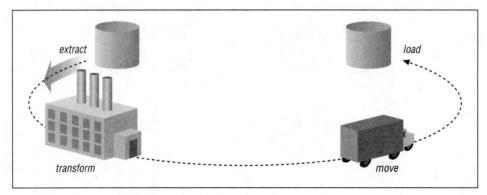

Figure 8-2. Extract, transform, move, load (preferred approach)

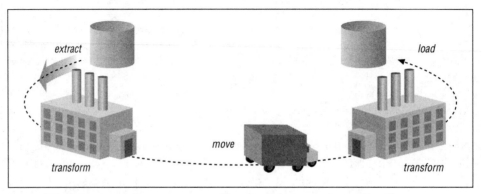

Figure 8-3. Extract, transform, move, transform, load (compromise approach)

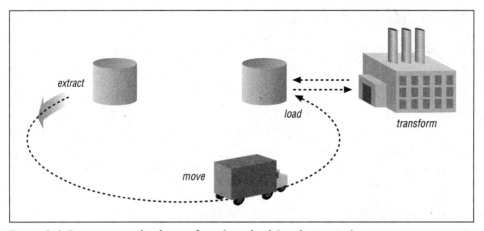

Figure 8-4. Extract, move, load, transform (standard Oracle practice)

have to consider multiple transformation steps; this is essential when there are separate transformation tasks which are better performed on different hosts. In many cases, those transformation steps which require reference data from the originating host can be bundled into the extract stage (for example, substitution of a pointer with a foreign key value).

In general, the most efficient way to organize the processing is to perform the transformations before the data is moved, but any attempt to add to the workload of a legacy system is usually resisted (for the reasons discussed at the beginning of this chapter). We must assume, therefore, that the data will emerge from the move process in pretty much the same state that it left the extract process. We may be able to get a character conversion from EBCDIC to ASCII, and we would certainly hope that any packed decimal values have been converted to text, but other than that we must expect that the rest of the transformation is our responsibility.

It is highly desirable that all data transmission should be in text format; it makes life *much* easier for the people involved, and only a tiny amount more difficult for the machines which incur data conversion overheads at the originating end. With Oracle's internal representation of dates and numbers, datatype conversions are absolutely inevitable at the receiving end for numeric data.

| *NOTE* | Oracle's former SQL and performance guru Chris Ellis once persuaded a consultant to render every single column in a data logging table as VARCHAR despite the fact that all of the values in the table were numeric. His logic was that since all of the access was from 3GL code and datatype conversion was inevitable, it might as well be under the control of the 3GL. The data certainly loaded much faster in character form! |

Data Transformation

We must expect to have to impose two types of transformations in the data load process:

- Changes of structure
- Changes of value

The principal thrust of this section is to persuade you that, contrary to common practice, the best approach is to impose both of these types of change *before* the data is loaded into Oracle. If you delay the transformation until after the (initial) load, you are simply guaranteeing that much of the data will have to be loaded twice, once incorrectly and then again correctly. Oracle7's insert performance is pretty good, but it is still *much* faster to perform only the exact number of inserts that are required to achieve the required task. The standard Oracle flow shown in Figure 8-4 (extract, move, load, transform) is particularly inefficient because it performs (at least) one unnecessary insert and one unnecessary fetch for every record loaded. In practice, we tend to find that multiple passes are required of a work table, adding to the overhead.

There are a number of other issues that have to be considered. These include:

- Referential integrity

- Transaction size

- Data placement

Let's consider a simple case.

> You have to load orders and order lines from a corporate database mainframe that permits a maximum of 20 lines per order. The mainframe team has offered you a text file which contains a single record for each order, with the order header data followed by the details of up to 20 order lines. The file contains adequate delimiters for you to load this data into a work table using SQL*Loader, but you have to adjust the order status code from the mainframe values to the values used in the Oracle application and also convert the order lines to hold unit price from holding unit price × quantity. How do you proceed?

The solution we most often see employed is that after loading the text file into a work table using SQL*Loader, a SQL*Plus script is run, which takes the order header data from the work table and inserts it into the *orders* table using an SQL statement something like this:

```
INSERT INTO orders ( order_no
                   , cust_no
                   , order_status
                   , ...
                   )
            SELECT order_no
                 , cust_no
                 , decode ( order_status
                          , '1' , 'OPEN'
                          , '2' , 'PAID'
                          , '3' , 'CANC'
                          , '4' , 'HELD'
                          , '??'
                          )
                 , ...
            FROM work_table;
```

This will work, but it is going to create all of the order records in a single transaction, which for high volumes will require a very large rollback segment. We will have to follow this with 20 further SQL statements of the general form:

```
INSERT INTO order_lines ( order_no
                        , line_no
                        , product_code
                        , quantity
                        , unit_price
                        , ...
                        )
                 SELECT order_no
                      , 01
                      , product_code_01
                      , quantity_01
                      , round( line_price_01
                              / quantity_01, 2)
                      , ...
                 FROM work_table
                 WHERE product_code_01 IS NOT NULL;
```

At this point, we have correctly loaded both the *orders* and *order_lines* tables, but we have the following issues:

- We've made 21 full table scans of an unnecessary work table.

- We've either performed the whole operation in a single transaction, or we've had to commit partial orders (i.e., committed an order record when not all of its lines had been posted). And remember, a single transaction may require a large rollback segment and will fail the entire load in the event of a single failure (such as a constraint violation).

- We've just about guaranteed that for each order every one of its order lines will be in a different physical database block.

One alternative is to not use SQL*Loader at all, but instead to write a 3GL program that reads the text file, and for each line in the text file inserts one row into *orders* and between one and 20 rows into *order_lines*. The inserts are made using the array interface, and the program commits after every (say) 50 orders to keep the rollback segment requirement under control.

Another alternative[*] is to use an intermediate C program, or perhaps just an *awk* script. This massages the text file received from the mainframe, translating the order status code and dividing price by quantity so that the resulting text file can indeed be handled directly via SQL*Loader using that program's support for header and detail records.

---

[*] One of many valuable additions and corrections made by Graham Wood during his review of a draft of this book

Both of these solutions are more difficult in that they require a 3GL program (or at least an *awk* script), but they are much more efficient and much safer. Using a direct approach offers several advantages:

- The only database operations are those which are required (i.e., inserts into the two tables).

- Rollback segment usage and recovery time can be controlled. (It may take several hours to restart the instance if there is an uncontrolled shutdown during the SQL*Plus process described above.)

- Incomplete orders are never committed.

- The order lines for any given order will have a strong tendency to be adjacent within the order lines table.

The key to both forms of the direct solution is to use a 3GL to perform both code translation and any field value adjustments. Too many project teams try to save time and money by making this type of value adjustment using a SQL*Plus script after the load, and in many cases compound the problem further by using a lookup table; for example:

```
INSERT INTO orders ( order_no
                   , cust_no
                   , order_status
                   , ...
                   )
         SELECT w.order_no
              , w.cust_no
              , o.new_code
              , ...
         FROM   work_table w
              , order_status_codes o
         WHERE   o.old_code = w.order_status;
```

With only a single join condition this will perform reasonably well, but once two or three more such lookups are added, the performance of the query starts to degrade quite markedly.

If it is unsafe to hard-code the translation inside a 3GL program to read the text file, the join can trivially be made data-driven. The 3GL program reads all the rows from the table *order_status_codes* into memory (in an array or linked-list structure) before starting to read the file, and replaces the codes as it goes, using its own table lookup in working storage. The 3GL program can also report those records with invalid codes, whereas the SQL solution shown will silently ignore any row in *orders* whose *order_status* is not present in *order_status_codes*. And that is *not* what you want!

Sooner or later, someone reading this is going to point out that most of the disadvantages of the SQL*Plus solution can be avoided by using PL/SQL. The plan here is that you still load into the work table, but instead of 21 passes of the work table you make a single pass in a PL/SQL cursor loop performing all of the required operations. This should be a lot cheaper to code and test than the 3GL program. It will allow you to control the commit interval and to avoid committing inconsistent data, and it will also get the *order_lines* rows as close together as will the 3GL approach. That's the good news. The bad news is that the PL/SQL loop will be seriously slow. If you were dealing with less than, say, 100,000 rows then you might be able to afford to throw processing power or elapsed time at the problem, but if you need to take on large volumes of data in short elapsed times, PL/SQL cursor loops are simply not going to deliver the goods.

File Formats

When a flat file interface is used for a data load, it is usually in one of two formats: either fixed-length or variable-length records. Variable-length records usually have some form of delimiter around the fields. Example 8-1 shows some examples, illustrating the same data in fixed- and variable-length format.

The first example demonstrates fixed-length records, where each field is blank-padded to a fixed length and the corresponding fields start in the same position in all lines of the file. Fixed-length record files tend to be the favored format for most COBOL programmers.

The second example illustrates the same data in variable format. The length of the record depends on the length of the fields. Each field is delimited by chosen characters (double quote in this case) and is separated with a separator character (comma in this case). If the delimiter character can legitimately appear in the text of the data, then there needs to be a means of telling the loader program to interpret the character literally. For example, if we want to load the value *Nicholas "Nic" Banger*, we would use something like **"Nicholas \"Nic\" Banger"**, where \ is the control character meaning "treat the next character literally". Of course we have to ensure that our data load program recognizes this convention.

Example 8-1. Fixed- and Variable-Length Records in Load Format

```
Fixed-length records
Widdrington     Tommy       11-11-72   164 04-26-90 Y
Magilton        James       01-24-68   195 02-19-93 N
Hopper          Neil        05-04-70   180 12-06-91 Y

Variable-length records
"Widdrington","Tommy","11-11-72","164","04-26-90","Y"
"Magilton","James","01-24-68","195","02-19-93","N"
"Hopper","Neil","05-04-70","18012-06-91","Y"
```

Null values are usually represented by blanks in fixed-length records and by a pair of delimiters ("" in the example) in variable-length records.

While we are on the subject of record layouts, note that is a useful idea to embed comments in the file and to agree on the proper means of doing so. This is a particularly useful tool when creating test data for the load utilities because it allows each line to be preceded with a description of what aspect it is testing and the expected outcome. You can choose your own format for comments – so long as your chosen loader program recognizes it, but starting the line with two hyphens is a common format; for example:

```
-- This is a comment
```

SQL*Loader supports this type of comment.

One problem that does occur with "lines" is that on many proprietary systems there is a physical limit on line length. This is usually set to some value that the designer felt would never fit on any fixed-pitch printer, and the older the operating system the shorter the limit is likely to be.

If you are faced with this problem, the solution may be to simply write records to the transport file in multiple lines; depending on the precise nature of the operation you may decide to use a fixed or variable number of lines, and you may or may not need to span individual fields over line boundaries.

The other problem, which can get quite tedious, is handling data with embedded newline characters. Our favorite approaches to this, in order of preference, are

- Do not have embedded newlines in strings.

- Use the UNIX convention of \n, and similarly record embedded tabs as \t.

After adding only a few complexities of the types discussed above, you may find it essential to load using a 3GL program, or at least to use a 3GL program to preprocess the load file so that SQL*Loader can handle it.

Ordering, Recovery, and Commit Frequency

If you are handling large volumes of data, it is common sense to break the process up into a series of smaller, more manageable loads. In such a situation, it may be imperative that the loads be completed in the correct order. This can be enforced by having a load sequence number as part of the header of the load file and checking it against a table in the database.

For example, suppose that we are loading a file with a header record such as HDR,,CUST LOAD,4. The number 4 indicates that this load is the fourth in the sequence and should not be started until load 3 is complete. An example of a table used to control data loads is shown in Table 8-1 in which each load is given a sequence and a name. Against each load we record the pathname of the external file from which the load was taken, and its status. In this example, the load process also keeps a record of the point in the input file that the active load has reached. This number would be updated at each commit point during the load. It is a useful mechanism for recovering a long load. If a load is restarted, it can determine from the load control table the point it reached and simply "fast forward" to that point in the file before it commences loading again. Using a load control file and the recovery mechanism we've outlined here is only viable if you are writing your own 3GL load process. But it may be worth using a 3GL simply to get this degree of control, and to be able to perform accurate restarts without compromising referential integrity.

Table 8-1. A Sample Load Control Table

LOAD SEQ	LOAD NAME	STATUS	RECORD NO.	FILE
1	CUS	COMPLETE		t:\load\cus_1.dat
2	CUS	COMPLETE		t:\load\cus_2.dat
3	ORD	COMPLETE		t:\load\ord_1.dat
4	ORD	RUNNING	1500	t:\load\ord_2.dat
5	LIN	PENDING		t:\load\lin_1.dat

Using SQL*Loader

When you are evaluating the requirements of your inbound external interfaces, one of the questions you will need to tackle is what tool to use for achieving the load. This section focuses on SQL*Loader.

SQL*Loader Vs. 3GL

We have already looked at a number of the issues surrounding the selection of tools for a data take-on, but we have not yet presented a direct comparison of the two most efficient methods. These are:

- SQL*Loader to input the data directly into live tables, relying on either or both preprocessing and database constraints to ensure data integrity

- 3GL code such as Pro*C or Pro*COBOL to read the transmission media, validate, adjust, and insert/update

The options are listed in order of runtime performance, fastest first. The SQL*Loader direct path option is without doubt the fastest method of inserting data into an Oracle table.

Pro*C programs tend to be markedly more expensive to code and test than (for example) PL/SQL code, but for any volume of data, they are almost certain to be several times faster than PL/SQL, provided that they are run on the same platform as the database instance, and they use Oracle's array interface.

For the reasons discussed earlier in this chapter, we cannot recommend post-processing of tables after loading as a high-volume technique.

One final preprocessing point: if you know that there is a particular index key on which your application performs multirow retrievals, it may be well worth your while to sort the input data on this key before performing the load. This will result in (much) more efficient query operation when retrieving via what Oracle calls an *index scan.*

SQL*Loader Strengths and Weaknesses

SQL*Loader is a mature and extensively used product. It supports fixed- and variable-length format records and can handle a mixture of character (normally ASCII) and binary data. It also has an internal sequence generator to generate unique IDs for rows. Note this is not the same as an Oracle7 sequence so after loading, any sequence used by the application to assign keys to the table must be altered to start from the maximum value in the table after the load has completed. SQL*Loader is ideal for simple data loads and can do a lot of entity integrity checking for you. For instance, it will reject records with missing mandatory columns and invalid data format.

Its main weaknesses are its inability to:

- Perform updates

- Perform data transformations

- Enforce referential integrity; although since Oracle7 can enforce foreign key and unique key constraints at database level, this weakness is no longer critical

SQL*Loader lacks the ability to specify any logic, apart from allowing you to apply conditions to the data to filter certain rows out of the load. If you want complex conditions on the load, or derived values, then SQL*Loader cannot really deliver. Designers and coders are famous for bright ideas, and have tried to overcome these weaknesses by a number of methods, including writing special triggers against the table that are intended to be enabled only for the duration of the load. Tricks such as this only rarely give adequate performance, and the "trigger trick" is especially unsafe, as there is no way whatever of ensuring either that the trigger is there when it is required or that it is not there when it is not required.

SQL*Loader's biggest advantage is its ability to perform *direct path* loading. Using this feature, the loader writes whole database blocks directly to the database, cutting out the middle men such as SQL execution and data cache management. This breaks Ted Codd's subversion rule for relational databases, but it gives such a performance improvement that nobody cares!

SQL*Loader's direct path option is definitely the way to go for high-volume loads where high throughput is essential and concurrency is expendable. To make the load go even faster, direct path loading uses a series of strategies to make index updating and constraint checking more efficient. Triggers do not fire during direct path loading, and all referential integrity constraints are disabled. The new index entries are simply pushed into silos or buffer. Once all the data blocks have been created, the silos are sorted on index key and are merged into the respective indexes.

At this point, the user can attempt to re-enable the constraints, probably using the EXCEPTIONS INTO option to record all violations which have been introduced, and can again enjoy all the benefits of the database triggers on the table.

WARNING   Before deciding to use direct path loading, you must recognise two important restrictions. Even triggers which are enabled do not fire during a direct path load, and only other SQL*Loader streams can access a table being loaded via direct path.

Oracle7 to Oracle7: A Special Case

There is one data migration method that we have yet to discuss, and which in reality forms part of the distributed database discussion in Chapter 12. When we can directly query the data we are trying to take on, then we have a series of rather different considerations to apply. This will obviously be the case if the data is already in tables owned by another application in the same database, but it may also be in another Oracle database elsewhere in our network or in a database that is accessible through SQL*Net and Oracle's gateway technology, or even through one of the data cartridges being produced for the Network Computing Architecture. From the programming standpoint, all of these options (except the last, which is procedural) can be made to look exactly the same using synonyms. That is, we can write queries to reference an object called PRICE_MASTER whether that object is actually:

*   A table in the local schema

- A synonym for a table in another schema in the same physical database, and against which we have been granted query access

- A synonym that uses a database link to reference a table in another Oracle database

- A synonym that uses a database link to reference an object in a non-Oracle database accessed through a transparent gateway

Although it is not possible to distinguish between these last two cases by inspecting either the synonym or the database link, quite different considerations apply because the foreign data server implied by the final case above may have totally different performance characteristics compared with an Oracle server. In particular, certain query operations which appear entirely reasonable to an experienced Oracle programmer may incur excessive overheads in the foreign environment.

The other major consideration for every case except the first case is the speed and message turnaround time of the network link. The great attraction of being able to perform your data take-on by simply coding:

```
INSERT INTO local_orders
    SELECT * FROM orders@hq
    WHERE processing_office = 'my location'.

DELETE FROM order@hq
    WHERE processing_office = 'my location'.

COMMIT;
```

will be reduced if the table takes longer to transmit over the network than it would have taken to key the data in by hand. We must also warn that deleting a high percentage of the rows in a table is not normally recommended.

The big issue in this case, as before, is going to be whether the data can be acquired from a SQL query in the form in which it is required, or whether it is going to need pre- or post-processing. The INSERT...SELECT... statement is highly efficient since the data never has to be converted from Oracle's internal format and because (on platforms such as UNIX where Oracle uses a two-task architecture) no context switches are incurred switching backwards and forwards from user process to Oracle process. On the other hand, if some data conversion or checking needs to be applied, then placing the data in a work table and cross-posting it may prove unacceptably inefficient.

However, since the data can be acquired through SQL query, it is again possible to write a 3GL program that issues the remote query (instead of reading a text file), carries out the required processing, and then inserts the data into the local database.

If you do this frequently (rather than as a one-off or as a required exercise), then we are probably discussing a true distributed database rather than a data feed or take-on. If you are tempted to go straight to Chapter 12 for the details, we should warn you that distributed databases share a number of design issues with client/server architectures, which is the subject of Chapter 11; we recommend that you read that chapter first.

Outbound Data

All of the emphasis in this chapter so far has been on inbound data. To be honest, this is where the majority of the issues lie. However we'd like to believe that the data in *our* application is pretty useful too, and from time to time we'll be asked to make it available to other applications in some format or other.

The observations made in the previous sections apply equally here. If we want to give another Oracle database read access to our data, we can consider a database link or a snapshot, depending on how up-to-date the data is required to be on the other system. We are once again in the realm of distributed database and we refer you to Chapter 12.

If the receiving database is non-Oracle or if networking is not a viable option, we will have to extract the data and transmit it, probably as a text file. We could use any of the following to achieve this:

- Oracle's EXPort utility
- SQL*Plus scripts
- A 3GL program
- A report writer

The choice that you make will depend on the complexity of the requirements. For instance, SQL*Plus is fairly good at producing simple text files with fixed-length records, but if all you need to do is to take an entire table from one Oracle database to another, an export file should suffice. Using a sophisticated and fully featured reporting product may be overkill. Also, certain reporting tools run only on the client platform and our guess is that you really don't want to be running a "data dump" application across a network. Our normal preference, once again, is for a 3GL tool that can fetch the data efficiently in arrays and gives a higher degree of control.

In cases where several denormalized extracts are required from the same data, it may be more efficient to extract the data from "live" tables into a set of denormalized tables that are specifically designed for the extract and then to produce the extract files directly from the copy table. This approach will also yield a consistent set of extract files which may be important in some reporting applications.

If a cross-load is periodic, then you have to consider whether to produce a complete refresh of the data every time or to transmit only the incremental changes since the last time. We recommend the complete refresh for a number of reasons:

- All data that is subject to extract must be timestamped on every change and these timestamps have to be maintained either by our application or by triggers. Use of a trigger-maintained log table to record the timestamp data is an alternative.

- Deletion has to be tackled either by using logical deletion or by the use of a trigger-maintained change log. On balance, we would recommend the log.

The use of a change log for a table is certainly feasible, but it is a major undertaking. It will also suffer from performance problems at the receiving end if any significant percentage of the source table is changed during a refresh interval. A fully engineered approach would be designed to revert to a complete refresh above some computed break-even value. For a fuller discussion of the steps required to implement a workable solution, we recommend study of Oracle's snapshot mechanism, which has the features required to reliably migrate changes from one table to another.

As we've said, our advice is to go for full extracts if you possibly can, even if the tables involved are large and the level of change is relatively small. However, the person who has to deal with input of the data at the other end may not agree!

9

Deciding on Object Placement and Storage

This chapter takes a look at the physical elements of database design. As a software project progresses through the design phase into the build phase, you will need to turn your attention to the physical properties of the system you're designing and the production environment that the new application will serve. Depending on the size and the scale of the project, the designer (or design team) will work together with the database administration team (or DBA) and possibly with a systems management team as well. The main purpose of this coming together is to undertake sizing and performance tuning exercises, along with capacity planning and a rollout strategy. On smaller projects, you may have to carry out these tasks alone, with no additional expert help. We will look at some of the issues and decisions that have to be made and give some specific guidelines for you to use as a starting point.

The following list itemizes some of the tasks that you will need to tackle during this stage of design:

- Decisions about physical storage properties (use of clusters, physical file placement, etc.)

- Sizing of database objects (tables, indexes, rollback segments, etc.)

- Sizing of the System Global Area (SGA)

- Implementation and cutover plan

- Creation of the installation scripts

Specifying Object Placement

This is a very general heading that covers a multitude of sins. We have to make plans to determine where everything will be physically housed in the system.

What do we mean by "everything"? Here is a list of some "things," both internal to the database and external:

- Tables
- Indexes
- Clusters (if any)
- Data dictionary, including all of our stored PL/SQL (functions, packages, procedures, and triggers)
- Rollback segments
- Redo logs
- Control files
- Executable programs
- Database files
- Initialization parameter files
- Program-generated log files
- Program-generated output
- Scripts
- Oracle runtime executables

All these objects (and others) need sizing (described in the next section) and placement somewhere in the system. The goals of object placement should be to:

- Promote recoverability
- Optimize performance
- Maintain flexibility

For any external file, remember that using operating system environment variables instead of hard-coding the pathname makes files easier to locate and to move.

Oracle7 has an option (redo log groups) that allows you to instruct Oracle to produce multiple copies of each redo log. This option was not available in prior versions of Oracle, and the current redo log became the single point of failure; if you had an unrecoverable error while writing to the redo log file, then you had a high probability of losing a previously committed transaction. Unless you are writing your redo logs to mirrored or shadowed disks, we strongly recommend that you use the duplex option (and that the copies be held on separate physical disk volumes—which may be difficult to guarantee if you are using a logical volume manager).

While on the subject of separate disk volumes, note that there may be some work to do in planning the placement of database objects to optimize performance. It is widely considered to be good practice to place tables on separate disks from their indexes as this is alleged to cut down on disk head movement when a table is being frequently accessed through its index. This effect is, however, quite minor and we do not specifically recommend it.

We have seen project teams waste vast quantities of time and effort planning the physical placement of their database objects. We'd like to eliminate the pain of this process. Unfortunately there is no good basis for this planning other than using knowledge, rather than hypotheses, about how applications work, which tables and indexes they use, and which applications may run in parallel with other applications. Improvements in operating systems technology has meant that, in general, entirely adequate I/O balancing can be achieved by using a logical volume manager and allowing it to distribute the database container files across the devices. As always, nothing is for free, and using a volume manager does mean that any disk failure is likely to cause the loss of many tablespaces since each drive will be carrying many tablespaces and each tablespace will be *striped* across many drives. Striping techniques are discussed in detail in Chapter 14, *Designing for Parallel Processing*.

NOTE   This practice does not apply if you are using RAID disk technology, since RAID itself can provide load balancing. RAID is discussed in detail in Chapter 14.

The distribution of application and software code modules needs some thought and planning prior to implementation. This is especially true in a client/server or distributed environment. For instance, when we create a new release of an application for a client/server system, it is likely that there will be dependent changes on both client and server. The implication here is that the server upgrade must be synchronized with *all* clients. This can be a logistical nightmare! One option for overcoming this problem is to hold all the software modules on the server on a shared disk to which all the clients have access. This solution has performance implications but may be xsacceptable on a LAN. There is a move towards this type of configuration, with the ultimate being the network computer (NC); the NC loads all of its software from the network (actually the Internet).

Another area where design input may be required is when allocating database objects to tablespaces. If the DBA is planning to selectively take tablespaces off-line (possibly for backup purposes) the designer can identify dependencies between the objects in those tablespaces and the objects that are required to be online by certain applications.

Sizing

Sizing is a task that is predominantly the responsibility of the DBA. However, the sizing process starts very early in the project life cycle.

Sizing of Tables

When we identify an entity in the analysis phase we will almost certainly indicate how many occurrences we will have initially and at what rate our occurrence will grow (or shrink) over a year. These figures are rough estimates, since they are being made at a time when we don't really know how large each row in the resulting table will be on average.

During design, when we turn entities into tables, we carry the volumes across, although there are some additional tasks to perform where the mapping of entity to table is not one to one. With tables, we can start to estimate the total space requirements. We have to estimate the average row size by asking ourselves questions such as "What percentage of rows will have a null in this column?" and "What will be the average size of the contents of this VARCHAR2(50) column?" We also need to determine to what extent rows will grow when updated by providing values for columns that were previously null and by increasing the length of variable-length character columns. The answers to these questions will dictate the amount of space that we will leave in blocks for row expansion.

Sizing of Rollback Segments

At this stage, the DBA will start to think about sizing the rollback segments. You and your design team should definitely have some input into this process. The DBA will not have much (if any) knowledge about the transaction sizes of the programs in the application. A common configuration is to have a series of small rollback segments available for online transactions and a large one that is used for batch processes. However, if the schedule of jobs during the night is different from that during the day, it can be beneficial to have a different configuration of rollback segments during the night.

You can give the DBA insight into the type of reports and batch programs that are scheduled to run at night, together with online requirements for rollback segments during the day. Take care; some of these situations can be tricky. For example, the conventional wisdom is that OLTP systems only require quite short rollback segments. This is true for pure OLTP, but as soon as some user launches a long-running query which is visiting blocks that are being updated by the OLTP application, we suddenly need rollback segments that are long enough not to wrap around during the course of the query. If you need to find out how often your rollback segments are wrapping around, monitor the column WRAPS in the system virtual table V$ROLLSTAT.

Sizing of Memory and the SGA

In addition to all the media storage sizing tasks, memory also needs to be accurately sized, and here the designer may have to play a leading role. The project schedule may dictate that orders for equipment have to be placed well in advance of system test or production. It is essential to size the application correctly in terms of memory usage, particularly if you are ordering new client machines for the application. In a client/server configuration, both the client and the server need to be specified in terms of hardware requirements, but if we get the client configuration wrong it will be costly since we have to multiply the cost of correcting it by the number of client systems we have.

Oracle gives us some guidelines for server and client configurations. For instance, Oracle Forms runtime Version 4.5 on an Intel or equivalent PC requires a minimum of 8 megabytes memory and recommends at least 12 megabytes. In practice, for most serious applications 8 megabytes is not enough, so do we order 12 megabytes, 16 megabytes, or more? If we don't have enough of the application written to run some load and performance tests when we place the order, we will have to "best guess" it. And we usually get it wrong! There is no substitute for experience—ideally of the target application but, failing that, of a substantially similar application. However you decide to size memory, do not take the salesman's recommendation unless it comes with a watertight guarantee that he will pay for any upgrade required if it turns out to be wrong.

Now let's take a quick look at server-side memory. Again, Oracle provides some standard metrics of how much physical memory you should have per concurrent user. Of course this figure is rough since so much depends on the nature of the application. For instance, if you are planning to use stored procedures that manipulate large PL/SQL tables, you may need to add some contingency to the Oracle-supplied guideline. However, there is a rule of thumb which says that you will never use less than 1.5 megabytes per connected user. People will talk to you about Oracle's multithreaded server (MTS), improvements in memory consumption in Version 7.3, and any number of complex rational arguments about how this number could be lower, but experience suggests that it hardly ever is. With complex, feature-rich applications, the number may drift up towards 5 megabytes per connected user, and the more stored PL/SQL is used, the larger the SGA needs to be in order to cache the compiled code. You may need to think in terms of a cache in excess of 100 megabytes for a complex, feature-rich application.

The finer points about sizing and tuning of the SGA are outside the scope of this book. There are other books that deal with this subject. It is generally something that is done by tweaking the live application; no amount of theorizing or bench-marking during design or development will get it right.

Specifying Storage Parameters

Whenever you create a database storage object (a rollback segment, cluster, table, or index), you are allowed to specify a set of physical attributes. In addition, these parameters can (and should) be supplied when you create primary and unique key constraints; they apply to the index created to support the constraints.

The following table creation script specifies most of the available physical attributes, including a full STORAGE clause.

```
— sample create table script

CREATE TABLE rules
   ( rule#   NUMBER        NOT NULL
     CONSTRAINT rules_pk    PRIMARY KEY
     USING INDEX TABLESPACE user_indexes
                 PCTFREE 0
                 STORAGE (INITIAL 100K NEXT 100K PCTINCREASE 0)
   , comment VARCHAR2(1000) NOT NULL
   )
   TABLESPACE users
   PCTFREE  20
   PCTUSED   0
   INITRANS  1
   MAXTRANS 10
   STORAGE ( INITIAL 1M NEXT 1M PCTINCREASE 0
             MINEXTENTS 10 MAXEXTENTS 100
             FREELISTS 10 FREELIST GROUPS 5 );
```

We recommend that your site adopt the following policies for storage:

- Do not ordinarily use STORAGE clauses within your DDL INITIAL and NEXT values for the tablespace.

- Always set PCTINCREASE to zero because any other value is liable to cause tablespace free space fragmentation.

- For each tablespace, set the values of INITIAL and NEXT equal to each other.

The following sections provide some additional guidelines.

INITIAL and NEXT

Once we've established the policies stated above, your DBA can create tablespaces for small objects (with a default INITIAL and NEXT of 10K), for medium objects (100K), and so on. Under these circumstances classic tablespace fragmentation will be impossible. Objects might not have all of their extents in contiguous space, but this does not matter.

MAXEXTENTS and MINEXTENTS

Particularly in Version 7.3, where the number of extents per object is no longer limited by the size of the segment header block, we may wish to set the object's maximum number of extents (MAXEXTENTS) to prevent it from growing out of control. Less often, we may want to ensure a minimum size for the object using MINEXTENTS. Space management is not so expensive in Oracle that we can't afford to add an occasional extent in real time, so the only normal reason for using MINEXTENTS is to reserve space for an object to expand in a tablespace that might otherwise fill up. If you think about it, this is illogical because it means that some other object is going to fail to expand, which may be an equally serious problem.

FREELISTS and FREELIST GROUPS

The FREELISTS and FREELIST GROUPS options are important for multiprocessor and parallel server environments, respectively. Since this book is aimed at designers, rather than DBAs, we'll only comment that using these options where they are not required can cause as much difficulty as failing to use them where they are required. If you are expecting to run on an SMP platform or in an Oracle parallel server environment, then it is important that you tell the DBA which tables are expected to be subject to multiple processes inserting into them at the same time, and give some idea of the degree of parallelism.

PCTFREE and PCTUSED

This leaves us with the critically underused parameters PCTFREE and PCTUSED. Taking the simpler case first, PCTFREE on an index applies only at index creation time and specifies the amount of distributed free space that should be left within the leaf blocks. Sensible use of this attribute can greatly speed index maintenance in applications where new index keys are randomly distributed with respect to the existing keys. A surname index on an employee table is a good example of such a case, assuming that your company's hiring policy does not discriminate on the basis of the first letter of the surname. If we had 10,000 employees and expected a further 2,000 to join in the course of the life of the index, then a good value for PCTFREE might be 25, which should almost guarantee that no index leaf blocks will have to be split.

If we are building an index on a key where every new value is higher than all current values (for example, a key based on an ascending sequence), then the only sensible value for PCTFREE is zero.

With tables (and clusters), PCTFREE is used for all insertions and instructs the database engine to leave at least that percentage of the block free following row insertion. The effect is to leave somewhat more, typically PCTFREE + 1/2 average row length. This distributed free space is available for use by rows in the block, which expands as a result of update operations. The following simple UPDATE statement can be guaranteed to increase row length since a null is turning into a 37-character string.

```
UPDATE parts_master p
SET    p.descr = 'No description available at ' || TO_CHAR(SYSDATE)
WHERE  p.descr IS NULL;
```

For tables on which updates are not performed, PCTFREE 0 is recommended as a way to save disk space (and thus to speed up full table scans). For tables that are updated, we recommend that you establish the likely row lengths at creation and after update, and to pass a suggested value for PCTFREE to the DBA. Failure to set it high enough will result in *row migration.*

What is row migration? When a row expands to the point where there is no longer enough space for it in the block into which it was originally inserted, it is removed from that block and reinserted into the current insert block for the table (or for the free list being used by the transaction, if the table has multiple free lists). This operation is somewhat time-consuming in its own right and, what's more, migrated rows are permanently inefficient for indexed access because index entries will continue to reference the original block where there is a *stub row* containing the rowid of the new row. Not even dropping and recreating the index will change this behavior, which adds one block visit to every indexed access to the row.

The PCTUSED attribute is used by DELETE (and UPDATE) processing to determine the point at which the block will be put onto a free space list (i.e., become available for row insertion). As soon as the space used in the block goes below this percentage, the block becomes available once again. Clearly, if PCTFREE and PCTFREE are too close to each other, then blocks are liable to be moving on and off the free space list too frequently. Many Oracle versions contain defensive code to prevent this from happening, and the intentional result is that blocks become "lost" to the free space mechanism. We cannot overemphasize that if you get too greedy with PCTUSED, it will bite you, and we recommend setting it to zero for all but the most unusual situations.

The most effective way to recoup the space used by deleted rows in a table is to schedule an outage and reorganize the table. We know that this option isn't always available to you, but that doesn't alter the fact that it really is the preferred option.

Creating Scripts

A script is a file that is run by a user to save the tedium of having to type in lots of commands. There are scripts for Oracle tools such as SQL*Loader, SQL*Plus, SQL*DBA, and Server Manager line mode, plus operating system scripts such as UNIX shell scripts. Most projects have a set of helpful scripts that you can use to create the test and live environments and sometimes to create some data. If you are using a CASE tool, that tool should create most (or at least some) of the scripts for you from information held in the repository.

Many of the scripts that you develop will evolve during the design and build stages and will be used for real during systems test and production. Here are some typical types of situations that require the development of utility scripts:

- Setting up new accounts and granting access to roles and/or users to database objects.

- Creating synonyms (public or private) to allow reference to database objects in another schema without requiring the schema prefix (EMP rather than SCOTT.EMP).

- Setting up reference data that does not change and therefore can't justify a maintenance screen to populate it; this is sometimes referred to as "seed" data.

- Checking the integrity of data where it is not protected by a constraint or trigger. In fact, these scripts are invariably created regardless of other protection since triggers and constraints tend to be occasionally dropped or disabled during development.

- Putting a "developer friendly" wrapper around a source control system.

- Creating packages and procedures.

- Automatically cutting a new release from the latest version of all source code (including database-resident code).

Implementation Planning

At some point, all this good stuff we are developing has to hit the live environment. There may be a manager or a team in charge of implementation since it can be a huge logistical task. The designer can provide valuable assistance to the planning process with knowledge of how the system works and how the various components fit together.

There are various approaches to implementation and cut-over. The "big bang" approach drops the whole new application on the entire user community in one go. Alternatively, a heavily phased approach will first give a subset of users a small part of the application and build up the user community and the functionality in a slow and controlled manner. As you would expect, both approaches have advantages and disadvantages.

If your new system is replacing a legacy system, then there is an advantage in getting all the users on as quickly as possible. In the interim, you will be running the old and the new systems in parallel and having to keep them synchronized. Believe us, you don't want to be doing this for too long unless you want a lot of gray hairs! If the system is a brand new application and is highly complex or will be totally unfamiliar to many of the users, then a phased rollout would be more applicable.

It is likely that you will be asked for input into a cutover plan. In particular the times that initial data loads will take have to be estimated. Quite often, the new system has to be fully commissioned over a weekend or holiday period and there is a limited time window to get all the base data on board.

Most implementation plans require some form of fallback strategy just in case things don't go as planned (do they ever?). As a designer, your knowledge and experience will help to determine the point of no return at which it is either impossible to go back or it will be easier to go forward and complete the cutover, even if it is late or not fully functional.

10

Safeguarding Your Data

If you are anything like most of the database designers we've met, you would rather ignore the topics we describe in this chapter; these are:

- Archiving

- Auditing

- Security

- Backup

These topics are usually regarded as "peripheral" or "non-mainstream," but they are absolutely critical to safeguarding your precious data. There are two basic ways of safeguarding data. First, it should be protected from unauthorized or malicious access, and second, it should be kept safe so that it always available to legitimate users. We'll describe both of these goals in the following sections.

The topics discussed in this chapter have two common characteristics:

- You will need to use both risk analysis and cost/benefit analysis to determine how much effort you'll have to put into providing the various services we describe.

- You will need to take each of these topics seriously from the start, including them in your project plan and making them a formal part of your acceptance criteria. It is all too easy to avoid the problems these topics present, and to defer even considering them until the development is well under way (this is usually much too late). We prefer to tackle these topics as early as possible and to design them into the overall system architecture. Be warned: if you choose to ignore this advice (as many projects do), then there is a very good chance that your venture will fail (as many projects do).

Throughout this chapter we will look at solutions ranging from the most simple (which is also usually the least functional) to the most complex and all-encompassing. Most "real world" systems will be somewhere between the two extremes.

Archiving

What is archiving? Usually, it means storing data so it is not available for immediate access, but is in a form that allows it to be retrieved if it is needed later on. Perhaps the most common of all oversights in Oracle projects these days is the assumption that archiving is something that you start to worry about when the disks are almost full and the hardware budget is empty! Until that unhappy day arrives, we keep adding more files to the tablespaces whenever they are full, and we hope that all will be well. When we can't find any more space (or, in current releases of Oracle, when our main detail table reaches its maximum number of extents), then we decide what we are going to do about it.

There are a number of reasons why this is a risky approach. The most important are these:

- Most archiving methods require that the application be taken offline while the actual archival is in progress. With good design, these outages can be minimized, but to keep your users from being disrupted, it's prudent to schedule the archiving (and therefore the outages) for periods when the user community is able to cope with downtime.

- Unless the application was designed to cope with archiving, it may not operate correctly after the data has been removed. This is a classic problem with totally normalized data structures which do not contain derived fields such as balances. Of course, this problem can be solved by introducing "brought forward" transactions, but unless these are already in use, then the application will have to be retested before such transactions can be introduced into a production system.

- The application may slow down unacceptably because of the continual need to scan data that is not contributing to the result. The infamous SQL statement that follows is a case in point:

```
SELECT MAX(transaction_date)
  FROM transactions
 WHERE account_id = :account;
```

   The more transactions there are for the account, the slower this query will run.

- Unless users have been warned that data will be aged out of the application and have bought into the advantages of the archive policy, there is likely to be a severe negative reaction when data disappears "without warning." Users always claim that there was no warning!

In many applications, data ages very quickly. New data is frequently queried and updated; then, as it grows old, it becomes less interesting, and it is referenced less frequently. It isn't only the audit trail (described later in this chapter) that is a candidate for archiving (indeed, in some cases the audit trail might be one type of data that we want to keep indefinitely). Transaction data can also clutter up systems, even in these days of terabytes of online storage. As capacity grows, so does the amount of data that we record. And in many cases, the amount we record grows faster than the size of the data store.

Archiving Options

Archiving isn't a single type of operation. Archiving can actually mean many different things, depending on your particular data and environment:

- Losing the data altogether (dropping or deleting it without keeping any copies)

- Removing the data from any possibility of immediate access, but preserving it on some offline medium from which it could (at least in theory) be restored

- Making the data inaccessible to production systems, but allowing access to it from MIS and EIS environments such as a data warehouse or OLAP service

- Maintaining full access to the data for query, but placing it into a read-only state to avoid having to include it in the standard backup cycle

The following sections look at each of these options.

Losing the data

You might argue that losing your data is not really an acceptable option. It's true that the cost of spinning out a tape that nobody is ever likely to read might be considered the single premium on an insurance policy that just might pay out one day. And neither you nor we want to be in the position of having to admit that we have deliberately thrown away a few hundred gigabytes of corporate data. However, there are cases in many applications, especially EIS or data warehouse applications, where the cost of keeping the data is greater than the perceived benefit of having it available for query. In such cases, the data is politely lost.

A typical requirement of an EIS system might read something like this:

> The full details of all subscriber-dialed calls shall be available for query for at least two years after the event.

After some investigation, we decide that we must keep these details for up to 27 months, and that once every three months we will delete all rows that are more than 24 months old. In the particular company we're dealing with, this means that we may have to delete a little over ten percent of the rows in a 500 million-row table.

However, there is a very efficient way of organizing this kind of deletion, which is to *horizontally partition* the table into a series of tables, each of which covers three months' worth of calls, and then to externalize the complete set of data using a UNION ALL view such as the following:

```
CREATE OR REPLACE VIEW calls AS
SELECT * FROM calls_95q1
 UNION ALL
SELECT * FROM calls_95q2
 UNION ALL
SELECT * FROM calls_95q3
 UNION ALL
SELECT * FROM calls_95q4
 UNION ALL
SELECT * FROM calls_96q1
 UNION ALL
SELECT * FROM calls_96q2
 UNION ALL
SELECT * FROM calls_96q3
 UNION ALL
SELECT * FROM calls_96q4
 UNION ALL
SELECT * FROM calls_97q1;
```

With versions prior to 7.3, there are a number of difficulties with such a view, especially when you (or an ad hoc user) try to join to it. It may be necessary to provide a series of other views with the join already coded in to each individual query. With Version 7.0, we saw cases where the only approach that would perform acceptably was to issue the queries individually and perform the UNION within the application. With Version 7.3, queries using this approach, called *manual partitioning,* are optimized quite well providing that a series of restrictive conditions have been met. In essence, these restrictions are that the definitions of the individual tables must be identical in every way other than their names and storage specifications.

Once we've set up this structure, losing the data (archiving) is easy. We simply do this:

1. Create a new table (*calls_97q2*).

2. Recreate the view, dropping out the reference to *calls_95q1* and adding a reference to *calls_97q2.*

3. Drop the table *calls_95q1.*

All of this can be done in under a second, whereas deleting 50 million rows will take rather more than a second.

This approach also offers considerable advantages for data loading from the operational systems. It is discussed further in Chapter 13, *Designing for Data Warehouses*.

Taking the data permanently offline

There are several problems with taking data permanently offline. In addition to being time-consuming, there is no guarantee whatever that we will be able to read the archive if it is ever removed from its vault and brought back to the machine room. Not only might the media have degraded, but after any protracted period of time there is the problem of finding a device which is capable of mounting and reading the media. Even if we can overcome that problem, we must then find software that's capable of processing what is on the media.[*]

To be fair to Oracle Corporation, there is good backward compatibility from Version 6 onwards, but that doesn't mean that you can simply take an image copy from an old version, download it onto a disk, and expect either the current version of the RDBMS or the current version of your application to process it without having to go through some upgrade process.

You might conclude that it would be prudent to include in your archive backup a complete software environment, including not only Oracle and your application, but also a copy of the operating system. That assumes, of course, that all of this good code is going to be capable of executing on whatever hardware the organization finds itself using in two months, or two years, or 20 years' time. You can see that we consider this whole area to be a nightmare!

Over the years many organizations have made it a practice to archive to microfilm (or, more likely, microfiche) rather than to tape because the medium can be read with simpler technology, requires no software whatever, and is believed to degrade much more slowly than magnetic media. Unfortunately, the only ways of searching microfiche are by using whatever index was shipped with it or by reading every "page." If you are trying to find one suspect entry in an archive of 10 million transactions, or if you need to present a summary, microfiche doesn't seem to be the solution. In addition, the recording densities now being achieved by magnetic and optical digital media are so high that the photographic media, which were originally introduced to save space and material, are starting to look bulky and expensive.

---

[*] Surely the authors are not the only people in the world who still have data on 5 1/4-inch disks (and neither of us has 5 1/4-floppy drives on our home PCs)! And there must be hundreds of image copies of Oracle Version 5 databases sitting in secure stores around the world.

Moving the data to another application

Moving our data to another application may sound like an easy way to go, except, of course, that the data warehouse may also run out of space—taking us right back to either one of the previous two options. In a large organization, that might be someone else's problem! But, quite seriously, migration of data from operational systems into MIS and EIS systems is a valid form of archiving from the viewpoint of the administrator of the operational system.

One warning: if data has been handed off to another store where it is known to have been loaded successfully, and if that data is no longer required for operational purposes in the original store, then it should be removed from the original store.

Moving the data to read-only space within the same application

This option is not really archiving at all unless the data is restructured in some way as part of the migration. It is, however, a valuable technique for reducing the volume of the regular backup cycle, since a read-only tablespace needs to be backed up only once (immediately after the ALTER TABLESPACE...READ ONLY).

How to Archive

What is the best solution? Our recommendation is that you should archive one copy of the data on magnetic media in a form that minimizes the amount of software required to use it. For both structured and textual data, this means extracting the data in a text format—that is, viewing the archive as a report that contains the entire contents of every record. Just to be on the safe side, the format should be self-describing (that's just a formal way of saying that the fields should be clearly labeled). An archive in this type of format will take considerably longer to produce than an image copy or an export (via the EXP utility), and it may require a significant development effort to reload it on an as-yet-unknown platform. However, you are at least giving yourself (or your successors) a sporting chance.

As part of this archive subproject you *must* create an archive restore, which loads your text format into a table. The archive and restore are now very easy, though time-consuming, to test.

Suppose that you archive a table (*old_x*), and then restore it to another table (*new_x*). If the following query executes without error and returns zero, then you will know that both your archive and restore routines work.

```
(SELECT * FROM new_x
   MINUS
 SELECT * FROM old_x
 )
```

```
      UNION ALL
  (SELECT * FROM old_x
     MINUS
   SELECT * FROM new_x
  );
```

This query, although elegant, will take a significant amount of both time and sort space for a long table. Nevertheless, it will be considerably faster than 3GL or PL/SQL compare loops.

NOTE   The set operations used in this example are yet another example of a genuinely useful piece of code that is not available to you if the table contains LONG or LONG RAW columns.

Note also that this comparison cannot be validly performed without a sort because there is no guarantee that the order of the rows in the original table will be the same as the order of the rows in the restored table. Indeed, if parallel processing is used to speed up both the unload and reload processing, we can almost guarantee that the rows will not be in the same order.

When to Archive

Rather than waiting for our disks to fill up, we need to have a clear policy about when we should archive our data—in other words, when the cost of keeping the data online is no longer justified. Most users and analysts tend to express this policy the other way round, for example:

Order line data must be kept available for online query for 24 months from the date of payment in full, and for 48 months from the date of dispatch if any payment is outstanding.

An organization may have a statutory or legal requirement to keep certain data for a length of time, but that only tells us the earliest point at which we can legally remove the data. It does not tell when we *should* remove it.

If we have timestamps on our data to tell us when it was last updated, we could check those to find data which has not changed for, say, three years. Unfortunately, we won't be able to find out when it was last queried!

Your users may wish to browse the data and use their own business knowledge to mark which customers have gone out of business, which data is known to be obsolete, and other similar facts. Periodic routines can then scan the data for marked entries and can archive them and all subordinate data (such as the customers' orders). Of course, you and we both know that the user will never get around to doing this, but we don't have to say so!

Should You Archive to a File or a Table?

Good question! The pros and cons of files and tables are each pretty obvious. Using files will free up precious database space (and disk space as well when the file, in turn, is archived to tape). If we are desperate to retrieve the data, then maybe we can use a gateway so we can still query the data using SQL—though it is unlikely that we will find a gateway that can read directly from tape, or that will access serial files which are in report format.

Archiving to a table really begs the question since, as we've discussed, neither a tablespace image backup nor even an export offers much certainty that you will definitely be able to retrieve the data many years in the future.

Can You Change Your Mind and Put the Archived Data Back?

Another good question! If you are designing modules to archive data, then you can also design and write modules to resurrect the data. Among the many things that you will have to watch out for in this case are unique keys—another record with the same key may have happened along in the interim.

One way to avoid this key duplication is to leave a skeleton row behind when you archive. We have seen this done, but we don't like it. When you do this, you have to leave some data behind in all the mandatory columns, and the row still occupies space. Further, even if all queries on the table contain a predicate such as ARCHIVED = 'N'. the skeleton rows are still likely to be processed during query execution.

We prefer to think of archiving as a one-way street. It makes life so much simpler and avoids false expectations.

Archiving Recommendations

As we've said throughout this section, don't assume that archiving will be easy. And just in case you last longer in this job than in your previous positions, don't be tempted to assume that you will be long gone before archiving rears its ugly head! In summary, our archiving recommendations are:

- Design it in from the start.
- Archive by entity, not by table. If a single entity maps to two tables, they should be archived in the same operation.
- Take particular care over the impact on referential integrity. You cannot leave "orphan" rows in the database by archiving parent rows but leaving their children—you have to define *archive groups* of related tables.

- If you use files, do so in a self-describing format (in essence, report files).

- Implement archiving as part of the main application, and test it as part of the acceptance suite.

Auditing

What is auditing and how does it relate to security? Auditing is about finding out who did what and whether they were allowed to do it; security is about stopping them from doing wrong in the first place. In any system that contains the opportunity for gain (e.g., a system which maintains loan records), you must be sure that either your auditing or your security is watertight; of course, it is infinitely better if both are perfect. Although auditing and security are linked, they are clearly separate activities; we discuss security later in this chapter. Unfortunately, as we shall see, there are a number of real-world restrictions on what we can achieve using Oracle7.

The term *auditing* is often used within IT to mean the recording of the *audit trail*. The audit trail is a separate set of records produced by the system—a set that is prohibitively difficult to attack. Sometimes, these terms are used interchangeably. In this section, however, we have tried to be precise: we refer to the audit trail when we are discussing record keeping, and to auditing when we are discussing the use of the audit trail to provide a reporting function.

Let's consider why we need an audit trail (though obviously this varies from system to system). The main purpose of the trail is to provide the means to detect any activity that might compromise system integrity. Put another way, we need to be able to discover both fraudulent entries and unapproved query access. For some reason, many organizations work harder to detect one of these than they do to detect the other.

What's in the Audit Trail?

What information should your system write to the audit trail? In theory, anything that happens within the system is a candidate for being recorded. Logins and logoffs are especially important to audit, as are updates to your data. The auditing of queries is somewhat problematic unless the queries are made through stored procedures, in which case an audit trail can be built in. Let's look at a few examples.

Most organizations record all logins to the system and report those that occur outside normal working hours, or those that are performed via dial-up access (assuming that we can tell). We might make a separate record of all financial transactions where money is posted out of the system. One way of doing this is by

---

What Do Auditors Really Want?

One of the most difficult aspects of putting audit controls onto a system is determining the requirements and ensuring exactly what the right level of audit information should be in the database. Some systems architects make their own assumptions without even asking anybody. This is not a good idea. We recommend that you go to the auditors in your organization and ask them what their auditing requirements are. Actually, one of the authors did this recently, and the answer he got was this: "We need to be able to track every change made to the data, and to be able to access the audit data in any way we wish." The only surprise was that he was surprised; they seemed to be such reasonable people!

Why not give them everything they want? The implications of exceeding reasonable audit requirements are that you increase the size of your database many-fold and that you add considerable runtime overhead in collecting a great deal of information that may never be used.

In this particular case, we eventually managed to agree that only financial transactions needed a full audit trail, and that a series of predefined reports, together with an ad hoc query tool, would be adequate for the auditors to do their investigations.

---

picking "accounts" or "events" at random and cross-checking them against the receiving system to ensure that the books balance. Another way is to pick out all of the transactions involving large amounts of money. Of course, anything we find through an audit is already over and done with. As we've said, audit is inextricably connected with security. It is far better to prevent a fraud or a security violation from ever occurring by imposing a tight security policy rather than by catching it after the event with audit controls.

Some organizations may also use audit controls to measure workflow and departmental or individual performance. For instance, the audit trail may tell us that an order was first logged on the system on April 21 (from *created_dt* on ORDERS), but that the goods were not dispatched until June 14 (from *created_dt* on DISPATCHES). By producing aggregates of these differences, managers can deduce work performance statistics. However, it is our belief that this is a potentially dangerous practice. There are often legitimate reasons why data entry is deferred and bears no reality to the date on which an event occurred. If work measurement statistics are required, then there should be columns on the table (separate from audit columns) for recording the relevant information (such as dispatch date).

The Most Basic Form of Audit Trail

Let's look at a minimalist solution to audit. In this example we assume that we are concerned only with recording access to data—specifically, who created each row and who last modified each row (if anyone). To most of our tables, we could add four additional columns:

```
...
, created_byVARCHAR2(30)NOT NULL
, created_dtDATE          NOT NULL
, updated_byVARCHAR2(30)
, updated_dtDATE
...
```

These columns are populated automatically by triggers on the tables, for example:

```
CREATE OR REPLACE TRIGGER t1_bir BEFORE INSERT ON t1
FOR EACH ROW
BEGIN
  :new.created_by := USER;
  :new.created_dt := SYSDATE;
END t1_bir;
/

CREATE OR REPLACE TRIGGER t1_bur BEFORE UPDATE ON t1
FOR EACH ROW
BEGIN
  :new.updated_by := USER;
  :new.updated_dt := SYSDATE;
END t1_bir;
/
```

Projects that use this form of audit trail normally exclude standing reference data tables, presumably on the assumption that it does not matter when such data changes. A client once suggested to one of us that audit trails were not necessary on such data "because it rarely changes." We asked immediately how he knew that it rarely changed when he had no audit trail, but we were unable to get a clear answer.

The "before insert" trigger could be replaced by DEFAULT clauses on the *created_ by, created_dt* columns. Either way, this is a solution that is very simple to implement and is not that costly in terms of runtime overhead or additional storage within the database.

Another advantage of this level of audit is that all of the information is held in the live transaction tables. This makes it easy to perform audit inquiries on our data, such as a listing of total order value by creator. So what are the drawbacks? Let's list them individually:

1. With these columns, we can determine only the creator and the last person to modify the row. All trace of intermediate modifications is forever lost.

2. We are able to see who last modified a row, and when they modified it, but we cannot tell what columns were changed. Was it simply a status column that was updated, or was an amount altered (or both)? We just don't know.

3. We can see who created a row, and who last updated it, but if a row is deleted, we lose all trace of it (including creation and modification details).

4. If we have generic user accounts such as "DATA ENTRY CLERK" that many users share on the system, using the user name to stamp records won't be much help in identifying the actual person who logged in. Also, if we have remote users who are accessing tables on our system using distributed transactions, the user account that is used to stamp the record may be a general proxy account used by remote users. If this is the case, our audit information similarly won't tell us much that is of use.

5. When we load data from another system (whether during initial take-on or on a periodic basis), if we have these triggers enabled, then all the loaded data will have the user name that the batch process used to connect to Oracle as its creator. This may be desirable, but often it is preferable to disable the triggers during data load and to carry across the creator (and time of creation) from the original system.

6. We are recording only creation and insertion events. We have no record of select activity, and we don't know who is accessing what data for read-only.

7. Our audit trail doesn't help us understand what else was done in the same transaction except by trying to join on username and time; the time, of course, does not stay constant for the duration of a transaction.

Using the Oracle7 Audit Features

Up to this point, we've discussed auditing only in a general way. In this section, we'll look at some of the standard audit features that are delivered with Oracle7. Initially these features may appear to be quite powerful and flexible. Unfortunately, on closer examination, we see that many of them aren't very helpful. They tend to only record events without logging the data values associated with the event. Chocolate teapots come to mind.[*]

Some of Oracle7's built-in audit options can be rather useful. With auditing enabled at the instance level, the command:

```
AUDIT SESSION;
```

will log all connections to the database and disconnections from it, both successful and unsuccessful. This may be useful if you suspect that you may have a hacker, but unfortunately it tells you nothing about what the user is doing between the connect and the disconnect. All you can gather is when and for how long the user was connected, and when and how often some unknown person failed to connect.

Let's assume that most of the data in our database is fairly innocuous and of little interest to the casual (or not so casual) user, but that we have one exception: a PAYROLL table that contains sensitive information. Obviously, we will implement a security policy that restricts access to this table to only certain privileged users (we'll discuss this in some detail later on in the section about security issues). However, people get careless with their passwords or may leave their screens logged on when they are not at their desks. We can supplement the security on this table by auditing activity on it via the following command:

```
AUDIT ALL ON LIVE.PAYROLL BY ACCESS;
```

This statement will cause Oracle to log the "details" of all activity against the PAYROLL table, with the BY ACCESS clause ensuring that there is a log entry for every access, not just one entry per access type per session. Oracle logs all enabled audit activity to the single table SYS.AUD$, which can become very cluttered if you have a lot of audit trails enabled. Fortunately, Oracle provides a series of views that enable you to examine the contents of AUD$ in a structured series of subsets (see CATAUDIT.SQL).

If we examine the audit views, we will see that we can query the accesses to PAYROLL by user, by type of access, and by date and time of access. We are still restricted, however, in that we can't tell if an update simply changed some of the personal details in the table (e.g., change of address) or if it altered a salary. Unfortunately, the Oracle audit facility can only tell us so much. If we suspect that someone is connecting as a user with the PAYROLL role, altering a salary prior to the payroll run, and then altering it back afterwards, we need a lot more information than Oracle auditing can give us.

The reason that Oracle auditing has to be enabled at both the instance level and by AUDIT statements is delightfully simple. If the system tablespace fills up with auditing enabled and there is no more room to make audit entries, then it is

---

* This book contains more than one reference to chocolate teapots, and of course there is no such thing. However there is an old English saying, "*as much use as a chocolate teapot*," which means, of course, that it is of absolutely no use at all. One of us worked many years ago for the UK subsidiary of a North American software manufacturer whose R&D facility was always referred to by UK staff as *the chocolate teapot factory.*

impossible to free up any space. Why? Because to do so you would have to make an audit entry and there is no room to make one.

The solution is to crash the instance (it is unlikely that you will be able to perform a SHUTDOWN NORMAL under these circumstances) and to restart it with auditing disabled at the instance level so that you (or your DBA) can come to grips with freeing up some space. Of course, while this is going on you are running without auditing.

If this has ever happened to you, you will realize why log analyzer software is so appealing to computer auditors. With such analyzers, every database change made is in the redo log, and the logs have ascending serial numbers so the auditor can tell if a log is missing. The log also contains both the old and new data values for updates, and the old values for deleted records. If you are really sophisticated, you can use a log analyzer to check on whether any tables have been altered without the changes appearing in their audit log!

As usual, however, there are a couple of problems. You simply are not guaranteed to know which user made the change, because the user ID is not logged, and there is no data whatever on queries. At the time of writing, one of us has been engaged in a study to try to find a way of determining the user ID from the redo log. The conclusion, sadly, is that it cannot reliably be done.

Using Triggers for Further Audit

In this section, we'll build on the previous example, but will further extend our auditing. This time we will introduce an additional table that will hold a complete chronological log of all changes made to the SALARY column of our PAYROLL table. Because there is some overhead in recording this information, some sites might enable this table only periodically—either to collect random samples or only when they suspect there is a problem. This last approach is known, technically, as "closing the stable door after the horse has bolted." Our opinion is that if you need an audit trail, then you need a *permanent* audit trail.

Sample SQL to create the log table and the code for the trigger to maintain it are illustrated in the following PL/SQL extract. Note that the primary key of the audit table uses date and time: it seems reasonable to suggest that nobody's salary should be changed twice in the same second, and if it is, then you are justified in your concern about security!

```
CREATE TABLE salary_change_log
(emp#            NUMBER(10)    NOT NULL
,transaction_dt  DATE          NOT NULL
,user_name       VARCHAR2(30)  NOT NULL
,old_sal_value   NUMBER(8,2)   NOT NULL
,new_sal_value   NUMBER(8,2)   NOT NULL
```

```
    ,CONSTRAINT scl_pk PRIMARY KEY (emp#, transaction_dt)
    );

    CREATE OR REPLACE TRIGGER pay_aur AFTER UPDATE ON payroll
    FOR EACH ROW
    BEGIN
       IF :old.emp#   <> :new.emp#
       THEN RAISE_APPLICATION_ERROR(-20000,
           'Illegal primary key change attempted on table PAYROLL'.;
       END IF;
       IF :old.salary <> :new.salary THEN
          BEGIN
             INSERT INTO salary_change_log ( emp#
                                           , transaction_dt
                                           , user_name
                                           , old_sal_value
                                           , new_sal_value
                                           )   VALUES
                                           ( :new.emp_no
                                           , SYSDATE
                                           , USER
                                           , :old.salary
                                           , :new.salary
                                           );
          END;
       END IF;
    END pay_aur;
    /
```

Now if somebody attempts to alter a salary on either side of a payroll run, our trigger will catch it—or will it? An alternative to updating the row is to delete it and reinsert it, and indeed this will have to be done if the user wants to change the employee number. Unfortunately, we are not intercepting deletions or insertions, and perhaps we should. The table definition and code in Example 10-1 is a more general version of the salary log table and a new trigger that captures all three events.

If you take the time to look through this example, you will see that we have used a single trigger that tests for insert, update, and delete rather than using a separate trigger for each event. Opinions differ on which is the best approach. On balance, we prefer to keep the implementation of the audit rules for any particular table in one (and only one) place.

There is a great deal that could be improved in our example. For example, many auditors will ask that the audit entries be sequentially numbered per employee so that they can tell if any have been deleted. There are two issues here: first, we have to decide how to implement the requirement, and second, we might want to find out why the auditors believe that someone with enough system knowledge to remove audit entries would not have enough knowledge to "downdate" later entries. For now, we'll pursue only the first of these issues, numbering the audit

Example 10-1. An Audit Table and Trigger to Capture the Information

```
CREATE TABLE salary_change_log
(emp#              NUMBER(10)    NOT NULL
,transaction_dt DATE            NOT NULL
,user_name       VARCHAR2(30) NOT NULL
,dml_type        CHAR(1)        NOT NULL
 CONSTRAINT scl_dml_type CHECK (dml_type IN ('I', 'U', 'D'))
,old_sal_value   NUMBER(8,2)
,CONSTRAINT scl_old_sal
   CHECK (  DECODE(dml_type, 'I', 0, 'U', 1, 'D', 1, 0)
         = DECODE(old_sal_value, null, 0, 1) )
,new_sal_value   NUMBER(8,2)
,CONSTRAINT scl_new_sal
   CHECK (  DECODE(dml_type, 'I', 1, 'U', 1, 'D', 0, 0)
         = DECODE(new_sal_value, null, 0, 1) )
,CONSTRAINT scl_pk PRIMARY KEY (emp#, transaction_dt)
);

CREATE OR REPLACE TRIGGER pay_aud
AFTER INSERT OR UPDATE OR DELETE ON payroll
FOR EACH ROW
DECLARE
  l_dml_typ salary_change_log.dml_type%TYPE;

BEGIN
  IF :old.emp#   <> :new.emp#  — fails if either is null
  THEN RAISE_APPLICATION_ERROR(-20000,
     'Illegal primary key change attempted on table PAYROLL');
  END IF;
  IF UPDATING ('SALARY') THEN
    l_dml_typ := 'U';
  ELSIF INSERTING THEN
    l_dml_typ := 'I';
  ELSE — deleting
    l_dml_typ := 'D';
  END IF;
  IF l_dml_typ IS NOT NULL
  THEN INSERT INTO salary_change_log
                    ( emp#
                    , transaction_dt
                    , user_name
                    , dml_type
                    , old_sal_value
                    , new_sal_value
                    )   VALUES
                    ( :new.emp#
                    , SYSDATE
                    , USER
                    , l_dml_typ
                    , :old.salary
                    , :new.salary
                    );
  END IF;
END pay_aud;
/
```

entries so that the primary key becomes (*emp#*, *change#*) with the change numbers starting at one (or zero) and extending upwards with no gaps.

It's pretty simple really: we just add a column to the PAYROLL table that tells us the highest change number for each employee. Then, when we want to write an audit record, we read the PAYROLL entry for the employee, grab the current number, add one to it, update the PAYROLL table, and insert the new row into the audit table. Nice try, but you will hit a brick wall called the "mutating table constraint." The workaround to this constraint is shown in Appendix B, *Tricks of the Trade*.

At this point, we may be confident that we have shown our auditors that we can record *anything* that happens to a row (except, of course, the people querying it). But they're never satisfied. They have a great idea: we should extend our auditing to a log of every change to every column in every table. How about this? Not only would we use an enormous amount of database space storing all this data, and considerable CPU power creating the audit trail records, but we would also have to write (and test) huge amounts of trigger code. (It took us long enough to debug the "pay_aud" example in Example 10-1 and we've both had a fair amount of practice at both designing and writing audit triggers.)

We make three recommendations in this area:

1. Try to avoid auditing row insertion in full; the row can normally provide its own record of its values.

2. Do not try to use only one audit table; SQL does not handle meta-structures at all well, and it will be much easier to have a separate audit table for each table design. If you have two tables with identical column definitions (partitioned data), then they can share an audit table if you wish.

3. Use a generator to create the audit triggers. If they need maintenance for any reason, maintain the generator and rebuild the triggers rather than trying to fix the generated code. This is one of these lessons that you can learn the easy way (by reading our book and following our advice) or the hard way (by explaining to your Chief Executive why a simple specification change caused a two-year overrun).

An Alternative Approach

A very workable alternative to creating audit logs for updates and deletes is never to change any data (i.e., no updates to base data) and never to delete rows except during archiving operations. With these two rules in place (and enforced by triggers), you can never lose data, and never lose sight of an interim state which may have only existed for a few hours.

But how is this possible? One way to make such an approach feasible is to hold derived records. Thus, in our payroll example, we would have a derived record (maintained only by triggers) which gave the current value of each attribute for each employee and a detail table showing every interim state that the row had experienced during its entire life, complete with a timestamp and updating user ID. Put another way, the application writes to the audit trail and the triggers maintain the "real data." Many people have great difficulty adapting to this approach, but it can be highly effective and, once it is understood, it actually raises fewer implementation problems than does the more conventional solution. Of course, it also uses a great deal of space and is not directly supported by RAD (Rapid Application Development) toolkits.

Other issues raised by this design technique are discussed in Chapter 17, *Metrics, Prototypes, and Specifications.*

Auditing Hints

This section contains several additional hints for auditing.

Do not disable audit triggers

Triggers can, of course, be disabled and there will be a strong temptation to do this while certain "trusted" batch processes are running. This is potentially disastrous because there is no foolproof way to prevent another (not trusted) process from accessing the data while the trigger is disabled.

A better approach is data-driven trigger suppression, where the trigger asks a packaged procedure if it is to act or not act. The package contains a persistent package variable which can be set by another procedure, and if this has been set correctly, the package can tell the trigger not to write its audit entries. This may sound insecure, but it is not nearly as insecure as the practice of disabling audit triggers. If necessary, password and cryptographic techniques can be used to ensure that the requester is entitled to suppress the trigger action.

Finding the user name

Many Oracle sites use generic login IDs (e.g., PRODUCTION), and may have several hundred users all attached to Oracle with the same Oracle user name. In fact, this is a requirement for effective use of a transaction processing (TP) manager environment. As a result, auditing based on the Oracle user name is not always very useful. The solution, as in the previous subsection, is to use a package with a persistent variable and to insist that the user establish his or her identity to this package before the audit triggers will permit updates to the audited tables. This approach, which is discussed in the security section later in this chapter, is not widely favored within the Oracle community, but is highly effective.

The role of log analysis in auditing

If you have a redo log analyzer available to you, then one of the checks you can make is whether the triggers have fired or not. Thus, if we were using a trigger to record all changes to the PAYROLL table, we could analyze the redo log to make sure that every operation against that table was accompanied by an audit entry.

The redo logs, which are preserved using redo log archiving by almost all sites running updates to sensitive data, offer a great deal to an auditor:

- The logs are not within the database, so no level of privilege in Oracle will allow access to them through SQL. They can be accessed only from the operating system at file level.

- They contain rigorous sequencing so it is easy to tell if a log is missing.

- They contain the new values and old values associated with *every* DML operation, with the exception of direct path loading and unrecoverable copies from one table to another.

- They are essentially free, because Oracle is going to write them regardless of whether you can find a use for them.

This all sounds too good to be true, and it is. Unfortunately, there are two enormous snags. First, there is no formal support from Oracle for processing redo logs, and second, although all of the data values are there in full, it is impossible to determine which user issued the statement.

WARNING   We have also seen sites attempt to utilize the fact that the V$SQLAR-EA view holds the last SQL statement in the SQL_TEXT column. We would strongly advise against attempting this; it is fraught with many dangers and loopholes. Only the first 1,000 characters of SQL statements are visible through this mechanism. All the recursive SQL statements are included in here and are impossible to distinguish from user-issued SQL. Bind variables are not evaluated, so you can't see the actual column values in many cases. Also, since it contains the SQL issued by all users of the system, it is difficult to tell who issued what.

Security

If our audit facilities are our system police, then the security surrounding the system is the crime prevention unit. Please give the security of your system the respect it deserves—it's far better to prevent a violation than to catch the violator after the event.

In Oracle7, security features can be divided into two distinct areas:

- *Access security* dictates who gets into our application, and how much of it they can use (or how much is available to them) once they are in.

- *Data security* determines which tables a user can reference and what they can do to the tables. In some cases, data security may extend to the row and column level, but typically it is used to give access rights (query, insert, update, delete) to the entire table.

Given a good security policy that covers both access and data, it should be possible to create a reasonably secure production environment that prevents any unauthorized access, either to data or to programs.

NOTE   If you are designing for a particularly sensitive installation, the facilities described in this section may not be adequate. The Trusted Oracle product is aimed at sites where a higher level of security is required. This product is beyond the scope of this book, but you can find many manuals available from Oracle on the subject.

Access Security

Oracle7 has a variety of mechanisms for identifying and verifying users; the simplest is to insist that every user provide a user name and a password when he or she first connects. This verification must occur regardless of the frontend tool that is being used to access the database. The idea is that until the user has a valid connection, he can't use any of the facilities in the database. The user name and password are checked against entries in the table SYS.USER$ into which the password is encrypted using a one-way algorithm. DBAs see only the encrypted password in the table (nobody sees the decrypted password). We don't know of anyone yet who has managed to decrypt a password in an Oracle environment.

Most users expect to have to log in to a system only once (and rightly so). If they have provided a user name and password to log in to the operating system—especially if the operating system security is good—why should they be expected to provide another user name and password to connect to Oracle? To address this concern, Oracle introduced a mechanism which has become known as *OPS$ logins*: using this mechanism, if a user provides a blank user name (and no password), Oracle will connect to the database as the appropriate Oracle user, accepting the operating system's authentication of user identity. These accounts are called OPS$ accounts, because in Version 5 the Oracle user name was always the operating system user name prefixed with OPS$. In current versions, the prefix is an instance-level parameter and may be null, so that the operating system and Oracle user names can be the same.

OPS$ accounts (we'll continue to refer to them in this way) are useful under many circumstances, but they do have their limitations. For a start, older PC operating systems such as MS-Windows 3.1 and OS/2 do not have a user login facility. The Oracle workaround for this environment is to specify the default user name in a configuration file, but this is only as secure as the physical security of the machine. Without taking some additional steps, anyone who can get access to your PC can use your default Oracle user name.

OPS$ accounts may also be totally insecure in client/server environments where the client machines do require you to log in. The problem is that many workstations are administered by the user, or at least the user knows the system administration password (under UNIX the *root* password) and can therefore add new users to his machine. This opens the door to attacking database security through such methods as "spoofing" and "phreaking."

Spoofing means creating a user who is known to exist and have privilege elsewhere in the network. This allows you (or anyone else with sufficient knowledge) to create an account for the user on a machine they control, and then to attach to another machine where that user name bears some privilege. In some connection systems, this is partially prevented by allowing connections only from certain machines. This requirement has led to the second method, *phreaking*, which means configuring your machine so that it identifies itself to the server as one of the machines permitted to connect.

Given these threats, it is hardly surprising that Oracle provides a server initialization parameter to prevent client machines from using OPS$ logins. Our advice is to disable remote OPS$ logins.

We should also make a brief point about the great strength of OPS$ logins, which is that they make certain types of impersonation much more difficult. In particular, they prevent DBAs from changing user passwords in order to connect to the database as a particular user to make some helpful adjustment (which then gets audited as having been performed by that user rather than the DBA). It is even possible for a knowledgeable DBA to then reset the user's password back to its original value even though that value is unknown to the DBA. It has little to do with design; just in case you find this difficult to believe, the code is shown below:

```
SQL> connect sys/whatever
SQL> col password new_value &pw
SQL> SELECT password FROM dba_users WHERE username = 'USER_A'.
```

```
PASSWORD
_____

88F10186D82B38F2

SQL> alter user user_a identified by xx; — change password

User altered.

SQL> connect user_a/xx
Connected.
SQL> alter user user_a identified by values '&pw'.

User altered.

SQL> — user_a's password now reset to its original value
```

One further point about client/server security. If you are allowing connections across a wide area network, there is a possibility that a determined hacker could monitor the data between the client and the server in the hope of seeing a connection request and using the same request to hack into the system. There is a client parameter, ORA_ENCRYPT_LOGIN, that may help in this case. When this parameter is set, it causes the login string to be encrypted between client and server. Note also that SQL*Net Secure Network Services Release 2.0 and above support industry-standard authentication services such as Kerberos and Sesame.

Unfortunately, Oracle7 has no facility for aging passwords—that is, forcing the user to enter a new password periodically. If you want to use such a feature in your system (and it's a very good idea), you will have to write it yourself. You may also want to keep a recent history of passwords (or at least their encrypted values) to prevent their reuse.

Unlike many systems, Oracle imposes no delay when returning a connection failure due to an invalid password. This means that combinatorial techniques (or just trying every first name you know) can be an effective way to break into databases which use conventional Oracle authentication. Ideally, you will also ensure that in your system at least six characters are used in all passwords and that at least one is nonalphabetic; unfortunately to do this you must write code as part of your application which handles all password changes. If some ingenious hacker puts an "audit trail" into that code to allow them to record all password changes, you really will have a security problem.

Despite our warnings, the ideal solution might still seem to be to call a user-written routine to perform the login process. This could check (in a table) the date and time of the most recent password change for the user, and enforce a change if it has expired. A further advantage of encapsulating the login process in this way is that we can disable an account if repeated logins are attempted with an invalid password. The major problem with this approach is that it depends on cooperative client processes. We can make all our project-written applications connect in this way, but we cannot force ad hoc query tools or third-party applications to do so.

Access security and menus

In most database applications there are a number of different categories of users who use different parts of the system and have different rights to see and modify data. In a simple case, there may only be two classes of users: those who enter the data (data entry clerks) and the managers who perform queries against the data. The managers have no interest in entering the data, and we would not allow data entry clerks to run the reports. In this case, the data entry clerks and managers can have entirely separate applications because there is no overlap in functionality, and the two applications can share a common database.

In more realistic cases, there will be several categories of users, and there will be overlaps in the functionality to which they must have access. In such cases, you can often save duplication of effort by having a single application with a menu or toolbar that varies from user to user depending on their assigned roles. Most development tools enable you to dynamically alter menu contents at runtime, depending on the user. Unfortunately, some tools resolve the permissions at build time rather than at runtime; we strongly recommend that you use a tool that looks up user rights in real time. It uses more network and server capacity, but it allows a much prompter reaction to security concerns.

Our preference is to hide items from users who don't have access rather than graying them out. Showing such items on the screen in any form simply lets the user know that the facilities are there, and may provide an incentive to find a "back door" entry into them.

On the subject of back door entry, we advise that in addition to a tailored menu, each application checks that the user who invoked it actually has the privilege to run it. If they do not, the application should terminate and record the violation in a *threat log*.

Batch processes

We have dealt with the subject of restricting interactive users, but we also have to validate the submission of batch jobs and reports. We may wish to restrict some users from running or scheduling certain jobs or reports through a batch queue. The mechanism used to enforce this will depend upon the particular batch scheduler in your environment. These controls should be applied both at the submission stage and at runtime. The check should be performed at submission because it is pointless to allow users to submit jobs that will fail at some point in the future because the submitting user has insufficient privilege. For extra security, though, the check should also be enforced at runtime just in case someone has found a way around the submission system.

Batch processes, including reporting processes, cannot always run using the identity of the submitting user. Even when that user has permission to run the job, he may not know any database password that gives him sufficient privilege to access some of the tables used. This issue of whether users are aware of the database passwords being used on their behalf becomes critical at sites where SQL*Plus is available to end users.

We continue to be amazed by the number of sites that do not adequately protect major batch updating jobs from being run by unauthorized users. If you think that rogue users could do you damage if they started issuing online transactions, imagine what they could do to you if they can initiate a bulk update using their own driver files!

Data Security

Once we are confident that only authorized users can connect to our database and that they can run only modules that they have been explicitly granted the privilege to run, we need to look at the next level of security—restricting their access to the data.

The introduction of *roles* in Oracle7 has been an enormous advance in data security. Prior to Oracle7, each user had to be explicitly granted access rights on every database object that they were permitted to use. This process has been simplified by granting access to a set of objects to the role and then granting use of the role to the appropriate users. Through the GRANT mechanism we can enable SELECT, INSERT, UPDATE, and DELETE privileges to users on database objects such as tables. In itself, this doesn't give us much flexibility. We may wish to restrict users to *parts* of a table—slicing the table horizontally (restricting the user to certain rows), vertically (restricting the user to certain columns), or both. How can we do this?

Let's continue our example of the PAYROLL table. We don't want all our users to see the SALARY column, and we might want to restrict users so they can see only the records of people in their own department. Table 10-1 uses shading to show a restricted view of the table.

The phrase "a restricted view" gives us a hint of one means of meeting this requirement. We can define a view and give users access to the view, but not to the underlying table (PAYROLL). They will be able to query the table, but only

Table 10-1. PAYROLL: A Restricted View of a Table (Visible Section Indicated by Shading)

ID	NAME	DEPT	PAYMENT_PERIOD	SALARY
1	JONES	10	WEEKLY	120
2	KIRKUP	10	MONTHLY	900
3	DAVIES	10	WEEKLY	150
4	ARMSTRONG	20	MONTHLY	1030
5	KEMP	20	MONTHLY	1005
6	FISHER	30	WEEKLY	150

through the view which restricts their access. A suitable view, V_PAYROLL, is shown below:

```
CREATE VIEW v_payroll AS
SELECT id
       ,name
       ,dept
       ,payment_period
FROM    payroll
WHERE   dept = (SELECT dept
               FROM   mysys_users
               WHERE  username = USER)
WITH CHECK OPTION;
```

This example does not project the SALARY column, so salaries will not be accessible through the view, and the predicate clause ensures that users can query PAYROLL details only for their own department.

There are a couple of potential pitfalls with this solution. First, we must ensure that users cannot simply update MYSYS_USERS to change their department and in this way query records from another department. Second, users could use this view to update, insert, or delete rows in PAYROLL, even if they are not within the user's department, had we not used the qualifier WITH CHECK OPTION to disallow this function.

NOTE   The view V_PAYROLL is unlikely to be an updateable view because it is almost certain that the SALARY column will have the constraint NOT NULL applied to it. Nevertheless, we strongly recommend that the WITH CHECK OPTION be used on all restrictive views since many more views become updateable in Version 7.3.

The use of views to restrict views of data works quite well, but if we have a large table with complex security requirements, we may have to create many views of the same table and to force applications to decide which is appropriate for the current user. Putting such logic in application code is not really desirable, so we need to explore alternative solutions.

Using packages

We can encapsulate all operations on the PAYROLL table in a stored package, or we could develop some triggers. Let's first examine the package solution. The package has methods (procedures/functions) that let us operate on the table or query back rows from the table. The contents and structure of the table are not directly accessible to the user, who has execute permission on the package but no authority to access the table. The owner of the package has full access to PAYROLL, but the calling user does not. When a user executes a stored procedure, or indeed uses a view, it operates with the access permissions of its owner.

Example 10-2 shows our first attempt at the package. The package *k_payroll* ensures that records can be deleted only by the manager of a department and that only the manager of the department can set the *salary*.

Example 10-2. First Attempt at a Package to Implement Data Access Security

```
CREATE OR REPLACE PACKAGE k_payroll AS
my_dept payroll.dept%TYPE;
mgr      BOOLEAN;

PROCEDURE del (p_emp_id INTEGER);
PROCEDURE ins (p_emp_id INTEGER, p_name VARCHAR2
              ,p_dept INTEGER, p_payment_period VARCHAR2
              ,p_salary INTEGER);
PROCEDURE upd (p_emp_id INTEGER, p_name VARCHAR2
              ,p_payment_period VARCHAR2 ,p_salary INTEGER);
END k_payroll;
/

CREATE OR REPLACE PACKAGE BODY k_payroll AS
mgr_flag payroll.mgr_flag%TYPE;
CURSOR  c_me IS
        SELECT dept,
               mgr_flag
        FROM   mysys_users
        WHERE  username = USER;

FUNCTION checkdept (p_emp_id INTEGER) RETURN BOOLEAN IS
dept payroll.dept%TYPE;
  CURSOR c_payroll IS
        SELECT pay.dept
        FROM   payroll pay
        WHERE  id = p_emp_id;
BEGIN
  OPEN  c_payroll;
  FETCH c_payroll INTO dept;
  CLOSE c_payroll;
```

Example 10-2. First Attempt at a Package to Implement Data Access Security (continued)

```
   IF dept <> my_dept THEN
     RETURN FALSE;
   END IF;

   RETURN TRUE;
END checkdept;

PROCEDURE del (p_emp_id INTEGER) IS
— Only Departmental Managers can delete their employees
— Payroll records
BEGIN
  IF checkdept(p_emp_id) AND mgr THEN
    DELETE payroll
    WHERE  id = p_emp_id;
  ELSE
    raise_application_error (-20001, 'Insufficient Privilege');
  END IF;

END del;

PROCEDURE ins (p_emp_id INTEGER, p_name VARCHAR2
               ,p_dept INTEGER, p_payment_period VARCHAR2
               ,p_salary INTEGER) IS
— Can only insert Payroll records in your own dept
— Only manager can set salary (otherwise set to null)
   l_salary payroll.salary%TYPE;
BEGIN
   IF NOT checkdept(p_emp_id) THEN
      raise_application_error (-20001, 'Insufficient Privilege');
   END IF;

   IF NOT mgr THEN
     l_salary := NULL;
   ELSE
     l_salary := p_salary;
   END IF;

   INSERT INTO payroll (id,name,dept,payment_period,salary)
   VALUES (p_emp_id,p_name,p_dept,p_payment_period,l_salary);
END ins;

PROCEDURE upd (p_emp_id INTEGER, p_name VARCHAR2
               ,p_payment_period VARCHAR2 ,p_salary INTEGER) IS
— Can only update Payroll records in your own dept
— Only manager can update salary (otherwise left as it was)
— Cannot change dept

l_salary payroll.salary%TYPE;

CURSOR c_old_salary IS
        SELECT pay.salary
        FROM   payroll pay
        WHERE  id = p_emp_id;
```

Example 10-2. First Attempt at a Package to Implement Data Access Security (continued)

```
BEGIN
  IF NOT checkdept(p_emp_id) THEN
     raise_application_error (-20001, 'Insufficient Privilege');
  END IF;

  IF NOT mgr THEN
    OPEN c_old_salary;
    FETCH c_old_salary INTO l_salary;
    CLOSE c_old_salary;
  ELSE
    l_salary := p_salary;
  END IF;

  UPDATE payroll
  SET    name = p_name
        ,payment_period = p_payment_period
        ,salary = l_salary
  WHERE id = p_emp_id;
END upd;
- Package initialization code
BEGIN
  OPEN  c_me;
  FETCH c_me
  INTO  my_dept
       ,mgr_flag;
  CLOSE c_me;
  IF mgr_flag = 'Y' THEN
    mgr := TRUE;
  ELSE
    mgr := FALSE;
  END IF;

END k_payroll;
/
```

Using triggers

While well encapsulated, the solution shown in the previous section is not ideal. It has too much encoded knowledge of the PAYROLL table, which means that every time we modify the structure of PAYROLL, we have to maintain the package. Also, we haven't tackled the most tricky problem yet—that of supporting queries through the package. In fact, the functionality delivered by this package as it stands is much easier to code as triggers: using triggers gives us much better protection against the impact of changes to the table structure.

One apparent advantage of the package is that we can use persistent variables to hold information about the user (his department, and whether or not he is a manager) rather than having to requery it each time, but we can call a package from inside our triggers so we can still get that optimization.

The real advantage of triggers in this case (provided the triggers are enabled), however, is that they are inescapable: everyone has to play by the same rules. Remember, we are now discussing *data* security rather than *access* security so we should apply our procedural rules to the *data*. And that requires triggers.

Before we go on to tackle the thorny issue of queries, let's examine a trigger solution that uses some of the package *k_payroll*, but replaces much of it. The triggers are listed in Example 10-3 and replace the functions INSERT, DELETE, and UPDATE in *k_payroll*. The package is kept to allow us to take advantage of common code and persistent variables.

Example 10-3. Triggers to Enforce Security on PAYROLL

```
CREATE OR REPLACE TRIGGER pay_bir BEFORE INSERT ON payroll
FOR EACH ROW
BEGIN
  IF :new.dept <> k_payroll.my_dept THEN
    raise_application_error (-20001, "Insufficient Privileges");
  END IF;
  IF NOT k_payroll.mgr THEN
    :new.salary := NULL;
  END IF;
END pay_bir;
/


CREATE OR REPLACE TRIGGER pay_bdr BEFORE DELETE ON payroll
FOR EACH ROW
BEGIN
  IF :new.dept <> k_payroll.my_dept
  OR NOT k_payroll.mgr THEN
    raise_application_error (-20001, 'Insufficient Privileges');
  END IF;
END pay_bdr;
/


CREATE OR REPLACE TRIGGER pay_bur BEFORE UPDATE ON payroll
FOR EACH ROW
BEGIN
  IF :new.dept <> k_payroll.my_dept THEN
    raise_application_error (-20001, "Insufficient Privileges");
  END IF;
  IF NOT K_PAYROLL.mgr THEN
    :new.salary := :old.salary;
  END IF;
  IF :new.dept <> :old.dept THEN
raise_application_error (-20002, "Cannot transfer department");
  END IF;

END pay_bur;
/
```

We are now left with the different issue of how to get procedural control over data access when our database engine has no SELECT triggers. The most obvious approach is to encapsulate the queries in a package, but this has a series of significant disadvantages, some of them dependent on the particular Oracle7 release being used. The most important disadvantages are:

- Very few development tools support the use of procedures for data retrieval.

- Even fewer ad hoc retrieval tools support them (and this is where we are most likely to need the best support).

- Unless all attributes are to be returned on every call (which can impose an undue CPU load), there are major issues to be resolved in terms of how the attribute list is specified and how it is handed to the calling program.

- It is difficult to design a good interface for user-supplied predicates that does not require a parser in the procedure in order to issue efficient queries.

- Array fetching through procedures is supported only in the latest releases of PL/SQL.

- Even once the predicate syntax has been agreed upon, the procedure must use dynamic SQL within PL/SQL, which is available from Version 7.1 onwards, but is both tedious and tricky to code.

These problems have been tackled with considerable success in heavily engineered projects, but they are daunting hurdles for most projects. PL/SQL Version 2.3 has greatly improved support for passing cursors, but as yet there is little real-world experience using this version.

Before we get too distressed, however, let us return briefly to the subject of views, and observe that from Version 7.1 onwards we can call PL/SQL functions from within SQL expressions. There are some implementation difficulties in this area in Version 7.1 (bugs to you and me), but with 7.2 and higher we can reliably code calls to user functions in SQL expressions and have these functions themselves issue SQL. The general principle is illustrated by the example:

```
CREATE VIEW v_payroll AS
SELECT id
     , name
     , dept
     , payment_period
FROM   payroll
WHERE  V_UTIL.CHECK_ACCESS(dept_code => dept) = 'Y'
WITH CHECK OPTION;
```

We assume that the user has made an earlier call to another part of the *v_util* package to register his or her ID, and this approach has the enormous benefit that it is independent of the user name used to connect to the database. On the assumption that you have read enough of our PL/SQL for one chapter, we have left out the code for the function *v_util.check_access* but it can be as simple or as complex as you need.

Backup

It should be obvious to everybody why we need backups. If we suffer a failure or catastrophe with our computer system or data and we have no recent backup, we will lose data. Most organizations need their data, and many will go out of business if it is permanently lost or unavailable for a protracted period; in some applications the corporate survival window is said to be as low as four hours. There are all kinds of failures. No matter how fault-tolerant your hardware and software is, it may fail to protect you from a terrorist attack, a flood, or an earthquake.

Your Backup Strategy

It may not be so obvious why we need an application-specific backup strategy for each project. The truth is that data security is expensive, and we want to tune our investment to match both the importance of the data and the nature of the systems operation. Let's look at the two extremes in backup requirements.

The high end

By their very nature, some systems require 24-hour operation seven days a week (the so-called 24x7 systems). Any downtime is liable to cost the organization a serious amount of money. In such cases, it's essential to make a substantial investment in redundant hardware to fall back on in case of failure. If the main system fails, the backup hardware immediately takes over with little, if any, effect on the user community. In a case of this kind, the backup mechanism needs to be a continuous feed of transactions from the live machine to the standby system so that the standby is always up to date. The Oracle7 symmetric replication technology described in Chapter 12, *Designing for Distributed Databases*, is an effective, although expensive, mechanism for this type of backup. If the loss of a few minutes' work is acceptable at your site, archiving redo logs to the backup site and immediately applying them is another effective option.

The low end

At the other end of the spectrum, some systems are used mainly for query purposes and their data is rarely altered. These systems may not need backing up at all if all the data contained in them can be reconstituted from other production systems (as is often the case with a data warehouse application). However, we have to weigh the cost of having to reconstitute the entire database (from multiple sources spread among many locations) against the cost of the occasional backup.

As you can imagine, the vast majority of systems have requirements somewhere between these two extremes. Our job as designers is to determine exactly what the requirements are by asking questions of key users and operational staff. The following lists contain some sample questions that might help in clarifying the backup requirements for a system.

To users:

- What hours of the day and days of the week is the system required to be fully available?

- Is it acceptable to have occasional periods of planned downtime?

- Is it acceptable to have periods of limited or restricted availability?

- Is there any data which will be unavailable from manual sources following a crash? (This is often the case with telephone order entry systems and data acquisition from sensors and automated feeds.)

- If it is available, what is the acceptable amount of data to be rekeyed in the event of a major failure?

- What is an acceptable time frame to get the system operational again in the event of a failure?

To operations:

- Is there a schedule of nightly batch jobs? (Perhaps the designer should answer this one!)

- When (if ever) will the system be manned by operations and support staff?

- What other applications will be running on the same hardware or across the same network?

- Is there a disaster recovery plan, and is this system covered by it?

- Is there redundant hardware or hardware with spare capacity available?

- What sustained transfer rate can be relied upon for backup? (This is a radically different question from asking for the device transfer rate or network bandwidth.)

- Is there an offsite facility for storing backup media?

- Is there a policy for cycling backup media?

Once we have obtained answers to our questions, we should have a good understanding of the requirements and the framework and we can start proposing solutions. What are the options we have at our disposal?

Image Copies

The Oracle database is stored in a series of operating system files. In terms of backup and recovery, the most important files are these:

- Data files
- Control files
- Redo log files

These can be backed up using standard operating system backup or copy utilities. We refer to this type of backup as a *database image backup*. Please note that each database image backup must consist of all three sets of files, that the sets must be complete, and that they must only be restored as a set. If you try to mix and match from different sets of files, it will all end in tears. Oracle Worldwide Support can help you out of most, but not all, of the problems that you may encounter if you do not have a complete and valid set of data files, control files, and redo log files, but it is a much smarter idea to make sure that you have a complete set in the first place.

If these files are backed up to removable media such as tape (which they should be), they can be moved offsite. When a database file backup is taken, it is essential that the data that is backed up be a single snapshot in time; otherwise, our backups will be about as useful as a chocolate teapot or an ashtray on a motorbike! This means that we have to take the database down while we perform the backup (unless we are running in *archivelog mode*—more on this later). Operating system backup utilities tend to be quick, so the downtime should be relatively short. If your intention is to back up to a slow device such as a tape drive or to use some form of compression on the files, it is best to do a quick disk-to-disk image copy first so that the database can be brought back up. Then run the backup from the copy, as illustrated in Figure 10-1. This is not always practical because of space limitations.

On some platforms, you can achieve the same goal using mirrored or shadowed disks. You'll follow a procedure something like this one:

1. Shut down the database instance.
2. Suspend mirroring.
3. Restart the database instance, now updating only one copy of the data.
4. Take the backup from the copy that is no longer being updated.
5. Resume mirroring.

This approach has great intuitive appeal, but in practice it has many disadvantages. Before you decide to adopt this strategy, you must find out how long it will

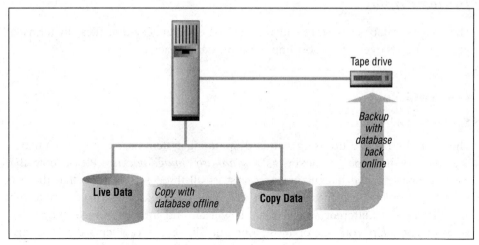

Figure 10-1. Backup using an intermediate copy to speed up the process

take to resynchronize the mirrored copy in step 5. We have seen platforms on which it could take several days and, of course, all the time that you run without the mirrored copy you have no fail-safe protection against media failure.

Image copy backups are relatively quick and easy to perform, but they do have some disadvantages. When it comes to restoring from an operating system backup it is all or nothing: the database is fully restored to the state it was in when the backup was taken, or to some later point in time if you have a set of archived redo logs. This presents problems when a single table needs to be restored without affecting the rest of the database. If a table is accidentally dropped, or if some rows in it are corrupted by application error or user action, then the following steps are required to recover it:

1. Back up the current database.

2. Restore the most recent backup (prior to the one just taken).

3. Save a copy of the table, typically using Oracle's export utility.

4. Restore the backup taken in step 1.

5. Recreate the table saved in step 3, typically using Oracle's import utility.

This process is not only extremely time-consuming for large data volumes, it is quite likely to fail as the result of violations of referential integrity constraints; we strongly urge you not to undertake this type of recovery without first making an in-depth study of the implications for your particular table structure.[*] The cautions about referential integrity continue to apply, but for the repair of localized damage, the process is much faster.

Export/Import

As an alternative (or supplement) to image copy backups we can use Oracle's export utility (EXP). EXPort creates an image of Oracle database objects in an external format, and it offers much more flexibility than image copies. With this utility, we can do any of the following:

- Export a single database object such as a table.
- Export selected database objects owned by a specified user.
- Export the entire schema of a user.
- Back up the whole database.

A useful feature of the corresponding import utility (IMP) is that we don't have to import everything that was exported. Therefore, if we did a complete system export, we can use it to retrieve a single table for our hapless user who accidentally dropped a table or deleted 1,000 rows that he really meant to keep! A further advantage of EXPort is that it implicitly checks the logical integrity of our data. Since the utility reads the data by accessing the tables row by row, it ensures that all rows are intact and that no corruption has occurred. An image copy backup will simply copy corrupt blocks, although these are comfortingly rare with Oracle7.

As you would probably expect, exports take much longer to complete than image copies. When we say much longer, we mean *much* longer. Thus, EXPort is not realistically feasible for very large databases (VLDBs) because the time to export is prohibitively long. The utility also requires that the database be up, and you must make sure that there are no users altering the data while the export is in progress. EXPort can be run in read-consistent mode to allow other users access to the database at the same time, but when updating is taking place, this can cause the export to fail after several hours with a read consistency failure ("snapshot too old"). There is no approach that can be guaranteed to prevent this error.

The IMPort utility takes truly incredible amounts of time, made worse by the requirement both to rebuild all indexes on imported tables and to re-enable all declarative constraints. Even if you can just about fit the export into your operating schedule, you may find that the import time (which will always be greater than the export time) renders the export unusable.

Finally, remember that each time you run EXPort it expects to write all of its output into a single file. If you are still running a version of UNIX with a file size

---

* Since one of us works for BMC Software, we can't resist pointing out that BMC's SQL*Trax product allows the type of damage detailed here to be repaired using the redo log to find out what was done, and to undo it.

limit of two gigabytes, this can present a major problem to the backup of a 30-gigabyte table.

Archivelog Mode

Let's assume that we have a relatively small data base and can afford to take weekly exports and nightly offline file copy backups. What happens if we have a serious disk error at five p.m.? Have we lost a day's work?

The answer is no, so long as we are running in archivelog mode and have managed to preserve all of the redo log files generated since the previous file copy backup. This mode is set in the Oracle initialization file (INIT.ORA) and, when used correctly. it allows us to recover or reapply transactions using roll-forward recovery. So we can restore from the image copy backup and then use the (archived) redo logs to roll the backup forward to either the end of the logs or to some specified point in time. We briefly explain the mechanism in this section, but for more details refer to the *Oracle7 Server Administrator's Guide.*

When a user issues the SQL COMMIT command, any changes that the user has made are likely to still be held in memory (in changed or "dirty" database buffers within the System Global Area, or SGA). Because memory is volatile, the changes have to be written to disk before the commit operation is considered complete. Since writing potentially many blocks to the database could be an expensive operation (in relative terms), the changes (and only the changes) are written to a sequential file called the *redo log*. Once all of the changes have been written, the commit is complete. The actual database blocks are (eventually) written back to the database by a background process called the *database writer* (*DBWR*), but this writing is not synchronized with the transaction.

The redo log itself is actually a series of files which are written to in a circular fashion. The first one is written to until it fills up, then the second is written to until it fills up, and so on until the last one fills up, at which point the first one is overwritten. Archivelog mode means that no redo log file will be overwritten until it has been copied (archived). In the event of a serious crash, the data can be recovered by mounting the last backup. Upon startup, Oracle7 will prompt you to apply the redo logs in the correct order and will recover all data up to the last commit on the last available redo log. In the event of complete machine loss, this will be the last redo log which was archived off the machine onto some transportable medium such as tape.

For most production sites, archivelog mode is an absolute must; users do not want to have to repeat a day's work under any circumstances. There is another advantage of archivelog mode. It is the key part of the mechanism that allows you to take operating system backups while the database is fully operational. These are referred to as *hot backups*. The DBA tells Oracle that a tablespace is about to be backed up using the following SQL statement:

```
ALTER TABLESPACE...BEGIN BACKUP
```

for one or more tablespaces. The backups are then taken of the files comprising the tablespace(s) and the DBA finally informs Oracle that the backup has completed by issuing the SQL statement:

```
ALTER TABLESPACE...END BACKUP
```

DBAs usually get quite good at handling hot backups but they frequently remain deeply mysterious to the rest of the project team. The essential point to bear in mind is that in the interval between the ALTER TABLESPACE...BEGIN BACKUP and the matching ALTER TABLESPACE...END BACKUP the Oracle instance will have written to a number of redo logs and that each of these logs must be applied following a restore of a hot backup.

TIP   A hot backup can only be used to recover to a point in time after it was taken, whereas the traditional offline or cold backup can be used to recover to the point in time before it was taken or, if a complete set of archived redo logs is available, any later point in time.

Standby Sites

The final backup option that we will consider is keeping a standby configuration up to date with the primary site in real time. This is an expensive option, requiring us to have a "spare" database on another machine, often at another site. In the event of failure of the primary machine, the standby machine assumes the role of the failed server and users are switched across.

NOTE   Please do not assume that any of this is easy. Before planning such an approach, you must find out exactly how the users get switched across, how much work they personally have to do (including signing on again), and how long it all takes. There is plenty of marketing collateral around that makes it all sound just as natural as having breakfast, but in reality there are many serious pitfalls to avoid.

On some platforms you can keep a standby current by using remote mirrored or shadowed disks. If the primary site is lost, a processor at the standby site starts an instance to run against the mirror, and this instance startup will first roll back any transactions which were in progress at the time that the primary system failed.

A less satisfactory approach is to use Oracle's *symmetric replication* to make tables on the standby machine shadow those on the live machine. There are several issues with this:

- In Versions 7.1.6 and 7.2, symmetric replication is an asynchronous mechanism and there is no way of guaranteeing the maximum amount of time it will take to propagate a change.

- Version 7.3 offers synchronous symmetric replication (using two-phase commit), so the standby is kept fully up to date but now, of course, the primary site cannot run without its standby online unless you allow the primary to run without replication. Since you were presumably going to allow the backup to run without replication, this may be entirely acceptable.

- Symmetric replication imposes a considerable performance overhead which you should measure before committing to using it. Synchronous symmetric replication over a wide area network may have an unacceptable impact on response time.

A further option is to move archived redo logs from one site to another, typically over a network, and to immediately apply them. This does not keep the standby machine fully up to date, but it has the great merit of requiring no active involvement from the primary other than transmitting the redo logs. This strategy, which has been used with considerable success since Oracle Version 6 days, is now officially supported by Oracle *provided that no other use is made of the standby database*. Although it is asynchronous, and the backup database can be up to one complete redo log behind the primary, it is now possible to limit the maximum time exposure by issuing the SQL command ALTER SYSTEM SWITCH REDO LOG at fixed intervals, and to limit the maximum volume of lost updates by keeping the redo log file size down.

Backup Summary

The following list provides a quick summary of the recommendations we've made in this section:

- Image copies, with the use of archivelog mode and online backups, are enough to fulfill the backup strategies of most sites. Generally, policy decisions are made by the DBA; however, as a designer you can provide invaluable insight into application and user requirements and constraints for backup. Once you've decided on the mechanics, you'll need to think about how long you need to keep older backups and, therefore, how frequently you will be recycling your backup media. The DBA and operations staff also need to sort out issues such as mounting the backup media at the appropriate times and arranging for offsite storage of backups.

- Export (via the EXP utility) will generally not be a key part of your backup strategy (unless you have a small database). We hesitate to specify an exact size, but suggest that almost anything that runs into gigabytes is going to present significant performance problems if you try to recover it using the import (IMP) utility.

- Standby databases can be kept fully up to date using two-phase commit, and this can be automated using database triggers as is done through Oracle's Version 7.3. symmetric replication support. Asynchronous propagation will give much better performance at the cost of some data loss on failure of the primary site.

The transmission of archived redo logs has almost no performance cost at the primary site. For this reason, it is an attractive scheme even though it has the very real potential for data loss with a typical window of around five minutes. The availability of parallel recovery from Version 7.1 onwards makes archive log transmission more feasible than it used to be. (Earlier versions often took longer to apply a log than they did to generate it!)

III

Designing for Specific Architectures

This part of the book discusses design issues for a number of specific Oracle architectures and environments. If you are designing for client/server, distributed databases, data warehouses, or parallel processing, you will find that there are many special considerations.

- Chapter 11, *Designing for Client/Server*, applies Oracle7 design methods to the client/server model. We examine a variety of techniques for distributing the processing to optimize performance and usability.

- Chapter 12, *Designing for Distributed Databases*, takes the data distribution model a step further and looks at the why and how of distributed databases. We examine the various options available with Oracle7 and consider which should be employed in various scenarios.

- Chapter 13, *Designing for Data Warehouses*, looks at the steps involved in setting up and maintaining a data warehouse. We look at dimensional modeling and the various techniques involved in getting the data into the warehouse and extracting it out again.

- Chapter 14, *Designing for Parallel Processing*, describes parallel processing concepts, looks at practical applications of Oracle's Parallel Query Option and Oracle Parallel Server, and discusses such technologies as disk striping and RAID.

11

Designing for Client/Server

Client/server has been one of the hot technical topics of the last five or six years. In the Oracle world, many of the early client/server applications were nothing short of disastrous; one high-profile internal Oracle application gave *three-minute* response times to the most trivial query. It was deployed as a live application for only about three hours before being scrapped. A good number of the people involved in the development of this application still work at Oracle Corporation, but the application is never discussed—it has simply been erased from the corporate consciousness! Many of the factors which led to this disaster have been countered by improvements in hardware and in more recent releases of the software, but some of the key factors remain issues today. As we progress through this chapter, we'll make occasional references back to this failed application to illustrate the importance to the designer of taking account of the special features of a distributed client/server environment.

There are two keys to successful design of client/server applications:

- Careful consideration of the number of message round trips, especially where a wide area network (WAN) may be used—this was the key factor that ensured the failure of the application mentioned above.

- Rigid separation of the business of managing the user interface (the role of the client) from the business of managing the data (the role of the server)— getting this wrong is the major cause of high message traffic between client and server.

Client/server is not a magic cure for overloaded servers, but neither is it snake oil. Used carefully, it gives the designer a cost-effective way of presenting a high-quality responsive interface to the user.

Why Client/Server?

As Microsoft Windows 3.1 emerged as the dominant desktop operating system, we started to see attractive, easy-to-use personal applications, such as word processing and spreadsheets, on the desktop. Available document preparation tools were rapidly extended to include both desktop processing (DTP) and presentation packages. The character or block mode interfaces still being used to access applications running on corporate and departmental servers started to look much less attractive than the interfaces used to access the personal applications. Also, in many cases, the server was critically overloaded. Not only was it handling a heavy database load, but in many cases every keystroke on a connected terminal caused a CPU interrupt on the server to handle the I/O and echo the character back.

The perception grew that by putting "cheap MIPS" on the desktop, then somehow the load on the server could be reduced. Sadly, this central plank of the client/server platform is not necessarily true. A rather more accurate assessment is that, *with careful design*, client/server can offer a much improved user interface without any significant increase in the server workload. One of the great fallacies of client/server is that it will bring a massive increase in server throughput.

Moving to client/server does provide one very clear advantage—the opportunity to offer a *graphical user interface (GUI)* front-end without having to upgrade the servers. It has become obvious that in many (possibly most) applications, a GUI interface has come to be regarded as mandatory—not just a design option—for the simple reason that users of PC applications have become used to them. Users who are going to run server-based applications from their PCs now expect them to behave a lot more like native Windows applications than native server applications.

In most environments, client/server has become inevitable. Your task as a designer is to achieve it in such a way that it works, gives adequate performance, and can be maintained. This chapter tries to guide you through the various design considerations you'll need to address to create a satisfactory client/server application. But first we need to be clear about the meaning of the term itself.

What Is Client/Server?

The term, "client/server," has come to mean accessing a departmental or corporate database from a PC or workstation. However, a client/server architecture does not demand the use of separate hardware. Instead, it is a software architecture in which one set of software components (the clients) use messages to ask another set of software components (the servers) to do things. The servers carry out the required actions and return their results to the clients, again using messages. Both the clients and the servers send their messages not using addresses (as one might expect), but instead using names. The clients, in particular, send their requests to named services rather than to specific machines, relying on some form of *name resolution* to determine the physical server to be used.

Because client/server communication is carried out by messages, the client program and the service can easily be on different machines; also, because the client program knows the service only by name, it is not aware of the hardware identity of the server on which the service is provided. A series of levels of software make this all work out. Clearly, deep down inside the machine, something has to know where the service really is. In an Oracle SQL*Net V2 environment, this information is typically in the file named *tnsnames.ora*.

The key to client/server is that the client sends messages to named services. Doing so has a number of significant advantages:

1. The client process and the server process do not need to be on the same physical machine, though it is perfectly acceptable (to this definition) if they are.

2. The client process and the server process do not need to be running on the same type of hardware or even running under the same operating system, provided that it is possible for them to send messages to each other. Turning this around, the client and the server have no need to know about the other's hardware and software environments. Indeed, making assumptions about these environments is a major cause of difficulty in client/server applications, because apparently trivial changes in the client or server may then render the overall system inoperable.

3. The process can continue ad infinitum; a client can make a request to a named service, which passes it off to another named service, and so on, as sketched in Figure 11-1. The client is completely unaware that the first server has involved other parties (except, of course, that all network operations take time, and this "subcontracting" of the provision of the service often results in unacceptable response time). One of the roles of the cartridges that plug into Oracle's Network Computing Architecture (NCA) (which we describe briefly

in Chapter 12) is to make it much simpler for designers and coders to distribute functionality in this way.

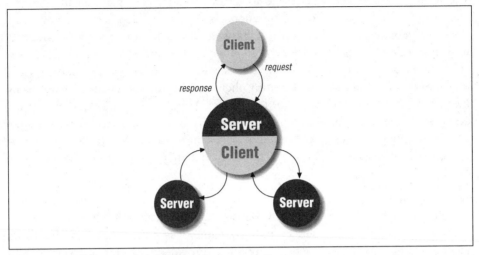

Figure 11-1. Schematic of nested client/server operation

All of these points describe *encapsulation*. This highly desirable state of affairs is one of the keys to all successful design, and it is absolutely critical to the success of any application of client/server techniques. The message processing involved in client/server should be quite familiar to anyone who has used a World Wide Web browser such as Netscape or Microsoft Internet Explorer; these are client/server applications which use the HTTP protocol. Web browsers also illustrate the power of being able to use multiple servers. More traditional client/server applications, especially those using Oracle tools and database servers, have tended to have each client connected to one and only one server.

What Kind of Hardware?

The client/server implementations seen in the late 1980s and the early to mid 1990s have typically used a fairly powerful workstation that runs some form of windowing software and that communicates with a server which was some type of mid-range minicomputer. Initially, the workstations were UNIX variants running Motif; now, they are much more likely to be Intel-based PCs running MS Windows 3.x or MS Windows95. At the time of writing, we're seeing an increasing use of MS Windows NT Workstations used as the client operating system. We're also seeing a growing use of web technology, a technology that renders the nature of the client device invisible—not only to the server but also, with languages such as Java, to the developer of the code that will be running on the client.

In many of the original client/server implementations, the server was a large Digital VAX running VMS. Today, the normal server is a UNIX variant (typically SVR4 running on SPARC, Alpha, Intel, or PowerPC chips), usually with a high MIPS rating, and vast quantities of online storage (disk). We are also starting to see MS-Windows NT Server in this role. The more recent the server, the more likely it is to have multiple CPUs and to support several gigabytes of real memory. Many earlier servers were critically limited by both CPU power and real memory.

Both the client and the server are invariably connected to a LAN which they use as their message highway. In some applications, the client and the server may be on the same physical LAN, though more typically they will communicate through an *intranet*, which is a bounded set of linked networks. Although Ethernet is the predominant technology in Oracle client/server systems, token ring is also used. The client and the server may use any of a variety of communications protocols, including the ubiquitous TCP/IP, which is very widely supported. With Oracle's multiprotocol interchange software, the client and the server may be using different protocols, with translation services being provided by the interchange. At present there are only a limited number of applications which truly operate over the *Internet* which, at its simplest, is an unbounded set of linked networks sharing common protocols. As soon as coverage is extended to the Internet, then we start finding client devices connected over dial-up lines, often at very low bandwidth.

The heavy reliance on LAN technology has become an issue for many organizations that want to support remote users dialing in from home or from a customer site. These organizations have often developed two application suites that fulfilled the same basic tasks. One set of applications would support online users who could connect directly to the LAN. The second set would involve some form of high-level upload/download protocol that exchanged information between client and server in a relatively short session, and enabled users to work largely offline. Things would be so much easier if the remote users could be treated like local users. Since SQL*Net can operate over many protocols, including Winsock, it has always been possible to run, say, Oracle Forms across a dial-up line. The problem has been that both the speed of the line and the message transmission delays often rendered the application unusable! With the emergence of faster modems and technologies such as ISDN, this is now becoming less of an issue. Nevertheless, it's something you need to consider during design. The application must run acceptably over the slowest link that it is required to support.

If the client and the server are not on the same physical LAN, then the LANs must be linked in some way, and this will frequently involve a *bridge* operating over a WAN. These bridges may be three orders of magnitude slower than the LANs which they are linking—although, as we shall see, network bandwidth is not normally a limiting factor in client/server performance. A much more important characteristic is the *round trip time*. It was round trip time that totally doomed the Oracle internal application we mentioned earlier.

Basic Design Issues for Client/Server

There are two main design issues that we need to address in any client/server application: minimizing round trips and carefully selecting the location of processing. The two are irrevocably linked, but certain work *has* to be done in a particular place.

In the final analysis, all operations which involve a physical hardware device such as a disk, a display, or a keyboard must be serviced by the system to which that device is connected; this is true even when the operation is being undertaken at the direct request of some other system. In client/server processing, we should expect to find this happening quite frequently—one system (usually the client) needs something done and makes a request of a server. In almost every case, the client will wait for the server's response before proceeding.

Now we begin to see why the number of round trips and the round trip time are so vital to client/server performance. If the round trip time is half a second and if, during some processing, we ask for service ten times, then we will spend a minimum of five seconds waiting even if the server is responding instantly to each individual request. You may have experienced exactly this effect when you used a Web browser with 15 or 20 "document done" messages appearing before you finally could see the resulting page.

The solution to the round trip problem is to make as few requests as possible or, more correctly, to make compound requests such as "Do A, then do B, then do C, then send me the answer." The use of PL/SQL stored procedures within the database makes this form of request much easier to achieve with Oracle. With Web browsers, the solution is more likely to lie in the way that the server is delivering its response to the original client request.

Over and over again, we hear both managers and technicians talking about the speed or bandwidth of their network as though this was the critical factor for client/server processing. This is not always the case. Using SQL*Net, most of the messages which are sent between the client and the server are quite short (tens or hundreds of bytes, rather than thousands or millions). So the speed with which the network can transmit a one-megabyte file is almost completely irrelevant—which is possibly why network suppliers are so fond of quoting it! The key statistics are the round trip time and the server's maximum packet rate. The round trip time can be measured on most TCP/IP networks using the command *ping hostname* (or *ping -s hostname* if *ping* merely tells you that the host is alive). The time will range from around one millisecond (with both client and server on the same LAN) to perhaps 400msec (where an X.25 bridge is being used). The maximum packet rate will typically be between 1000 and 2000 packets per second, and this represents an absolute hardware limit for the network interface card.

Network bandwidth becomes critical only when long messages must be sent from the server to the client. One feature of any good client/server design is that it minimizes the number of bitmaps being transferred. Home page developers take note: most visitors to your home page arrive in the hope of finding data rather than art. Most users of traditional client/server applications are similarly motivated.

Designing for Client/Server

Our goal as designers of client/server applications is simple and attractive: design your system so that both client and server undertake the tasks that they are good at (and therefore avoid the tasks at which they are not so good). Typically, a client is good at providing an attractive application interface, and a server is good at handling shared data. The obvious solution is to implement the application interface on the client and to perform all operations using shared data on the server(s). To keep the number of packets down, you will bundle up your shared data requests and execute many of them in a single round trip. It sounds so easy, but life is never quite that simple.

A Client/Server Workload Model

The breakdown shown in Figure 11-2 was originally proposed by the Gartner Group to show the variety of ways in which the workload can be divided between the client and the server.

The original breakdown was useful, and can be extended to cover three-tier architectures, but it failed to show the common error of having presentation, logic, and data management all distributed between client and server. The more rigorously you can apply encapsulation to your design, the less likely you are to find small fragments of presentation management logic buried deep in the data management code—and often, quite large segments of the data management task coded directly into the presentation layer. This kind of undisciplined behavior results in complex application code that is highly sensitive to change and that often proves impossible to maintain with any reliability. Unfortunately, this style is common within Oracle projects; this is largely a legacy of SQL*Forms Versions 2 and 3, which encouraged the coding of so-called key triggers (presentation or interface management) which were free to contain SQL statements and database procedure calls.

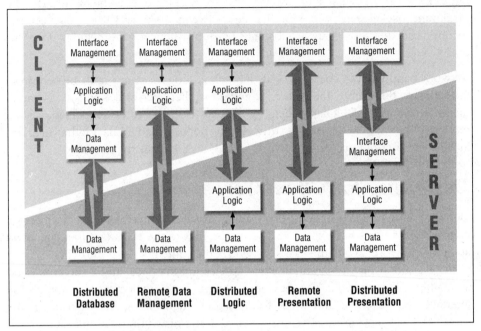

Figure 11-2. Types of client/server computing

Because SQL*Forms Version 2 had so little data transformation capability, programmers also found it necessary to embed formatting rules in the data management code (the SQL). This practice is still prevalent today in Forms triggers containing statements such as this one:

```
SELECT INITCAP(cust_name)
  INTO cust_name
  FROM custs
 WHERE cust_id = :cust_id;
```

This trivial example mixes a presentation requirement (of interest only to the client) with a data management operation (which must be executed on the server). If the retrieval logic is now encapsulated on the server using a procedure call such as the following:

```
...
    :cust_name := CUSTOMERS.FETCH_NAME(:cust_id);
...
```

we find ourselves hiding the data transformation within the package or having to pass formatting codes into the server. It is much simpler and more consistent to simply return the data from the server in its stored form and to apply any required formatting in the client.

Figure 11-2 also does not show n-tier architectures; in these, application management layers which provide the application logic sit between the client and the data server.

The Importance of "Thin Clients"

In Chapter 16, *Determining Where to Locate the Processing,* we will talk about the difference between an interface and a process. Our approach to client/server processing is completely consistent with our discussion there. In an Oracle client/server application, we should be aiming for something between distributed logic and remote presentation (see Figure 11-2), with the client handling only those issues that relate directly to the user interface, and the server handling everything else; this includes all query and update processing and the enforcement of both data and business rules.

Let's deal with the black-and-white areas before exploring the gray ones. Clearly, the client is adept at managing the presentation of data to the user, whether it's in graphical form, as a spreadsheet, or as a bitmapped form-based screen. The client handles all keyboard and mouse events, paints the screen image, and allows the user to manipulate and navigate between objects that are presented on the screen. You would not want your client software requesting masses of raw data (such as entire tables) from the server and having to sort out the data which is of interest from that which is not. Not only would this create excessive network traffic, it would greatly increase the server load. And yet, we have met many designers who appeared to have an irrational belief that data could be extracted from a database and transmitted over a network without causing any significant server load; in fact, both operations can prove very expensive.

The Oracle database server is optimized for selective retrieval—for performing relational operations such as filtering, projection, and join against large volumes of data. The server software is designed to accept requests, process them, and return the status and/or data with the minimum turnaround time.

What you don't want your server to be doing is drawing screen images or running personal productivity tools. Nobody in his or her right mind would recommend such an approach. Yet it's surprising how many sites we've come across where all the client software is contained on a shared drive on the server. Why? Because it makes software distribution easier and ensures that all clients are running the same version. Client software tends to be segmented into the basic core functions in an executable file with many subroutines in link libraries (known as dynamic link libraries or DLLs in Microsoft Windows parlance). Every time a subroutine is called and the DLL is not in memory, then a potentially large binary file has to be downloaded from the server. This may be happening with alarming regularity if the client does not have enough memory.

Now that we've told you that downloading executables is a problem for the conventional PC, we have to acknowledge that this appears to be the direction in which the industry is moving. This movement was first driven by the Web, and also now by Oracle's sponsorship of the *Network Computer (NC)*.

Oracle's Network Computer

What is the NC all about? The principle is that when you are using any Web browser which supports Java, if you have an NC, the client device carries only the enabling software; the rest of the required code comes down the line, along with the data, in the form of *applets*. To make this approach successful, the size of these applets must be carefully matched to the available bandwidth, and the client device must aggressively cache the applets it receives so they don't have to be downloaded again the next time they are needed. This, in turn, raises the issue of cache coherency—that is, ensuring that the client's cache is up to date. If you are using Netscape, this is generally fudged by simply setting to one day the time after which the cache entries are forced to expire. In this way, the client will only have to use an out-of-date page for a maximum of 24 hours.

Traditional client/server systems tend to have only one client type but, increasingly, we find a need to provide application service both to traditional workstations and through Web browsers. In this type of environment, it is much cleaner to have none of the application logic on the client.

SQL*Net Basics

In Oracle, the high-level protocol that occurs across SQL*Net is very simple. Essentially, the client submits SQL statements or PL/SQL anonymous blocks to the server for execution; the server processes them and sends data back to the client. If the statement is a SELECT, then the rows are returned (in response to a FETCH issued from the client). For DML statements and PL/SQL blocks, the data returned is the completion status of the statement and any output parameters. This is illustrated in Figure 11-3.

Oracle has had a full client/server architecture since Version 5, and the system uses this architecture even when the client and server are on the same physical machine. Normally, Oracle uses a two-task architecture in which the client and the server are two separate processes (even if they are on the same machine). On some platforms, they can be combined into a single process although this is not normally recommended because of the risk that the application program might corrupt the SGA and therefore the database itself. Many proprietary operating

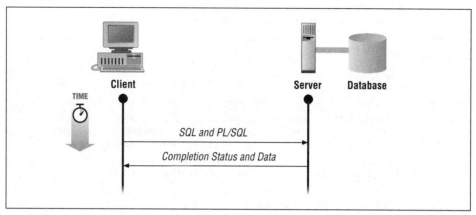

Figure 11-3. The high-level protocol of Oracle client/server

systems, including IBM's MVS and Digital's VMS, allow *privileged libraries*. With these, an application can call a library routine, such as the database server, which has the privilege of looking at the SGA even though the calling program does not. Note that for online transaction processing (OLTP), Oracle's single-task architecture is often about 20% faster than its two-task architecture because of the dramatic reduction in operating system context switches.

In Oracle7, Oracle's developers took a number of important steps to make their client/server architecture more efficient. In many cases, the number of network pairs (round trips from client to server and back) required to execute a single statement has been cut from four to one.

Anatomy of a SQL Statement

Let's examine the anatomy of a SQL statement in an Oracle database to help us understand the effect our applications have on network traffic.

Consider the following SELECT statement:

```
SELECT  ord.id
      , ord.value
  INTO  :ord_id
      , :ord_val
  FROM  orders ord
  WHERE ord.cust_id = :ord.cust_id
    and ord.value   > :threshold;
```

The processing of this simple statement can be broken into five stages: parse, define, bind, execute, and fetch. Unless Oracle's deferred call features are being used, each stage requires at least one network message pair in order to complete. For instance, to complete the parse stage, the client typically sends the statement text to the server, and the server responds with a status code signaling success or failure. (The stages listed in this section should be very familiar to anyone who has programmed using the Oracle Call Interface (OCI) where they have to be coded explicitly.)

NOTE　　Most of Oracle's client tools perform a series of transformations on SQL statements before issuing them to the server. Typically, they remove unnecessary white space, render the statement in uppercase, and number bind variable references. In addition, they typically remove INTO clauses because that part of the operation is performed by the client. Thus, the example statement above might be sent to the server as:

```
SELECT ord.id,ord.value
  FROM orders ord
 WHERE ord.cust_id=:1 AND ord.value>:2
```

No transformations are applied by SQL*Plus, SQL*DBA, or Server Manager.

Here is a brief description of each of the five stages of processing a SQL statement.

Parse

Sends the SQL statement as a text string to the server. The server examines the string, breaks it down, and validates it. The validation is not purely syntactic; Oracle also verifies that all objects which are referenced in the statement actually exist in the database and are accessible to the calling user. Obviously, table names, column names, view names, and sequences are validated. Validation of the referenced objects will require recursive SQL if new SQL statements have to be generated to perform the validation. The parse produces a *parse tree*, an internal representation of the SQL that is held on the server.

Define

The client requests the properties of all variables in the select list (ORDERS.ID and ORDERS.VALUE in this example). To respond, the server uses the parse tree built during the parse stage.

Bind

The client determines the actual value of any bind values in the statement (*:ord_id* in the example) and passes their values to the server.

Execute

The client requests the server to process the statement and produce a set of results. At this point, no result data is returned to the client, only a status. Since this query contains a FOR UPDATE clause, all of the rows must be visited and locked for the execute phase to complete, but the result set still resides on the server. If variables have been bound, then the server's first action is to ask the client to supply the current values of the bind variables. In very old versions, this was done one variable at a time, but Version 5.1 introduced *speedbind*, which requested all of the required values in a single operation. In Oracle7, the library code on the client (knowing that the bind values are required in order to execute the statement) sends them automatically with the execute request.

Fetch

The client requests the server to transmit a subset of the data resulting from the execution of the query. The amount of data returned is governed by the array size (dimension) of the select list variables. Generally, fetches are repeated to fetch subsequent result data until the required amount of data is retrieved (for example, to fill a buffer or screen) or until an end-of-fetch is returned. This is under application control.

Now let's consider some refinements to this model of SQL execution and look at its effect on our design when we are designing for a client/server architecture.

1. If a SQL statement is repeatedly executed, it is not usually necessary to parse or define it again; both client and server can remember the statement from the previous occasion. A rebind is only necessary if the addresses (not the values) of any bind variable have changed since the previous iteration.

2. DML statements (INSERT, UPDATE, and DELETE) do not require a fetch. The statement completes when executed.

3. Oracle has a mechanism known as the Deferred Call Interface, sometimes referred to as UPIALL. This protocol bundles the parse, define, and bind with the execute by holding them on the client and releasing them only when the execute is issued. This can considerably reduce network traffic and improve the overall throughput and response time on a client/server system by employing fewer data packets (although those used are of a greater size). It is used in the more recent Oracle-supplied tools such as Oracle Forms 4.0 and 4.5. If you are using Pro*C for development, then you should install Version 1.6 or 2.0 or above to ensure that you utilize this technology.

4. PL/SQL blocks are similar to DML statements in that no fetch is required. The block is simply executed. All host variable references in a PL/SQL block are treated as bind variables (even if they are fetched into within the block). Using a PL/SQL block to group SQL statements is a good way to cut down on network traffic. As an example, let's take a client application that needs to update the balance of two account tables by 10%:

```
UPDATE  checking_accounts cac
SET     cac.balance = cac.balance * 1.1
WHERE   cac.cus_id = :cus_id;
```

```
UPDATE savings_accounts sac
SET    sac.balance = sac.balance * 1.1
WHERE  sac.cus_id = :cus_id;
```

Even with full call bundling, this will take two message pairs, one for each SQL statement. If the two statements are surrounded with a BEGIN...END pair to form a single PL/SQL block, then only one message pair is required in the best case. (An even better practice would be to encapsulate the application action and move the two statements to the server as a stored procedure; to perform the application action a program would execute an anonymous block containing the stored procedure call.)

Performing a client/server operation in one message pair is good practice in all cases. This should always be your objective if a wide area network is likely to be present between the client and server.

Cutting in the Middle Man[*]

The term "middleware" seems to be enjoying much vogue at the moment. Like many fashionable terms, it is overused; vendors seem to be climbing over each other to jump on the bandwagon with "middleware" products such as ODBC drivers.

How shall we define middleware for the purposes of this book? In our client/server examples we have considered a front-end (client) application firing SQL and PL/SQL at the back-end (server) database. Middleware is a layer of software that sits between the client and the server. It may reside on the server or the client or it may have its own dedicated hardware. It may utilize a TP manager such as Tuxedo or CICS to maximize throughput.

One of the main *raisons d'être* for middleware is to make the front-end application database-independent. The client may have its own high-level language or protocol with which it communicates with the middleware. It couldn't care less whether the middleware passes it on to an Oracle database or a Sybase database. If the middleware product generates SQL that is strictly ANSI-92 compliant, it becomes an even simpler task to swap the back-end database product. Even if portability to another database vendor is not an issue, middleware can protect the client software from changes made to the database structure on the server. In other words, it is another technique for achieving encapsulation.

The trivial example in Figure 11-4 demonstrates the theory. The middleware receives a high-level call from the client via an *application programmatic inter-*

---

* Perhaps in these days of political correctness we should say "Cutting in the middle person," but we prefer the sound of the traditional version and leave it unamended and without apology.

face (API) and translates it into a SQL statement. In this simple example, the middleware does not need to convert the return data from the server; it simply passes it on to the client. The middleware has to have considerable intelligence or an extremely sophisticated mapping layer defined in order to perform these translations of calls into SQL.

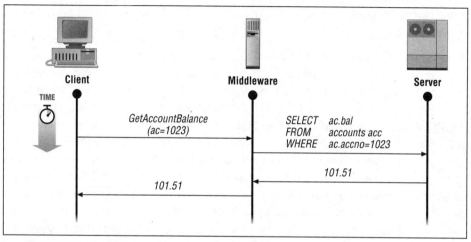

Figure 11-4. Using middleware between client and server

One relatively cheap and straightforward implementation of a middleware solution would be to use only stored procedure/function calls from the client and to develop an entire library or package of procedures and functions to service all application requests. Sometimes this solution is partially implemented, with the client application retaining all SELECT statements which can return multiple rows. However, Version 7.2 brought the ability to pass cursors between applications allowing multirow SELECTs to be sent for execution on the server and the results passed back in a reasonably elegant manner. Support for this functionality has been considerably improved in Version 7.3 and PL/SQL Version 2.3. In addition to reducing network overhead, this design approach makes use of shared cursors and potentially reduces parse overheads.

WARNING   As we've mentioned, providing packages of application services to reduce the amount of mapping required in the middleware gets more complex when support is required for multirow queries. It gets an order of magnitude more complex when the end user requires a full ad hoc query capability. We recommend that you not try to tackle this at project level.

If the advantage of middleware is the ability to avoid database lock-in for your applications, what are the costs and risks? Certainly, diagnosing problems can be a bit of a challenge with the addition of another layer that may be a potential cause of the problems. You may also pay with performance since the middleware has to service requests individually and may not be able to multitask. The result may be that requests are queued, awaiting the middleware, thus introducing an unwelcome bottleneck. Use of a TP manager to drive the middleware should reduce these risks.

One particular side-effect of middleware that can give rise to performance problems involves the use of hints in SQL statements. Some ODBC drivers "streamline" SQL by cutting out comments before dispatching them to the server. But hints for the cost-based optimizer in Oracle7 are contained in comments! More generally, ODBC drivers often reformat your SQL, and this can negate other methods of tuning that you have used. To generalize even further, sometimes the application on the client has knowledge about the amount or content of the expected data that can't easily be expressed to or translated by a generic middleware component. This leads to a temptation to write middleware components for specific applications—which rather negates the purpose of the middleware. It may be a very sound approach, however, to introduce an application logic layer that isolates the interface management on the client from the data management on the database server.

The introduction of such a middle layer means, however, that you have now moved from a simple client/server architecture to a three-tier architecture. Although such architectures have significant theoretical advantages, they have not been well supported by Oracle tools, nor have they been used widely within the Oracle community, though Oracle's Network Computing Architecture should provide direct support three-tier processing. (This topic is also discussed in Chapter 16, *Determining Where to Locate the Processing*.)

Special Design Considerations

This section describes various characteristics of the client/server environment that you need to be aware of when you design applications for this environment.

Caching of Nonvolatile Data on the Client

As we stated earlier in this chapter, there are a number of gray areas in the field of client/server design.

Consider a static lookup table such as fiscal months for an enterprise which is too steeped in its own bureaucracy and accounting practices to use proper calendar months. Table 11-1 shows a sample table:

Table 11-1. A Table of Fiscal Months

FISCAL MONTHS

FISCAL_MONTH	START	END
1	05-APR-1996	05-MAY-1996
2	06-MAY-1996	04-JUN-1996
3	05-JUN-1996	07-JUL-1996
etc..	etc...	etc...

Suppose that many of the key business entities reference FISCAL_MONTH as a foreign key. On client applications, there is a frequent requirement to pop up a list of FISCAL MONTHS so the user can point and click on the relevant one. Each time this operation occurs, the client requests the data from the server even though invariably it hasn't changed since the previous time.

Clearly, we are using network and server CPU resources to perform unnecessary data transfers. The obvious solution is to retrieve the data the first time it is required by the user interface code, and then to hold it locally on the client to service subsequent requests. If the data volumes are small, the client software could make the data request to the server as part of the application startup on the client so that the user interface can rely on the cache always being present. The particular mechanism that is used depends upon the client software. In a Visual C++ application, for instance, you can allocate memory dynamically and hold the data in a linked list of structures. In Oracle Forms 4.5, you can use *record groups* to hold the cached values.

There may be a strong temptation to hold the cached table data in a local disk file, especially when you are writing the client-side code in a 3GL. We normally recommend against this practice because it is, in effect, the project implementation of a distributed database server. In particular, the volume of cached data is normally relatively low (a few kilobytes), and caching in memory consumes only a trivial amount of additional memory. The reason the caches can be kept small is that we have predicated their existence on the assertion that the same data is being continually redisplayed. With the exception of multimedia data, frequently displayed data is, of necessity, short.

Let's look at an arbitrary example, such as a parts descriptions table. We might find that although there are as many as 100,000 parts listed, only perhaps 100 of these are frequently retrieved by any given client. If we could also establish the assertion that parts descriptions are never changed during client/server processing (or that using a marginally out-of-date description does not expose the enterprise to any significant risk), then we might chose to implement either a *rolling cache* or a *least recently used* cache algorithm at the client.

With a rolling cache, each request is first checked to see whether the data is within the cache. If it is already there, it is retrieved from the cache; otherwise, the data is retrieved from the server and is added to the cache before being returned to the interface code. In all cases, the data is passed back to the caller from the cache rather than directly from the server. Each data item (in this case, part description) will be retrieved only once per client session. Unfortunately, if the client sessions run for long periods of time, then not only can the caches get out of date, but they can also get very large. Fortunately, both of these problems can be solved if you have the time and energy to design and code a suitable solution.

You can typically address the problem of a continually growing cache by setting a maximum cache size and keeping only the most recently used items. This is usually called a *least recently used (LRU) algorithm* because when the cache is full and a new entry must be added to it, then the least recently used entry is overwritten.

Cache consistency is a larger problem. You can address this one either by automatically deleting cached items after a specified time interval (such as 30 minutes) or by using a trigger at the server to maintain the date and time of the latest change to the underlying table. The client code can periodically check this derived field and voluntarily invalidate its cache if any changes have been made to the server-side data since the start of cache loading. If the client operating system can accept remote requests (RPCs), then the cache can be automatically invalidated by the server when a change occurs. However, this is a heavily engineered solution which can itself give rise to significant performance problems if there are a high number of clients or if there are frequent changes to the cached objects.

The biggest problem with all such caches, whether trivially simple or highly complex, is that without some form of middleware to hide them, the user interface code must be aware of the existence of the cache and how to request data from it. Therefore, whether or not you use middleware, retrieval of data that might be locally cached must not be through SQL unless there is a database instance running on the client; in this case, we are dealing not just with client/server but also with a distributed database. (This topic is described briefly in the next section from the point of view of client/server processing; the wider implications of data distribution are discussed in Chapter 12, *Designing for Distributed Databases.*)

Application caches provide the most benefits in client/server applications that have an intervening wide area network. The technique can also save significant CPU resource usage even when the client and server code coexist on the same machine. However, the larger a proposed cache becomes and the more complex the suggested cache management algorithm, the more strongly we suggest that you look at alternative design solutions; these may include the use of a distributed database. After all, a cache of the type we have been discussing is nothing more or less than a project-built memory-resident database—and Oracle has already spent a great deal of time and money implementing server code to provide a database server. The Oracle server may have an enormous memory footprint and may require considerable administrative attention, but it does work. A highly complex project-built cache manager may not.

Client-Side Cache—A Case Study

If you are familiar with Netscape Navigator, you should also be used to the concept of a client-side rolling cache. You are also quite likely to have met the problem of cache coherency. In its user options, Navigator allows the user to decide whether pages that have been downloaded should be preserved locally (on disk) and for how long they may be kept. This feature is extremely useful in avoiding the network delays inherent in downloading home pages which feature several hundred kilobytes of bitmapped graphics.

Client/Server and Distributed Databases

What if we have large populations of nonvolatile data, such as product descriptions where there are no frequently referenced occurrences that we can cache? If we can't predict which records will be required, then the only way to eliminate the message traffic for this data is to hold a copy of it in persistent store either at the client or, as we shall see shortly, closer to the client than the central server.

Taking data out of the database and putting it into external files can give rise to all manner of headaches. We could perhaps refresh the files every night so that they never get too far out of sync, but the advantage of keeping your data in the database is that the RDBMS itself guarantees the integrity of your data. As soon as you start relying on data held outside the database, you lay yourself open to having integrity compromised. For instance, someone could come along and inadvertently or maliciously edit your local file. If part of the network is down one night and you miss your nightly update, it's possible that your file will be out of sync with everybody else's. Of course, you could build application scripts which crawl their way around the network, checking the currency of each copy, but this whole exercise is about reducing network traffic!

Very few database-oriented client tools are particularly adept at file I/O. You must also consider how you are going to achieve adequate query processing. Let's accept that if we need to hold significant data locally, then we should hold it in a database (either Oracle or non-Oracle). For purposes of this discussion, we are going to assume that the local database is either a version of Oracle which supports the Distributed Database Option or that it is capable of interworking with this option. This is important because very few developers are comfortable working with multiple database connections open at the same time. Also, as far as we know, few of the Rapid Application Development (RAD) tools in common use give full support to multiple simultaneous database connections. Normally, multiple connections are supported only from 3GLs (and, as an oddity, the little-used SQL*Plus COPY command).

If we have both a local and a remote database, and if we must operate with only one database connection, then we *must* connect to the local database because that is the only way that we can reach it without causing message traffic. Remember, we are trying to reduce message traffic. For each user, his local database engine is the control point for all database activity. The two major implications of this are that any use of location transparency may (and probably will) cause cross-network joins and distributed transactions requiring the use of the two-phase commit (2PC) feature (described in Chapter 12).

Although each successive sub-version of Oracle7 has improved the performance of cross-network joins, we still caution against blindly trusting that these joins will be optimized as expected. We also advise you to check the precise level of optimization implemented in the release(s) that you are running. If there is a non-Oracle server in the equation with access through gateway products, then you should investigate even more carefully.

In the most extreme case we've encountered, a Microsoft Access application was joining a local table in Access to an Oracle table on a remote server. It turned out that the entire Oracle table was being transferred from the server to the client where the join was performed, despite the fact that the SQL statement contained a predicate which, if evaluated on the server, would have returned only one row.

NOTE   The latest versions of the Oracle optimizer are capable of exporting
              a join to a remote server; earlier versions always performed the join
              at the controlling instance.

Introducing a Second Database Tier

By now, many of you will be worrying that we're proposing that Oracle be installed on every client in a client/server network. Aside from the capital cost in terms of both Oracle licenses and having sufficient hardware to run the instances with acceptable local performance, the cost of ownership is likely to render such an approach impractical—there would simply be too many Oracle databases to administer. In addition, even a small update volume to the distributed reference tables could cause a major network load.

There is a halfway house which has worked well for a number of sites. If we accept that message round trip times over a LAN normally don't cause any performance problems, then we can see that having to go over a LAN for our lookups on reference tables should be completely affordable. So, in any environment where we have groups of users attached to the same or closely adjacent LANs. it may make good sense to put a local lookup database onto the LAN and have all references to the main server handled through this intermediate server. This configuration is illustrated in Figure 11-5.

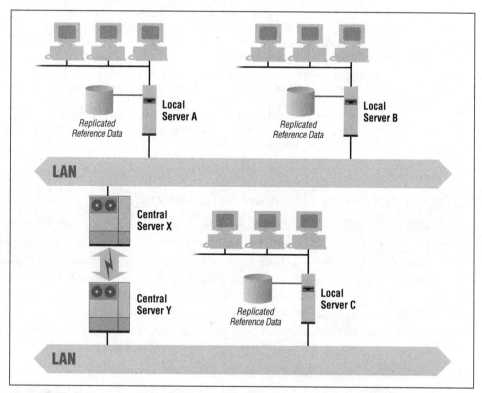

Figure 11-5. Utilizing local database servers for reference data on a network

Their reference data can be kept up to date using either snapshots or symmetric replication, and they can relieve the main or central server of a major part of the query load while also reducing the number of round trips over the WAN. If we assume that most update transactions from the client will perform their updates only at the main server, then the two-phase commit overhead is low because the main server will be invited by the intermediate server to perform an atomic commit. (Snapshots and symmetric replication are described in detail in Chapter 12.)

If you are adopting this architecture, we strongly recommend that you make it transparent through the use of synonyms in the intermediate databases. In this way, clients at remote sites that aren't large enough to justify a local server can connect directly to the main server and run an identical version of the application. Making the data distribution transparent to the application will also allow the DBA to revise the distribution strategy without having to change the application.

TIP   In some client/server environments, you may need to consider application authentication—that is, demanding that the application identify its version in a secure manner to the server-side code. These problems may be reduced by using Web browsers or Network Computers as the client technology because the client logic is in an applet downloaded from a server.

Although this is somewhat outside the scope of this book, we'll also point out that the use of other forms of intermediate servers, especially file servers, can greatly reduce the administrative overhead of application software distribution. These servers also make it harder for an individual user to replace the authorized version of a client application with an unauthorized version.

Using Views to Cut Down on Network Traffic

Let's consider a variation on the message traffic problem. Suppose that we have an application that displays a grid (sometimes known as a multirow block) of orders. One column of the ORDERS table is *cus_id*, which contains the unique identifier of the customer who placed the order. Our application needs to display the more meaningful customer name which must be retrieved from the table CUSTOMERS. For the sake of argument, assume that this application is to be developed in Oracle Forms 4.0/4.5 and that it will look similar to that shown in Figure 11-6.

Obviously, since Customer Name is not a column of ORDERS, we need to write (or generate) some code to handle the field. We need to look up the value when

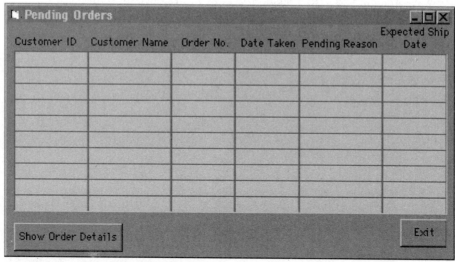

Figure 11-6. Sample screen showing a set of orders

retrieving an order, and possibly provide a list of values on the field so the user can select the customer from a list of names when inserting new orders.

Your first instinct, especially if you are long in the tooth Forms hackers like us, may be to implement the query functionality as a *post-query trigger.*

```
POST-QUERY
SELECT cus.name
INTO   :ord.cus_name
FROM   customers cus
WHERE  cus.id = :ord.cus_id
```

This is a simple and highly effective indexed lookup, but it fires once for every row that is displayed on the form. So for our simple form, we have to make one additional round trip to the server per row on the multirow form just to get the customer name. The impact of this is much greater than you might realize at first, because Oracle Forms makes good use of the array fetch to fetch all of the rows for each screen-full in a single round trip. So, if there are 10 rows per screen, our simple trigger can increase the message traffic from 1 to 11 round trips.

NOTE   This assumes that ten rows are fetched and ten rows displayed. By default, Oracle Forms initially fetches one row more than can be displayed in the block. It does this to make the most efficient use of the array interface and to correctly show whether there are additional rows available.

One way of getting back to a single round trip to retrieve all of the data for many rows is to define a view and base the form on the view rather than the ORDERS table. The view is a join of CUSTOMERS and ORDERS defined as follows:

```
CREATE OR REPLACE VIEW v_orders
      ( id
      , cus_id
      , cus_name
      , date_taken
      , pending_reason
      ...
      ) AS
SELECT ord.id
      , ord.cus_id
      , cus.name
      , ord.date_taken
      , ord.pending_reason
      ...
   FROM orders ord
      , customers cus
   WHERE ord.cus_id = cus.id;
```

The customer name column, *cus_name*, is now a base field on the form, and the server can feed the client the data in a single fetch. However, a series of issues arise concerning both query efficiency and updatable views. Our position on each of these is highly release-dependent; as you would hope and expect, the later the release, the less the problem.

In every Oracle release prior to 7.3, views that contain joins cannot be subject to DML, which means that INSERT, UPDATE, and DELETE are not permitted. Version 7.3 supports updatable views, although, as you might expect, there are a number of restrictions. In any view, the columns which can be updated must come from a single table, and that table must be *key preserved*. At its simplest, this means that the join key(s) cannot be updated.

Until or unless you have Version 7.3 (or higher), you will have to code or generate ON-INSERT, ON-UPDATE, and ON-DELETE triggers in your form to perform updates through a block based on a join view—or, indeed, on any non-updatable view. These triggers, which are normally quite straightforward to code, simply issue explicit DML against the underlying tables of the view. In many cases, it is only necessary to issue DML against one such table. In our example case, this would almost certainly be the ORDERS table since it's extremely unlikely that we would use a multirow ORDERS block to amend customer names.

WARNING These explicit ON-triggers will, of course, continue to work perfectly well even after you migrate to 7.3 whether or not your view turns out to be updatable. There is now a distinct inelegance, however, because your form (or, more precisely, your block) now relies on the definition of the view. If, for some reason, you were to recode the view V_ORDERS to select from the table ORDERS2, and you did not also recode the Forms triggers, then the triggers would attempt to update the wrong table. If you were lucky, this would result in an error. If it is not your lucky day, you will end up applying the update to the wrong table, which is not good news.

An UPDATE or DELETE will probably fail, provided that it attempts to reference the target row using rowid (reference by rowid is standard practice for Forms UPDATE and DELETE operations on base table rows), but an INSERT is quite likely to succeed!

View Optimization

The query optimization issues are more problematical. Most complex multirow blocks must perform lookups against not just one, but many other tables. Often, the foreign key allows null values (the relationship is optional), so the view must be coded with outer joins. The initial reaction of both developer and user to view-based blocks is usually positive because it is trivially possible to use any of the fields as the basis for a query, removing the traditional problems associated with "non-base table queries." Unfortunately, although the solution is functionally rich and also causes minimal message traffic, it can have severe implications for both server load and response time.

The simple view quoted in the following definition may help as an example. In order to keep this example reasonably short, we've omitted a number of the columns which one would expect to see in an ORDERS table. However, it does show both the basis for a "star join" and the use of outer joins to handle code fields which may be null.

```
CREATE OR REPLACE VIEW v_orders
      ( id
      , settlement_currency
      , quotation_currency
      , sales_office
      , customer_name
) AS
SELECT ord.id
      , cc1.name
      , cc2.name
      , sof.name
      , cus.name
```

```
FROM    orders     ord
        , currencies cc1
        , currencies cc2
        , sales_offs sof
        , customers  cus
WHERE   ord.cus_id = cus.id
AND     ord.se_cur = cc1.code
AND     ord.qu_cur = cc2.code(+)
AND     ord.sof_id = sof.id(+);
```

Star joins are so-called because they can be represented like a star network. In the following example, there is a star query against the view V_ORDERS.

```
SELECT id
       , customer_name
FROM    v_orders
WHERE   se_cur = 'UK Pounds'
AND     qu_cur = 'US Dollars'
AND     sof_id = 'North America'.
```

We have selective predicates against three tables; each has a join predicate to ORDERS, but has no relationships with the other tables. The ORDERS table is at the center of the star. The best strategy for the join is to:

1. Execute query steps against the currencies tables (twice) and the sales office table.

2. Form a Cartesian product of the results of these queries (and, in this case, the Cartesian product will have only one row).

3. Use the Cartesian product to join to the ORDERS table.

4. Join from the ORDERS table to the CUSTOMERS table.

Steps 1, 2, and 3 are the star join, and versions prior to 7.3 produce poor query plans for star queries. Unfortunately, even the use of hints does not particularly help for two reasons: First, the query engines in earlier releases do not have a really good strategy available to them for the hint to select; second, in most Forms applications, it is difficult to predict which of the possible arguments will be supplied (since these are entered as query criteria) and this will change the required plan. For instance, we cannot use the same sequence of table references if the two currency names and the customer name (but not the Sales Office) have been specified. Without star join logic in the query engine, the best approach to a star join is to code it procedurally.

The problem with outer joins is that Oracle's query optimizer will never produce a query plan that goes "the wrong way" across an outer join. This is the case even if a predicate is present that shows that no outer join need be made for the data being retrieved. In this example, therefore, the existence of the outer joins means that the star query strategy cannot, in fact, be used. The join order will be:

1. Execute the query against the CURRENCIES table to get code for quotation currency.

2. Use this code to join to the ORDERS table.

3. Join from the ORDERS table to the CUSTOMERS table, the CURRENCIES table, and the SALES_OFFS tables, executing filters against the second and third tables after the joins.

If, as seems likely, very few orders are quoted in U.S. dollars but are settled in UK pounds, this will be a highly inefficient query plan. The solution, as ever, is to take procedural control over the join. We can do this in one of two places, the client or the server.

If we implement the procedural solution in the client, then we are going to increase message traffic—and our original motivation for basing the block on a view was to decrease the number of required network round trips. If we were to base the block on a view, but prevent all use of the view by adding ON-SELECT, ON-FETCH, and ON-LOCK triggers which call server-side PL/SQL procedures, then we could fully encapsulate the query logic on the server. This would guarantee that the round trips would be limited to one to initiate the processing, and one per row. For a single-row block, this approach is completely acceptable. However, the more rows that have to be populated in a multirow block, the less acceptable it becomes. Nevertheless, it still offers a considerable reduction in the number of messages if the alternative is to use many field-level triggers to perform the lookups, and it allows the complexity of non-base table queries to be handled in server-side logic rather than client-side logic.

Three procedures are required, and these should be in a package which uses a persistent package cursor. In our example, the procedures might be declared as follows:

```
CREATE OR REPLACE PACKAGE order_query IS

    PROCEDURE params
            ( ord_id               IN   NUMBER
            , settlement_currency  IN   VARCHAR2
            , quotation_currency   IN   VARCHAR2
            , sales_office         IN   VARCHAR2
            , customer_name        IN   VARCHAR2
            );

    FUNCTION  fetch_row
            ( row_id               OUT  VARCHAR2
            , ord_id               OUT  NUMBER
            , settlement_currency  OUT  VARCHAR2
```

```
                    , quotation_currency   OUT VARCHAR2
                    , sales_office         OUT VARCHAR2
                    , customer_name        OUT VARCHAR2
                    ) RETURN BOOLEAN;

        FUNCTION  lock_row
                    (row_id               IN VARCHAR2
                    ) RETURN BOOLEAN;


        ...


        END order_query;
```

The implementation cost of this full encapsulation approach is high because the server-side procedure must use dynamic SQL to build the queries required for each combination of supplied field values. However, the techniques required are well documented and, in most cases, the resulting code results in a reasonable reduction in message traffic. It also offers the best opportunity for minimizing the query execution overhead.

We recommend that you consider taking this approach for all heavily used client applications where you are concerned about the number of message round trips and where you must support query through non-base table fields. If all queries can be restricted to specifying base table fields as parameters, then the simpler expedient of using a join view as the base table for the forms block is likely to prove effective.

We are aware of at least one project which set out to reduce the message traffic by having the FETCH_ROW function return several rows, with each variable passed back containing a list of values packed into a single string. This requires extra code on both the server side and the client side. Although this is both inelegant and CPU-consumptive, it can reduce the number of round trips to the same level as for views (one per screen-full).

Data Validation in a Client/Server Environment

In the heady days of Oracle6, developers got into the habit of coding all of the business rules and constraints into the applications because there was nowhere else to put them. More often than not, the same code would have to be repeated in several applications, with all the problems that this entailed for maintenance and consistency.

With Oracle7, we now have the ability to define procedures, constraints, and triggers in the database, so we need to write them only once and can enforce them globally. However, there remain strong arguments for implementing data validation within the user interface as well as within the database server.

Client applications can either validate data as it is entered or can defer validation until the operator decides to commit the changes. There are arguments for both methods. The choice depends largely on the nature of the application and the expertise of the end users. Most applications use a mixture of the two techniques, validating individual fields at entry but deferring cross-field and cross-record validation until the commit is signaled.

It is certainly frustrating for a user to spend time keying a lot of detail into a form only to be told when committing that the first field he entered was invalid. If it isn't possible to recover, the user has to throw away the work—which does not make for happy users or for a popular system. On the other hand, if the form validates data as it is entered, then the designer has to choose between duplicating validation on the client or making frequent calls to the server, thus increasing network traffic. In our opinion, this extra traffic is preferable to the duplication of code, and we favor server-side validation wherever it is affordable. The use of intermediate servers (as described in the previous section) can help to reduce the impact of this approach on message traffic.

One drawback of the immediate validation of data is that valid data (we hope the vast majority of data) may be validated twice. The second validation occurs when a row is committed and the validation trigger on the table fires. As we have stressed in a number of places in this book, we don't want to take this trigger off since it's the main guardian of the integrity of our database; in particular, it protects the database against users with access to ad hoc tools. This is illustrated in Figure 11-7, an example in which a credit limit cannot exceed the amount shown.

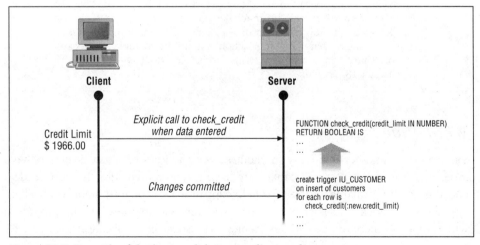

Figure 11-7. Example of duplicate validation in client and server

The *check_credit* function is called twice—first, explicitly from the form to provide immediate feedback on data entry, and second, implicitly by the trigger when an insert or update event occurs on the table.

Another reason sometimes given for implementing validation at the client end is that it can provide the user with more meaningful error messages than those that come from the server on constraint violation or trigger failure. We believe that this argument is facile. The client software can and should intercept messages and translate them rather than having to contain and perform the detailed validation logic.

What is important is that you have a comprehensive set of GUI development standards that clearly define a consistent approach to validation that is enforced throughout the application. Forms that were originally developed in Oracle Forms Version 3 or earlier and are converted using a conversion tool still tend to behave like a Forms 3 program despite having the appearance of a GUI. They still have a lot of the validation on navigational events. These converted forms do not tend to mix well with forms that were developed from scratch in Forms 4.5. The converted forms are very likely to need rewriting. Likewise, it is an appealing concept (especially for marketing departments within application vendors) to have the same source code for both character- and GUI-based versions of the same application, but we believe that this is basically a pipe-dream because of the compromises you have to make.

TIP   Remember that as long as there is good trigger-based data integrity
               enforcement, client-side validation does not need to take locks. By
               having your application avoid taking locks until the last possible mo-
               ment, your users will be much less likely to encounter lock con-
               flicts, though they will from time to time get commit-time messages
               telling them that their transaction cannot be completed because
               something has changed. This topic is discussed further in
               Chapter 18, *Locking*.

What Time Is It?

Time presents another quandary in client/server applications. Most designers have a requirement (or at least think that they have a requirement) for the current date and time to be available in the client. Except in a DCE environment, each client has a system clock and each server has a system clock; these clocks provide a wide range of uncoordinated times. Which one does the application pick to use?

Coupled with the problem that the same point in time is stated differently in different time zones, this whole situation is something of a mess.

NOTE   The Distributed Computing Environment (DCE) is a standard that specifies how a *cell* of networked machines may interwork. In this context, a cell may be loosely described as *a group of machines with a common purpose.* One of the requirements of DCE is that the cell must have a minimum of three *time servers,* and an algorithm is available to request time in a manner which is guaranteed to give a consistent value across the entire cell.

              Oracle supports the use of DCE and can be configured to derive SYSDATE using DCE time services. Of course, there is a performance overhead associated with using DCE.

If you simply wish to date- and time-stamp a new or updated row, you can dispatch a SQL statement to the server with the SYSDATE pseudo-column used to supply the data value. SYSDATE will be evaluated and the server's date and time supplied; this approach clearly works for time-stamping and is acceptable for the vast majority of applications. A sample SQL statement of this type is shown here:

```
UPDATE orders or
SET    ord.tot_amount = ord.tot_amount * 1.01
       ,ord.latest_update_dt = SYSDATE
WHERE  ord.cus_id = 1024;
```

But suppose that the applications require the user to actually see the time stamp on the record before deciding whether or not to commit it. Now there is a choice! The application may request the date and time from the server, or may request it from the local client clock. The actual mechanism for doing this will vary from application tool to application tool. Many people are surprised to find out that when a local PL/SQL procedure running in an Oracle Forms application references SYSDATE, it causes a call to the server to retrieve the current value. The only means of referencing the local clock is by using the $$DATE$$ or $$DATETIME$$ values as defaults for Forms items.

TIP   Don't mix these two approaches—that is, don't use $$DATETIME$$ to default a date and time and then use SYSDATE to perform validation on it. The two may have little in common except their format.

Most client tools provide a call to get the current time from the client clock. For instance, Visual Basic has the *Now* function.

When you are making a choice about where to obtain the time, be sure to consider what the application is doing and exactly what the time is required for. We recommend that wherever the time is to be posted to the database, you should use server time; if your database is distributed, you should code carefully to take the time from the most central server. As a general rule (which has little to do with client/server), any procedure which uses time should acquire it once and only once so that each time it posts is the same. Few things are more frustrating than trying to code a join on a timestamp only to discover that the particular time in question mysteriously spans two or three seconds because SYSDATE has been referenced more than once within the same long-running transaction.

If your application contains scheduling components where events are intended to be coordinated between network nodes, it is even more important to use a single clock or some form of network time service. Again, remember that if you opt for a single clock, it should be the one on the most central server.

12

Designing for Distributed Databases

This chapter continues our examination of how to extend design techniques to take networking into account. In Chapter 11, *Designing for Client/Server*, we discussed the effect of the client/server model on Oracle design. The next logical step is to look at the impact of distributing the data storage and management to more than one server. As soon as you do this, for whatever reason, you have entered the weird and wonderful world of the distributed database.

When Should You Use Distributed Databases?

There are many factors you need to consider in deciding whether or not to use a distributed database design. Of these, we think the following are the most important:

- The desire to place frequently referenced data close to client applications that need to reference it, thus minimizing network round trips and access time

- The desire to place volatile data in a single place, thus minimizing the problems inherent in having multiple updatable copies of the data

- A reduction of the impact of a single point of failure such as a server going down

If these factors are key to the success of your applications, then distributed data-base may be for you. Don't enter into it lightly, however—designing a distributed database is not a trivial task, nor is maintaining such a database once it is up and running. There are many ways to achieve data distribution. In this chapter, we'll lead you through the maze and, we hope, give you enough information so you can make an informed decision.

Chapter 11 gave an example of a specific type of three-tier architecture, client-server-server. The purpose of this example was to show how a local server could take advantage of the responsiveness of a local area network to satisfy requests for access to (relatively) static data, which was replicated through the middle tier, with the more volatile data held on central server(s) where it could be more easily shared.

Although Chapter 11 did not explore all of the implications, the example shown in Figure 12-1 has two linked central servers, each directly connected to a number of intermediate servers. For purposes of this discussion, let's assume that the link shown between these two servers is necessary—that is, that it is not possible to divide up the central data in such a way that all of the records of interest to the clients of A and B can be held on X and that all of the data of interest to clients of C can be held on Y.

Figure 12-1, then, is our sample distributed database application; it holds five copies of the reference data and two copies of the operational data. Although it is still a relatively simple topology, this example can be used to illustrate the key features and problems found in distributed database applications. These include:

- Data consistency—making sure that whichever client is used at any given point in time, the user is presented with the correct and consistent data and that any updates made from that client are secured at commit.

- Performance—making sure that both the overall throughput and the respon-siveness of the application at each client meet the requirements.

- Availability—making sure that the application is sufficiently reliable.

Evolution of Oracle Support for Data Distribution

Oracle began to offer partial support for distributed database with Oracle Version 5.1 and SQL*Net, which allowed remote queries through database links. With SQL*Net suitably configured, the data dictionary entries shown in the following example could be used to achieve the twin goals of *location transparency* and *location independence*.

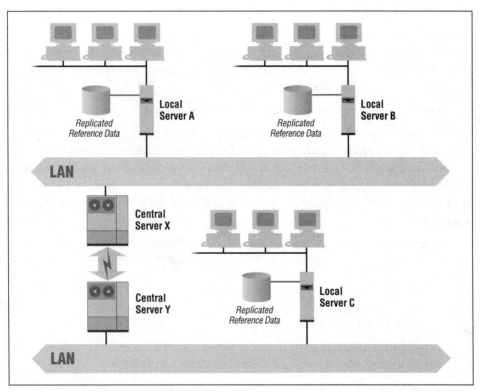

Figure 12-1. A typical network topology

```
CREATE PUBLIC DATABASE LINK elsewhere
    CONNECT TO system IDENTIFIED BY manager
    USING 'T:hp34:appdev'.

CREATE PUBLIC SYNONYM dept. FOR scott.dept@elsewhere;
CREATE PUBLIC SYNONYM emp  FOR scott.emp@elsewhere;
```

What do these terms mean? With these entries in the data dictionary, the SQL statement that follows will retrieve the required data from EMP and DEPT just as though both of the tables were in the database to which the user connected. The location of the tables, that is, the database in which they reside, is *transparent* to the writer of the query even though it did have to be known to the administrator who made data dictionary entries. In addition, these required entries were made *independently* of the target database and tables.

```
SELECT d.dname
     , e.ename
  FROM emp  e
     , dept d
 WHERE d.deptno = 10
   AND d.deptno = e.deptno;
```

Database Links

Database links represent the only mechanism for referencing an object in a database other than the one to which the application is connected. Their use can be *implicit* through a synonym, as in the previous example, or *explicit,* as in the next example:

```
SELECT ename FROM emp@elsewhere WHERE empno = 7319;
```

As the syntax suggests, each database link that is in use requires a connection to be made to the remote database in question. In Oracle, database connections are expensive in terms of both the CPU used to create them and the memory used to maintain them. A total of four database connections are required to execute the next query, one for the original connection and three for connections via the database links.

```
   SELECT c.cust_name    — get customer, product name, quantity
        , p.prod_name    — for any product where the customer has
        , SUM(l.qty)     — bought and paid for over 100 pieces
     FROM custs@hq       c
        , ordrs@sales    o
        , lines@sales    l
        , prods@mktg     p
    WHERE o.cust_id = c.cust_id
      AND l.ord_id  = o.ord_id
      AND p.prod_id = l.prod_id
      AND l.qty_id >= 100
      AND o.status  = 'PAID'.
```

When there are "popular" servers—those which are the subject of many open database links—the total number of open Oracle connections to these machines may become high enough to cause excessive paging. Later releases of Oracle7 not only allow the administrator to set the maximum number of database links that a process may have open (via the INIT.ORA parameter DB_LINKS), but also allow a session to close a database link (which it has used but which it does not wish to retain as an open link) that is using resources at the remote server. The commands for this example are shown here:

```
ALTER SESSION CLOSE DATABASE LINK hq;
ALTER SESSION CLOSE DATABASE LINK sales;
ALTER SESSION CLOSE DATABASE LINK mktg;
```

Unfortunately, connecting to Oracle uses a significant amount of CPU at the server end of the link, and so it may not be efficient to close a database link if there is any substantial probability that you'll need it again in the immediate future. The one megabyte or so of memory being tied up at the remote server may be a lesser evil than incurring additional connect and disconnect overheads later on. On the other hand, if the remote servers are resource-critical, and if you know that the links are unlikely to be reused, then closing them will conserve resources. It will also destroy location transparency and will require a richer application than most designers or coders might choose to implement.

Distributed Joins

In Versions 5 and 6 of Oracle, remote access through database links could be used only for queries. In addition, there were a number of performance problems which particularly affected joins. In many cases, entire tables would be fetched across the network in order to perform a join in the server to which the user had connected. This was not a major problem with a 14-row EMP table, but it did present a major hurdle to the scalability of applications which used distributed queries.

NOTE   The solution to the remote join problem illustrated in the EMP and DEPT example above was to create a join view at the remote database, create a local synonym for this view, and then retrieve through this view. Distributed joins have caused performance problems throughout the history of distributed database support. The strategies have improved with time, and the later releases of Oracle7 generate execution plans that are adequate in the majority of simpler cases.

We recommend against the use of *any* distributed join without first testing it at production data volumes. If the performance is not satisfactory, you can then consider various options:

- The join can be recoded to reference one or more views, as mentioned in the previous Note, to move key parts of the query optimization to servers where they will be optimized more effectively.

- The join can be performed by the application, using remote SQL as appropriate. We have seen a number of cases in which this strategy was effective, but the network overhead will increase progressively with the number of remote queries and fetches that have to be issued. The technique is best employed when the remote data can be acquired in one, or very few, discrete queries.

- The distribution of the join can be altered by moving one or more of the tables to a different database (or replicating the data in some way). This solution requires a fundamental change to the design, and several different distribution strategies may have to be tried before an effective one is found. This is why we are so anxious to test the proposed distributed join early in the project cycle.

This last approach brings us to the heart of the issue of distributed database design:

> The data distribution policy should be driven by the application's performance and availability requirements rather than by enterprise politics.

It is our experience that executive committees frequently mandate a data distribution policy, but they rarely (if ever) take steps to establish its feasibility. In many real-world cases, the data distribution policy is set on the basis of *data ownership*, a totally meaningless concept with which most senior managers feel blissfully happy. Many user managers also suffer from an obsession with being physically close to their data. As children, they probably used to cling tightly to their teddy bears and refused to sleep alone!

If you find that your management cannot be prevented from discussing the relationship of various departments or individuals to parts of the data domain, then you will find it most helpful if you teach them to use terms like *responsibility* and *access requirements*. If you are told that some division *owns* the Parts Stock data, and that this data must therefore be physically stored in the main warehouse, then ask a more senior manager the following:

- Is the warehouse manager solely responsible for the accuracy of the data?

- Has any member of the warehouse staff has ever lost a file from his PC?

- Will the manager take personal responsibility for providing secure access to the parts data by whomever needs access to it?

If you want to implement well-designed applications, it can be very useful to be an external consultant; it makes it so much easier to ask these kinds of pointed questions!

Remote Updates

The inability of Versions 5 and 6 to support remote updates could, of course, be very simply overcome in a 3GL by making explicit connections to more than one database instance. With these connections in place, a program can update wherever it chooses, but it also has to issue an explicit commit to each of the instances at which it has issued any DML. This approach is still feasible with the current releases of Oracle. However, developers have rarely taken this approach (either now or then) for two very good reasons: no courses (at least none we're aware of) teach multiple connections and no RAD tools directly support these connections. As a result, they are normally available only from a 3GL.[*] The steps required are shown below (using the embedded SQL syntax supported by Pro*C):

```
EXEC SQL CONNECT :user_and_passwd AT :local_db;
EXEC SQL CONNECT :user_and_passwd AT :remote_db;
    . . .
EXEC SQL DELETE FROM dept AT :remote_db WHERE deptno = :dept;
EXEC SQL DELETE FROM emp  AT :local_db  WHERE deptno = :dept;
    . . .
EXEC SQL AT :remote_db COMMIT WORK;
EXEC SQL AT :local_db  COMMIT WORK;
```

This approach raises the (largely theoretical) problem of what to do if the second commit were to fail, because by then the first commit cannot be undone and we will have orphaned records (employees whose department no longer exists). Whatever pragmatic steps we take to overcome this situation, we are left with the unfortunate fact that for at least some period of time, an inconsistent distributed database will be exposed to other users.

The reason we describe this problem as "largely theoretical" is that all of Oracle's checking is done when the DML is issued, so the risk that a commit will fail is very low; it will normally occur only when the redo log cannot be written for some reason. However, if we take the full family of problems from which this solution can suffer—especially when several instances are involved—then we do want the database engine to solve them for us. The solution is the *two-phase commit*, often referred to as *2PC*.

Two-Phase Commit

With the two-phase commit solution, we can rewrite our example as follows:

```
EXEC SQL CONNECT :user_and_passwd;
    . . .
EXEC SQL DELETE FROM dept@remote_db WHERE deptno = :dept;
EXEC SQL DELETE FROM emp            WHERE deptno = :dept;
    . . .
EXEC SQL COMMIT WORK;
```

Not only does the software guarantee that the entire transaction is either completely committed or completely rolled back, but we can (if we wish) also regain the advantages of location transparency and location independence by using synonyms in place of the explicit use of database links.

How the two-phase commit works is a major subject in its own right, and in a later section we'll look at some of the characteristics of Oracle's support for 2PC.

---

[*] Although it is true that RAD tools do not support multiple connects, note that the SQL*Plus COPY command is implemented using multiple connects.

At this point, we'll just outline the essential logic of the feature: When the commit is issued, one of the database instances involved in the transaction takes on the role of being the coordinator. This instance selects one of the instances as the *commit point* and instructs all of the other instances involved (which may include itself if it is not the commit point) to prepare. In effect, it asks:

"If I were to ask you to commit, could you do so?"

This is the first phase.

Once all of the other instances have agreed to commit, the commit point is asked to perform a normal commit. Depending on the result of this commit, the coordinator asks all of the other instances to either commit or to roll back. This the second phase.

Of course all manner of things can go wrong. Individual servers can fail at any point in the process; network links can fail at any point in the process; and the software has to be able to guarantee the integrity of the data whatever happens. The net result is that not only is there considerable message traffic, but also potentially persistent block level locks are taken.

Oracle7 Data Distribution Features

After Oracle released an implementation of two-phase commit in Version 7.0, the company used this base functionality to provide a series of features to help projects to implement data distribution. The most important of these are listed here; in parentheses is the number of the release in which the feature first appeared:

*   Remote DML (7.0)
*   Synchronous remote procedure calls (7.0)
*   Snapshots (7.0)
*   Unlimited triggers per table (7.1)
*   Asynchronous remote procedure calls (7.1.6)
*   Consistent snapshots (7.1.6)
*   Updatable snapshots (7.1.6)
*   Asynchronous symmetric replication (7.1.6)
*   Synchronous symmetric replication (7.3)

Each of these features is discussed later in this chapter. With the exception of unlimited triggers per table, they require licensing and installation of Oracle's Distributed Option, and the last three items listed also require that Oracle's Data

Replication Support be installed. Both the Distributed Option and the Data Replication Support are typically available at extra cost; contact your account manager for Oracle's current policies on pricing and packaging of these components.

Six Entity Properties Essential to Resolving Data Distribution

Before we describe the issues relevant to design that are presented by each of the Oracle features listed above, we need to take a look at the ways in which analysis can help us to refine our views on how to distribute data within an application. Or course, the documentation prepared during the analysis phase should refer to entities, rather than tables. The analysts need to define, for each entity, the following properties relevant to planning data distribution:

Availability
How much of the time the information needs to be available

Reliability
How important it is to have access to the current value

Visibility
How widely query authority is granted

Accessibility
How often the information needs to be queried

Mutability
How widely change authority is granted

Volatility
How often the information needs to be changed

If the entity can be partitioned, the analysis should also provide the *fragmentation schema* describing the following:

- Any mappings which may be used to partition the entity into fragments.

- How the fragments are defined.

- From where each fragment will be queried and updated—that is, the fragment's visibility, accessibility, mutability, and volatility. If none of these properties differ from one fragment to another, then partitioning may not be useful.

We call these properties the six *ilities*. With all six and the fragmentation schemas available for each entity, some data distribution decisions can be very easy indeed. The intrepid designer (or either you or us if we can't find an intrepid designer) takes the logical view of the spread of the patterns of data access, and uses this view to make decisions about the physical location of data in the network. The designer needs to consider and balance such things as controlling redundancy, minimizing the impact of system and network outages, maintaining the accuracy of the data, optimizing response time, and making the whole distributed schema simple (or at least possible) to administer.

Let's look at several types of data and see what properties they have.

Lookup table example

As we've mentioned earlier in this book, an application often contains reference or *lookup* tables. These tables have several important characteristics:

- They are used continually by everyone.
- They are hardly ever changed.
- When they are changed, they are changed only by a single person in a named staff position.
- It is not absolutely essential to have the latest version of such tables.

The entities on which these tables were based would be described as having all of the following properties:

- Maximum availability
- Low reliability
- High visibility
- High accessibility
- Minimum mutability
- Very low volatility

Instances of this data can safely reside on every server in our network provided that we have some reliable means of (eventually) propagating changes. In this case, we would also regard all but one of the copies as read-only, except for the purpose of copying changes from the one copy that is updatable.

The fact that distribution is feasible does not, of course, mean that we have to distribute the data. However, if doing so would reduce the round trips on a wide area network, distribution would be attractive in this case. We would consider using Oracle's snapshot mechanism (which we'll describe in detail later on) to implement change distribution. Snapshots can be configured so that only the changes are propagated when the snapshot is refreshed. Figure 12-2 illustrates this type of data distribution.

Employee data example

At another extreme, we might have employee data for which queries must be guaranteed to return the current value. The data is used only in a monthly net pay

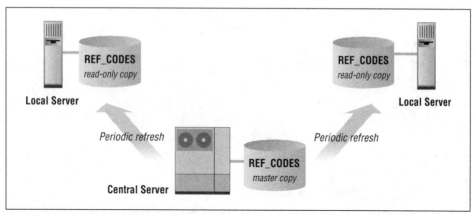

Figure 12-2. Distributing reference data

calculation and for ad hoc queries by divisional managers. The divisional managers may access records only for their own staff, and the data may only be changed by the divisional payroll clerks. The analysis for the underlying entities for such data would reflect all of the following properties:

- Medium availability

- Maximum reliability

- Minimum visibility (because access is limited to a specific division)

- Medium accessibility

- Low mutability

- Low volatility

This data needs to exist only on the server used by the divisional payroll; except for backup, there is no requirement for copies on other servers. The data is *horizontally partitioned*, and no specific support is required from the database engines. The partitioning enforces some of the access and security requirements since the divisional managers can see only payroll data that is on the server to which they are physically connected. We assume in this example that each regional server has its own local payroll application. If this is not the case, then there would be some requirement for distributed support. This configuration is illustrated in Figure 12-3.

The first and second cases often exist side by side within the same application. Our payroll can be expected to use a number of code sets (which are centrally maintained), in addition to its employee records (whose maintenance is performed by the site responsible for the data). We may need to propagate summary data to a central or headquarters server.

Figure 12-3. Horizontally partitioned data

Oracle's current support for distributed databases has no direct support for this type of central summarization, although the data structures can be adapted to allow Oracle's updatable snapshot mechanism to propagate summary data to the "master." In this case, that master needs be protected against update!

Insurance claims example

One of the authors recently worked on a development where this technology is being employed. The application is an insurance claims system where claims are created and owned by one of seven regional offices. The head office function does not itself create claims, but it does run audit and MIS queries against all claims. This is probably going to be implemented (it is still in the design phase) using updatable snapshots with the master on the head office system and each of the regions having its own horizontal slice.

The irony of this design is that all inserts and updates are performed on the snapshots, and the master table is only used for query. One of the neat aspects of the system is that in the (rare) event that a claim is transferred from one region to another, a simple update on the snapshot (on the column that defines the segmentation—the owning region) causes the claim to be removed from one horizontal partition and to appear on another within a short time frame. The only problem with this is that in the interim (between disappearing and reappearing), the claim does not appear to belong to any region and can be found only by directly querying the master table. Figure 12-4 shows the proposed arrangement.

We tend to prefer a locally implemented solution, which may or may not use the two-phase commit feature. Our feeling is that there has to be some limit on the extent to which one "bends" a design in order to use a product feature when it is reasonably straightforward to implement a custom solution.

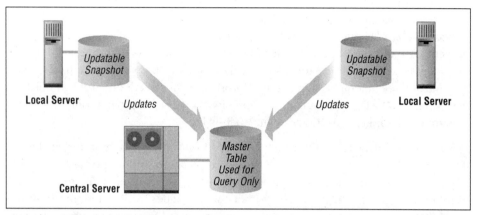

Figure 12-4. Using updatable snapshots for propagated summary data

Worldwide update access example

Let's consider the example of an airline flight booking system in which worldwide update access to current data is required. The simple and effective solution here is not to distribute the data at all, but to bring all access requests into a central server of sufficient power and connectivity to service the worldwide load. If you've ever wondered how the centralized mainframe continues to survive in such a downsized, distributed, and open systems world, then you might now have the answer. At the time we are writing, it is still almost impossibly difficult to service more than about 2,000 clients (simultaneous users) from a single Oracle database.

It is also almost equally difficult to support 100,000 simultaneous users on a single mainframe installation, but this level of service is required by a number of enterprises around the world and they have been achieving it day in and day out for some years with well over 99% uptime.

You (or your management) may dismiss the mainframe option out of hand, for a number of understandable reasons:

- Hardware cost
- Survivability
- Network traffic
- Development cost
- Development timescales

If the mainframe is not an option, you may be a candidate for symmetric replication. With this feature, there are multiple (master) copies to which changes may be made; these changes are propagated to the other masters either asynchronously or synchronously. We caution, however, that unless you approach such projects with great care—not to mention healthy skepticism—the savings in development cost and development timescales will be rather less than predicted. Going the open systems relational route can easily cost more than a mainframe project if the initial three attempts at making it work are all based on rapid application development (RAD) tools that have previously been deployed only for small departmental applications. Once again, such is life.

In some cases, data distribution will be forced onto a project by the decades-old trend toward departmental servers. If a new application, running on a new server, requires access to existing data held on an existing server, then some form of data distribution is inevitable. Your analysis of the six "ilities" will determine how this distribution is to be achieved. In some cases, it will be feasible to operate the new system with its own copy of the "shared" data, refreshed in bulk perhaps as infrequently as once per month. Data warehouses and EIS systems which have no updating function whatever normally operate with periodic refreshes of this type. In some cases, the degree of data transformation applied during the transfer will be so great that the result may not even be classed as a distributed database. Instead, you can view it simply as one application passing data to another in the traditional manner of 1960s tape-based data processing. In other cases, it will be necessary for each application to make changes to the data that are available to the other application in real time. In this latter case, the volumes of query and update from each server will determine whether there should be one copy or two.

Selecting a Data Distribution Strategy

So far, we've looked at the general principles of data distribution. We've also looked at the six "ilities" which must be specified as part of the analysis documentation for effective design decisions to be made about how to distribute data within a particular application. Now we're ready to discuss Oracle's support for remote updating in more detail, and to look at how to apply this support to various scenarios.

Before we get into the details of a feature-by-feature discussion, let's agree on why we might consider using data distribution in the first place: the purpose of introducing data distribution into a design is either

- To reduce network load or server load, or
- To increase availability

That's it. There are no other reasons for even considering data distribution. For every proposed data distribution topology, we must aggressively check that the design will not impose an unacceptable load on any of the network legs, servers, or network cards, and that it will not reduce availability to below-acceptable levels.

NOTE   In this chapter, we say little about Oracle's Gateway products or Oracle's Network Computing Architecture. The various gateways vary in both their support of the full functionality of an Oracle server, and of their efficiency in executing the features they do support. As so often in this book, we recommend exhaustive testing under realistic conditions before committing to the use of any distributed solution. This is especially true for one which involves heterogeneous server technologies. The Network Computing Architecture provides the ability to make encapsulated requests to "data cartridges." This feature may make distributed solutions easier to assemble, but at present it seems unlikely to address the issues of efficiency or availability.

To take a pathological example, let's consider an imaginary order processing system in which the orders are held on the local server at the nearest office to the specified delivery address for the order, but in which the customer records are held at the sales office which took the first order from that customer. There is no way of telling from a customer ID which server the record is on, so in order to look up a customer who is not on the local server, all of the other servers must be interrogated, typically through a view defined as:

```
CREATE VIEW all_customers (cust_loc, cust_id, cust_name, ...) AS
    SELECT 'LOCAL'      , cust_id, cust_name, ...
    FROM customers  — from local DB, New York
UNION ALL
    SELECT 'LONDON'     , cust_id, cust_name, ...
     FROM customers@london
UNION ALL
    SELECT 'TOKYO'     , cust_id, cust_name, ...
     FROM customers@tokyo
UNION ALL
    SELECT 'SYDNEY'      , cust_id, cust_name, ...
   FROM customers@sydney
UNION ALL
    SELECT 'LOS ANGELES'. CUST_ID, CUST_NAME, ...
     FROM customers@la;
```

With this view in place, coding the query to find a customer is easy. In order to retrieve any customer, we need to visit every database. If any of the required databases are down, the query will produce an error even if the required data can be read. But at least it was easy to code!

Updating a customer record once it has been retrieved is more difficult because the program (or at least some PL/SQL implicitly or explicitly called by the program) will have to direct the update to the appropriate server—which is why the view is helpfully coded to report the location.

Either the view or the synonyms used by the queries within the view will have to be different at each site unless you are willing to code the query on the local database using a database link. This will adversely affect performance because the query will have to establish a second connection to the local database rather than using the perfectly good connection that it already has.

But all of these problems fade into insignificance next to the performance and availability implications of the view. Even if you use the parallel query option (described in Chapter 14), this query is not parallelized. Each query will take place after the previous one has been resolved, and the query will produce an error if any one of the databases is not available for query.

Based on our simple reason for introducing distribution, this proposal clearly fails. Why? Because it will perform worse than having the customer database held on one nominated server, and it will have lower availability than having the customer database held on one nominated server. To be honest, there are various steps we could take to make the distribution more survivable, but they all involve writing extra code simply to reduce the negative impact of an unwise and unnecessary design decision. We believe that it would be easier to get the design right in the first place.

The discussion in the following sections is aimed at helping you to do exactly that. Remember, though, to succeed in using these features, you must know the six "ilities" for your data. At best, guesswork will not help you; at worst, it will render the design inoperable.

More Details on Two-Phase Commit

Oracle's two-phase commit support works pretty much as described in the section earlier in this chapter, but it has a number of additional characteristics that every designer should be aware of.

Two-phase commit requirement

The first issue is a Catch-22. As the commit processing starts, the coordinator asks each of the instances visited in the transaction whether it actually made any changes or applied any locks. Those which have not made changes or applied locks play no further part in the proceedings. Suppose that we issue only one command using the database link *chicago*:

```
UPDATE emp@chicago SET sal=sal*1.05 WHERE deptno = 26;
```

If there are no employees in Department 26 recorded in the Chicago version of the table, then when the coordinator asks the Chicago instance whether it made any changes, it will report that no changes were made. As a result, if a transaction makes changes at only one database instance (even if that instance is remote), a two-phase commit is not required. The Catch-22 is that using Oracle you must have the Distributed Option (which includes two-phase commit) in order to detect that a two-phase commit is not required. In other words, you cannot update through a database link even in those cases where two-phase commit is not required—unless you have two-phase commit installed!

In-doubt data

The second issue is that between the prepare and the commit, data is said to be *in doubt.* Once the prepare has been received at a database where an update was made, there is no way of telling whether that data is committed or not unless the second phase is signaled by the coordinator with its commit or rollback. For this reason, Oracle uses block-level locking to prevent access to this data because it cannot tell whether or not to apply read consistency. Normally, these locks persist for only a few milliseconds in a local area network environment, and for a few hundred milliseconds using a wide area network. However, if some problem (such as a network failure) prevents the second phase from being completed, then this in-doubt data will remain inaccessible until the problem has been resolved. The problem can be resolved either by Oracle's built-in recovery mechanisms or by the DBA'. intervention using one of the SQL statements COMMIT FORCE or ROLLBACK FORCE.

WARNING   These persistent locks survive instance shutdowns, and will still be in force when the instance is restarted. They prevent all data access to the affected block, including queries.

The one instance that performs a conventional commit is called the *commit point,* and it does not have to place blocks into the in-doubt state. Clearly, the more important the database, the less you can afford to run the risk that your processing will encounter in-doubt data, so Oracle provides an INIT.ORA parameter, called COMMIT_POINT_STRENGTH, to help you. In any distributed transaction, the commit point will be the instance with the highest commit point strength, though we advise you to check the documentation carefully for an important exception to this rule when remote operations themselves involve remote operations.

Serial operations

The third issue is this: When you are trying to estimate the likely duration of a two-phase commit (or, worse still, a two-phase rollback), please bear in mind that the required operations are performed serially, not in parallel. Thus, a two-phase commit which has to coordinate three remote instances (each linked through an X.25 service with a message round trip time of 500 msec) can easily take four seconds (assuming that the coordinating instance is also the commit point).

WARNING   The reason for the caution about rolling back is that in Oracle, roll-back *always* takes longer than commit. In fact, Oracle never puts a rollback entry onto the redo log: when an instance is asked to roll back, it reads through the transaction's rollback entry chain. For each entry, it makes a redo log entry so that recovery will make the same (reverse) change, fetches the database block, and reverses the change. Then when all the rollback segment entries have been processed, it writes a commit to the redo log and flushes the buffer.

A commit, on the other hand, simply has to write a commit entry to the redo log and flush the buffer (and, in Version 7.3, release row-level locks if the changed blocks are still in memory).

Note also that to ensure recoverability Oracle takes redo and roll-back actions in what appears to be the "wrong order." The redo and rollback entries are made before making the change to which they refer. In this way, you can never have a change made without the entries to protect it.

Remote DML

We have used the phrase "remote DML" several times. By DML (Data Management Language) we mean only the following SQL statements:

```
INSERT
UPDATE
DELETE
SELECT...FOR UPDATE
LOCK
```

Oracle's distributed database support does not directly support remote DCL (Data Control Language—for example, GRANT and REVOKE) or remote DDL (Data Definition Language—for example, CREATE, ALTER, DROP). However, the symmetric replication support contains a PL/SQL package, DBMS_REPCAT, which is capable of executing the remote DDL required as part of setting up a distributed replication schema.

Despite this, if your application logic calls for the process to be able to create tables, issue grants, truncate tables, or indeed perform anything other than queries and the five DML statements listed, then you will *not* be able to execute the required statements at a remote node. Of course, we'd respond by asking why you think you need to be able to execute such statements as part of normal transaction logic. We'd also remind you that in Oracle, DDL statements have two implicit commits:

- When you issue a DDL statement, any current transaction for the session is committed.

- When the DDL statement completes, it commits (or rolls back if it encountered an error).

Thus, DDL always terminates the current transaction.

Synchronous Remote Procedure Calls (RPCs)

In addition to being able to issue remote DML, we can also call a remote procedure either through a synonym or by explicitly supplying the database link:

```
   ...
   success := stock.alloc@stores( cust_id =>  'C155'
                                  , part_no =>  'AC7/95'
                                  , qty     =>  6
                        );
   ...
```

This is a particularly powerful way in which to issue remote DML and even remote queries, because it both reduces the number of network round trips (it requires only one round trip no matter how much work has to be done at the remote site) and provides *encapsulation*. Within our local environment, we only have to know what needs to be done, not the data structures which are required in order to do it.

TIP   We strongly recommend that you code any cross-application references using remote procedure calls in order to prevent the condition known as *schema gridlock* where there are several applications each using remote queries and remote DML to access each other's data.

                If access is coded directly in SQL, then each application is dependent on the stability of the schema in another application and no schema can be changed without coordinated changes in all of the applications which reference it.

By using procedure calls rather than SQL, we can provide one level of isolation which will help to reduce the problem of schema gridlock. By using packaged procedures and functions, we can reduce the problem further by using *over-loading*. For example, if we decide to introduce a new version of the ALLOC function in which the "date needed" is a mandatory parameter, we can use over-loading to allow existing calls to continue to operate. This is illustrated in the code that follows.

Note that both the calling and called databases must support the Distributed Option, and therefore the *alloc* function may itself issue remote queries, DML, or procedure calls. Note also that this process can nest to any number of levels, with serious effects on both response time and availability.

```
...
   FUNCTION alloc ( cust_id IN NUMBER    — new cust id format
                  , part_no IN VARCHAR2 — stores part ref.
                  , qty     IN NUMBER    — number of units needed
                  , needed  IN DATE      — date on which needed
                  ) RETURN BOOLEAN IS
   BEGIN
     ....
   END; — alloc

   — for backward compatibility we provide the old format with
   — the customer id as a string and no date needed so that the
   — allocation has to be from stock which is already in the store

   FUNCTION alloc ( cust_id IN VARCHAR2
                  , part_no IN VARCHAR2
                  , qty     IN NUMBER
                  ) RETURN BOOLEAN IS
   BEGIN
     RETURN alloc(TO_NUMBER(cust_id), part_no, qty, TRUNC(SYSDATE));
   END; — alloc
...
```

There is another rather strange feature of remote procedure calls under versions 7.0, 7.1, and 7.2 which can cause errors that mysteriously go away the next time you try the same operation. At first, this might seem to be a highly desirable feature! Indeed, if all errors went away the second time you ran a process, programming would be much easier for us. Why this situation occurs using RPCs is a DBA topic rather than a design topic, so instead of explaining here exactly why this happens, we are just going to give designers a warning: be aware that if remotely called procedures or packages are changed, then to assure fully correct operation, you will need to recompile all other code which calls those code units. This happens automatically for references within the same data dictionary, but the mechanism used for invoking the required recompilation on remote nodes is less elegant in earlier versions.

Snapshots

As the name suggests, a *snapshot* is a copy of a table (or tables) taken at a point in time. It is defined by a query on a table or a set of tables (the snapshot master), and it may be simple or complex. The snapshot mechanism allows the DBA to define other schemas into which this snapshot is to be refreshed at some stated interval.

A *simple snapshot* is based on a query that neither performs a join nor contains any summary functions. A *complex snapshot* may contain either or both of these features. The important difference is that complex snapshots can be refreshed only by completely reloading them, whereas simple snapshots can be the subject of a *fast refresh* in which only the changes are transmitted.

At first glance, snapshots look really useful for keeping copies all around the network of such things as code tables—tables which everyone needs to query but which are rarely updated. Using the WHERE clause in the defining query, you can create simple snapshots which do not contain some of the rows of the master table (which may not be required at the remote site). Also, using the SELECT list, you can remove some of the columns for security reasons or simply because they are not necessary. Thus, a simple snapshot may be either (or both) a horizontal and a vertical subset of the master table, as illustrated in Figure 12-5.

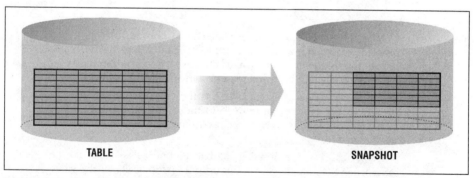

TABLE   **SNAPSHOT**

Figure 12-5. A snapshot which is both a vertical and horizontal partition of the table

The main problems with snapshots revolve around their efficiency (even with fast refresh) and the fact that any code referencing the snapshot can never be absolutely sure that it has the most up-to-date data. If reliability does not matter (how likely does that sound?) and if the server that carries the master can sustain the load of the triggers which are used to record all of the changes made, then simple snapshots with fast refresh can be very effective. But if large numbers of changes are made and the master then remains stable for long periods, it may be better to wait until the changes are complete; at that point, you can manually (or program-matically) force a full refresh.

WARNING   Before Version 7.3, the change recording for fast refreshes uses the rowid. Any form of maintenance on the snapshot which performed a reorganization, such as exporting and then importing, caused the referencing mechanism to become invalid. Whoops!

A further problem with Oracle's original snapshot support was that all snapshots were refreshed independently, and it was impossible to keep them in step. Thus, if a parent and a child table were both master tables for simple snapshots, it was not possible to maintain referential integrity between the snapshots—even when it was perfectly maintained between the two masters. Why? Because, quite simply, the snapshots could never guarantee to be taken with *exactly* the same read consistency point. An ingenious DBA might be able to find workarounds to this problem if the required refresh frequency is not too high, and if there are reason-ably long quiet periods on the server with the masters. It was clear, though, that Oracle's support was unsatisfactory in this important area. This problem has been addressed with the introduction of *snapshot groups*, which we describe later in this chapter.

WARNING   On the subject of setting refresh intervals, be aware of a potential problem of "creeping slippage," which occurs when the refresh is not run as frequently as you had intended when you originally set the interval. There are several reasons why this might occur.

One possible cause of this problem is the fact that the interval ap-plies from the end of one refresh to the start of the next, so you have to allow for the average elapsed time of a refresh when you set the interval.

A second cause is the fact that the background tasks which do the refreshes (SNP0, SNP1, etc.) wake up only periodically. If the value of the sleep period (the INIT.ORA parameter called JOB_QUEUE_IN-TERVAL) is large in relation to the refresh interval, slippage can oc-cur.

Consistent snapshots

As we mentioned earlier, to overcome the problems of snapshots of parent and child tables, Oracle now provides snapshot groups. These are the subject of a consistent refresh—that is, each member of the group will be refreshed as of the same point in time. This facility is certainly worth considering for code structures in which there are foreign key relationships.

Updatable snapshots

We have already seen that snapshots, which can be horizontal or vertical partitions of tables, can allow selected parts of a central master table to be distributed to the servers on which they are of interest.

In Version 7.1.6, snapshots became optionally updatable. This means that a simple snapshot which contains all of the NOT NULL columns from its master table can be updated, and the changes made will be propagated back to the parent. This propagation is performed later using a mechanism similar to the one discussed in the next section, "Asynchronous Symmetric Replication." If the master is never updated, and if the individual snapshot tables contain no overlaps, then this is a completely safe approach—one that provides a convenient way to manage data where the responsibility for different subsets can be assigned to different servers, but where query access is required to the entire data population.

However, as soon as it becomes possible to update the same record (row) in more than one physical database, then any asynchronous approach is liable to give rise to conflicts; we describe these conflicts and their resolution in the next section.

If you are using updatable snapshots, there are two particular "gotchas" that you need to be aware of.

- When an updatable snapshot is created, the constraints from the master table are not inherited (including foreign keys). You cannot manually create them on the snapshot itself, since it is a view of a table called SNAP$*<table name>*. It appears that you can recreate the constraints on the SNAP$ table. However, this is a manual process; as such, it may be prone to error. The implications of making an error are not nice. If you miss a constraint on the SNAP$ table, then it will be possible to create and commit a row which violates it. When the master is updated, the insert will fail and at some point the row will disappear without warning from the snapshot on which it was created. The only clue that there was a problem is in a log table (USLOG *$_<table name>*) on the site containing the master table.

- You have to be careful when you are creating triggers on updatable snapshots. Suppose that you have a trigger on an ORDER_LINES table which updates the total order value in the ORDERS table (a denormalized column). For instance, in the BEFORE INSERT trigger, we add the value of the new order item into the order value. You want this to occur at all sites, so in addition to defining the trigger on the master table, you also put it on the SNAP$ tables at all of the other sites. The trigger code is identical, so that on the snapshot sites it actually updates the view of ORDER_LINES. You include ORDERS and ORDER_LINES in a snapshot group so they are updated together. There is a problem, though: although the snapshot group guarantees that the two tables are refreshed from an identical point in time, the changes are applied in an arbitrary order. If the order is updated before the order line, then when the order line is inserted, the trigger on the master table will fire and the additive trigger will add the order line for a second time (rendering the value incorrect).

You can avoid having to apply the trigger a second time using the DBMS_SNAPSHOT.AM_I_A_REFRESH function, but there is a deeper problem here. A large amount of propagation of data is going on, and it's worth considering the option of not having the trigger on the SNAP$ table and allowing the change to filter down from the master site. This would be the preferred option if you can live with the total being wrong until the snapshot is fully synchronized with the master. Since this is unlikely, you may want to consider forgoing denormalization altogether in this case.

Distributed design is full of conundrums like this—you just have to keep an eye out for them all!

Unlimited Triggers per Table

The recording of changes to master tables is performed using triggers on the underlying tables. In Version 7.0, this caused a major problem. If the installation script for some piece of software wanted to place a trigger on a table (for example, a row BEFORE INSERT trigger) and if such a trigger already existed, then the resulting conflict could be resolved only by merging the two triggers into one. Very few, if any, install script authors were willing to adopt that solution, and the ability to have many triggers on a table with the same timing is a highly effective solution.

To try to discourage trigger coders from introducing any dependency on other triggers that may be known to exist, Oracle specifically states as "undefined" the order in which the triggers fire. We strongly support this approach; the whole idea of having multiple triggers is to allow different applications to do their own thing based on a particular type of change being made to a particular table.

Snapshots and replication both create triggers on the tables for which changes are to be propagated, and with the ability to have multiple triggers at each of the 12 possible events, these triggers can safely be created without disturbing any other trigger logic that is already being fired by the same event.

This feature, which arrived with Version 7.1, is part of the procedural option rather than the Distributed Option and is therefore effectively part of the base product (as we assume that very few users run without the Distributed Option).

Asynchronous Remote Procedure Calls

In this chapter, we have made several references to network round trips in a distributed environment, and to the problems which can be caused by network failures and instance shutdowns in that environment. Clearly, if an application that is running on one server needs data that is (only) held on another, it can access it only if both the network and the other server are available. An update, however, is a different matter. If you are willing to accept the fact that the update may not take place for some time (if at all), then you can greatly increase both availability and throughput by using asynchronous calls.

Your process calls a local service which notes the required call and places it in a queue. At some point in the future, the entries in the queue will be copied to the remote server and marked as sent (using two-phase commit). There is, of course, no guarantee whatever that the remote server will be able to execute them successfully.

Thus, if you were planning to use an asynchronous RPC for the stock allocation example, you would find it prudent to have the remote procedure issue an asynchronous RPC back to the original server stating the result of the operation. Every few hours (or few minutes, or few days, depending on the urgency) you might want to run a report showing all those stock allocations which had either failed or for which no acknowledgment had been received. This task might be part of the main application, or it might more conveniently be performed by an application management tool such as BMC PATROL. However it is done, this is pure design; it needs to be carried back to the analysis team to agree upon how the situation should be handled at the business level. If your business analysts are anything like the ones we work with, then the answer is likely to be that the stock should be allocated in real time so the problem will not exist!

If you receive such a response, then you should go back to the six "ilities" and arrive at a compromise that best meets the most important of the requirements.

Asynchronous Symmetric Replication

The asynchronous symmetric replication feature allows several copies of the same table to exist in different databases—and therefore, presumably, on different servers. No copy is the master: they are equal or symmetric. You can make changes to the individual replicate tables, and these changes are then propagated asynchronously to the other replicas of the same table. The time that it takes for a change to propagate depends to some extent on various parameters set by the DBA, but also on the availability of the databases to which the propagation is taking place. As a result, update conflicts can clearly occur. To handle these, Oracle provides both conflict detection and a series of conflict resolution options, including the ability to implement a set of custom rules in PL/SQL.

Oracle's conflict detection for updates is simple: both the old and new values are propagated. If at any of the sites the row does not currently have the old value that has been propagated, then there is an update conflict. Easy stuff. For many applications, the supplied conflict resolution rules can work well, especially the additive rule, which states: "Change the value by the same amount."

Suppose there are 50 of Part 37B in stock, and that we allocate 20 of them. We will then propagate a change which says that for Part 37B, the quantity was 50 but is now 30. If, on some other machine, we find that Part 37B has a quantity of 40, we simply reduce that to 20, making the same relative change that we made in the first place. Eventually, the change which reduced the quantity from 50 to 40 on the remote machine will be propagated back to our original machine where the same logic will reduce our figure of 30 to 20. So everyone is happy, unless we have a rule which says that the quantity can never be less than 30!

WARNING   We do, however, caution you against using time as a basis for con-
             flict resolution. Why? Because unless you are running in a DCE envi-
             ronment, it is extremely unlikely that the clocks on your servers are
             synchronized. Thus, using *latest* as your conflict resolution strategy
             pretty much equates to using *random choice* (which is not one of
             the Oracle options). In particular, if your network spans time zones
             you may wonder why all your Boston changes are overwritten by
             San Francisco!

Site priority also has its dangers when there are more than two sites in the network. Consider Figure 12-6. In this scenario, with a certain combination of circumstances, the sites end up out of sync, with site C disagreeing with A and B. Since A is the designated priority site, this would suggest that C is incorrect.

There are clearly a number of applications (including almost all financial processing) where the only acceptable way of dealing with conflicts is to prevent them from occurring in the first place. One of the techniques we can use to do this rejoices in the unlikely name *mediation of update rights*.

Using this approach, each row has a data attribute (column) which defines which server is allowed to update that column. The right is usually implied; thus, in an

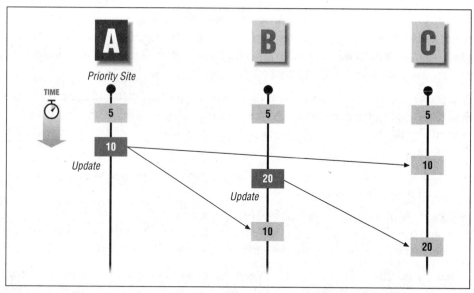

Figure 12-6. Potential problem with site priority conflict resolution

order processing system, *order_status* might be used to mediate update rights, as shown in Table 12-1:

Table 12-1. Using a Status Column to Define the Update Rights

Status	Meaning	Update Rights
	Order not yet created	Order Processing Departmental Server
IP	In preparation	Order Processing Departmental Server
CFD	Cleared for dispatch	Shipping Unit Departmental Server
CFI	Cleared for invoice (shipped)	Finance Unit Departmental Server

This works well provided that the update rights can be *pushed* when they need to move from one server to another. Thus, when the Shipping Unit Server updates the status to "Cleared for invoice," the record then becomes not updatable by that server. Indeed, for at least a few seconds and possibly for several hours (until the change is propagated to the Finance Unit Server and applied), this row will not be updatable by any server. Inspecting the six "ilities" allows you to determine whether or not this is a problem. This solution lends itself to a workflow application where a piece of work passes from department to department as the result of predefined transition events before eventually being archived.

But suppose an application needs to *pull* update rights—that is, it needs to update a record for which the server on which it is running does not have update rights. In this case, the best advice we can give is for you to imitate the design of the Sybase Replication Server. Determine which server does have update rights, and make a remote update on that server using two-phase commit. Depending on your level of perversity, you can simply change the update rights and wait for them to be propagated back to you so that you can make the required changes, or you can make the full change using the remote connection.

We prefer the latter approach even though it does mean that a change you have just made will not immediately be visible in the copy on the server from which it was made. If you consider this to be a major problem, you can solve it using the following:

- Additional tables—These contain the primary keys of the rows which have been remotely updated.

- Procedural lookup techniques—These check against the additional tables the primary key of every row retrieved; they then go off to the server where the change was originally made to retrieve the version as updated.

Solutions of this type start to get highly complex and can be subject to errors which are extremely difficult to debug and even more difficult to explain to the users. If you find yourself walking down this path, the best thing to do is to challenge your original data distribution decisions. Of course, this will be much easier if the decisions were, in fact, someone else's—and if the someone else is neither your immediate superior nor anyone else who has the power to determine your salary prospects!

A further alternative might be to use a two-phase commit transaction to change the update rights simultaneously in both the local copy of the table and the copy with the current update rights. Unfortunately, this causes the same change to be replicated in both directions, which can get rather confusing (an understatement).

This section would be incomplete without mention of both insert conflicts and delete conflicts. The latter are not much of a problem: if on propagating a delete it is discovered that the row has already been deleted in some other master, then this should be acceptable. The situation is as you would want it in that the data is no longer there. Insert contention is rather more serious and occurs when two rows have been inserted with the same primary key; application design should seek to prevent this, but if it occurs, then it will normally have to be reported to the users for manual resolution even if the two records are identical.

Synchronous Symmetric Replication

Support for the synchronous symmetric replication feature was new at the time we wrote this book. At this point, neither of us has had any practical experience with this feature, nor have we been able to find anyone outside Oracle Corporation who has used it. We have had, however, some involvement in a project implementation of this functionality which was successfully run in production under Version 7.0.

In applications where it is necessary to have multiple updatable copies of the same table in different databases and where both transaction and data integrity are of primary importance, then all copies need to be changed within the scope of the transaction. Synchronous symmetric replication achieves this goal, though the impact on both network load and server load is likely to be severe for any significant update volume.

Despite this problem, synchronous symmetric replication does represent the best means of ensuring the ability to efficiently retrieve the latest data at any of the sites. It provides both absolute reliability and higher availability than a single master table would, because only the local copy needs to be available to support queries. Query performance is optimal since all queries can be performed locally. The sting in the tail for this technique comes when the designer is forced to decide what approach to adopt when one or more of the databases is unavailable, and what to do when part of the network is unavailable.

In the first case (one of the databases is unavailable), it is usually adequate to keep running with as many of the servers as have survived provided that it will be feasible to bring the missing databases back into line once they are available again.

In the second case (part of the network is unavailable), a series of rules need to be in place as to which subsets are permitted to run in the face of network failures. To assure absolute reliability, these rules must be such that if any subset is running with updating permitted, then it is the *only* subset which is running. Moreover, all other copies of the table will be resynchronized before they too can rejoin the community. This is not easy stuff.

Mixing and Matching Approaches

As we have already said, you have to consider each table (or group of related tables) and perform a fragmentation analysis on it (or them). You have to decide where the data within the table should be located to optimize both performance and availability for the users who need to see and operate on it. If this analysis leads you to the decision that the data should be physically located at more than one site, then you need to determine how it should be either split or replicated among them. After you've done this, you can then make your choice from the various options we've presented in this chapter (bearing in mind the six "ilties").

Of course, what is best for one table may not be optimal for another. It is quite acceptable to come up with a solution that (within reason) mixes the technologies. A mixture of updatable and nonupdatable snapshots, plus a set of remote procedure calls, is a perfectly valid solution. There used to be a restriction that you couldn't mix snapshots and replicated tables within the same schema. We believe that this restriction has been removed in Version 7.3; nevertheless, we'd advise anyone contemplating such a design to think carefully about the level of complexity they wish to support and the job of administering the configuration.

A DBA Nightmare

Distributed databases, particularly the more advanced flavors, present interesting challenges for the DBA—even before the network failures start to happen! Creating the schemas is certainly not a trivial task, although the Replication Manager (supplied as part of Oracle Enterprise Manager with Version 7.3) makes it significantly easier. Although it is supplied with all platforms, this utility runs only under MS Windows NT.

Without Replication Manager, setting up replication requires the DBA to run a series of procedures, most of which have very long names; for example:

```
DBMS_REPCAT_AUTH.GRANT_SURROGATE_REPCAT('REMOTESYS');
```

These procedures are also very sensitive to the order in which they are run. Furthermore, most CASE products don't support definition of a distributed schema and invariably generate DDL that assumes that all objects will be defined within a single schema. This has to be hand-crafted to fit your distributed design.

Example Scenarios

Now that we have examined the distributed database options available to you, let's consider which of them would be the best fit for a number of simple scenarios. First, we will introduce a very simple network topology and table schema that we'll use to illustrate the design considerations that would influence the decision about which technologies to use. The network topology is illustrated in Figure 12-7 and the data model in Figure 12-8. For purposes of these examples, we assume that each node has a single instance running, where the instance name is identical to the node name.

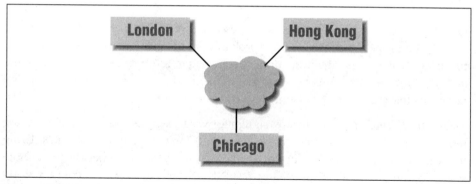

Figure 12-7. Simple network topology

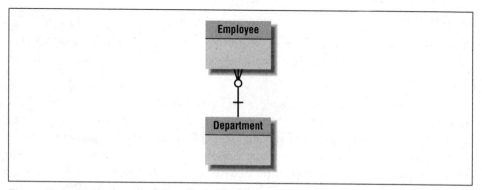

Figure 12-8. Simple data model

Scenario 1

The subsidiaries in the organization are run on an autonomous basis and have no need to access data from other subsidiaries. Each site is responsible for its own local employee and departmental data. However, a user at CHICAGO needs to produce periodic reports that are based on all employees in the organization.

This scenario is simple because the consolidated reports only need to read the data. In this case, you employ remote queries with *database links*. You would create two database links on CHICAGO for LONDON and HONG KONG, create a view that is a union of the three employee tables, and run the report against this view. Of course, if these reports are not run very frequently, you could avoid distributed database altogether and obtain periodic table dumps (such as exports) of the tables in LONDON and HONG KONG and load these in CHICAGO. As a DBA once said, "FedEx is the best network transport layer we've found for transferring large files."

Scenario 2

Our organization hires a new Human Resources VP who notices that when the Country Personnel Manager is away (probably on the golf course), any changes to the tables have to be deferred until the manager returns. The VP requires the ability to update the employee and department tables (from CHICAGO) on the occasions that the Country Personnel Manager is absent.

Again, this scenario is relatively straightforward because the updating of the remote data is done in discrete transactions that don't involve multiple sites. Using the database link that was set up for Scenario 1, the VP can connect to the remote system by putting @HONG_KONG or @LONDON on the end of his connect string when he wants to perform remote maintenance.

Scenario 3

The VP of Human Resources is now starting to consolidate a power base, and has dictated that updates to the salary column can only be made by the HR department in Chicago.

You could use the same solution as in Scenario 2 and simply control the update privilege with a trigger on the tables. However, let's assume that our demanding VP wants to be able to see and update all employees from a single screen-based application. Here, we can use a variant of the view described in Scenario 1 to view the data, but you certainly can't update through this view. You will have to include a pseudo-column in the view that defines the source node of the row and use this value and a bit of dynamic SQL to generate an appropriate UPDATE statement. You are now committed to two-phase commit.

Let's consider a new data model now since the one we've discussed up to now is unlikely to warrant any more complex solution for distributing the data among the nodes. Remember, we stated before that the only reasons for doing so are to reduce the network load or to increase availability, neither of which is likely to be an issue in this example. Our new data model is shown in Figure 12-9.

Scenario 4

Each country trades only in its own stocks. However, there are multinational companies that trade in all three countries and need to be able to call any local office and be told the current position of their global portfolio, as of the previous night (local time).

Let's consider Customer first. There is an associative relationship (pig's ear) on Customer that indicates that a Customer may have a parent Company. What's more, this Company may be in another country. You need to be able to attach a

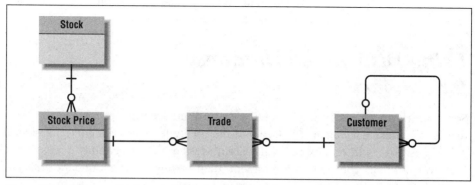

Figure 12-9. Data model for more complex distributed scenarios

local Customer to a remote one; however, this is not a time-critical operation, and you could live with nonlocal Customers not being updated immediately. Since Customers is well-partitioned across our sites and since there is no obvious master site, you would probably opt for a multimaster table that is replicated asynchronously. The only conflict that you would need to take into account is the unlikely event that one of your users links a company to a already-deleted parent from another country.

In this scenario, each site is interested only in local Stock and Price information, so you can implement discrete nondistributed tables for these. Trades might be a bit more difficult because of the requirement that each country must be able to give a reasonably accurate assessment of the global position of a multinational corporation. The preferred option here would be to implement Trades as a local table and to create a denormalized column on Customers that holds the current position (and is updated every time a trade occurs). This column can be maintained by a simple trigger. If the Customer has a parent, a further trigger should fire to update the parent. In this case, conflict is more likely. We recommend that you use the additive method of conflict resolution.

Scenario 5

This scenario is similar to 4, but now trading is allowed in foreign stock. It is vital to quote and use the most recent price when making a trade.

Customers and Trades can remain as in the previous example. However, because Stock Prices need to be fully synchronized at all times, you have no choice but to use synchronous symmetric replication for them. However, if part of the network fails, we can't update Stock Prices on any system. To reduce the impact of this, you either have to buy a lot of resilient and redundant equipment or create your own form of synchronous symmetric replication that can tolerate system failures and defer synchronization under certain controlled conditions. Or you might elect to have only one copy and invest in a fast network!

Using Distributed Databases for Fallback

Some sites seek to justify implementing a distributed design purely on the basis that it offers resilience against failure and the ability to operate a limited system if a server is taken out of service. With careful design, this is certainly a possibility. However, if this is your main requirement, then buying some redundant or stand-by hardware may be a cheaper (and easier) option.

The simple rule is that if any of your transactions rely on having another system respond in some way before it can commit, then you have a dependency and your level of service will be impaired in the event that a server or connection is lost. Clearly, synchronous RPCs and synchronous symmetric replication rely on the server responding as does two-phase commit. Snapshots and asynchronous symmetric replication are less sensitive, since with these features, the updates are always deferred and can be deferred a bit longer if the failure persists. However, if you are using updatable snapshots and the master site is down, there comes a point where the snapshots diverge and the chance of a conflict increases.

One of the authors has seen a plan for a disaster scenario plan in which one of the remote servers assumes the responsibility of the central site (which has most of the master tables) in the event of long failure of the central site. While it is pretending to be the central server, it continues to service its local user community. This has yet to be proved and the author remains somewhat skeptical, especially since the two servers involved are many miles apart. As with all disasters, we sincerely hope that it will never happen.

Other Design Considerations

This section describes a few additional considerations for distributed database design.

LONG Columns

Columns defined as LONG present some problems for distributed database design. Tables that contain long columns can't be replicated and can't participate in two-phase commit. Similarly, snapshots can't include LONG columns. In fact, this makes a lot of sense: would you want your network clogged up with huge bitmap images or graphics being replicated around your sites? But be aware that this restriction might affect your table design. For example, you may decide to store a BLOB data externally on a chosen server and develop your own routine to pull the data on demand.

Batch Updates

If you anticipate that your system will have periods of intense update—for example, the end of a financial period—then you need to consider the additional overhead that your distributed architecture will cause, and you need to determine a plan to minimize the effect. For instance, if you are using snapshots and you run a heavy overnight batch program on the master site, then it makes good sense to disable the snapshot mechanism prior to the run and do a full refresh after the run. This is not quite as straightforward as it seems since the refresh has to be initiated from the snapshot sites. In any event, we believe that a periodic manual reconciliation of the data is good for the health of your data!

Data Distribution Summary

As is the case with so many other technologies described in this book, the real trick in the distributed database arena is to be very clear indeed about what the enterprise really needs to achieve, what the available technology really does well, and what it does less well. Let's quickly summarize our main recommendations in this chapter.

Oracle's software support for distributed operation is impressive. Snapshots have the ability to keep copies of reference data around the network almost up to date, and this should reduce both message traffic and the load on the server(s) which would otherwise be carrying the only copy of the data. Synchronous replication can keep many copies of the same table up to date in different locations without conflict, albeit at a performance cost and with availability implications because loss of any component will prevent the updates from taking place as intended.

We feel that the only valid reason for using asynchronous RPCs and asynchronous symmetric replication is if the design is capable of avoiding conflict through mediation of update rights or of coping with the consequences of having an apparently successful operation be classified later on as being unsuccessful. Most designers and business analysts have considerable difficulties with this concept and, as a result, do not propose effective solutions.

Wherever there is a WAN, you must be aware of its performance (in terms of round trip time) and you must carefully assess the number of round trips required. Testing the application over a LAN will simply give a misleading result.

Oracle's Network Computing Architecture (NCA)

As Oracle7 evolves, and as we look forward to Oracle8, the company has announced its new Network Computing Architecture. At its simplest, this architecture involves three types of components:

- Client or presentation management

- Application management

- Data management

These three components talk to each other over a "software bus," which is an upgraded version of Oracle's network transport services. The user content of each of these components is supplied in "cartridges" which may be coded in a variety of languages ranging from the traditional C and C++ all the way to the latest industry success story of Java and Javascript. On the way from C to Java, Microsoft's Visual Basic and ActiveX are also supported.

Based on our initial inspection of NCA, this new architecture does not change any of our conclusions about design for Oracle—although the levels of transparency being offered by the cartridges may make it a little easier to recover from many possible design errors. What the new architecture does make clear is that Oracle is now ready to explicitly support n-tier environments. As soon as the task of data coordination is moved from the data server into the application server, we are likely (possibly even certain) to find that the responsibility for coordinating two-phase commit moves with it, even if all of the databases concerned are Oracle. However, to confuse the picture, cartridges are already becoming available which can be called from PL/SQL within the Oracle data server and which talk to external data stores, potentially leaving the coordination within the data server.

There is nothing within Oracle's NCA which will make obsolete traditional SQL-based development, but the intent is clearly that over time, new development should move toward use of the cartridge approach.

Most important of all is for the design team to know what levels of service they are required to meet—the six "ilities" we've said so much about in this chapter. Without this information it is difficult, if not impossible, to create an effective distributed data design. If you find that it's possible to meet the requirements without going to a distributed solution, then do so. Remember that the reason for introducing data distribution is to solve either a performance or an availability problem that would otherwise exist. Put another way: *If it ain't broke, don't fix it!*

13

Designing for Data Warehouses

This chapter looks at the specific issues you will need to consider when you design a data warehouse based on an underlying Oracle database. We'll examine why data warehouses have become so popular in recent years, and look at specific design issues for data warehouses—some of which challenge many of the deep-rooted relational design disciplines. We'll also examine the properties and special needs that set data warehouses apart from *online transaction processing* (OLTP) systems. Finally, we'll describe how to get data into the warehouse and how to extract it out again in a useful and meaningful format.

Why Data Warehouses?

Data warehousing is currently one of the hottest subjects in the information technology industry. As with other hot topics, suppliers are jumping on the bandwagon and offering solutions to problems that, until a few years ago, you weren't even aware that you had! Is it just mass hysteria or is there some foundation to all the talk about data warehousing? Read on and draw your own conclusions.

To understand where data warehousing sprang from, we need to give a very brief recent history of computing. When the authors began their careers in computing, the mainframe was king, applications were written in assembler language by "real" programmers, and there was invariably an enormous backlog of work. In the 1980s, the minicomputer rose to challenge and, some would say, depose the mainframe as king. This new champion gave rise to *departmental* or *workgroup* computing where applications specific to a business function were developed that could run in blissful isolation from the world around them (although they might grudgingly communicate with the "old technology" now and then). Even organizations that stayed essentially loyal to the centralized mainframe—for example, major airlines—started to develop their application suites in total isolation of one another.

This is where problems started to arise. Many organizations have ended up with an abundance of incompatible customer files or tables, none of which containing 100% of the customers and none of which synchronized with each other. Each individual version is accepted as being accurate by the code of a particular application suite (even if the users have their doubts). There are computer software vendors who simply cannot produce a definitive customer list, and there are many companies who can do so only by running several reports and merging the output. If any of this sounds familiar to you, then perhaps you too need a data warehouse!

Back to our history lesson. After the mini came the ubiquitous PC. Of equal importance was the huge advance in networking—both wide area networking and local area networking. *Interoperability* became a key issue; applications that were written in different tools against different databases (maybe on different platforms) now could share and/or exchange data. The islands of data suddenly had bridges between them. Advances were also made in storage technology, and it became cheap to retain old data and less costly to proliferate redundant copies of data. Fast multiprocessor servers became available at reasonable prices; when these server architectures were combined with intelligent database software, they were ideal for supporting complex queries against very large databases.

In an ideal world, you might want to rewrite many of the legacy mini and mainframe systems to make use of newer technologies such as client/server and distributed database. In the process of rewriting the systems, you'd completely rationalize and cleanse the data. Unfortunately, this is not a practical proposition for most sites. The rationale is this: although many incumbent systems may not be breaking the frontiers of technology, they nevertheless do the job for which they were designed, so why pay out all that money to rewrite them?

NOTE   Actually, one very good reason to rewrite these legacy systems is
              the impending millennium and all the problems associated with
              computer systems interpreting dates in the next century. See
              Appendix B, *Tricks of the Trade*, for a full discussion of this issue.

Lack of integrated and consistent data is not the only problem that users and executives are now facing. Most systems that were designed using traditional methods and techniques are not well-optimized for query. In particular, ad hoc inquiries that were not anticipated at design time may perform poorly—or they may simply be impossible to provide. A great deal of CPU and disk time can be spent in GROUP BY clauses summarizing data. Today's executives want systems which arm them with data in a format that can help them make strategic business decisions. They need the ability to view data from many different angles and across many dimensions. To achieve this goal, executives need more than a clever query tool—they need data in a format that is optimized for their purpose.

Traditional data modeling techniques are designed to achieve high performance in OLTP systems. If you go to a site that has been designed in the traditional way and attempt to find the answer to a simple question such as "How profitable was this organization in the Midwest region last year?" you would probably struggle to find the answer. First, you'll need an MIS professional (one who has a deep understanding of the data structures and the complex paths between them) to construct the query for you. Then, you'll find that the query involves joining a huge number of tables and has many complex predicates in the WHERE clause. The upshot of all of this is that the query ends up running like a bear in syrup! Worse still, the bear in question has to share a limited supply of honey (CPU power and I/O capacity) with your online users. What can be done?

What Is a Data Warehouse?

Data warehouses are an excellent way to address the problems we've described in the previous section. You can think of a data warehouse as sitting in the middle of all of the application-centric systems in your organization. The warehouse receives regular feeds of data from these systems and forms a consolidated view. The data may be a simple copy of the transactional data (in which case it is referred to as *atomic* data), or it may go through a transformation or aggregation process between its source and final destination (the warehouse). The data may be cut so that only a subset is taken at one time, or it may go through a translation process to make it compatible with data from other sources. The terms *slicing* and *dicing* are commonly used to described the data reduction and extraction techniques. The internal structure of the data warehouse is designed to make queries simple to define and efficient to execute; we'll describe the details of how this is achieved later in this chapter.

Almost every successful application of data warehousing uses dedicated servers. With these servers, the "queries from hell" which are a common feature of data warehousing affect only the users of the information service and do not slow down time-critical business operations.

Earlier, we alluded to the fact that powerful tools are required to enable users who are not *au fait* with the SQL language to define queries and perform *dimensional analysis* (basically "what if" scenarios) on the data. It should be possible to pose queries such as "What would be the effect on our sales if our main competitor decided to pull out of the market?" A new generation of end-user tools and engines known as *online analytical processing (OLAP)* is designed to tackle this type of projection and to aid users in walking around the database and then drilling down to more detailed analyses where they require them. However, be aware that Oracle's OLAP engine, part of the Universal Server in Version 7.3, does not directly use Oracle's relational database engine. (See the final section of this chapter for additional information.)

Figure 13-1 illustrates our definition of a data warehouse with a typical example.

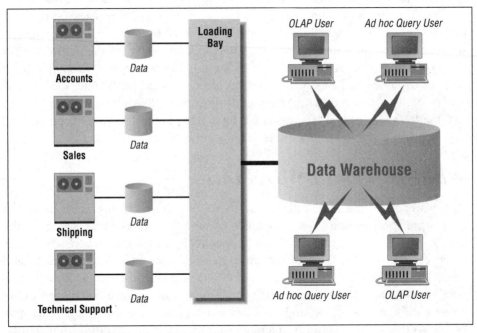

Figure 13-1. A typical data warehouse configuration

The data sources are many and varied, and the data is moved from the source systems into a *loading bay* from which it goes through a transformation and integration process and is loaded into the warehouse. Once data is in the warehouse, it is freely available for users to perform *data mining* operations with the OLAP tool.

The loading bay shown in Figure 13-1 is a conceptual object that is used to hold the incoming data in its raw format before applying it to the data warehouse. The data contained in the loading bay may be physically held as flat ASCII load files or in temporary holding tables in the database. These holding tables may be snapshots or replicated data tables from other sources. The loading bay data may even be held in some internal form in a product that handles the data transfer. While the data is in the loading bay, it is not available for analysis; it is not yet in the data warehouse.

By showing only a thin line, the diagram fails to do justice to the transformation process that gets the data from the loading bay into the warehouse. This is where the transformation and integration logic resides. If two feeder systems both hold customer details but use different identifiers, then the data must be reconciled and some of it may have to be amended or discarded. This process is often called *data scrubbing*.

The data warehouse itself is shown as a data store, but obviously it must reside on a computer somewhere. This is likely to be a powerful symmetric multiprocessor (SMP) machine, or it may be a massively parallel (MPP) machine. It may even be a distributed environment itself, or a three-tier architecture with an application server between the client and the data server. The designer must be involved in choosing and sizing the particular machine(s) that will hold the data warehouse. As we've mentioned, the data warehouse should live on a dedicated machine since complex queries in the warehouse would otherwise have an impact on the performance of the other applications.

Within the server is the data model. The structure of the data is the most important facet of the warehouse. It may (in the simplest case) be a direct copy of a single production database with some heavy denormalization applied to it. Or it may be a fairly complex schema that is the result of merging several production databases, applying some aggregations, and denormalizing the result. In such cases, there will almost certainly be *mismatch resolution intelligence* built into the cleaning or loading process.

If this is a "serious" warehouse, the data model will be a highly complex *star schema* drawn from a mixture of internal and external data sources, possibly including textural and/or multimedia data. (We'll tell you more about star schemas later in this chapter.)

Multidimensional Versus Spatial

The database underlying the data warehouse need not be relational. Many such databases are based on a *multidimensional* model rather than a relational one. Multidimensional servers are designed to optimize the storage and retrieval of dimensional data with a level of performance that would be hard to achieve with a relational architecture. However, multidimensional databases have proved not to scale too well and tend to underachieve with high data volumes and large numbers of dimensions.

In Version 7.3, Oracle has successfully implemented a series of extensions to its relational database engine so that if you select the spatial data option, the system directly supports spatial queries. Unfortunately, many Oracle staff (including some of their marketing executives!) appear confused about the difference between multidimensional support (referencing data on the basis of any number of foreign keys) and spatial support (referencing data on the basis of coordinates). This chapter is about the multidimensional problem; the data may also have spatial properties, but that is another problem.

To understand why the spatial problem is so nasty for a relational database, consider how you would index to support the following query that seeks out all oil wells in a given locality:

```
SELECT welled, latitude, longitude, total_barrels_produced
  FROM oil_wells
 WHERE latitude  BETWEEN :lat1   AND :lat2
   AND longitude BETWEEN :long1  AND :long2;
```

The only effective mechanism for addressing the problem efficiently is to invent a referencing system that divides the 3D space into a (large) number of blocks, each, say, 500 meters by 500 meters, and to store for each oil well the block in which the oil well is located. The query predicates can be transformed into a list of qualifying blocks, and this can be used as the basis for indexed access. Each oil well which is in a qualifying block is checked to see if it is actually inside the space described by the query predicates. Figure 13-2 sketches the general scheme.

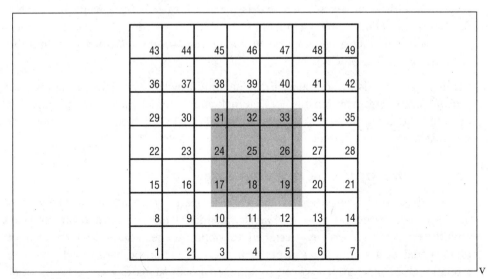

Figure 13-2. Getting from two dimensions to one (in figurelabel tag?)

The clause:

```
WHERE x BETWEEN 3.8 AND 5.3 AND y BETWEEN 2.2 AND 5.3;
```

becomes

```
WHERE block IN (10,11,12,17,18,19,24,25,26,31,32,33)
   AND x BETWEEN 3.8 AND 5.3 AND y BETWEEN 2.2 AND 5.3;
```

Unfortunately, the list of qualifying blocks can be very long indeed for some queries, so Oracle's Spatial Data Option uses a hierarchical mechanism. Clever stuff, and almost an essential buy if that is your problem—but it is not the subject of this chapter.

What Sets a Data Warehouse Apart?

A data warehouse may strike you as an expensive luxury. At first glance, it may appear that powerful query tools running against the live OLTP database could achieve the same effect. But in most cases, this is just not so. There are many reasons; some of the most significant are the following:

- Data on the OLTP system is constantly changing as the data entry processes capture new and updated data. You cannot effectively perform "what if" scenarios and other forms of analysis on data which is not static because you cannot validly compare the results. You may wish to hold some variables constant, while you change others, to see the effect. In the meantime, though, if the underlying data has changed, the comparisons are worthless. Oracle7 gives us the facility to view data in a read-consistent manner (using the SET TRANSACTION READ ONLY statement), but only in a relatively short time frame since it is limited by the size of the rollback segments.

- The data is often dispersed across the organization, held in heterogeneous computer environments at distant locations. Even with the benefit of distributed database technology, it would be technically challenging to accomplish an integrated view of this data without first migrating it. The performance implications of trying to run the queries are horrific!

- As we have already said, data in an OLTP database is usually designed and optimized for data entry and maintenance. Most of the navigation around the data is controlled by the OLTP applications. Providing for unanticipated access and navigation will not always be possible; where it is possible, it is likely to be slow.

- Many OLTP systems only record limited history (if any). This makes it unlikely to be useful for analyzing trends.

- Since the data is mostly used by applications written by IT people, it probably contains encoded values and obscure naming conventions. It probably also contains tables which have no real business purpose, but which were introduced to implement a physical design decision. All of this makes the data hard to be understood by end users. Such users are unable to see the wood for the trees; if they do see the wood, it doesn't make much sense to them without some translation process! The use of views can overcome this shortfall to a degree. However, view names and the names of columns within a view are restricted to 30 characters, and it is often difficult to express a meaningful name in this limited space. For instance, the column AUTO_ACK_YN on a table could be named SEND_AUTOMATIC_ACKNOWLEDGEMENT in a view. A good user query tool will allow more descriptive names, and may even allow names that have embedded spaces.

- Many OLTP systems implement data access and security control in the application itself, making the use of ad hoc query tools unsafe unless they also have a suitable security subsystem. Commonly, you will see a proliferation of view definitions to overcome this problem.

- When ad hoc queries are performed on live data, such queries may have to be restricted to certain times of the day that are not critical to the business operation. After all, you don't expect your query users to be well-versed in performance techniques, and there will be little to stop them from writing (or generating) the query from hell, prompting the online users to remark, "The system is slow again." You can try to solve these problems by only permitting ad hoc queries before 8:00 a.m. and after 6:00 p.m., but you are going to find it difficult to sell your system as a true on-demand query service, especially if the jobs have to be scheduled through an operations group!

Data warehouses did not come into being overnight. Rather, they evolved from *decision support systems* and *executive information systems.* Traditionally, DSS and EIS systems operated on data that was identical to the data in the operational system where the data was maintained; these systems accessed either the live data or a recent read-only copy of it. Data warehouses do not necessarily take direct copies of operational data from OLTP systems. The tables are based on operational data, but generally they include only detail pertinent to the decision-making process. The data belonging to your organization is of interest, but if it can be combined with general market data that includes your competitors, then such data takes on a whole new significance. The other data sources may be available from marketing agencies. Some external data is available as a continuous feed from service such as those provided by Reuters.

Why have data warehouses caught on in such a big way, what benefit do they give us, and how can the cost be justified? For strategic decision-making, it is imperative to have access to at least an enterprise-wide view of operational data, and in some cases, a market-wide view. To form a complete business picture, the users must be able to traverse the departmental boundaries and they must have available external data such as that relating to competitors. In this environment, historical data is as important as current data—therefore, both must be maintained. This consolidated view of the business, together with some intelligent data mining tools for performing ad hoc inquiry, provides us with a powerful armory for making informed business decisions. What kinds of decisions? A marketing executive may perform trend analysis on data in a data warehouse and identify a potential gap in the market that could be exploited.

Design Challenges

Data warehouses present some interesting design challenges. By their very nature, these warehouses are physical beasts; as such, they require strong design and DBA skills from an early stage to make them effective. Some of the properties of data warehouse that present these design challenges are the following:

- Warehouses tend to be large databases—often very large.

- They demand a high data throughput.

- Data must be physically stored in a way that is optimized for query.

- Many traditional design techniques don't apply to data warehouses because they presuppose that you want to optimize for OLTP or for update (warehoused data should *never* be updated directly, only indirectly as a result of receiving new data in the loading bay). This characteristic has the important consequence that it can be both desirable and safe to break third normal form (3NF).

The fact that a data warehouse is usually formed as the product of several production systems means that it is likely to accommodate a huge amount of data, often stretching into terabytes. Accurate sizing in design is critical—both in the initial sizing and in the growth rate of the data. It is not uncommon for a data warehouse to receive several gigabytes of new or revised data every day. This places a further stress on the code that moves data from the loading bay into the warehouse.

Traditional techniques such as data normalization are based on a basic need to avoid redundancy in order to balance query requirements against DML. As we saw in Chapter 3, *Data Modeling*, the process of normalization proliferates a large number of tables. And yet, a large number of small tables tends to be the antithesis of what best serves a data warehouse. For this reason, data warehouses challenge some of the deepest-rooted concepts of traditional relational design. Even entity modeling is not ideally suited to data warehouses, and this has given rise to a technique known as *dimensional modeling*, which produces databases that are easier to navigate and query. We'll discuss dimensional modeling later in this chapter. For the moment we'll simply note the concept of a *fact table*, structured to hold all of the facts with which the warehouse is concerned, such as stock movements or item sales.

It should be clear by now that implementing a data warehouse is not a case of simply going out and buying some query tools. It requires some serious work in scoping and designing the warehouse before you can even contemplate which tools are most suitable for inquiry on the data. If you are considering the first data warehousing project in your experience or that of your organization, we recommend that you set yourself a small and achievable scope to start with. If your first attempt sets out to develop a corporate-wide solution, the chances of success are heavily stacked against you. Instead, you should focus on a small well-defined area of the business that is achievable in a reasonable time scale and has a manageable data size. Once this has been successfully accomplished, you can then go on to conquer the world!

Oracle's Commitment to Data Warehousing

Oracle was uncharacteristically tardy in embracing the data warehouse concept. In the early 1990s, as customers started to implement data warehousing, Oracle was somewhat slow to provide explicit support. When it became clear that the company was falling behind specialist vendors such as Redbrick, Oracle launched a series of initiatives that were intended to give them the edge. This included the acquisition of the OLAP tool PC Express (now known as Oracle Express) from IRI software. Oracle also encouraged third parties to join forces with them. The company set up the Warehouse Technology Initiative (charmingly, though perhaps misleadingly known as WITI) and currently has more than 30 partners.

Oracle also recognized that Version 7.0 failed to meet the requirements of DW sites and started to specifically target data warehousing in each subsequent release.

Version 7.1 came with additions that facilitate both the data query and data take-on elements of warehousing. The parallel query option enables a large or complex query to utilize multiple processors in a multiprocessor environment. Release 7.1 also boasts a parallel load facility and a parallel index builder. The parallel loader enables rapid data take-on. Multiple SQL*Loader sessions can simultaneously load data into the same table using the *direct path* facility which yields huge savings in elapsed times for a load.

The data replication facility enables you to replicate a table in any of the operational databases. This is an alternative to providing a flat file data load facility to suck the data into the warehouse. This table may not be in the format that is ultimately required, but from the replicated table further transformations can be made to massage it into a more useful shape in another table. Effectively, the replicated table lies in the loading bay of the warehouse.

Version 7.2 was delivered with claims of twofold performance improvements in creating indexes and executing certain types of complex query. The improvements in index creation came largely from the fact that the buffer pool is bypassed. The CREATE INDEX command writes directly to the database blocks. Improvements in the CREATE TABLE...AS SELECT... command also allow the insert and query operations to run in parallel. This is beneficial when creating a roll-up table of summary data.

Version 7.3 has intelligence within the optimizer specifically for star joins, and it removes limitations on the number of extents in a database object. This release also has significant efficiency improvements in handling joins to UNION ALL views. This is particularly useful when a fact table in the warehouse has been partitioned but requires combining for certain queries that need to see a consolidated view of the data. Most importantly, Version 7.3 finally implements value distribution histograms so that the query optimizer can calculate the selectivity of an index operation against data whose distribution of values is skewed.

There are a number of additional features of Oracle7 that were not specifically designed for data warehouses but which may be of use. For example:

- For large heterogeneous networks, the many Gateway and Interchange products which Oracle provides (such as the Transparent Gateway to IBM DB2) can save the tedium of a dump to a flat file and subsequent reload, and the UNRECOVERABLE option on INSERT...SELECT... further reduces the overhead of such operations.

- Data that is required to be held in the warehouse is not necessarily all classical record-based data. There may also be large volumes of pure textual data, such as word processing documents and multimedia presentations. This unstructured data can be accommodated by integrating applications with Oracle Text Server and Oracle Media Server. The text server product, for instance, enables fast words-in-text searches on high volumes of unstructured data, and this can be a powerful data mining tool.

- Oracle also has its own offering in the data mining tools arena, with the Discoverer/2000 product group. Two products are available which are very similar in nature—Oracle Data Query 4 and Oracle Data Browser 2. In our opinion, this is an area where Oracle is still maturing.

Tales of Caution

Now that we've established some of the major benefits of data warehouses, we had better look at what can go wrong. Here are some warnings to take heed of before you jump on the data warehouse bandwagon!

- Data warehousing is a technology that you have to ease into gently. You should adopt an iterative approach, bringing in a single data feed at a time. If you go for the "Big Bang" approach, you are pretty much certain to encounter severe problems. You may not fail completely, but you will always have regrets about certain elements. The iterative approach, on the other hand, allows you to learn from previous steps and makes the task more manageable. However, you do need a basic infrastructure in place first—even on a small project—and you must condition your users to realize that although the real benefits from the data warehouse will come as the complexity and size are increased, you cannot get there in one step.

- Remember that the warehouse is pulling together data from the entire organization. In most organizations, what is referred to as a "widget" by sales is known as a "grommet" by production. Not only this, but the sales force knows instances of the widget/grommet by a three-digit code, and the production group uses a six-letter code. If you want to mix your widgets with your grommets, and report on them as the same thing (which in the real world they are) then you will have to get the organization to agree a standard set of terminology and data standards. Of course, you can introduce synonyms where something has more than one valid name, but that is also fraught with danger. The business must "buy in" to the technology, must be prepared to make quick decisions about data standards, and must be willing to make compromises.

- The previous point alludes to differences in naming and format of data. There may also be subtler but deeper-rooted anomalies. For instance, a *customer* to one part of the organization may be a *branch* or *department* of a parent customer to another part of the organization. Differences like this may be difficult to detect. When they are detected, they can be difficult to resolve to the satisfaction of the entire organization. We emphasize that the more data feeds you have, the more time you need to plan for resolving mismatch issues of these kinds. In addition, although it is nice to have a strong, well-constrained data model, it is not always possible because the data from the disparate sources may not match or fit together very well. For example, you may have to allow null values in a column that would normally be considered mandatory if you have one particular source which you cannot guarantee will always supply the data. Alternatively you may find yourself putting the text string "UNKNOWN" into mandatory columns.

- We advise you to undertake a data quality exercise on each of the feeder systems before you design the data warehouse. The last thing you want is for your executives and VPs to be making bold corporate decisions based upon data whose validity is in doubt. You may choose to filter the data from certain sources or to omit the source completely pending a cleanup of the data.

- Be aware that the data in your warehouse is liable to be high volume to start with, and will only grow over time. You *must* do some early capacity management planning to predict this volume and growth. You must also consider the system management issues that surround the administration of such vast data. Your DBA and your system administrator may very well need some help with this baby! The DBA should be involved in the project at an early stage. As we've pointed out, data warehouses are very physical by nature.

- We reiterate the point that you should start small and grow from there. As we've mentioned before, your first attempt at a data warehouse may be simply a denormalized copy of a single production database, combined with a flat file load interface and a set of simple data query tools.

Design Issues for Data Warehouses

Now that we understand what a data warehouse is, let's look at the design considerations.

Dimensional Modeling and Star Schemas

We've mentioned very briefly before that data warehouses may be modeled using the techniques of dimensional modeling and the star schema. To reiterate what we've said, traditional data modeling and database design methods do not tend to yield data structures that are optimized for mass query. You'll need to throw away some traditional ideas about design and learn some new techniques. Some of this section touches on analysis—we make no apology for this since it is essential to understand how these models are defined.

Like most concepts in the computing world, *star schema* has several aliases. It is also known as the *multidimensional schema, data cube,* and *star-join schema.* The reason that it is called a star schema is (surprisingly enough) because the data models resemble stars.

Facts and Dimensions

The star schema model consists of a central *fact table* surrounded by several *dimension tables.* Figure 13-3 illustrates the concept. The fact table is often physically many tables that are partitioned in some way. We will cover partitioning later in this chapter.

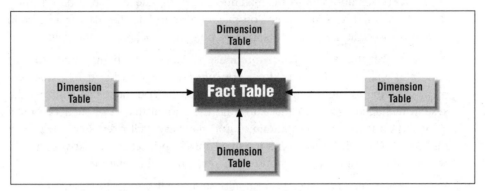

Figure 13-3. The star schema

The relationships between the fact table and the dimension tables must be simple and clear, such that there is only one possible join path between any two tables and that the meaning of the join is obvious and well understood. We always need to bear in mind that we are developing this system to enable the users to define their own queries. End user ad hoc query tools against traditional relational database have never really caught on to any great extent. Even if the columns are dressed up and given friendly names, the problem has always been that the relationships within the data model are both complex and plural. By plural, we mean that there is commonly more than one way to join two tables. Sometimes a query must include tables that are irrelevant to the business question, but which are necessary because they contain references to other tables required in the query, although some middleware products such as HP Intelligent Warehouse and Business Objects address this issue by providing a mapping layer. The other benefit of simple relationships is that it helps to improve our performance.

In doing the dimensional modeling, all our analyst has to do is identify the facts and their dimensions! Put simply, the facts tend to be the key business activities and influences on the business or sector of the business. If your organization (or department) has a mission statement, then what are the things within the business that have a major role in achieving that mission? To find candidates for inclusion, examine the entity models of the OLTP systems and especially examine reports that are run off the current systems specifically for executives and marketeers. The list you come up with will go through a refinement process and will eventually be agreed upon.

What about the dimensional tables? Put broadly, these are the elements which may exert some influence or give rise to trends over our facts. Dimensions can be broadly categorized as *people, places, things, and time* (see Figure 13-4).

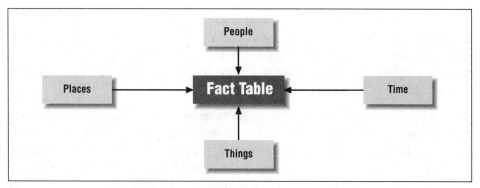

Figure 13-4. Dimensions categorized as people, places, things, and time

Think of the fact table in terms of a transaction history: it has a foreign key to each relevant dimension table. It pulls together the dimensions that gave rise to an event of significances, and it contains quantitative and qualitative information about the event. These foreign keys can be used in two ways:

1. They can be joined to the dimension table to retrieve descriptive information about the dimension.

2. They are the basis on which we commonly wish to summarize the fact table. For instance, we may sum the quantitative values from the fact table for a particular customer; providing that the customer name is part of the statement of the fact, this summing can be achieved without a join to any other table.

The fact table may also contain descriptive information, but this is less common—descriptions tend to reside in the dimension tables. In a sales scenario, a fact table might contain the quantity of a product that was sold, the monetary value of the transaction, and the foreign keys of the dimensions of the sale (which product, when it was sold, who sold it, and what method of payment was used).

The time dimension in a star schema has some interesting properties. It is quite likely that the fact will pertain to a period of time rather than a precise moment in time. Thus, the time dimension is usually a summary dimension. For example, it is unlikely (although possible) that the warehouse needs to record the details of every sale of every product in every location by every salesperson. It is far more likely that you would want to know the value of sales over a *month* by product, location, and salesperson. The choice of month as the unit is arbitrary in this case, of course; the unit could be a day, a week, or a quarter. We would normally choose the usual reporting period of the organization. However, there is clearly a trade off between holding a vast number of fact tables in the warehouse (that have to be summed in most queries) against missing seasonal trends due to summarizing over too long a period.

The time dimension is often the basis upon which the fact table is partitioned. Partitioning is often required to prevent a fact table from becoming too large and unmanageable. Time is used since it tends to give rise to even slices and is often the most logical dimension for partitioning. It is also the most likely basis for pruning the fact table (should you ever be able to get the enterprise to agree to remove data from their beloved warehouse).

The choice of the granularity for the time dimension (week, day, month, etc.) can be extremely important. If you choose a month, for instance, then your analysis tool may be able to summarize further and show the data aggregated across years. You may then wish to use drill-down techniques to represent the data over the quarters for a given year, and again down to months. Obviously, the drill-down cannot proceed to a lower level, since no data is held for any lower level. The granularity decision is an important one that has to balance the requirements for a more and more detailed breakdown against the size of the data warehouse and the load time required to populate it. If you choose to load every single transaction from your various OLTP databases into the warehouse, your users would probably be doing date-effective queries against the time dimension table with all the complexity of SQL and the potential pitfalls involved. (For a perspective on this, see Chapter 7, *Dealing with Temporal Data*.)

Some intelligent OLAP tools may formulate the queries for you, but behind the scenes is a potentially inefficient query. However, bear in mind that by summarizing you will always lose some information. It may be that certain sales regions are increasing sales significantly by keeping the sales offices open into the evening. By summarizing by sales date (and time) into month, you could miss this valuable insight.

Therefore, you will need to give due consideration to our time dimensions and make a decision in each case about the appropriate granularity to sum over when you are designing the warehouse.

Example Star Schema

Figure 13-5 illustrates the star schema for a sales system in which our fact table (SALES) is summarized by MONTH (time), PRODUCT (thing), SALESPERSON (person), and CUSTOMER (person). First of all, let's consider the number of rows in our fact table in a year (12 months). Suppose that we have 100 customers, five sales staff, and three products. The maximum total number of rows is the product of all of these numbers (100 x 5 x 3 x 12 = 45,000) rows. However, it is unlikely that all our sales staff sell all products to every customer each month, so the actual size will be considerably less. What this calculation serves to illustrate is that the fact table in this case is the Cartesian product of the dimensions minus any inapplicable rows. If almost all rows were populated, then many designers would opt to hold a record showing a zero volume for the cases which could logically be left out.

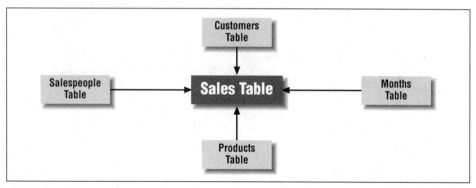

Figure 13-5. Star schema for a Sales system

Figure 13-6 shows the table definitions that are used to implement the star schema from Figure 13-5. Several points are worthy of note.

1. Surrogate keys tend to proliferate in dimension tables. This is simply because the table has often been created from several sources. It may be formed as a join of several tables from an OLTP system. It may be sourced from similar tables on several different OLTP systems that do not have identical keys. It is sometimes useful to give the dimension table a "real" key, as in the case of Months in the example. This makes the foreign key in the fact table more useful, since it enables analysis by year without performing a join back to Month.

2. Some of the dimension tables have what would be foreign keys to further tables in a traditional model. For instance Salesperson has a *bonus_scheme_id* and a *sales_office_id* field. Since the bonus scheme and the sales office are not considered to be dimensions of the Sales fact table (in this interpretation at least), they are not created as separate tables. Any details that are required can be included in the dimension table that they are related to. For instance, Salespeople includes the bonus scheme type. This is an example of redundant and unnormalized data that is characteristic of dimension tables.

A typical query against a star schema specifies details about the points of the star (the dimension) and summarizes the data about those points. This usually leads to several iterations of varying one of the dimensions in order to seek trend information in the data. You can do this by holding some dimensions constant while varying others or by joining the fact table to others to seek correlation between the fact table and the unconstrained dimensions. This technique is frequently referred to as drill-down and is supported by many of the available OLAP data

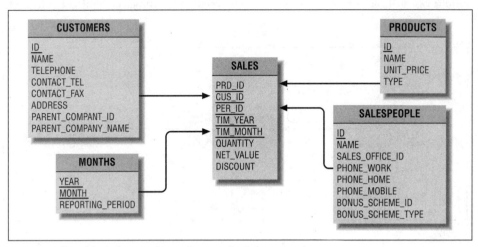

Figure 13-6. Table definitions to implement the Sales star schema

browsing tools. The following SELECT statement illustrates a typical query against the star schema from which variations may be made to the sales region, months, or product to seek out trends in the data. Note the characteristic simplicity of the SQL for a star schema; it uses only simple one-way equijoins from the dimension tables to the fact table to formulate it. The dimension tables have not been joined to one another to formulate the query—a sign of a good warehouse design.

```
SELECT SUM(sls.quantity)
       ,sls.month
       ,per.name
FROM   sales sls
       ,salespeople per
WHERE  sales.per_id = per.id
AND    sales.year = 1995
AND    sales.month BETWEEN 6 AND 7
AND    sales.prd_id = 33
AND    per.sales_office_id = 6
GROUP BY sls.month, per.name
```

The above query should optimize adequately, although you might need to experiment to get Oracle to pick the correct driving table. "Star queries," on the other hand—those in which there are predicates against more than one dimension table—optimize extremely badly in all Oracle versions prior to 7.3. We strongly advise you to implement a procedural solution (or use a query generator that generates one) if you have to support such queries against earlier versions.

Dimension Rollups

Although the query shown in the previous section is simple, it is also somewhat cryptic as it stands. It is not clear exactly what the product with an ID of 33 is.

This could be overcome by joining to the Products dimension and specifying the name instead. However, it is not possible to do this to specify the Sales Office by name rather than ID since, as we said, there is no Sales Office dimension. There are several options here:

1. Include the Sales Office name in addition to its ID on the Salespeople table.

2. Create a new dimension called "Sales Office."

3. Create a *dimension rollup* table.

Options 1 and 2 are fairly self-explanatory. If this type of query is common, then adding a separate dimension for Sales Office would be the recommended choice. But let's explore the third option—dimensional rollup. With this option, we somewhat break the classical star structure and we create a dimension rollup table that is related to the dimension table.

This is illustrated in Figure 13-7 and looks suspiciously like a normalization of the star schema. This approach is acceptable if it is a requirement to hold a lot of information about a Sales Office and to frequently summarize by Salespeople within Sales Office. You should keep the number of dimension rollup tables small; ideally, avoid them altogether because they make the SQL to extract data more complex.

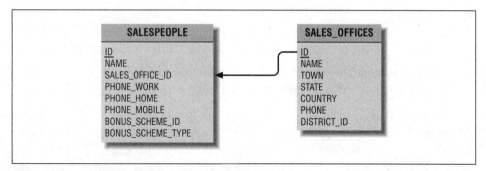

Figure 13-7. Introduction of a dimension rollup table

Partitioning

The term *partitioning* is used a lot in database-speak and it generally means the subsetting of data. There are horizontal partitions (slices) which take a subset of the rows, and vertical partitions (dices) which take a subset of the columns. In this chapter, where we talk about "partition" without qualifying it, we mean a horizontal partition. This is illustrated in Figure 13-8.

Most fact tables in a warehouse will have a data source that is subject to heavy transactions. In the example shown in Figures 13-5 and 13-6, the Sales table is the

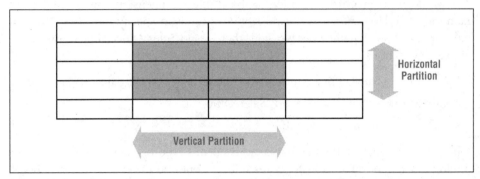

Figure 13-8. Horizontal and vertical partitioning

fact table. We hope that there is a healthy flow of new sales coming in through the Sales Offices each day! These new sales need to be brought into the data warehouse periodically. Later in this chapter, we'll explore mechanisms for bringing in the new data. Let's suppose that there are seven regional offices and we decide to load up the new sales data to the data warehouse once per day. The files could be loaded into a single Sales table, but this has several disadvantages:

- The table could become very large in a short period of time, making it difficult to administer and manage.

- The table may be unavailable to the query users while the load is in progress, depending on the techniques used to make the load process perform well.

- It is hard to separate off and discard data that has become old and lost its relevance without writing a purge facility that runs periodically.

To overcome these issues, we can partition the fact tables into smaller tables. In the example, instead of a single table for all sales data called SALES, there will be a table for each day called SALES_0101096, SALES_010296, SALES_010396, etc. Each table will contain the combined sales figures of the seven regional sales offices for the day in question. It would be possible to partition by Region (SALES_ NORTH, SALES_MIDWEST, etc.) but it really wouldn't make much sense in this case since doing so doesn't address most of the issues raised in our list. In most cases, the time dimension is the obvious one to use for partitioning.

When you are choosing the differentiating column for the partition, you'll find that it is best to opt for a partition key that makes loading easy. For this reason, Date Processed or Date Created tend to be better candidates than Date Applicable since the former fit more naturally into the cyclic load process. You might enter an order on the system that was actually taken from the customer last week or you might enter future or recurring orders. When it comes to extracting data to load into the data warehouse, you can't guarantee that you'll get all the data for a partition in a single hit if the partition is based on the order date, but you can guarantee this if it is based on the order processed date.

We've shown the beneficial effect that partitioning has on the load process. Let's look now at the effect on the data query process. On the face of it, there is a problem. To query or summarize the data for the whole of January 1996 requires a union of 31 tables: SALES_010196, SALES_010296, ...SALES_013196. You'd expect this large union to be cumbersome to code and inefficient to run. However, its cumbersome nature can be overcome by defining views that pre-create the large unions (but make absolutely certain that you use the UNION ALL set operator rather than UNION).

Some of the more sophisticated query tools allow you to define a meta-model of your data that describes the relationship between the partitioned tables that collectively define the fact table. The performance issues are dramatically addressed in Version 7.3 where join conditions can be "pushed down" into UNION ALL views provided that a series of restrictive conditions are met; essentially, the view must be on pure partitions—that is, the logical definitions of the partitions must be identical in every regard.

In addition, Version 7.3 can use its histograms of column values to determine which of the partitions to search by index and which to full table scan. This feature removes a previous major penalty for the inclusion of "redundant" partitions and forces the previous generation of query generators to attempt this optimization as part of query generation rather than leaving it to the query optimizer. With versions prior to 7.2, partitioning still has the advantages we've discussed under archiving in Chapter 10, *Safeguarding Your Data*. Still, we advise you not to attempt to join to the UNION ALL view; instead you will need a query generator that generates a complete query on each partition and forms a UNION ALL of the results.

It is possible to partition over more than one attribute (SALES_NORTH_0196, SALES_NORTH_0296, SALES_SOUTH_0196, etc.). However, doing so moves us away from the concept of keeping the design simple and gives rise to complexities when we combine the tables.

You could develop an end-of month routine to run on your data warehouse that extracts the data for the month and creates a new table (SALES_0196). This has obvious redundancy, but it could be used effectively if you also perform aggregation operations in the extract to summarize the data for a monthly view. When the user drills down, you start to use the daily partitions that make more detail available.

Defining an Aggregation Policy

As we have said, most data warehouses comprise a mixture of two types of data:

- Atomic data that maps directly to data from OLTP systems

- Aggregate data, that is, a summary of the data held in OLTP systems

We need to examine when, what, and how to aggregate.

When

Let's deal first with *when* since this is a relatively straightforward characteristic. The best time to aggregate data is during the transition from the loading bay to the warehouse. The second best (and more usual) approach is to load it into the fact table and then aggregate from there. An alternative is to create a load file of summary data at the same time the atomic data load file is created. But there are several problems with this alternate method:

- It may not be certain that all of the data will be validated successfully when it is loaded into the warehouse. This can lead to inconsistencies between the aggregate and the atomic data, since the aggregate data may not fail the validation in exactly the same pattern as the underlying data.

- Quite often, you will want to aggregate data that is not from a single source system or that did not come across in the same load set.

What

Next, let's deal with the less clear-cut issue of *what* aggregates to produce. The best way to answer this is to examine the likely uses for the data. This is difficult to ascertain since, until the data warehouse is operational, you don't really know how it will be used. However, if you've collected some opinions while gathering user requirements, this information can give you some vital clues. Look at some potential aggregation groups for our Sales example in Table 13-1. If we were to produce all possible combinations of aggregations, we would be producing an enormous number of new facts in the fact table. Clearly, we have to decide which are important and eliminate those which are not.

Remember that any aggregate that is not implemented in the warehouse can be derived at runtime from other aggregates or atomic data. Thus, any aggregate which has a subordinate aggregate with a small number of distinct occurrences is a good candidate for elimination. For instance, it is possible to determine the value for a quarter by simply summing three months, and to determine the value for all products by summing Core and Noncore (assuming that this is a mutually exclusive and exhaustive grouping).

Table 13-1. Candidates for Aggregation

PRODUCTS	SALES PERSON	CUSTOMER	PERIOD
All PRODUCTS	All SALES PERSONS	All CUSTOMERS	Year
Core/Noncore PRODUCTS	By Country, Region, and Sales Office	By Vertical Market	Quarter
PRODUCT Lines	Salaried/Commissioned	Multinational/ National	Month
	Direct/via Distributor	Top 20, 10, 5	Week
			Day

It's tempting to eliminate the aggregates that have lower granularity because, on the face of it, these result in the highest saving. For instance, since there are 365 days in a year, eliminating days may seem tempting (when multiplied by the number of Products, Sales Persons, Customers, etc.). However, in the example, the data is likely to be very sparse at this level (unless every Product is sold by every Sales Person to every Customer every day); in actual fact, the reduction may not be that significant.

It may not be possible to eliminate any of the complete categories that are shown in Table 13-1 since they may all be significant to various facets of the business; however, it's highly likely that certain combinations could be excluded. For instance, Sales made direct or via a distributor may only be required per Quarter and only for some Product lines, since it is likely that not all products are sold through both channels. Examining management reports that are produced on OLTP systems may give you some information that will help you decide what combinations of aggregates are significant.

How

Now let's consider *how* to aggregate. By this we mean where to physically store the aggregate data. Basically, we have a choice of three options:

1. In the same table as the base (nonaggregated) fact data

2. In a single fact table but separate from the base fact table

3. In separate tables for each aggregate created

As you would expect, there are arguments for each approach.

1. Option 1 is not really viable if the fact table is partitioned and gives rise to very large tables which can become unmanageable. When the aggregation process is in operation, it will be both reading from and writing to a potentially huge table; as a result, it may be very slow. Also, the aggregate rows

may not have the same structure as the atomic one, since some columns will be inappropriate at a summary level.

2. Option 2 may still have the problem that the table holding the aggregates may grow very large and is only viable if your various aggregates for a single fact table have the same format. This can be restrictive if you later want to add new aggregates.

3. Option 3 is probably the most attractive, but you need a good naming convention to keep track of all your table names, and a good meta-model to describe them to your query tools and end users. Effectively, your end user tools or your middleware should be made "aggregate aware," or your end users will have to bear the responsibility for spotting opportunities to use the derived data.

Combining Fact Tables

The fact tables defined in the schema are not necessarily totally isolated from each other. There may be occasions where they need to be joined. For instance, there may be an Invoice fact table and a Line Item fact table, and it may be useful to analyze combined information from the two. This can be achieved by creating a view that joins the tables. The view can be made known to the middleware or query tool and created as a fact table in its own right.

Extracting and Loading the Data

Perhaps the longest and most danger-fraught part of building a data warehouse is the production of the data extraction facilities from the feeder systems. It is very easy to underestimate the complexity and the problems that you will experience when planning the data migration. In Chapter 8, *Loading and Unloading Data*, we examined some of the general issues you'll encounter when you migrate and load data. This chapter focuses on the issues that are specific to a data warehouse.

You can view the data extraction and load process as a series of steps; some of these take place on the feeder system, and others take place on the data warehouse system.

Step 1: Read the Data

You first have to consider which systems have data which is of relevance and interest to the data warehouse. This might appear to be a very straightforward task; however, in some organizations there are a proliferation of PC databases that were created to make up for shortfalls in the production systems. These databases sit on the C drives of individual users' PCs and often contain really useful information. You have to decide whether such databases should be included in the load. In making this decision, you'll need to strike a balance among these various factors:

- The usefulness of the data.

- The difficulty of acquiring the data—PCs get switched off and moved with monotonous regularity, and when they are networked their IP addresses mysteriously change.

- The potential lack of integrity and authenticity of the data. User-written PC applications often have even less data validation than the official ones released by IT or MIS.

For the moment, let's ignore these personal databases and concentrate on the core systems of your organization. The most challenging part of the task often is finding documentation that describes the data items so you can determine which are important and what format they are in. This is particularly true if the application system was bought from a third party, and the vendor has a policy of not publishing layouts (the subject of much discussion in Appendix A, *Off-the-Shelf Packages*).

If you have no idea of the internal structure of the application, this does not necessarily mean that it cannot provide data to participate in the data warehouse. You may be able to use the contents of a report, or (if you are lucky) the application system may already have a facility to dump out data in a well-documented format. This may not be ideal, since it may not be exactly the data you are interested in, but it is better than nothing.

Once you have identified the data that you want, you need to decide how you are going to pull it out—and in what format you want it. By far the most common method is a flat file. These can be either fixed-length or delimited (described at length in Chapter 8). There is usually a choice of tools for creating such files. For instance, if the data is in an Oracle7 OLTP system, you can use SQL*Plus, a 3GL using the precompiler, Oracle Reports, or any of a number of third-party tools to create the file. Our experience is that a 3GL is the best bet, but it is also the most expensive option. Of course, you can try to write the extract in PL/SQL, but you might regret it for a number of reasons, including performance. For many simple columnar extracts, especially if there are no long text fields, it is difficult to do better than use SQL*Plus as follows:

```
set echo off termout off arraysize 100 pagesize 0
spool extract.lis
SELECT cust_id, order_no, order_value, sales_code, order_date
  FROM orders
/
```

```
    spool off
    exit
```

Where potentially long fields need to be trimmed and delimited, we recommend against the use of SQL for these operations. 3GLs do the job so much better.

There are a number of alternatives to flat files that you might want to examine. For instance, using the distributed database capabilities of SQL*Net or some of Oracle's Gateway products, you could read from the production system and write directly to tables on another system. In most cases, you should not insert directly into the data warehouse because you would be skipping some of the next steps, but rather you should insert into the loading bay.

Step 2: Filter the Data

Apart from the very first data extract, you do not really want the entire contents of the extract. Ideally, you want only records that have changed or been added since the last extract. Some data warehouses are completely flushed out and reloaded every time they are refreshed, but this is a practical proposition only for relatively small warehouses where the data is not refreshed very frequently or where a large percentage of the data is likely to have undergone some form of change between loads.

You need to determine what data has changed since the last extract. If you are very lucky, the source database has *date_changed* and *date_created* columns, and the filter can be put in the extract process. However, even this does not help you identify the records that have been deleted since the last load unless you are *extremely* lucky and the system has logical deletions that set a *date_deleted* column.

Assuming that you don't have the luxury of such a column, the only way to determine what has changed is by comparing one complete dump of the data with the previous one. This can be achieved by sorting the files by key order and comparing them line by line. There are tools that are specifically designed to do this for you. However, if you are a do-it-yourself type of person (we call them DIYs in the U.K.), a utility such as the UNIX *diff* command is invaluable.

Step 3: Ensure That Historic Data Is Not Lost

As we've already discussed, one of the differences between a data warehouse and a traditional application system is that in the data warehouse it is usually important to keep a full historic perspective. The fact that a product name was once changed from "Marathon" to "Snickers" is of little relevance to the Sales and Order Entry systems. However, it is of huge significance to the data warehouse because the change of brand name may have a significant impact on sales and market share—just the kind of thing you are hoping that the data warehouse will tell you. Let's assume that the name is simply an attribute in the sales applications and order entry and the product key is a numeric code. When there is a change in value of a significant attribute of the operational data, it is important not to simply overwrite the record in the dimension table in the data warehouse; instead, we want to create a derivative of it.

However, you now have a riddle to solve. Some queries will want to regard all facts for either product name as referring to the same dimension table row, whereas others will want to discriminate between the two. We suggest the use of a secondary foreign key column (a version number), although we recognize this is not an intuitive solution to the ad hoc query user.

This encoding of meaning into the keys of dimension tables can be useful when you are performing dimensional analysis, as you can choose whether or not to use the similarity of the keys in your queries (i.e., to treat them as the same product or separate products) without losing performance. You need to define the version numbers in the meta-data of the warehouse (more on meta-models later).

Step 4: Manipulate the Data

The format of the data as it comes out of feeds from the live systems is highly unlikely to be in exactly the format that is required for the data warehouse, which has highly denormalized data structures. The fact tables may be fairly close to the desired shape, but the dimension tables will probably need manipulation, and may need to be combined. For example, in the Sales example used throughout this chapter, the Sales Office is not created as a dimension but is merged into Sales Person. There may also be some summary and aggregation of the data in this step. However, as we have already mentioned, this is better left until the new data is in the warehouse.

We cannot over-stress that when you are combining data from different applications you will be forced to make compromises, and at times you will have to make arbitrary decisions. You may find, for example, that sales data from one subsidiary contains only the list price in force at the time of the sale but not the amount received, whereas the data from another subsidiary contains only the price realized and not the list price (which is no longer available). A third subsidiary may have both prices, but the data structures make it impossible to determine whether or not the money was ever received.

The solution you select from the choices in this example will depend in large measure on how the users are likely to interpret the data in the warehouse. In the abstract, there are no right answers.

Step 5: Move the Data

Next, you need to get the data from the source system into the loading bay of the data warehouse. There are many methods for achieving this goal, but generally some form of file transfer is used, especially if the machines are physically located a long way apart. In many cases, you will find that the data is moved prior to being manipulated because the warehouse project wants the data fully under its control as early as possible in the cycle. Another factor may be the extreme difficulty of getting any new 3GL code written for the mainframe, and of finding room for it in the operations cycle. However, in many cases the source system will be the best place to perform at least the initial transformations.

Step 6: Load the Data into the Data Warehouse

At last, the data goes from the loading bay into the warehouse itself and becomes accessible. Unless the data is to be "scatter loaded," with data from one source record being posted to many tables, SQL*Loader is almost certain to be the best option. As we have already said, the new parallel capabilities of SQL*Loader should ensure a reasonably efficient load, especially when the direct path option is used to bypass much of the overhead usually associated with inserting data into an Oracle table. The various options of SQL*Loader are discussed in Chapter 8.

You may be tempted to drop indexes and disable constraints on the table prior to the load, and then to re-enable them afterwards. However, the direct path loader handles the merge of the old and new index values efficiently. The issue of constraints is a thorny one, and many warehouses simply run without them. If your validation is good, then you should not be experiencing constraint violations. At the end of the day, the CPU and elapsed time costs of re-enabling them will be enormous.

Step 7: Sort Out Rejected Records

In our experience, a high proportion of loads generate exceptions. This may be for any of a number of reasons, some of which are explained in the following list:

- Dirty data in the original system that fails the stricter constraints of the data warehouse (though this should have been handled by the data scrubbing).

- Incorrect load order, such as trying to load a fact row that has a dimension value that has yet to be loaded. This probably indicates that the load process has a basic design flaw.

- Internal problems, such as lack of space in the data warehouse itself, and lack of a sort area for rebuilding indexes.

- Interrupted, aborted, or partially complete load.

- Duplicate data, which will again indicate a design problem or a program bug in your data validation.

Any data warehouse that contains a partial load should carry an explicit health warning sign in a table which is checked by the menu system that takes users into the query tool. Why? Because as soon as the incomplete data is used for analysis purposes, you are in trouble. The data will be used for making strategic decisions, and users will assume that it is valid. The regional VP of your Asia and Pacific area may not be very happy if he or she is sacked for a poor sales record because two of the country's sales figures didn't load!

When you have exceptions from the load, then you need to go through them, assess the importance of them, and attempt to fix them. If they can't be fixed, then it is useful to have a contingency plan—for example, restore the data warehouse from a recent backup. If you do take this drastic step, remember that the feeder systems need to be informed somehow so that they include the data again on the next extract.

Step 8: Derive Aggregates

For a discussion of this step, see the section called "Defining an Aggregation Policy," earlier in this chapter.

Step 9: Verify

Assuming either that the load was error-free or that you fixed the exceptions, you are nearly ready to roll. However, we advise you to run a series of verification checks before you allow the users on the system. These checks are designed to give you confidence in the data. They can merely be a set of simple SQL scripts that test for a few obvious things. For instance:

- If you sum up all the Sales across one dimension, then the figure should be the same as the sum across another dimension.

- The Sales for a given month should be equal to the sum of the Sales for the days in the month.

- The sum of Sales for every Region in the month should equal the sum of the Sales across all Salespeople for the months.

and so on. Because of the inherent redundancy in the data warehouse, there should be a large number of these types of checks that you can perform. We recommend that you pick a representative subset and make them as automated as possible.

Meta Data

When you employ a middleware product in your data warehouse it will invariably require *meta data* or a *meta model*. Put simply, meta data is data that describes other data. In terms of designing a data warehouse, it is a set of data structures which describes the data in the warehouse and identifies the sources. It contains mapping and transformation logic and may describe or name the processes which perform the transformation and integration (see Figure 13-9). This meta data may also provide the mapping layer for the ad hoc query or reporting tool that is used to mine the data. It can describe the data in terms that are meaningful to the end user, and it hides any complications within the underlying database structures. The meta data contains details of how you have partitioned your fact tables and what aggregates are available for each fact table. Using this information, an intelligent query tool or middleware engine can make sensible decisions about how to best structure an efficient query based on a user's search criteria. A well-maintained meta model is an invaluable tool, even if you aren't employing middleware that requires it.

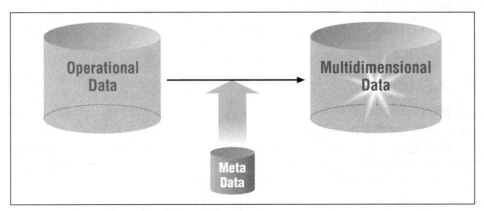

Figure 13-9. The important role of the meta data

Once you have defined the structure of your operational data, mapped it to source data from a data feed, and defined rules for transforming it, the next step is to actually extract and load it, as we've discussed above. You can go out and buy a tool to help automate the process or you can opt to do it yourself.

Transformation Types and Methods

It is hard to generalize completely, because we can guarantee that you will find an unanticipated transformation in each new data warehouse project that you undertake. However, let's look at a representative list of typical transformations that you may encounter.

Encoded Keys

Many systems have keys or identifiers for tables that encode a meaning of some kind. For example, a policy number in an insurance application may be composed as follows:

Policy Number = 92SWMV092

where:

92 = Year
SW = Region or Territory
MV = Policy Type
092 = Sequence Number

There is very useful information buried in this key. We describe it as *buried* information because you cannot easily build a query predicate based on it. Sure, you can use the standard Oracle wildcards and search for strings matching "_SW%" to locate all of the policies in the South West territory, but this is both cryptic and extremely inefficient. However, you may find an abundance of this type of structure in some of the older legacy systems that are your data source, and you will have to deal with them.

As part of the transformation process, you can expand this field out into several useful fields using lookup tables. The policy number in the example may be expanded as follows:

Policy Number	Year Policy Started	Sales Region	Policy Type
92SWBC092	1992	South West	Motor Vehicle

This new structure contains the same information (with some redundancy), but now it is in a much more usable format. This translation is often critical since some of this information will become dimensions in the data warehouse.

Flags in Multilingual Systems

Many data warehouses take a global view of a market. In multinational organizations, this means combining data from many countries, including non-English-speaking ones. The fact that descriptive data is in a foreign language may not intrinsically present a problem; however, there may well be a problem with encoded values. Strange as it may seem to English speakers, many French speakers seem prefer to use "O" and "N" where we would use "Y" and "N", using as their justification the unarguable fact that the French word "Oui" means "Yes" in English. The meta data needs to identify all columns that take their value from a list of values and to define the equivalent values for each language supported. During the transformation stage, you will need to translate all such values into a single target language.

Numeric Data Manipulation

Numeric data can come in a variety of formats. You may need to convert real numbers into integers, to remove spurious precision, and to allow for scientific notation (such as $6.2e17$). Mainframe systems that are producing binary files may well include packed decimal fields, and their character strings are more than likely to be in EBCDIC. If FTP or SQL*Net cannot be deployed to provide the required conversions, you will need to write a utility to handle this conversion task.

Date Manipulation

Oracle can cope with most external date formats, but not all. There are some pretty obscure representations, such as the number of elapsed days since a fixed point in time (such as 01/01/1970), which may need massaging into a format that an Oracle date mask can cope with.

Match and Merge of Keys

This is where you deal with the problem of the mismatch of data from disparate feeder systems. If you encounter something as trivial as products that have a 7-character alphanumeric code on the Sales system but a 9-character numeric code on the support system, then a simple lookup table will suffice (provided that there is a one-to-one relationship between the codes). If there is not, then you are back in the compromise business.

A more sticky problem is that of external data such as customers. The worst scenario for this problem arises when you have to merge several disparate Customer tables from data feeds into a single consolidated dimension table. First of all, you need to agree upon a structure of the consolidated table and the primary key. The table will contain all the common columns and some that occur only in some of the feeds. The key will normally be a surrogate one. The meta model needs to hold information mapping every field of all of the data feeds to a column in the consolidated dimension table. The difficult part is automating the matching process so that "Abc Inc." from one system matches "A.B.C. Inc." from another. Obviously, when an automated match cannot be made, you will need to manually map records from the feeds to one another. Be sure to retain the full details of this mapping for reference by future loads. Hold all of this detail in your meta model.

NOTE Name and address matching is a complex problem that is of great importance both to the direct mail industry and to a number of systems designed to detect attempted frauds. It is a highly specialized area and there are a number of companies that specialize in it.

Retrieving the Data via Data Mining and OLAP Tools

Tools that enable high-powered users to make both strategic and tactical business decisions are collectively known as *online analytical processing* (OLAP) tools. They enable the user to navigate around the data without knowledge of the underlying structure and present the data using familiar business terms. They allow the data to be viewed from a number of different perspectives or dimensions (a technique known as *pivoting*), and they support variance of a dimension with others kept static to allow modeling of "what if" scenarios. OLAP tools also let the user drill down into the data where a greater level of detail is required.

OLAP tools can be divided broadly into two categories:

• Multidimensional (MD-OLAP)

• Relational OLAP (ROLAP)

The difference is that MD-OLAP utilizes a multidimensional database architecture, whereas ROLAP supports an underlying relational database. For purposes of this book, we are considering only ROLAP, although we acknowledge that some OLAP tools have a multidimensional engine between the (relational) database and the front-end tool.

NOTE In Oracle7 Release 7.3, Oracle has incorporated a multidimensional engine (the Oracle Express Server) within the "Universal Server." However, this new engine operates in a totally separate space from the relational engine and at present isn't very well integrated. The multidimensional engine acts as an independent data store and a cache for data held in the relational back-end. Because the subject of this book is the Oracle relational database, we won't delve into the multidimensional engine.

The selection of an OLAP tool is an important part of the development process of data warehouses. We recommend that you make your choice as early as possible in the life cycle because certain design decisions may depend on your choice. For instance, you may be in a quandary about how much atomic data to hold and how many aggregates to maintain. Some OLAP tools can produce aggregates "on the fly" at runtime. If you hold monthly, but not quarterly, sales figures in the data warehouse, then a simple group summation can create the monthly figures. A more likely scenario would be that you have the required aggregation but want to show a particular dimension occurrence as a percentage of the total, or consolidated with another dimension. For instance:

- "What proportion of our sales of nondurable goods came from the Asia-Pacific region in September?"

- "Which of our operating departments spent over budget last year?"

- "Who are our top ten spending customers worldwide, and what percent of our revenue came from them?"

The bottom line is that the more adept your OLAP tool is at deriving this data, the less you will have to anticipate these type of questions.

14

Designing for Parallel Processing

In an Oracle environment, parallel processing is built around two specific products: the Oracle Parallel Query Option (PQO) and the Oracle Parallel Server (OPS). As we shall see in this chapter, these two very different pieces of software both set out to achieve the same goal—to apply as much hardware as is available to service the current workload. Although the similar names of these products sometimes leads to confusion between them, they are completely separate products. The potential confusion between the two is made worse by the ability of the Parallel Query Option to exploit the Parallel Server if it is also present.

What do these products do? Oracle's Parallel Query Option seeks to speed up full table scans (and only full table scans) by having several processes each do part of the work. This can be an advantage even on single-CPU machines, but on a machine with many CPUs and many disk controllers, the improvement in query time can be stunning.

Oracle Parallel Server allows separate Oracle instances to share a single physical database. This approach allows Oracle to support hardware where processors can share disk drives (or read and write to each other's drives in so-called *shared nothing* architectures) but cannot share memory, and thus cannot all access the same in-memory control structures.

Even if we don't run either of these products, there are ways that we can (and, in most cases, should) take many steps to achieve at least some parallelism in our processing. It is fortunate that we can get the benefits of parallelism without using PQO and OPS because, although both are brilliant examples of software engineering, they provide real benefit only in highly specific circumstances.

Many of the concepts discussed in this chapter apply to environments with a single CPU as well as to those where CPUs are in abundance! Before we examine how we can use this software, let's take a brief look at the problems we'd like to solve.

Why Do We Need Parallelism?

Normally, we run several processes inside our server. Some are part of the operating system (for example, the process that receives email); some are part of database operation (for example, Oracle's DBWR (database writer) process); and others are user processes where our SQL statements are interpreted and processed.

There is a crucial process called the scheduler, which runs under two very specific circumstances: in a single-processor machine, the scheduler takes over whenever either of the following conditions occurs:

- The process using the machine decides to surrender control, usually because it has to wait for some form of input or output (I/O).

- The process using the machine does not surrender control, but tries to keep on using it after the expiration of some deadline. The length of time the process is allowed to run for is known as its *time slice*, and this form of scheduling was originally known as *time slicing*.

Almost all processing has to stop and wait for I/O at frequent intervals. In normal Oracle operation it is very unusual for even a batch process to use much more than 50% of the available CPU power. Why? Because it spends the rest of its time waiting for database blocks to be read in from disk and (to a lesser extent) waiting for redo log entries to be written to disk.

When the CPU is performing an operation such as that shown in the following statement, our CPU utilization may only be able to reach single figures because we are spending more and more time waiting for table blocks to be read in from disk.

```
SELECT sales_region, COUNT(*), SUM(order_value)
FROM   orders
GROUP  BY sales_region;
```

However, this is not the end of the story, because the hardware may have the ability to perform many disk operations in parallel using multiple disk controllers. If we had spread this table out over many disk drives (a process called striping, discussed later in this chapter), then a monitoring tool such as BMC's PATROL product would see an almost idle CPU and a series of disk drives each working, but none anywhere near capacity. Without striping, and when only one query is running, we would expect to see only the drive containing the table being used at all, but not being driven to its full capacity, and an even more idle CPU. In this case, what is happening is that the CPU and the drive are working alternately.

Asynchronous readahead will help to alleviate this situation, but the maximum rate at which the CPU can acquire data will be limited by the single drive.

Rule one of "Bottleneckology" states that:

> At any given moment in time, a system can only have run out of one resource.

Although this rule is widely quoted and accepted, it is not absolutely true. Nevertheless, it can be assumed to be true for all normal design and tuning activity because its corollaries are both true and useful. If we have not yet run out of any resource, then we ought to be able to use more resources and thus go faster; once we've run out of one resource, we'll have to reduce our consumption of that one in order to go faster still.

Since we would like the answer to our queries as soon as possible, we want to be able to drive either CPU or disk I/O capacity to its maximum performance. In the example mentioned above, we are almost certain to reach the limits of the I/O subsystem before reaching the CPU limit of even a single processor. However, with other queries (especially those using functions and with complex predicate clauses), we may find that we can exhaust several CPUs while remaining within the capacity of our I/O subsystem. And, of course, the usage pattern does not remain constant for the life of the query: traditionally, Oracle processes a GROUP BY query such as the one in the example in three steps:

1. Full table scan to acquire the values

2. Sort to group all the values for each region

3. Aggregation (actually performed in the final merge phase of the sort)

If the instance tuning parameters allow the allocation of a large sort work area, then the process may move from being I/O-bound in step 1 to being CPU-bound in steps 2 and 3; we would like to organize execution to be able to take advantage of this.

Only recently have designers been forced to address the problems caused by Oracle's exhausting I/O capacity: except on the very largest systems, Oracle applications that have used parallel processing to push an application to its resource limits have traditionally run out of CPU, rather than I/O. However, over the past few years, a number of important factors have changed the performance profile:

- Processors have become significantly faster, and servers tend to have more processors than in the past.

- Databases have become significantly larger, requiring more I/O operations for a typical report or analysis query.

- Disks have become significantly larger, concentrating more I/O operations onto a single device.

- Disks have not become significantly faster.

In summary, then, we need parallelism so that while one of our processes is waiting for I/O, another can take over and start using either a CPU or a different I/O resource. We also need parallelism so that we can use more than one CPU and more than one I/O device at a time. To perform optimally, we need as many processes active simultaneously as it will take to guarantee that we will exhaust either our I/O capacity or our CPU capacity. As a rule of thumb, for online transaction processing, this normally requires between four and eight active processes per CPU.

Striping

Striping is a term used to describe a technique of spreading data across disk drives. Imagine that we have four tables, each residing on a separate dedicated drive, as shown in Figure 14-1. Now imagine that it is month end, that all the departmental heads are desperately attempting to get their month-end figures in, and that accountants are equally desperately trying to analyze said figures. All of this data is stored in our database in table 1, which is taking considerable "hits." So much so that there is continuous contention for the drive, and user processes are held on a queue awaiting disk availability. Clearly, this is not an ideal scenario!

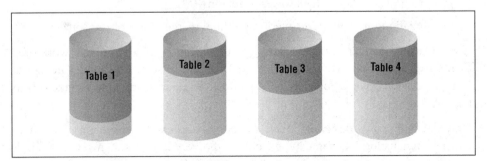

Figure 14-1. Four tables in a traditional disk configuration

How can we better spread out the I/O, regardless of which table is being used? We can lay each of the tables across each of the drives, as shown in Figure 14-2. This is known as disk striping.

With this new arrangement, it does not matter which table is "popular" at any particular time; we have at least some chance of spreading the I/O load across several drives. Clearly, without some special arrangement, such as the use of Oracle's Parallel Query Option, this distribution of tables will only be of benefit to

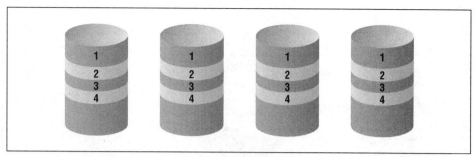

Figure 14-2. The same four tables an a striped configuration

our CPU or I/O utilization if there are multiple users all trying to access the table at the same time.

At one time, this striping would have been achieved by creating a series of database container files or UNIX raw partitions (as shown in Figure 14-2), and then using the CREATE TABLESPACE and ALTER TABLESPACE commands to create four tablespaces, each spanning four physical devices. Each table would then have been loaded into its own tablespace. For critical benchmarks or performance tests, tuners would even seek to load each table in a predetermined sequence designed to ensure that each process would use "its own" drive. For most real-world systems, it is unlikely that such an ideal loading pattern exists. However, there is a known weakness in this approach to striping, which is that it is quite difficult to control where *new* rows are inserted. In general, they will all go to the current insert block (or blocks) of the table, and they may tend to reside on the same physical disk. If this occurs, and if there are high insertion rates into the table or the most recent rows are those most frequently queried, then the striping will turn out to be largely ineffective.

Fortunately, the latest generation of operating systems relieves the designer of these constraints. Many current versions of UNIX contain a *logical volume manager*, which allows the system administrator to create logical disks from all or parts of the physical disk domain. In most cases, the logical volume manager will also provide striping by spreading the blocks of the logical disk across the physical disks in such a way that a random pattern of access to any of the data in the logical volume will generate an equal load on each disk.

A great benefit of using a logical volume manager is that it applies to all files on the disks, not only those containing the Oracle database. This reduces the effect that other (non-Oracle) applications may have on disk contention, and it may also reduce disk bottlenecks writing trace files and report output.

From the designer's point of view, the logical volume can be visualized as shown in Figure 14-3.

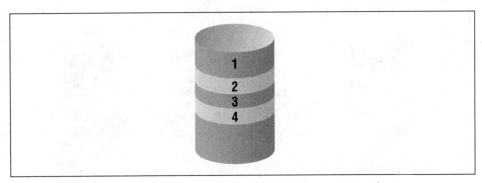

Figure 14-3. A logical volume (as seen through a logical volume manager)

This is a much simpler model to deal with than manual striping, and it is frequently much more effective. We cannot recommend that you impose the load of manual striping on your system administration function unless you have an environment in which total I/O throughput to a single object is becoming a problem *and* your operating system has no provision for creating logical volumes.

RAID, Mirroring, and Performance

RAID (*R*edundant *A*rrays of *I*nexpensive *D*isks) technology is widely adopted as an enhancer of both data integrity and performance. Our experience of RAID has been that it has both benefits and costs.

One feature normally found in such arrays is that the RAID controller implements "logical volumes," such as those we described, except that in this case the mapping is performed in the controller, and the operating system does not need to be aware of the underlying physical arrangement.

RAID controllers can also be used to implement *disk mirroring*, a process in which each write is made to two separate drives. These pairs of drives mirror each other and reduce the probability of data loss due to drive failure. When a disk block is requested by the server, it can be read from either of the drives on which it is resident, delaying the onset of drive contention. This is RAID 1.

RAID proponents also promote the advantages of RAID 5, an arrangement whereby blocks written to disk are not written conventionally into a single place on disk, but instead are distributed across a number of drives using a particular algorithm. This algorithm means that the record can be fully reconstructed in the event that any one of the drives fails. Such a mechanism uses about 40% fewer disk drives than RAID 1 for the same nominal capacity, while still offering the ability to sustain failure of a physical drive with no data loss. That's the good news.

However, to write a single block to disk we have to involve five drives, and to read a single block we require service from four drives. In the worst case, we can reduce our effective I/O throughput by around 70%. That's the bad news.

Our conclusion about RAID is that it can be a cost-effective way of buying mass storage. However, before you use configurations other than RAID 0 and RAID 1, we advise you to carefully consider both the costs and the benefits of the technology.

Designing to Achieve Parallelism

Even when you expect your application to run only on a single processor CPU with a limited number of disk drives, it is still worth looking to see if you can increase performance by introducing parallelism. At the very least, consider whether parallelism will ensure that if your hardware is upgraded, the application performance will increase rather than remain constant.

As a very rough rule of thumb, for a typical batch processing or reporting application running on its own on a server with medium-rated CPUs and fast disks, we would expect to get no better than the following levels of CPU utilization:

Number of Processes per CPU	Overall CPU Utilization
1	<50%
2	~75%
3	~85%
3+	>90%

On a ten-CPU system, a single batch process will use less than 50% of one CPU or less than 5% of the total CPU power. As many of the critical processes within applications continue to be designed as single-stream batch tasks, we begin to see that there might be a considerable advantage in performing parallel processing whenever possible. In other words, instead of having our single processor use less than 50% of one CPU (which does all the work serially), we would hope to take advantage of the other CPUs. In doing so, we'll increase the overall throughput of our report or process.

Creating and Maintaining Indexes

Both index maintenance and index creation are time-consuming processes, and many sites have indexes which are routinely dropped and recreated for performance reasons. For example, if a long batch job is going to update an indexed column in each row of a million-row table, but it does not use the index to query the table within the job, then it will invariably be faster to drop the index, run the batch job, and recreate the index.

But what if there are three such indexes to be recreated on the same or different tables? Especially if a logical volume manager has been used to stripe the tables, why not initiate all of the index recreates in parallel? (Yes, Oracle does allow multiple indexes to be built on the same table at the same time, and has done so since Version 6.)

Most system administrators and tuners are unwilling to do this because of concerns about "head contention." They worry that, whereas a single index create could scan the table by moving the heads across the disk in a linear manner, with several scans in progress at once, the heads will be continuously moving backwards and forwards across the disk and thus wasting time. Our advice is to try this approach on your own hardware against your own data. Our experiences have been almost uniformly positive.

After seeing that parallel index builds give better performance, if you continue to worry about head contention, you will have to construct a model that is more complex than simply looking at disk head movement. In reality, an index build alternates between episodes of intensive I/O and episodes of intensive computing. The cost of moving the heads is trivial compared with the advantage of getting some I/O done during an episode in which the first task would have left the disk idle while computing.

Batch Processing

Traditionally, batch processing in Oracle applications has been specified and implemented as single stream without considering whether or not the sequence imposed is required. As with index re-creation, the simplest way to get some parallel processing going is to simply initiate more than one job at a time. Viewed from a UNIX shell script, this may be as simple as changing the script

```
aged_debts min_age=30 level=4 offices=all connect=scott/tiger

pick_list_print stores=all connect=scott/tiger
```

to:

```
nohup aged_debts min_age=30 level=4 offices=all connect=scott/tiger &

nohup pick_list_print stores=all connect=scott/tiger &
```

Those not familiar with UNIX may need a little explanation: the & at the end of the line causes the line to be run asynchronously, and the command *nohup* causes the requested process to be independent of the script that started it. The job will continue to run even if the user who started it logs out of the system before the job has completed.

If we are sure that there is no dependency between these two tasks—that is, neither task queries data which might be changed by the other—then this is a perfectly safe optimization. Depending on device and CPU contention, we may save anything up to the elapsed time of the shorter job.

However if our server is a symmetric multiprocessor architecture machine with (say) six processors, then in order to exploit the available power, we are going to have to find many more than two processes to run in parallel. One of the most powerful design techniques for doing this is to abandon the notion of performing the entire business function within a single run, and to start the same program many times, each process performing part of the overall job. In an organization that supports four offices and three stores, the script might become similar to the following:

```
nohup aged_debts min_age=30 level=4 offices=NY connect=scott/tiger &
nohup aged_debts min_age=30 level=4 offices=LA connect=scott/tiger &
nohup aged_debts min_age=30 level=4 offices=UK connect=scott/tiger &
nohup aged_debts min_age=30 level=4 offices=HK connect=scott/tiger &

nohup pick_list_print stores=US connect=scott/tiger &
nohup pick_list_print stores=UK connect=scott/tiger &
nohup pick_list_print stores=HK connect=scott/tiger &
```

At this point, if we have any sense, we start to get worried. If we add another office or another store, someone is going to have to remember to change the script to include the new site. Instead, we should tackle this problem by building the job stream dynamically; a trivial implementation example is shown below:

```
rem must set define to avoid & being parsed by SQL*Plus
set echo off feedback off pagesize 0 define #
spool pick_list_print_init
SELECT 'nohup pick_list_print stores ='
     || STORE_CODE
     || ' connect=scott/tiger &'
  FROM stores;
!pick_list_print_init
```

With some more control logic built around this script to ensure that the required runs have taken place, we can build a robust data-driven mechanism for running almost any task in parallel with itself. Even in cases where a final summary stage is required, the bulk of the processing can be performed in parallel by doing the following:

- Each of the parallel streams posts its contribution to a holding table.

- A summary stage waits until the posting is complete.

- The summary stage builds the summary.

This process is illustrated in Figure 14-4.

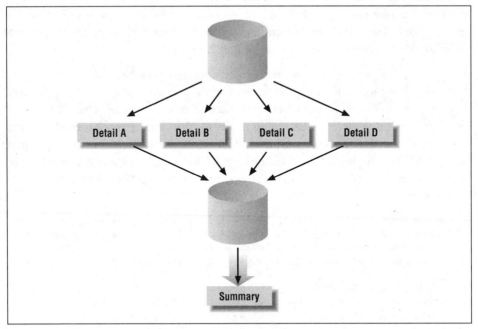

Figure 14-4. Batch processing in parallel streams with a summary process

Splitting a batch stream into parallel processes is beneficial, especially when there is a single large table driving the main query. It can be particularly effective when you have multiple CPUs on your system. However, there are a few things that you should bear in mind:

- Even though the streams may be partitioned in a way that ensures that they process different segments of the data, there is a risk that lock contention could occur on (say) a common parent row with a denormalized aggregate column.

- If one of the streams encounters an error and fails for some reason, then the entire process should be considered to have failed. However, some of the other processes may have completed and committed their processing. You will need to give careful consideration to recovery and restart when you are splitting a batch stream into parallel processes.

- It is not an easy job to split the load evenly. Our previous example used office and store locations, but this could be a very uneven split. The following section proposes a solution to this problem, but it involves considerable development effort to implement.

It is worth repeating a point we made earlier in the chapter. Provided that we have been able to distribute our data out across several drives that can be accessed simultaneously, these techniques will improve our batch processing speed regardless of whether the task is CPU-hungry or I/O-hungry. The objective is to use as much as possible of the available resource.

Case Study: Oracle Payroll

As we mentioned in Chapter 5, *Choosing Datatypes and Nulls,* the first release of Oracle Payroll ran under Oracle Version 6. In order to provide the required degree of customization and flexibility, this product used dynamic PL/SQL anonymous blocks to perform the detail payroll calculations. To say that this approach initially caused performance difficulties would be an understatement! The beta sites reported it took up to ten seconds per employee to calculate a paycheck.

Studies by the product team showed that part of the problem was the parsing of the anonymous PL/SQL blocks. They concluded that implementation of a large cursor cache within the calculation engine would ease this problem. However, it was apparent that the Version 1 PL/SQL engine was simply CPU-consumptive when making calculations. The team also noted that all of the beta customers were running on Sequent hardware, and that each had at least four processors. Thus, they made a decision to make the calculation process run in parallel.

The team investigated the use of various tactics, but in the end they decided to perform the allocation in real time. It was not sensible to pre-allocate employees to a particular process. There were two reasons. First, different employees could require wildly different amounts of processing; second, there was real danger that one process would be assigned all of the "difficult cases" and would end several hours after the others. This variation in processing times can be understood if you think about the difference between calculating pay for:

- An office worker who has worked a standard month and who pays neither local nor state income tax.

- A salesman whose commission structure was changed during the month, who pays both local and state taxes, and whose old and new commission schemes give different rates of commission for different product lines with rate enhancements once stated targets are met.

The process architecture that the team eventually arrived at allowed any number of pay calculation processes to be started. Each process made calls to an "allocator," which took an exclusive lock on the allocation table, allocated 20 employees to that process, and then recorded the allocation before committing and returning to the calculation process. After calculating the pay for these 20 employees, the process would call the allocator again, and would continue in this manner until the allocator told it that there was nobody left to pay. At this point, the process would insert its summary data into the database and complete.

It was clearly possible for the pay calculation processes to encounter contention trying to allocate employees, but the allocation lock was typically held for only 10% of the total elapsed time, and contention for this lock was insignificant. Parallel pay calculation was an immediate success, with order of magnitude improvements in performance at the beta sites.

But, unfortunately, there was a sting in the tail. Every so often, a pay calculation process would terminate unexpectedly with the unwelcome message:

```
ORA-00060 : deadlock detected while waiting for resource
```

Much time was spent investigating the allocator to determine how it was that it could allocate the same employee to more than one pay calculation process. After a few weeks, the team realized that the deadlocks were internal to Oracle. All that was necessary was to issue a ROLLBACK, sleep for a few seconds, and then try again. The technique for handling deadlocks was well known to the build team, but they had not bothered to implement it because they had convinced themselves that deadlocks would not occur. This is like riding a motorcycle without a safety helmet because you have convinced yourself that you are not going to have an accident!

TIP   Deadlocks of this type are very rare, and occur only when several
                processes try to take row-level locks in the same block at the same
                time. Eventually, Oracle runs out of space to record who is holding
                the lock and waits for one of the other processes to either commit
                or roll back. If you are very, very unlucky, it picks a process which
                is already waiting for one of your locks and the result is a deadlock.

                We are not saying that there is any limit on the total number of row-
                level locks that can be held (the limit is the number of rows in the
                distributed database), only that there is a limit on the number of dif-
                ferent processes which can hold locks within the same block at the
                same time. This limit varies with the amount of free space in the
                block, and is always greater than or equal to the value of the INIT-
                TRANS parameter for the object.

                This problem is rare, but it can occur. As a result, we strongly rec-
                ommend that all program designs take deadlocks into consideration.

Parallel Query Option (PQO)

Oracle's Parallel Query Option is a product that can help speed up full table scans, and their associated processing, by breaking these scans into pieces and allocating the pieces to a pool of processes. PQO was first made available in Version 7.1. Like the allocator described in the previous section for Oracle Payroll, the latest versions of PQO perform the allocation dynamically. They also deliberately allocate different-size units of work to the processes in the pool to reduce the likelihood that several processes will come back asking for more work at the same time.

PQO Pros and Cons

Suppose that we have the following query:

```
SELECT region_name
     , count(*)
  FROM customers
 WHERE industry_code = 'HW'
 GROUP BY region_name
```

If the predicate clause selects 5% (for example) of the table requiring visits to 4% of the table blocks, we might find that on an otherwise idle machine we can execute this query faster using PQO than we can using an index. However, this decrease in elapsed time is going to come at a cost—the query is going to drive either the I/O subsystem or the CPU to its maximum throughput. This is desirable if there is only one user on the machine, but is much less attractive if there are 50 order entry users all waiting to input new business while our query is running.

PQO goes further than the Oracle Payroll allocator in that it takes a query like the previous one and parallelizes both the data acquisition phase (the full table scan) and the sort phase; it then overlaps them so that the sorting starts while the scan is still in progress. The final merge pass in the sort is the single-threaded summary phase; as we described earlier, this is required when a parallelized process is required to produce a summary result. The resulting structure is shown in Figure 14-5.

What is the result of all of this processing? Not only can we leverage any striping that we've managed to apply to the table, but we can also get most of the sorting done while we are still working our way through the data.

The word "Query" in the product name is somewhat misleading; one powerful use of PQO is to allow indexes to be built much more quickly than they could be using a conventional full table scan. As we discussed earlier, such a scan alternates between being I/O bound and being CPU bound (on a single CPU). PQO does an excellent job of overlapping the I/O and CPU activity, and also allows multiple CPUs to be employed.

If you've read this far in this book, you've realized by now that we never get very far recommending a feature before we start issuing warnings and explaining some

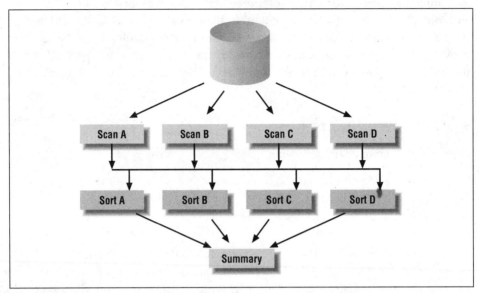

Figure 14-5. Outline of Parallel Query operation

of the disadvantages. Our first warning is that the word "Option" in the product name is *not* misleading. At the time we are writing, PQO carries a significant extra cost. Before deciding that this feature is going to solve all your query performance problems, you must be aware of the following:

- PQO works only on full table scans; most queries (particularly those used in online processing) are better served by using an index and forgoing the chance to be parallel.

- PQO is *designed* to hog resources; bearing in mind the limitations of UNIX schedulers, be aware that a single PQO user can effectively take over the server.

- PQO can be awkward to set up and tune; the control mechanism has no way of accepting an instruction such as the following: "My machine works best with 20 servers, so if there is only one parallel query in progress, give it 20 servers; however if other users come along, then take processes away from the first user and give each user an approximately equal number of servers up to a maximum of five parallel queries in progress at one time."

Where Should You Set the Degree of Parallelism?

The current implementation of the Parallel Query Option encourages the application process that is issuing the query to request a particular number of parallel threads (via the PARALLEL parameter). Unfortunately, doing this embeds an important tuning parameter into the application code. The application issuing the query may very well have a view on whether or not the operation is suitable for using a parallel scan. But the selection of the number of threads (the degree of parallelism) needs to be made on the basis of a number of factors which may not be known at the time the query is written, and which may not even be within the scope of the query writer. These factors include the following:

- The hardware on which the query is running, in particular:
  — The number of CPUs
  — The number of I/O controllers
  — The number of drives
- The extent to which the objects have been striped
- The other load on the machine

In general, we recommend that the PARALLEL clause and the PARALLEL hint should set neither the degree of parallelism nor the number of instances. The recommended forms are:

```
CREATE TABLE new_history
            TABLESPACE temp
            PARALLEL (DEGREE DEFAULT)
AS SELECT *
     FROM history h
    WHERE h.entry_date > SYSDATE - 730
       OR h.active = 'Y'
       OR h.type   = 'SECURE'.

SELECT /*+ FULL(H) PARALLEL (H, DEFAULT, DEFAULT) */
         h.type
       , count(*)
   FROM history h
  WHERE h.active = 'Y'
  GROUP BY h.type
  ORDER BY 2 DESC;
```

A possible exception is the use of INSTANCES 1 to prevent an operation from being exported to other hosts in an Oracle Parallel Server environment. This is recommended especially when you are building indexes on a host that is reserved for MIS or EIS queries. It can readily be set as the default parameter within the INIT.ORA file for the instance. It may also be appropriate to set the degree of parallelism above the normal installation default for queries or index build operations that you plan to perform on an otherwise empty machine. Indeed this CREATE TABLE statement might well be the first stage in a table reorganization running in a clustered environment—one where you assume that the table creation is allowed to take over the entire local host, but it is not acceptable to export parts of the query to other hosts. With four processors on the local host, the following modified statement might be preferable.

```
CREATE TABLE new_history
            TABLESPACE temp
            PARALLEL (DEGREE 20 INSTANCES 1)
AS SELECT *
    FROM history h
   WHERE h.entry_date > sysdate - 730
      OR h.active = 'Y'
      OR H.TYPE   = 'SECURE'.
```

Conclusions About PQO

We believe that the Parallel Query Option is best used for index creation and for summary queries that cause a substantial portion of a large (or very large) table to be visited (either because no suitable index exists or because a significant proportion of the total rows in the table qualify for inclusion in the processing). Despite the difficulty in specifying how the instance should perform its server allocation, PQO is very smart software technology. In an environment where there are multiple CPUs and multiple I/O paths, it offers the designer the opportunity to scan and sort large volumes of data in a fraction of the time that would be taken using conventional query optimization.

Oracle Parallel Server (OPS)

As we've mentioned, the Oracle Parallel Server option is a completely separate feature from the Parallel Query Option described in the previous section. Parallel Server allows separate Oracle instances to share a single physical database.

Symmetric Multiprocessing (SMP)

Hardware manufacturers have developed a series of architectures that seek to provide more powerful machines using components which are manufactured in large quantities. There is an underlying cost imperative here. At any given point in time, there are PC and workstation processor chips of a given speed being manufactured at very high volumes. Because of the high volumes, these chips have a low factory gate price. To produce a chip with 10 times the power may cost 10,000 times as much, or may simply not be feasible with current technology. So the way of producing very powerful machines at low cost is to get lots of low-cost chips running in parallel.

In a symmetric multiprocessor architecture, many processors share a memory bus. A typical SMP configuration is shown in Figure 14-6.

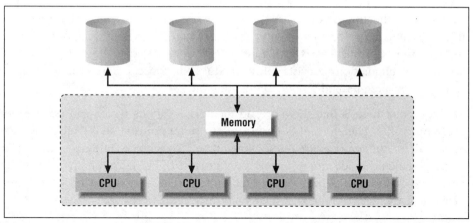

Figure 14-6. An SMP configuration

Unfortunately, as the number of processors increases, these architectures suffer from memory bus contention. This effect is compounded by the operation of the Oracle Server software, which makes heavy use the System Global Area (SGA) in shared memory, minimizing the impact of memory caches at the processor level. At some point (which will vary from one proprietary architecture to another), adding more processors ceases to be effective. Then what? The next route to increasing total processing power without requiring a faster processor is to "cluster" a series of hosts, which may themselves be SMP machines. This is shown in Figure 14-7.

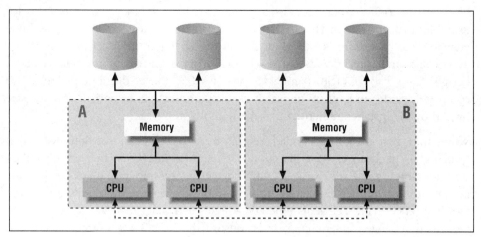

Figure 14-7. A cluster configuration

The cluster shown in Figure 14-7 consists of two SMP machines. For simplicity, we've shown each of the two hosts or nodes having the same number of processors, and each having access to all of the disk drives. Neither of these features is mandatory or even usual. When two separate machines share disks in this way, they are said to be *loosely coupled*. When CPUs share memory (such as the two CPUs in machine B in Figure 14-7) they are said to be *tightly coupled*. When a configuration consists of a mixture of loosely and tightly coupled systems, it is often termed a *hybrid* configuration.

The key point here is that there are no memory locations which can be seen by every processor. Therefore, it is impossible to run a conventional Oracle instance across all of the processors at the same time. A database instance running in Oracle's standard mode can run on Host A *or* Host B, but not on both at the same time. The dotted line at the bottom linking the processors is part of a local area network (LAN); let's look next at the significance of this network.

Oracle Parallel Server allows instances running on separate hosts within a cluster to share a database; the instances are said to be running in *shared mode*. The trick here is to ensure that a process looking at Oracle's shared memory region (the SGA) on one host sees an up-to-date picture, and that is that it is aware of any relevant changes made in memory on the other machine. To achieve this, the two (or more) instances use a Distributed Lock Manager (DLM). This lock manager typically uses a local area network to signal the lock requests, and the network technology is normally switched Ethernet connections.

At its simplest, whenever an instance wants to look at something in memory that might have been changed by another instance, it takes a share lock on the resource. Whenever it wants to change an area of memory, such as a database block in the buffer pool, it takes an exclusive lock. If an instance is told, for example, that another instance needs a lock on a database buffer that has been changed, the procedure is: the instance that has changed the block has to write it out to disk and surrender its exclusive lock. This is known as *pinging*. A major design feature of Oracle Parallel Server is that these distributed locks are completely independent of transactions and transaction boundaries. They are owned by the instance rather than by the transaction.

When they first meet the Parallel Server, most people can see intuitively that "pinging" is likely to cause contention between the instances. In particular, they start to worry about the disk I/O traffic caused by moving blocks from one instance to another. Unfortunately, this is rarely (if ever) the most severe problem they will encounter. The real difficulty is that each time an instance is about to look at or change something, it must ensure that it has the correct distributed lock; *this factor alone means that in shared mode an instance will generally run about 10% slower than in exclusive mode*. However, if it does not have the required lock, it must use the LAN to signal all of the other instances and they must reply. Even if no disk I/O has to take place, the result is a high level of distributed lock traffic. As we saw in Chapter 11, *Designing for Client/Server* and Chapter 12, *Designing for Distributed Databases*, there are very real limits on the rate at which a node can send and receive messages over an Ethernet.

OPS contains a number of design features that can limit the number of blocks which must be passed back and forth. In particular, tables may have sets of free lists called *free list groups*. When each instance uses its own free list group, both free list contention and current insert block contention are minimized. In addition, the DBA can divide the database blocks into groups by data file; in this way, the required number of distributed locks is reduced by covering a group of blocks with a single lock. It is common to cover all of the reference tables with a single lock; once each instance has a share lock on the reference data, they can all cache that data in memory without further distributed lock activity. Of course, under this arrangement, if anyone tries to update any row in the reference tables, then all the other nodes will have to abandon all their cached reference tables.

Sequences can cause a major problem, and so we recommend that you be careful to ensure that sequences are cached (the CACHE parameter value should be large enough for at least five minutes' operation at peak throughput) and that all sequences which are used cluster-wide are specified as NOORDER. A better solution is to ensure that each sequence is referenced by only one of the instances.

Index maintenance is the problem that dooms many OPS sites. Unfortunately, to make any changes to an index, an Oracle instance may have to "ping" an index branch block. Doing so invalidates that instance's copies of all blocks below that branch block in the index tree. The end result is that in a conventional cluster, you cannot afford to have the same index being maintained with any frequency from more than one instance. If you try to break this rule, your system may perform less work with two hosts than it did with one. It is that simple.

As the designer, you must take responsibility for ensuring that the work is partitioned across the cluster. We are not saying that other hosts can *never* maintain an index normally maintained by a particular instance, but we are very clearly saying that if they do it too often, the result will be catastrophic. It takes tests to determine the value of "too often" for any particular hardware, but the finding is likely to be that the lock should not be transferred more than two or three times per second. If it is never transferred at all, so much the better.

How can you design to live within this restriction, and still exploit the CPU power of the cluster?

1. Try very hard to segment the workload. If necessary, horizontally partition data entry tables and use a periodic consolidation task to gather the data.

2. Practice expectation control; help your users to understand that clustered hosts and Oracle Parallel Server are not magic, but just clever technology doing its best in an imperfect world.

Massively Parallel Processors: An Attempt to Change the Rules

Massively Parallel Processors (MPPs), always seem to be tomorrow's technology. Despite the billions of dollars invested (some would say wasted) in trying to get them to the point of commercial acceptance, there is still little to show in terms of an installed base. Although there are no standards in the world of MPPs, a number of clear trends are emerging in terms of the architecture choices and construction techniques. The MPP world is also learning that the scalar world (you and us) is not prepared to rewrite every single line of code they ever wrote just for the privilege of running on a machine that has 8192 processors, each with 64MB of memory, in a box about the same size as a microwave oven (and nearly as hot to the touch!).

Since it seems unlikely that many of you will be confronted with having to design applications for MPPs in the immediate future, we will simply note that MPP architectures offer certain special benefits to the OPS, in addition to enormous bang per buck:

- MPPs are, in general, designed to handle distributed locks efficiently. To cut down on the circuitry, the ways in which this is done are rather more complex than just connecting every CPU to every other CPU, but they certainly do not use simple LAN networks. We have seen claims of DLM rates in excess of 20,000 lock operations per second—where a typical cluster is limited to a few hundred. On the other hand, we have also seen a prototype MPP which could manage fewer than 100 lock operations per second!

- MPPs often allow memory-to-memory transfers between processor memories; indeed, some MPP architectures have only a limited number of processors with access to the disk farm, making such memory-to-memory operations essential for the worker processors to achieve any I/O. As we've mentioned, architectures where there is no shared memory and no shared disk are usually referred to as *shared nothing*.

- We are increasingly seeing NUMA (Non-Uniform Memory Architecture) machines, which allow large caches to be held in a memory field which sits between onboard processor memory and the disk farm. A simple NUMA machine is shown in Figure 14-8.

Some visionaries (including Larry Ellison, founder and CEO of Oracle Corporation) have suggested that with such an architecture, disks can be relegated to the

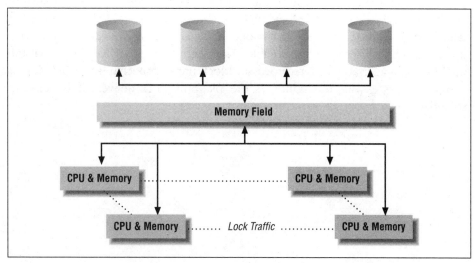

Figure 14-8. Simple NUMA (Non-Uniform Memory Architecture) configuration

role of a backup medium. For most applications, however, fully memory-resident databases are still some way off.

Once MPPs start to be used for major applications the ground rules for the design and implementation of high performance systems will certainly change. If MPPs also make large memory-resident databases feasible, then even more of our current design principles will require fundamental review.

The design of online transaction processes may not need radical change. Indeed, such an architecture (with perhaps 256 processors rather than the four shown in Figure 14-8) is better able than today's hardware to cope with the traditional "connection per user" approach found in Oracle applications and assumed by many (if not most) of the high-productivity application development tools.

The fundamental challenge is to find a way of spreading the work for a set-oriented process out across enough processors to take advantage of the computing power available. *Such algorithms do not, themselves, need to be efficient.* If our traditional approach to a report or a batch update uses only one of even just four processors, then an approach which uses 100% more CPU but is capable of running all four processors simultaneously should complete in half the time. This may be counter-intuitive, but it is the reality of the situation.

Conclusions About OPS

Oracle Parallel Server is exciting technology, but it is not a realistic option in every case. If the design of the application does not allow the effects of pinging to be kept under control (normally by partitioning the update load across the clustered hosts), we advise you not to use OPS. If massively parallel architectures are being deployed, a technology such as Oracle Parallel Server is essential for data sharing, and it's unlikely that work load partitioning will be feasible. High ping rates will, therefore, be inevitable. The platform must deliver both a distributed lock manager and an interprocessor block transfer mechanism which are fast enough to cope with the traffic. If the platform can't deliver, don't use this solution.

IV

Designing the Code Modules

Earlier parts of this book have focused on the design of the Oracle database. But designers also need to be concerned with the design of the code modules. This part of the book describes a variety of design issues in this category.

- Chapter 15, *Introduction to Code Design*, describes the basic concepts of code module design.

- Chapter 16, *Determining Where to Locate the Processing*, looks at an innovative way of partitioning the logic of an application.

- Chapter 17, *Metrics, Prototypes, and Specifications*, describes the formal side of code design; in particular, this chapter focuses on how you can ensure that your modules meet the requirements.

- Chapter 18, *Locking*, contains information that will help you minimize contention within your applications.

- Chapter 19, *Selecting the Toolset*, compares the merits of the various categories of front-end products that can support an Oracle back end.

- Chapter 20, *Designing Screens, Reports, Batch Programs, and More*, deals with specific design issues for screens, reports, batch programs, error handling, navigation, and online help.

15

Introduction to Code Design

Although the main focus of this book is database design, it is true that the most perfectly designed database in the world is of little use without some code somewhere to access it. And not just any code! Today's sophisticated users expect front-end programs that are both powerful and quick. The focus of this part of the book is on designing the code modules that complement the database.

In this chapter, we will first examine the information about functions that is input into the design from the analysis. We will then consider how we map the functions that are organized by business requirement into a set of module definitions that are structured in such a way that we can build them into program units without writing redundant or duplicate code and without huge complex modules if we can avoid it. We will also consider modules that have to be designed and built that are not directly in support of the business requirements. We call these the *system modules* and include in our definition items such as a print manager and an archival process. Finally, we will consider the relative merits of a CASE tool in module design and build, with particular emphasis on code generators.

Generally, module design takes place in parallel with database design. If there are separate design teams for the two design tasks, it is essential that there be good communication between the two teams because there are always many cross-dependencies. For instance, why hold a derived TOTAL_DEBITS column in a parent table if no module is ever going to use it for query? Very few data model decisions can be made in isolation; each option is generally to the benefit of some modules and to the detriment of others. As designers, we have to balance the consequences and be pragmatic.

How do we go about designing code modules? Usually, it is done in many stages, with refinements being made at each stage as you gain more knowledge about how the system will work. Often the refinement is a direct consequence of proto-types that are built during the design. We will start by looking at the very beginning of design.

Analysis Deliverables

Let's look at the specific functional deliverables from analysis that will be our starting point in design. Remember, as we discussed in Chapter 1, we have to take these deliverables in whatever form they're in and transform them into a set of precise module definitions. Typically, we will start with a set of function specifications that state, in business terms, what is required. We may also be given a list of dependencies between the functions and the events that trigger the functions. The analyst may also prepare a list of design issues that were identified during analysis; the usefulness of this list varies from analyst to analyst. In general, we prefer that analysts stick to analysis rather than design (just as both the analysts and the programmers would prefer that the designers stick to design!).

The amount of information in, and the content of, functional analysis varies considerably between both methodologies and individual projects. Some analysts like to draw screen layouts. If it keeps them happy that's fine, but past experience has taught us that the final product will probably not bear any resemblance whatever to their drawings. Similarly, the final code will probably not bear any resemblance whatever to any SQL statements or pseudocode so helpfully provided by the designers.

Function Hierarchies

We'll begin by looking at the *function hierarchy*. This is an analysis technique which states the requirements at the highest level and then iteratively breaks each statement down into smaller components until the "atomic" functions have been identified. Figure 15-1 shows an excerpt from the function hierarchy for claims handling in a hypothetical insurance application. In this simplified diagram, we show only the claims function of the application, and in the text we expand on only one of the functions (Step 2.2).

If the concept of *atomic functions* is new to you, then the simplest test is to ask whether it makes sense to perform only part of the function. Thus in Step 2.2.5 (Authorize Repairs) we have an atomic function. The repair is either authorized or it is not. There is no middle ground. Atomic functions will therefore tend to be associated with commit units in the eventual modules, and you should certainly investigate carefully if you find that you are calling for a commit in the middle of servicing an atomic function.

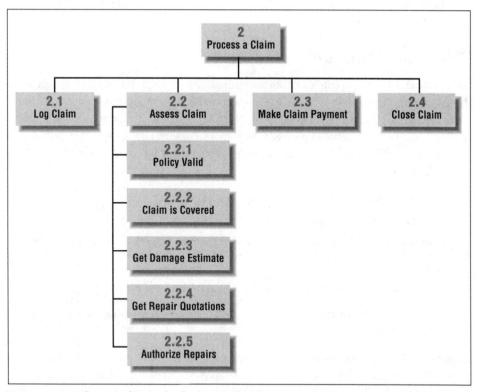

Figure 15-1. A function hierarchy for handling claims

You need to keep some important points in mind when you are reviewing the function hierarchy.

1. The analysis will describe business functions, and not all of them will be directly or even indirectly supported by the computer application. Some will be executed as purely manual procedures.

2. Because we are dealing with a hierarchy, rather than a lattice or network, there is a strong tendency to find functions that occur in more than one place in the hierarchy. These different instances of the same function will, of course, have different numbers because of the way the tree is labeled.

   In the classic application of Oracle Method, such duplication indicates an analysis error. Specifically, it usually indicates that the analyst has confused function with mechanism. Thus, we may find that a claim notification by post is described in a different part of the hierarchy from a claim notification by telephone. This is clearly an error where the mechanism (the postal service, the telephone system) has been confused with the function (receipt of a notification of a claim). If there are differences in procedure for the two types of notification, then these can be detailed under the single function "Receive claim notification."

Function Definitions

In addition to developing the function hierarchy (which has only brief descriptions of the functions), the analyst must write a textual explanation of each function. This may not be necessary at every level in the hierarchy, but it is essential at both the top level (Process Claim in our example) and at the bottom, or atomic, level (2.2.1–2.2.5 in the example). Example 15-1 contains a sample of a description.

Example 15-1. A Brief Sample of a Functional Definition

2.2.2 Check that the Claim is Covered

Obtain and record all the *Claims Details* including any *Third Party* or *Witness* details. Examine the *Policy* for *Exclusion Clauses* and determine if they apply to this *Claim*.

If an applicable *Exclusion Clause* is found, then close the *Claim* and generate a *Standard Letter* to the *Claimant*. If no such *Exclusion Clause* is found, then change the status of the *Claim* to "Awaiting Estimate" and assign and inform a Loss Adjuster.

In this description we have conveniently highlighted the entities by underlining them. If you are lucky, the analysts who ship you specifications will adopt the same approach. If they don't do so, this will be a useful exercise for you to perform as part of accepting the specification because it gives a clear picture of which entities are referenced by a function. Make sure that you understand the descriptions fully, and verify that they are clear, concise, and unambiguous. This is part of the analysis QA and sign-off process that was outlined in Chapter 1.

NOTE   The entity names used in Example 15-1 are not normalized; they
            have been worded to make the example clear, rather than to fully
            agree with any particular methodology.

Other Deliverables

The other essential deliverable—don't attempt design without it—is the entity model. You need to know both what the enterprise is trying to do (functions) and the information that has to be handled to achieve it (entities).

Highlighting entity names in functional descriptions helps us understand the impact of the functions, but a more rigorous approach to developing this understanding is to construct a complete matrix of functions against entities showing usage. The matrix format allows us to look at the information for a particular function or for a particular entity, and the matrix allows a QA check to ensure that each entity has a constructor or source (a function that creates instances of it), is referenced (used), and has a destructor. In many cases, the destructor is the archiving suite, but in many more cases it is simply absent. As we've mentioned earlier in this book, the analysis terms for entity references use the acronym CRUD for Create, Reference, Update, and Delete.

Sometimes the information is further broken down to give a function/attribute matrix. This level of detail takes a long time to produce, and we question whether it is always worth the expense. The transformations made during design mean that the function/attribute matrix will often bear little resemblance to the eventual module/column matrix, which most definitely *is* useful. However, such a cross-reference does permit a useful analysis QA step, which is to check that each attribute in the entity model has both a source and a use. It may also be very helpful in determining whether it would make sense to split a table into two (vertical partitioning). If the cross-reference shows that one set of attributes is used by a discrete set of functions and another set is used by an entirely different set of functions, then you may well have two entities which share a primary key.

Data flow diagrams and entity life history diagrams (both discussed in Chapter 3, *Data Modeling*) can also be helpful in understanding the functions and how they fit into the overall processing cycle.

Mapping Functions to Modules

Analysts should focus on the tangible deliverables to users, the functional side. As designers we should pay more heed to the operational side, the database that is the engine of the application. This difference in emphasis is not necessarily a bad thing. To guard against the dangers inherent in the difference in emphasis we recommend the four-stage approach illustrated in Figure 15-2:

1. Start the analysis by looking at the functions.
2. Complete the analysis with an entity model to support the functions.
3. Start the design by proposing a schema to support the entity model.
4. Complete the design with the module specifications that implement the functions against the schema.

Once we have read through the functional descriptions, checked them, and understood them, we can start mapping them onto modules that will be computer-based. In some cases the mapping from an atomic function to a computer-based module will be one-to-one, but this is more the exception than the rule. Indeed,

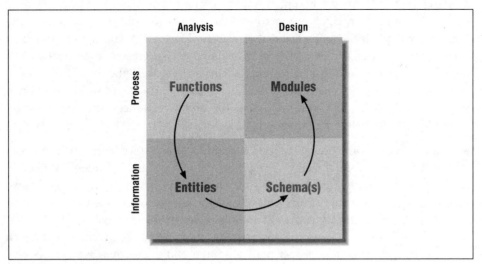

Figure 15-2. The steps required to reach the module design stage

the more one-to-one mappings we find, the more suspicious we become that no true analysis has been performed and that the alleged analysis is, in fact, a design. Figure 15-3 shows a typical mapping.

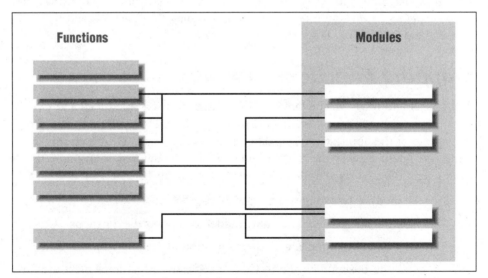

Figure 15-3. The maze effect of mapping functions to modules

Some functions are sufficiently similar in their mechanical action that they can and should be combined into a single common module even if their effect or context is radically different. Others are complex and need to be split up into smaller and more manageable components. There may be data rules wrapped up in functional descriptions that can be implemented as table constraints or triggers, rather than as application modules, thus enforcing them across the entire system (rather than being confined within an application). Some functions will be resolved as a purely manual process and will not be mapped to modules at all.

Unfortunately, there are no shortcuts or simple answers to performing this task. It takes time, patience, and experience. Rarely will we get the breakdown of functions into modules exactly "right" the first time, whatever "right" is. We must expect to change our minds about the number and composition of modules on several occasions during the design process. However, it is critical to get it right (or at least pretty nearly so) before we start to create the modules themselves. The penalty for failure is, at best, a poorly performing application that is difficult to maintain; more likely, it is an application that simply does not work as required.

In our function-to-module mapping (and therefore in our module design), we should be continually working to leverage those Oracle7 features which are going to help us create a better application (and to avoid any that might prejudice it). The features we should be looking to deploy include:

- Declarative constraints: to implement data rules without procedural code

- Database triggers: to enforce data rules procedurally across all parts of the application

- Stored procedures: to encapsulate common business functions

- Commonality of SQL (best achieved through the use of stored procedures): to exploit the shared SQL area

Don't Forget the System Modules

The focus of module design is on producing functionality that satisfies the business requirements that were identified in the analysis. There are a good number of peripheral processes that you should consider that don't come directly from a stated business function. For instance, you will have to be able to print from within most of your applications. Providing such facilities is often far from trivial, and if you must implement the solution for yourselves, then you need the work required to be part of your estimates and specifications. Often, these system functions turn out to be the most demanding modules within the application.

The extent to which you need to design and develop these system functions for yourselves depends on the requirements, the capabilities of the target operating system and infrastructure, and the availability and applicability of affordable off-the-shelf utilities that you can buy to do the job. Typical candidates are:

- Batch queue manager/job scheduler

- Print queue manager

- Data browse facility or ad-hoc query tool

- File system directory manager

- Menu/module integrator

- Automated backup procedures

- Automated recovery procedures

- Facility for granting and revoking access to users

- Facility for setting up the environment for a new user

- Facility for enabling users to change their password

- Application management facilities

Some of these functions can be handled by the operating system, but operating systems differ widely in their ability to deliver—for example, how flexible is a particular system's print queue handling? We must also consider whether users will have access to the operating system features that are available. Even if they do, will users have to quit the application to look at a print queue, and then re-invoke that application? Will the users be able to make sense of a UNIX print queue from the *lpstat* command? (Indeed, can anybody?) Even though an operating system may appear at first glance to support some of the functions you need, there is often further work to do (particularly on print queues), even if it only involves writing a user-friendly shell around some of the system functions.

Remember also that you may be designing for a heterogeneous environment (in other words, more than one target operating system). In a client-server environment, some applications will require local printing and others may require printing to be carried out on a remote server. You need to decide if it is feasible (or even desirable) to make this transparent to the users.

A data browse facility is a common requirement in contemporary projects. Users are more computer-aware than they have been in the past, and they want to harness the power on their desktops. They expect to process information in innovative and unusual ways. You have an important decision to make here. Do you want your users running MIS queries against your operational data and potentially slowing down the other online operations? Alternatively, do you want to extract data and put it in a copy database or a data warehouse? Chapter 13, *Designing for Data Warehouses*, contains a discussion of this subject.

Back to the query tools. There are a wealth of products that you can buy: Oracle Data Query, Oracle Data Browser (collectively known as Discoverer/2000), Business Objects, and Cognos Impromptu are good examples. Don't fall into the trap of thinking that you simply can install these tools on users' PCs and then walk away. The products require considerable setup to make them usable. For instance, you need to give meaningful pseudonyms to columns and to create logical views (either within the product or as Oracle views) to hide some of the complexity of the database. An example of this is pre-joining two or more tables within a view. This activity is sometimes referred to as creating the *mapping layer* for the product; in Business Objects it is called a "universe"—just to emphasize how important it is!

Many people will look at some of the elements in the system modules list and say, "That's a DBA or administrative function; why should we write project code to handle functions such as backup, recovery, setting an environment, and granting new users?" You may be able to sustain this view if you are running on a large server, but it will probably prove inadequate if you are designing small workgroup and desktop systems that are intended to be "turnkey."[*]

Your end user is probably not going to get the budget to hire a full-time DBA to administer Personal Oracle7 on a single-user PC or on a Novell network with three users. If you have 10,000 such installations within your enterprise, you can be pretty darn sure that you will not have full-time DBAs with the spare time to look after each one. As a result, these days there is a common requirement to write a user-friendly interface for such functions; the interface handles a simple job and hides the underlying complexity. Oracle itself has recognized this fact and is getting better at providing these features in the core product, but they are not quite there yet, so there may well be further functionality for you to add. In a large network with many nodes, you may opt to purchase a remote application management tool such as BMC's PATROL to supplement the services available in Oracle Enterprise Manager.

Application Management

Application management is a topic in itself.[†] It is unarguable that the delivery of mission critical applications is too important to be left to chance and needs to be managed. Not only does the general health of the server platforms and database instances need to be monitored, there may be aspects of application operation,

---

[*] Rather than "turkey" as offered by one spell-checker—we had no idea spell-checkers had such an advanced sense of humor.

[†] One of the authors of this book is a member of PATROL Research and Development within BMC Software and can safely be considered to be rather biased in this area.

such as the lengths of various work queues, which need to be monitored on a regular basis with automatic action being taken if they exceed preset thresholds. In many organizations there are several dozen, and in some cases several hundred, application and database servers which must all be continuously monitored by a small team of administrators.

One of the functions of an Application management tool is to use intelligent agents to operate locally on each server, remitting information as required to one or more management consoles. Among the criteria by which a management tool may be judged are its ability to adapt to handle different management goals, the load that it imposes on the managed systems, the amount of network traffic that it imposes communicating with its consoles, and the ability of its agents to run autonomously (i.e., to manage the server even in the absence of a management console).

In many cases, the local agent on the server can perform its monitoring and management *nonintrusively*, using normal system features to monitor for various types of problems: a trivial example might be to issue the following query once per minute and to send an email message to the user(s) if any failed jobs are found:

```
SELECT job
     , log_user
  FROM dba_jobs
 WHERE broken = 'Y';
```

NOTE   The above query has been deliberately left incomplete for clarity; in the real monitoring application on which this is based a filter is applied to avoid reselecting jobs that have already been reported as broken, and the query also reports jobs that were previously flagged as broken and are no longer in that state.

Nonintrusive monitoring will meet the entire application management need for many systems, but in some cases it is desirable for the application itself to be able to call the management tool to notify certain events which are apparent in program logic, but which are either not detectable from the database or excessively difficult or expensive to uncover through database queries.

Source and Version Control

It is important for any project to manage its source code well. Disasters can easily happen if you don't. For instance, if two developers can work on the same piece of code concurrently, then the changes made by one will likely be overwritten and lost. In an Oracle project it is equally important to control and manage iterations of the database definitions and keep them in step with source code versions.

Source code control is all about controlling code while it is being developed. Version control is about bringing together compatible versions of code and the database definition for the purpose of creating a release for the system test or production environment.

Database Control

We generally recommend that you pull together a first-cut database design as quickly as possible. This may be the fully normalized logical model produced in analysis with any structures that cannot be resolved directly implemented in the relational model. Chapter 3 gives a detailed discussion of these structures and explains how they can be resolved in table design. The purpose of this task is to allow for prototyping, demonstrations, and experiments. It is also extremely useful to develop scripts to populate some or all of the standing or nonvolatile data such as lookup values, and to populate some of the core tables with sample data. Good quality sample data can be vital; it can alleviate dependencies between modules where one module cannot be unit tested because it relies heavily on data that is created by a module that hasn't been developed yet.

It goes without saying (but we will stress it anyway) that any code developed against this first-cut has a good chance of ending its days in the trash can! For this reason, we sometimes use the term "iterative development" in place of the word "prototype" to focus management's mind on the unpalatable fact that, however much they like the first cut, it is going to have to be trashed. If they resist, ask them how they'd feel about flying in a prototype aircraft!

An account on a live database instance somewhere on the corporate network will not normally suffice as a development workbench. You really should have your own Oracle7 instance, preferably your own dedicated server. You should plan during design for the requirements of build and test, where you will probably need several instances, each of which may have several schemas. On the other hand, we recommend against giving each developer his or her own instance because we have found that it can be very difficult to keep the schemas compatible. Code developed against an out-of-date table design is unlikely to work against the correct one. The issue of releasing database versions to developers is a sticky one.

We've found that the best approach (certainly in an Oracle development environment) is to give each developer his own schema (which in Oracle7 is the same as a username) and to insist that the developers use synonyms to reference objects in a shared schema which is maintained by the development DBA. It is a relatively simple exercise to check which private objects any schema is referencing.

One of the crucial standards that you must agree upon is how frequently to reissue database updates and what mechanism should be used for performing the reissue. You can never please everyone on this one! There will always be one person who is held up waiting for changes and another person who is debugging a critical piece of code, threatening to kill you if you overwrite the database now!

One good approach is to have a circular list of instances or schemas so that the development DBA maintains, say, the last five definitions, overwriting the oldest each time that a new one is issued. This requires good communication; team members must get adequate notice of impending changes and a complete list of the changes to be made. It does have the merit of preventing the "mix and match" approach which can result from the synonym-based approach described earlier, (although some find that it is this ability that makes the synonym-based approach so useful).

Source Code Control

Before build starts, you will need to have a source control system of some kind identified, installed, and tested. You will also need *make* or project files or other procedures that reliably run partial or complete regeneration of the application. Source code control is a relatively well-known area for C and C++ code, but few of the RAD tools interface well, if at all, to either source code control systems or to *make*.

If source code generators are being used, the real "source code" may be a repository or design dictionary rather than source code held in pure text files. Both Oracle Developer/2000 and Microsoft Visual Basic are examples of this. Even where pure text files are used—in SQL*Forms 2.x and 3.0 INP files, for example— a source code control system may not know how to insert its control information into the file without rendering the file invalid to the tool that is intended to read it.

Source control can be an even more complex issue in client-server environments, where some of the code must be compiled on the client and other parts have to be compiled on the server. This requires planning and technical innovation to ensure that the two environments are kept in step.

Source code control may be difficult, but it is essential. You run a severe risk of losing key changes if two programmers can work on the same file at the same time, and you must do what you can to control the risk. On smaller projects, a simple registry application may be sufficient. Under this scheme, the team members agree to record in a database the name of each file they are modifying, and team members never change a copy of a file shown in the registry as being subject to change by someone else. This approach is very simple, it relies on cooperation, but it has been used successfully on projects.

We recommend that you keep all database object creation scripts under source control; this makes it possible to revert to old versions and to determine which version of the database goes with which program source code version. There are check sum encoding techniques for assigning a unique number to a database schema definition and determining its value at runtime.[*]

You should also maintain scripts or export files to create standing data such as reference codes under source control. Unfortunately, none of the check sum encoding methods we have seen support these static parts of the data. They deal only with structure.

An administrator and/or DBA will need to provide logins and accounts for developers and testers. The design team, in liaison with the DBA, should ensure that every class of user in the target system is represented and usable by system test.

Template Code

Generation of *skeleton* or *template* applications in some or all of the chosen build tools can be a productive design task. It can certainly cut some of the donkey work out of the build process and can ensure a level of consistency in the modules. The concept is that the designer provides a "bare bones" program (hence the name skeleton) with any code or objects that are common to all modules. The builder then starts each new module from the skeleton. Of course, if you are using an object-oriented methodology, then what you will do is to create classes of objects from which the builders will derive their own classes.

Let's look at an example where we are using Oracle Forms to develop our screens, and we develop a structure like that shown in Figure 15-4. We have two skeletons on which we can base a new form that we need to develop. One is for straightforward forms and the other is for more complex ones. We have a catalogue of PL/SQL libraries that can be used by other (non-Oracle Forms) applications as well.

New code modules (forms) are built from a copy of the template and, as such, they inherit common functionality (such as a toolbar) from the skeleton. The objects in the skeleton are mainly references to libraries and a reference form. This means that we can change some of the common objects and that the forms based on the template only need a recompilation to inherit the changes.

---

[*] See "Database Fingerprinting" by Chris Johnson, *Database Programming and Design*, September 1995.

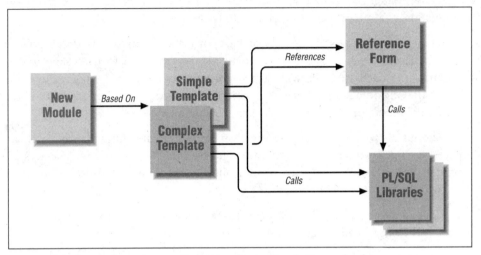

Figure 15-4. A typical template configuration for an Oracle Forms development

TIP   As a general rule, as much as possible of your common code
       should be referenced, rather than copied. The difference is that
       code which is referenced can be changed in a single place and the
       changes will be inherited by all applications with a simple recom-
       pile (or maybe no explicit action at all!). As soon as any code is cop-
       ied, you will inevitably end up with different versions in different
       places. No amount of testing of your template before developers
       start to use it will guarantee that it won't be necessary to change it
       at some point. Make life easy for yourself and use references wher-
       ever you can.

Designing for Testing

There is a school of thought that says the planning of system and acceptance tests
should commence during analysis. This makes a lot of sense, since the project
sponsor and key users can sign off on what are acceptable test criteria for the
project. In practice, however, such planning is often left until design or even later.
The problem with this deferment is that you will end up with a set of tests that
validate that you have built what you thought was wanted; the earlier in the cycle
that the final acceptance criteria are specified, the more likely they are to reflect
the requirement rather than the solution. Both of us have seen altogether too
many systems which passed all their acceptance tests, but simply did not do the
job that was required of them.

During design, you should come up with standards for module (unit) testing and a strategy or plan for integration and system testing. Boring, yes. But it has to be done. It takes a certain type of person to actually relish having anything to do with testing!

Develop Test Strategies

Your test strategy should incorporate the following categories of testing:

- Unit or module testing

- Link testing (interface between two or more related modules)

- System testing

- Acceptance testing (often performed by the user)

- Regression testing (a series of "old" tests to ensure that your enhancements haven't inadvertently put an unwanted spanner in the works)

- Performance or high-load and stress testing

You also need to develop standards for documenting a test plan and for recording the individual test runs made against the plan.

Develop Harnesses

Some modules cannot be unit tested in isolation (if they are strictly internal routines). These may require a dedicated test harness to be built to allow unit testing to proceed. All required test harnesses should be identified as part of the deliverables from the build stage. You must also make sure that each harness has an estimate of the time taken to both write and test them. Test harnesses can easily consume 25% of the programming effort on a project, and they are often cruelly difficult to test themselves!

Note also that if the internal routines ever start exhibiting bugs, or need to be upgraded in any way, then you (or your poor successors) will need the test harnesses again. For this reason successful projects often regard their test support code as just "another part of the system" and make sure that it is easily accessible from the GUI to any user with the privileges required to use it. This may be a good moment to remind you of our credo: *work smarter, not harder.*

CASE Products in Run Unit Design

What about using CASE tools in the design of applications? Let's look briefly at what level of functional description should be entered into a CASE product and how useful code generators are. We'll also consider the balance between the effort to put the detail into a tool and the amount of payback we'll get from using it.

In general, CASE tools support the data modeling side of analysis and design to a much higher degree than they support the functional side. Sadly, many of the best-selling tools support only *data modeling* and not *entity modeling,* causing projects to start with design rather than with formal analysis.

Most CASE products are able to generate code but can create only very "data-centric" applications. For instance, if you have an orders table defined in the repository, most tools will generate a small maintenance program to query, insert, update, and delete orders. Some tools may even generate a simple master-detail application that lets you maintain both orders and order lines. However, few go beyond this.

These criticisms are less true of Oracle's Designer/2000 which, despite its name, gives explicit support to the analysis activities that should precede design. Also, this product was designed to allow code generation and is therefore strong in the area of module definition and module/attribute cross-referencing.

When you are evaluating the use of CASE technology on a project, be sure to consider how you want to use it.

- Do you want to use it simply as a repository for data definitions?
- Do you want to extend it to house module definitions as well?
- Do you want to generate from module definitions into code?

In making a choice of repository, you will need to answer the following questions:

- How many of the applications are straightforward database manipulations and how many have complex logic that cannot be generated?
- How much of the "donkey work" of your application code can be achieved by having templates and libraries of code?
- How likely are you to have to make changes to the schema which could be made easier by accurate cross-referencing within a repository or, better still, incorporated by regeneration of the affected code?
- Are you using RAD methods, and would a generator aid the prototype iterations?

Generators are becoming more sophisticated, and Oracle is aiming for 100% generation of 100% of the code in major applications. This goal is grand, but in the world of 100% generation, only achieving 99.95% represents total failure (even though it might be extremely useful in a project setting). Oracle and their competitors are still a long way from achieving 100%, in part because of the extreme difficulty of deriving an adequate data model for functional requirements. Meanwhile, back in the present...If you have a large number of simple modules to code, a generator is likely to save you time and may also give you more consistent code. If, on the other hand, you have a small number of modules from hell to create, then a generator can be a positive hindrance as the first task will undoubtedly be to take out unwanted generated code!

However, there is now much higher acceptance of generator technology than there has ever been before. In most projects that employ generators, the generators are used to create the simple data maintenance modules and for first cuts of the more complex ones. Once the code has been amended by developers, it is rarely reverse-engineered back into the repository for subsequent amendment and regeneration.

TIP   You may remember that we started with the idea of working smarter, not harder. Spending three months battling with a generator to get it to do something that it does not want to do, and then having to admit defeat, is not very smart if it would have taken less than three weeks to write the module by hand!

Most of us are worried what the generators will do with our code and just don't trust them enough yet!

The $64,000 question about any CASE tool coupled to a generator is this: If you can establish that the generator is capable of generating modules of the complexity that you need, is the effort that you will have to put into entering data into the repository less than the effort that will be required to create the same modules, fully documented, using conventional methods?

16

Determining Where to Locate the Processing

In previous chapters of this book we've examined the design of the database, sometimes referred to in modern parlance as the back end. In the chapters in Part IV we look at the design of program units, sometimes called the front end. The front end encompasses the screens and reports that are supported by the database. In a traditional database application the two ends are well-defined; the back end contains the tables, indexes, and views, and the front end contains the formatting and application logic.

This chapter briefly explores the considerations that require designers to separate carefully the management of the user interface from the actual processing that is to be performed. These concepts are central to many of the suggestions we make in the chapters about specific architectures—in particular, the discussion of client/server issues in Chapter 11, *Designing for Client/Server*. That chapter focuses on the particular problems which arise when the user interface is separated by a network from the database.

Data Rules vs. Process Rules vs. Interface Rules

Many applications systems suffer from a blurring of the distinction between data rules, process rules, and interface rules. In this section we try to differentiate them.

Defining the Types of Rules

What do the three different types of rules mean? Put simply:

- *Data rules* tell us about conditions that the data must meet. These rules apply to every instance of the data to which they relate. They are normally derived from the data model.

- *Process rules* tell us what the application may (and may not) do. These rules are normally derived from the function model.

- *Interface rules* tell us how the application should look to the end user; such rules affect only the user's view of the application and leave the processing unchanged. Interface rules are derived from the user interface specification.

Rules should be atomic—that is, compound rules should be broken down into their constituent parts, and you must investigate all rules to ensure that they are justified.

Rather than refining and expanding the definitions of these three terms, let's consider a series of examples. To give you something to do, we'll first present the rules without any comments to give you a chance to form your own opinions about which category a particular rule falls into. Then we'll present them a second time with our comments.

Here is the set of rules for you to think about.

- The sex of a person must be either 'F' or 'M'.

- Each order must be for one and only one customer.

- Each order line must be part of one and only one order, and must be for one and only one product code.

- A benefit is not to be paid to any person with more than $16,000 in savings.

- Only a manager can authorize an ex-gratia payment.

- Any trading that occurs on a Sunday goes into the account books for the following Monday.

- The system initiates an availability search for the required product from the code entered, and updates the screen with the description and price. If a cheaper equivalent brand is found, this brand is substituted on the screen in place of the original.

- If a user retrieves an unauthorized order whose value exceeds his or her specified authorization limit, the **Authorize** button on the screen must be grayed out.

- Each payment has a unique system-allocated reference number.

- All currency codes should be expanded to show their full name next to the code when entered.

- Updates to payment records are not permitted.

Interface-Process vs. Client/Server

Because Oracle7 has both stored procedures and triggers, in a client/server environment much of the logic can (and should) be resident in the database on the server. Technically, Oracle7 uses a client/server model even when both the client (application program) and the server (database engine) reside on the same machine. Why? Because these two entities communicate with each other using messages rather than conventional call structures. This message interface allows the two parts—the application program and the database engine—to execute as separate processes. These separate processes may be on the same machine (usually referred to as the "two-task" architecture) or on separate machines linked by a network. It is this last case that people are normally referring to when they talk about client/server.

- All changes to customer records require that a customer change audit entry is made.

We hope that at least some of you have made an effort to match up rules with types. If you only glanced at them, we'd like to try to persuade you to go back and take one more look because this section covers a number of issues that we believe are absolutely essential to effective design. These examples present a series of issues that we have often seen make the difference between project success and project failure.

That said, whether or not you've really tried to analyze the examples for yourself, let's proceed with our analysis of each of these rules.

The sex of a person must be either 'F' or 'M'.
> This is a data rule, and can be implemented using a check constraint. Every time we have a column value for the sex of a person, then the value must be present and the value must be either 'F' or 'M'. There may, of course, be an analysis or design error; we may need to allow for the value to be absent.

> Cliff Longman was one of our one-time colleagues at Oracle, and was for many years architect of Oracle's CASE products. He used to say in his Strategic Business Analysis class, "It is a rule and it is definitive; it may be wrong but in that case it is definitively wrong." This is a critical feature of any rule: it states categorically how the application is going to behave whether or not the rule is correctly formed. That is why we must be so careful to get it right.

Each order must be for one and only one customer.
> This is a data rule, and can be implemented using a combination of a foreign key constraint and a NOT NULL constraint.

Each order line must be part of one and only one order, and must be for one and only one product code.

This is not one, but two, data rules, each of which can be implemented using a combination of a foreign key constraint and a NOT NULL constraint. Reviewing and possibly changing the design would be much easier if we stated two distinct rules, each of which could stand or fall on its own merits.

A benefit is not to be paid to any person with more than $16,000 in savings.

This is a process rule. It makes no statement about the database contents or definitions, but rather expresses what may or may not take place. If the rule is to be automated at all (it might be a clerical check), then it should be implemented within the application and not the interface or the database.

Only a manager can authorize an ex-gratia payment.

This is a process rule. At the moment when the payment is authorized, the application should check that the user is suitably empowered, that is, is a manager. Many designers try to implement rules like this as data rules, but that is not correct because the relationship is temporal (dependent on time) rather than being independent of time (as is the case in the first three examples).

Any trading that occurs on a Sunday goes into the account books for the following Monday.

This is actually two rules. The first rule is that trading entries may not be made in the account books for Sundays; this is a data rule which can be enforced by a check constraint. The second rule is a process rule which explains to the application how to adjust the date so that it becomes acceptable; it must detect all dates which are Sunday and add one to them. By splitting the rules in this way, we avoid having to create a situation in which we have an INSERT statement in the application which supplies a value for a column only to find that a different value has appeared in the resulting database row. This form of statement subversion was specifically illegal in the beta versions of Oracle7 Version 7.0, but was permitted in the production version as a result of customer pressure. Many of us feel that this relaxation was a poorly advised concession by Oracle to permit their customers to perpetrate design errors!

A better solution to the problem may be to hold two dates, *transaction_date* and *effective_date*, and to have a data rule that makes the *effective_date* a derived field. In this case, the rule can be transformed into a data rule, and the process logic can be absolved of the requirement to specify the effective date.

The system initiates an availability search for the required product from the code entered and updates the screen with the description and price. If a cheaper equivalent brand is found, this is substituted on the screen in place of the original.

This is actually a process rule. It states that (within some part of the application) a request to retrieve product details should retrieve those of the cheapest alternative. The second sentence is completely irrelevant and should be removed from the rule. If our system operates with any reasonable response time, the users will never be able to read the original display because it will get overwritten too quickly. We are missing the process rules (and probably data rules) that would tell us how to find a cheaper equivalent brand, but for the sake of this discussion we'll assume that these are present elsewhere in the specifications.

If a user retrieves an unauthorized order whose value exceeds their specified Authorization Limit, the Authorize button on the screen must be grayed out.

There are probably three rules here, two general and one specific. There is probably one general rule that disabled screen features must be so indicated, and a second one that for buttons this is done by graying them out. The third rule is that the Authorize facility is to be disabled under the specified circumstance. Of course, there may also be function key or menu equivalents of the Authorize button, and these must adhere to some other general rules.

But if we leave it there, then we are relying on the interface code to enforce authorization levels, and we must also introduce a process rule that a user cannot authorize orders beyond his personal authorization limit. This rule will be enforced within the data manager as part of a stored procedure in addition to being enforced in the interface. This issue of double coverage of rules is discussed in the next section of this chapter.

Each payment has a unique system-allocated reference number.

Again, this is two rules masquerading as one. The first (must be unique) is a simple data rule that can be enforced using a primary or unique key constraint. The second rule requires the processing to allocate a reference number. We would assume that the data design provides a mechanism for doing this which might be an Oracle sequence or, if more control is required and the accountants are averse to gaps in the sequence, perhaps a single row table which contains the next available number.

Anyone who knows Oracle well could, of course, argue that the processing does not need to be aware of this allocation mechanism. Why? Because we can write a pre-insert trigger that operates at row level and applies the system-allocated reference number. Unfortunately, this means that the process cannot retrieve, or link other records to, the record that it has just created because it does not know the reference number! The tenacious SQL warrior then codes the trigger to store the allocated number into a persistent package variable from which the application can retrieve it.

Whenever you see structures like this in trigger and procedure code, it is almost certain that the design and implementation teams have confused data rules and process rules. When we are designing for a distributed architecture, we should clarify the rule. Are the reference numbers unique within the site/office or unique across the organization?

All currency codes should be expanded to show their full name next to the code when entered.

This is a pure interface rule taken from the user interface specification of a real world system. At first glance, it seems like a perfectly reasonable and sensible request, but a trivial investigation reveals that the users of the system habitually refer to the currencies by their codes rather than by their full names. They neither need nor want a system which tells them that when they enter the code "USD," what they really mean is "United States Dollars."

Most organizations have sets of acronyms or abbreviations that become part of the language and culture. New users who aren't yet familiar with the parlance can rely on online help or a pop-up list of values for assistance in identifying the correct code, but most users simply want to enter the code they are familiar with. Lookup and display of the descriptive text uses up screen space and takes time, especially where the data has not been cached within the interface and requires a reference to the database engine. Caching is discussed further in Chapter 11.

Updates to payment records are not permitted.

This is a data rule that should be enforced with a simple pre-update trigger at statement level which raises an application error.

All changes to customer records require that a customer change audit entry is made.

This is a data rule that should be enforced by a pre-update trigger at row level on the customer table.

Implications for Documentation and Approval Cycles

Although the three sets of rules we've defined in the previous section are strongly interconnected, it is important to separate their documentation for presentation to users and, even more important, for seeking user approval and sign-off. We should be aiming for three deliverables (or sets of deliverables) from design.

- The *interface design* is primarily for the user community. It tells the users what they will see and how they will interact with it. It is not cluttered and confused with any technical detail. User acceptance and sign-off is more likely to occur quickly for a concise, simple, and relevant document than for one that requires them to understand the enabling technology.

- The *process design* refers to the interface design and specifies how both it, and the services it requires, are to be implemented.

- The *data design* specifies the underlying database objects against which the processing must operate.

During the design phase, you can prototype the user interface in a way that ensures that it is what the user wants, but be careful not to prototype an interface that assumes services that the processing cannot deliver.

The restricting factor is generally performance. You might develop an Interface design which uses a Graphical Interface System (GIS) to display a street map and which allows the user to select an area by drawing a rubber band, then hitting a button to perform an update against all residents in that area. On the prototype, this operation will be instantaneous (since it does nothing under the covers). In the real system, however, there may be a complex process involved in locating the residents on the basis of postal area, or it may simply be that the update itself takes a significant amount of time for a heavily populated area. The corollary to this scenario is that when we go live, the search may have to be submitted to batch. The result is that the process has forced a change to the interface. Given that it was the interface design that your users accepted and are demanding that you deliver, this constitutes a serious project failure.

Logic Placement

The placement of the code (or declarations) to implement the three types of rules we've described in the previous section is an important issue.

What Goes Where?

Where do we actually place the three types of rules in our code?

- Interface rules should be implemented in the "front end," regardless of whether that front end is a Visual Basic or Delphi program, an Oracle Form, or a report writer.

- Process rules should be implemented as procedures called from the front end, but should not be a necessary part of the front end.

- Data rules should be implemented in the database manager itself by declarative constraints or triggers.

A brief inspection of these three statements shows us that although the locations of the interface rules and the data rules are precisely specified, the location of the process rules is left somewhat open (even though there is a carefully worded restriction that any process rule which is in the front end should not be there by necessity). Thus, any procedure that implements a process rule must be separate from, and not dependent on, any code that implements an interface rule.

When these nondependent process procedures are written in PL/SQL, Oracle Forms has the attractive feature of allowing them to be dragged from the front end and dropped into the back end. Although this capability is powerful and makes the point that process rules can exist in either the client space or the server space, its application is rather limited by the fact that Oracle Forms currently only supports PL/SQL Version 1 rather than the much later and considerably improved PL/SQL Version 2.x, which is present with the procedural option in Oracle7.

Multiple Coverage

This is all very well and good, but after a while our users start asking for prompter feedback about illegal data values. If we take a simple data rule such as our first example:

> The sex of a person must be either 'F' or 'M'.

it would be entirely reasonable for the interface specification to say that this rule is to be validated as soon as the user moves to the next field. (This example assumes that the data is literally entered rather than being selected from a radio group that is itself a form of local enforcement in the interface.)

The designer may feel that he or she is confronted with a choice between implementing the check as an interface rule in the interface or implementing it as a data rule in the data server. In fact, this choice does not exist; there are actually two rules operating in different environments, and both rules must be implemented. The interface rule must be implemented because prompt feedback is required by the users, and the data rule must be implemented because the server must not rely on the interface to enforce data integrity.

When we present this discussion of rules to any group of programmers or designers, they usually become concerned about both the performance overhead and the possibility of the two rules getting out of step. Let's deal with these two issues in turn. The redundant check is the one in the interface, and (especially in client/server environments) there isn't typically any shortage of CPU in the front end. In addition, the test is essentially trivial to perform. If we accept the argument that the check must be performed in the back end whether or not it is performed in the front end, then the performance concern is answered.

Figure 16-1 illustrates a rule implemented in the database and in the interface—in this case, a Visual Basic program.

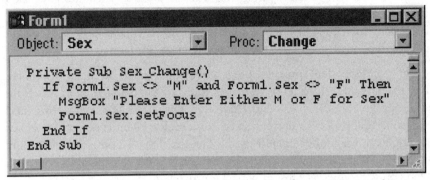

Figure 16-1. Implementation of the same rule in the database and the interface (Visual Basic)

If the rules get out of step, we actually gain an advantage. Consider a case where the interface insists that the value is either 'f' or 'm' and the database insists that it is either 'F' or 'M'. Any value which gets past the check in the interface will fail in the database, and it will become completely impossible to enter or modify a value for the *sex* field using that interface. The interface code, or at least part of it, has become inoperable. This fact will quickly highlight the problem and lead to some attention being given to fix it. Compare this with the situation we'd be in if the check were not in the database. In this case, an errant application could readily set lower case values and corrupt the database.

Most designers and DBAs would rather that something stopped working than that it did the wrong thing, though many users will take a more short-sighted view. They should be resisted!

```
CREATE TABLE emp
(empno ..
,..
,sex CHAR(1) NOT NULL CONSTRAINT (emp_cc1)
                    CHECK (sex IN ('.'.'.'.)
,..
```

Locking Issues

If we elect to implement rule enforcement in the interface, we must be very careful about locking (described in detail in Chapter 18). Suppose that we have the following rule:

> No debits may be issued against a customer account if the value of the current balance minus the debit amount exceeds the account overdraft limit.

Now suppose that we are using a screen to enter a debit and that the interface is enforcing this rule. The interface does the following:

1. Retrieves account details, including overdraft limit and current balance.

2. Allows the user to enter details of the new debit (payee, date, amount, etc.)

3. If (balance – debit amount > overdraft limit), then commits the transaction; otherwise, issues an error and rolls back.

The problem with this implementation is that the rule can be broken if, in the elapsed time between steps 1 and 3, other committed transactions are posted to the account or if another user updates the credit limit. The likelihood of this occurring may be significant since at step 2 we are waiting for the user to enter data on the screen.

We could try to resolve the situation with a "preemptive" or "pessimistic" lock in step 1 using SELECT...FOR UPDATE, but the lock would have to remain in force while we are waiting for the user to enter the details on the screen.

WARNING   Even this approach will not work if the account balance is not stored on the account record as a derived value (presumably maintained by triggers). If the account balance is queried by performing a summary operation, then the only way of guaranteeing that the result of the check stays true is to take a share lock on every table whose contents may contribute to the result. Holding table-level share locks across user I/O on volatile tables is not a performance-enhancing technique!

There is a similar and frequently encountered problem with the entry of unique keys. It is technically impossible for the interface to guarantee the uniqueness of an entered key without either:

- Actually performing the required DML operation, or

- Taking a share lock on the table against which the DML will eventually be performed

A highly effective solution to all of these problems is to perform the check from the interface without a lock and then to repeat the checking in the process logic at commit time. (In many cases the process logic does not need to explicitly repeat the check because issuing the DML will perform the checking implicitly.)

This concept of having two types of checking (which we call *advisory checking* and *mandatory checking*) can be implemented to allow almost any type of transaction to safely proceed without having to take locks across terminal I/O, and it also provides a high level of feedback to the user. However, nothing in this world comes free. In addition to the message traffic and the CPU load of the database requests required to make the advisory checks, there is also the risk that the advisory check will get it wrong.

The advisory check may pass and then the eventual commit fail as a result of the mandatory check (because, for example, another user commits a transaction which uses up the credit that your transaction found available, but did not lock). Also, under some circumstances, the check can report a violation where the commit would have succeeded. For this reason we recommend that whenever you use advisory checking, then the way that you report a check failure should allow the user to continue (at his discretion) following an advisory message. In an environment in which a user can have multiple transactions in flight at the same time, this will also allow that user the opportunity to overcome the problem in a parallel transaction—for example, by increasing the customer's credit limit.

Good user training and carefully written online help will make this approach much more acceptable to the user base. The few anomalies that will occur are a small price to pay for coupling adequate performance with the integrity of your data.

How Does This Relate to Three-Tier Architectures?

The discussion in this chapter is particularly relevant to the kind of three-tier architecture in which the application is separated into three parts:

- Managing the user interface
- Executing the processing rules
- Executing the data storage and retrieval functions

One consequence of using a three-tier architecture is that we have a clear opportunity to enforce a rigid separation of the process rules from the data rules. The former are implemented (exclusively) in the middle tier, and the latter (rather less exclusively) in the data management tier. One of the great strengths of a three-tier architecture is that it allows an application (the middle tier) to use several different data servers without any need for Gateway products to interface the data servers to each other.

Thus, in an extreme case, we could keep our customer records in conventional indexed files, our order records in an Oracle RdB database, and our stock records in an Oracle7 database. The main line of our application calls each database using native calls to retrieve the data, and the separate data universes remain unaware of one another's existence. Unfortunately, this means in turn that all referential integrity issues must now be handled by the application mainline; because none of the data stores is aware of the other, none can be responsible for maintaining cross-database constraints.

Although Oracle7 can operate as the data management tier in a three-tier architecture, it is more normally deployed in a two-tier architecture with the user interface code (the screen handler or report generator) communicating directly over SQL*Net to the database engine, and any middle tier provided by PL/SQL stored procedures, usually in the form of packages for performance and manageability.

Our strong recommendation for most Oracle7 applications is to code as follows:

- The interface rules in the front end tool (Oracle Forms, Powerbuilder, etc.)
- The process rules in PL/SQL packages
- The data rules as declarative constraints and triggers

Ideally, the tables themselves will not be available for direct insert, update, or delete from interface processes which will be forced to perform all DML through the stored PL/SQL code. Although this approach does not fit well with many of the RAD tools on the market (which tout their ability to generate DML code), it does allow the process rules to be concentrated in one place—the database engine—to be shared by all interfaces.

This ability to directly share a single copy of process rules between multiple interfaces can be a critical factor in ensuring the integrity of heavily distributed applications using multiple interfaces and can give rise to significant performance benefits.

Extending Connectivity

The wider connectivity is to be extended, the more sense it makes to ensure that the interface code is concerned solely with interface rules and any advisory checking that has been introduced. This separation will guarantee that users at different types of interface will achieve the same results from identical requests against identical data through different interfaces.

If connectivity is extended to the point where there are transactions which need to access many data servers of different types, then it may well be worth constructing a formal middle tier—either one of the data servers or, more likely, on a dedicated application server. This leads naturally to consideration of TP Managers such as Tuxedo and Encina. Although these are outside the scope of this book, it is worth mentioning again at this point that effective deployment of a TP Manager will normally require the use of *shared connections* within Oracle and that these, in turn, require the use of *atomic transactions* in order to be deployed efficiently.

The adoption of advisory checking rather than mandatory checking in the user interface means that the user interface can operate without taking locks right up to the point in time where the user wants to commit his changes. Thus, each call from the user interface can be passed to the appropriate data server as an atomic transaction.

17

Metrics, Prototypes, and Specifications

At some point during the design phase of every project, the project manager starts hounding you to answer questions like "How long will it take to build these modules?" and "What tools are you going to use to build them?" And that's if you're lucky. If you're unlucky, management will already have answered both of these questions to their own entire satisfaction—and your Mission Impossible will be to make their predictions come true! In this chapter, we'll try to help you fulfill your mission.

At a later point, the developers come to you asking "Just exactly how is this module I am writing supposed to work, and where is it called from?" You hope that you'll be able to produce a well-written specification that answers these questions and more.

Later still, during user acceptance testing, a user comes up to you and says, "This is the first system delivered by Information Systems that has really delivered what we wanted the first time." You reply (smugly), "That's why we invested the time prototyping it with you before we wrote a single line of code in earnest."

This chapter is all about some of the black arts of code design: estimating, specifying, and prototyping.

Developing Design and Build Metrics for Modules

Estimating how long it will take to complete a code module is notoriously difficult. A lot of designers underestimate module development time and, when this is scaled up by the number of modules, it is easy to see why some projects come in so late!

Most well-run projects tackle the need for time estimates at two levels of detail:

- At the first level, which takes as input the initial analysis documentation, the *technical architect* proposes an initial set of estimates and documents a set of assumptions. These assumptions should include both the tools to be used for the build and estimates of the hardware resources likely to be required for that build. Obviously, these estimates are "best guesses."

- The second set of estimates is much more detailed and must be prepared much later, after most of the detailed analysis, database design, and module design work has been performed.

To nobody's surprise, the two different approaches often lead to radically different answers. Your project manager knows this too, which is why he keeps knocking at your door (or sending you email messages) asking where the estimates are. Even if he isn't pressuring you, estimating is an essential exercise that you must go through in any case. Here's how to begin.

Make a list of your current set of modules, pencil in a set of tools in which to implement them (not necessarily binding at this stage), and assign each module a tool and a complexity. Don't invent eight or nine levels of complexity; use these four at the most:

- Simple
- Medium
- Complex
- Very complex

Why two categories of complex? To appease the project manager, you will apply standard metrics to most of the modules to work out the overall build estimates. However, in most systems there tend to be two or three modules (sometimes more!) that don't quite fit the model. These "megamodules" have to be evaluated and estimated separately (or designed out; in the next section you will be amazed to see just how easy it is to avoid superman modules with good analysis and design methodology).

What are these metrics? They are simply tables of estimated person days against each complexity for each software development tool that will be used for programming. In Table 17-1 we have split the metrics into three tasks: program design, build, and unit test.

Table 17-1. Sample Metrics for Oracle Forms 4.0/4.5

Oracle Forms 4/4.5	Program Design	Build	Unit Test
Simple	1	1	1
Medium	3	4	3
Complex	5	10	7
Very Complex	6 – 10	11 – 15	8 – 20

Don't pay too much attention to the specific figures shown here but do note that nothing takes less than one person day. Absolutely nothing. The actual figures vary from project to project and depend on many external influences. We should always include a large list of assumptions with our metrics to cover ourselves when the inevitable slippage starts to occur. Some examples of the assumptions that we may wish to record are these:

- Stability of the data model while module design/build is in progress
- Skill level of the developers
- Suitability of the chosen suite of development tools
- Use (or not) of code generators
- Adequacy of the development environment (hardware/software/network)
- Level of change in functionality absorbed during the build process

---

TIP   Be very suspicious of modules that have a high complexity rating but for which a relatively low function tool has been picked. There is a series of graphs used to express the effect of increased complexity on the development effort required with various types of tools, one of which is illustrated in Figure 17-1.

Like many such graphs, this one is suspiciously devoid of any scale on the axes. It does, however, make the point that once the going gets difficult, it gets very difficult indeed with certain types of tools.

So, we now have our first cut list of modules, the products we expect to use to implement them, and rough timescales for their development.

Banishing Megamodules

There are a number of different manifestations of the megamodule, which we describe in the following sections.

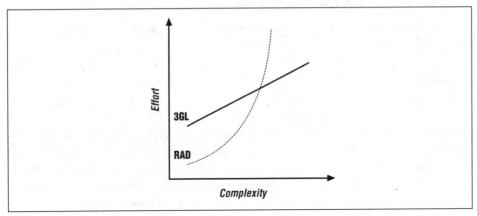

Figure 17-1. Effect of complexity on effort based on tool type

Sadly, the *megamodule* or *superman* screen is a common feature in online systems. On such screens we often find that several application functions are supported from within a single form. Indeed, in one famous Oracle Forms application, we were lucky enough to witness all DML (except reference table maintenance) contained in a single ON-COMMIT trigger of fiendish complexity. The justification was that "the users needed it to be that way." On the other hand, the reason that one of us was on site was that the users never stopped complaining about the poor performance and reliability of the form in question. The first part of the solution was to realize that the users were saying very clearly that they needed the application *not* to be that way. On another occasion, a proud developer showed us the entire application that he had developed in a single Oracle form with 70 screen pages!

WARNING   This objective of keeping complexity down is harder to achieve
            when using a RAD approach to development. What starts off as a
            relatively small module will often end up doing everything but mak-
            ing the coffee once the users start adding bits of functionality on
            during prototype review. This needs to be strictly controlled.

Batch Processing

Before we discuss the online manifestation of the megamodule in more detail, let's simply observe that such modules exist not only in forms but also in reports and batch jobs. In batch, there may be at least a partial justification, because by performing all of the required processing while a record (row) is in memory, it's often possible to save having to retrieve the same data in job after job during the overnight processing. Thus, a single walk through the customer or account data may perform a series of updating tasks and gather the data for a series of reports, possibly summarizing in memory under a series of headings and writing out these results at the end of the run.

As a historical note, we observe that the standard batch process design for the tape-based systems of the 1960s and early 1970s involved a serial pass of the master file, spinning off a series of (we hope, shorter) serial files to drive the remaining stages of the process. In the megamodule we do nothing as amateurish as writing serial data sets for later processing; we do it all right then and there.

The key to implementing such a job is to build the control structure for the main loop, and then to rigidly separate (encapsulate) each of the actions that is performed in each loop iteration; this allows any one of them to be modified without affecting any of the others. It may be totally obvious to the coder that step 24 is performed only in those cases where step 17 has found a particular condition, but life will be so much easier for everyone concerned (and especially the maintenance team) if you fail to fully optimize and do not have step 17 leave its conclusion in some secret place for step 24 to pick up. The simplest solution is to have both steps 17 and 24 test against the database for the condition (with luck, all the required SQL and data will still be in the SGA). If there is a major efficiency problem with both of these steps now having to retrieve the same data to make the same decision, then the decision should itself be encapsulated in a procedure that can record, unseen to either step, whether the required processing has already taken place.

Reports

In the case of reports, it is usually simpler just to build a series of similar reports than it is to try to build a single report that is capable of adapting itself to every possible requirement by the continual addition of more and more parameters. Indeed, if we are to assume that the reports are launched not by name but by menu option or some other device on the GUI, then the user doesn't care whether his or her choices are supported by one report module or one hundred report modules. The great advantage to the user of the latter approach is that if she requests a change to the heading format of one particular report, then (with luck) the heading will change only on that particular report, and no other reports will unexpectedly stop working. Most reporting tools will allow you to develop library code that can be shared among the report modules so that this approach doesn't necessarily imply a lack of reusability.

Online Applications

With online applications, a major cause of the megamodule is the fact that analysts and designers may impose unnecessary restrictions on the data model. For example, there may be a rule that a customer record may not exist without at least one order. Now the coder of the order entry screen will find it necessary to create a customer record which cannot be committed until the order is committed. Of course, the installation follows the standard that no DML is permitted until commit time in a form, so now the order entry has to use a flag to tell various data validation steps whether the current customer already exists in the database or will be created at commit time.

A much simpler solution is to allow customer records to exist without orders, and then to call the screen which creates them from the order processing screen when required. The called screen can then issue a commit (or rollback) before it returns. This, again, is encapsulation. If it really bothers you to have "customers" who have never done business with you, then invent a super-type called something like *known party* and state a rule that a *known party* becomes a *customer* when that party has had at least one order entered. Put another way, when over-simplistic analysis is the cause of your problem, then negotiate (or impose) a change to the analysis.

Each time that you see a megamodule on the horizon, ask yourself the simple question "What do I have to do to allow the processing to be broken up?" Neither of us has yet failed to find a way of doing exactly this, though we have at times had great difficulty convincing our colleagues that a simpler solution was a better way to proceed. Remember that design is about finding a cost-effective way to meet the user requirements within the constraints, and that the constraints usually include both cost and performance. Megamodules cost us dearly to implement and maintain, and they rarely perform well.

Shall We Prototype?

Prototypes are mockups of the real application or visualizations of concepts that are created specifically to demonstrate potential functionality, aid understanding, and solicit the opinions of users. It may be a working model, but it is only a model; it is not the "real thing" and must not be confused with reality. Very few of the zany concept cars that you see at motor shows become production models, but many of the concepts are carried forward into new production models. A prototype should be regarded as a tool to present ideas in visual fashion and to promote discussion and feedback. It is usually an iterative process; the prototype is refined in the light of feedback and is presented again.

The deliverables from a prototyping exercise may be a concrete set of screen designs, papers, and technical notes on how complex functionality is to be implemented. They may also include a "look-and-feel" standard that is signed off on by the user community.

This section discusses the value of the prototype and tries to reach a conclusion about when we should develop prototypes, how we should go about developing a prototype, and how much depth or functionality we should build into a prototype. We also look briefly at the important aspect of marketing the prototype to users so they understand exactly what they are seeing.

The arguments have been raging on for years about prototyping applications. Are they worth it? What do they achieve? Do they set unacceptably high levels of user expectation? Should they be throwaway or refined into part of the system? Are they too time-consuming?

We will try to address these questions, but first we must distinguish between two types of prototypes. Traditionally, a prototype was the vehicle for proving a concept or for demonstrating a particular capability to the user community and obtaining feedback. Such prototypes were nearly always disposable items, and they would be discarded once approved. With rapid application development (RAD) methods, however, the prototype goes through many iterations and eventually forms part (if not all) of the production system.

Prototyping with RAD

The RAD approach has the benefit that we are not wasting time by producing something only to throw it away later. It also means that what we have is generally a working model, rather than a series of empty screens with no functionality behind them. We are proving the process, not simply demonstrating screens that are no more than layouts.

With all its benefits, though, the RAD approach comes with several significant built-in costs, which include the following:

- If the code is to become the final product, it must be developed according to the project standards. This means that you must either have the standards ready before prototyping begins or suffer the cost of reworking the code when the standards are produced. Of course, this rework never happens, and a more likely scenario is that a set of vague standards are produced that have been bent to fit the existing code!

- A parallel cost is that the prototype itself will take longer to produce since more care must be taken. In reality, of course, an experienced technical auditor can spot those parts of an application that were prototyped early. They are the components that look rather awkward and nonstandard.

- Code that has been reworked several times tends to be messy. There is a high likelihood of obsolete code that is never called, variables that are no longer used, comments that are no longer valid, and sections of code that have been commented out. The flow of the code is not as logical as it would be if the code had been produced without all the changes.

Those who favor having the prototype progress through to production, which is also called *iterative development,* ask us if these problems really matter provided that the end product works properly. This is rather like asking if it really matters if your car is wrecked provided that the accident happens at the place you were headed for. You may be in the right place, but you are going to find it very difficult to get anywhere else until the vehicle has undergone extensive repairs.

We urge you not to fall for the seductive arguments in favor of iterative development. Unless your approach is 100% generator-based, you will end up with code that is extremely difficult to maintain, and we regard maintenance as inevitable. The use of generator technology can greatly ease these problems provided that after each iteration, the generated code is discarded and only the information in the repository is retained. This is, of course, nothing less than an automated method of recoding the component from scratch on each iteration.

- The iterative process must be controlled, and it must have clear objectives. Too often it becomes an auction between the developers, the analysts and the prospective users to see who can come up with the hottest new feature that can possibly be provided in the interface, rather than taking care of the underlying business. And at some point you have to draw the line and say, "We've got it." One way to put a time limit on the exercise is to use the time-box techniques discussed in Chapter 1, *Introduction*; another is to give each screen a fixed number of iterations after which no changes are accepted without very good justification.

- With today's 4GL and RAD tools, it is easy enough present attractive-looking data; the screen painter will allow you to show whatever you want to show. However, this is not the whole story. Underneath these screens there is (or will eventually be) an Oracle7 database. You have to be sure that the database can support the designs which are so easy to "paint," and we recommend that all data displayed in prototypes should actually be retrieved from the proposed schema rather than just assuming that retrieval is possible and hard-coding it. We have to consider the database as fluid for the duration of the prototyping exercise; the database is being RADed along with the screens.

This rather piecemeal approach doesn't always lead to the best designed database.

As designers we need to bear these points in mind when we are developing prototypes. We should make sure that we keep our build skills current since the design and build are heavily intertwined in a RAD development. There is little point in creating all the iterations ourselves and then handing them over to a builder for the final cut. After all, 90% of the work will have been done at this point.

If you want to know more about how Oracle Corporation believes that RAD can be deployed in an Oracle environment, we suggest the book by Dai Clegg and Richard Barker.[*]

Prototyping in a Non-RAD Development

In a more traditional development environment, we have a genuine choice of whether to prototype or not. In this environment, prototyping can serve two very distinct but important purposes:

- Helping the designers understand how (whether) the system will work

- Involving end users early in the project and helping them to "buy in"

User "buy-in" is vital. It is likely that the users have spent considerable time and effort talking about the system, even if only in purely theoretical terms. If, at an early stage, they can actually see and touch something, then they see a result of their hard labors, which feeds their motivation. They may not like the prototype, but smart designers view user complaints as constructive criticism and take account of their comments in a second pass. It is much better to have users reject an early prototype (when we can do something to fix it at minimal cost) than to have them find themselves unable to use the eventual system.

While prototyping some of the application, you will comes across many of the pitfalls and complexities of the system; the result is that you will be wiser the second time around when you are designing it (and maybe writing it) for real. How often have you finished a major piece of code and wished you could start it all again with the hindsight you've just gained by doing it the first time?

When you meet with users to demonstrate and discuss the prototype, it is particularly important to set the ground rules and the expectation levels. We must ensure that users don't get a false impression. Some prototypes look almost like the complete system, but in fact they are an almost completely hollow shell. If we show this kind of prototype to users and don't explain it very well, they may go

---

[*] Clegg, Dai and Richard Barker, *CASE Methods FastTrack: A RAD Approach*, Addison Wesley, 1994.

away with the expectation that they will get the system in a couple of weeks! A good demo of almost anything can get you a sale!

Most test data bears little resemblance to the real data, yet most users will criticize the data if they haven't been properly briefed. It's important to guide users into concentrating on the look and feel and usability of the screen, and on whether or not they meet the requirements of the business. We must add, though, that if you can come up with realistic data, it does show that you have a very good understanding of the environment in which the application will be used.

How many applications should we prototype, and how do we choose which ones? The answers obviously depend on the time and manpower available, but we can supply some general guidelines. Referring back to our two key reasons for prototyping, we remind you to concentrate on the "shop window" of the system to users (the look and feel) and the complex areas of functionality (technical *proof of concept*).

To establish the look and feel and style of the system, take two fairly simple and related screens. Code the prototypes to show the placement of data on the screen, the use of keyboard, function keys, and mouse, some kind of selection from a list, and (most importantly) navigation between the two applications.

Take an honest look at the system for both the most complex areas and the most critical areas in terms of the overall success of the system. If it is at all unclear how these will be implemented, then draw up a list of alternatives and try them out. This can be a lengthy process, so adopt it only if there is likely to be some tangible benefit in terms of performance or usability of the final system. You have to be realistic. It is likely that there are several approaches you could take to solve the most complex problem in the application. Pick perhaps two, and at most three, that look to be the most promising candidates and prototype these. At all costs remember KISS (Keep It Simple, Stupid); otherwise, you'll end up writing two or three complete application systems, which is exactly what you are trying to avoid. (Remember that the purpose of the prototypes is to avoid expensive mistakes.)

It is entirely normal, of course, for the most complex part of the application to be the most critical for its overall success. To improve your chances of success, you may wish to reread the section earlier in this chapter on avoiding megamodules!

Our final word on prototypes is (in the words of the Nike commercials) Just Do It! Memos, specs, and email messages just don't cut it when you have to explain proposals to users and involve them in the development process. Building a prototype is generally a worthwhile exercise, especially if the prototype is relatively small in relation to the entire system. It may even be worthwhile getting formal sign-off from the users involved that they are happy with the result of the proto-typing exercise.

Where Are My Specs? Guidelines for Module Specifications

Suppose that you have created your first-cut list of modules, done some estima-tions, created a couple of prototypes, written some libraries, and agreed upon how the system will look and how the complex areas will work. What's next? Now, unfortunately, you are entering the drudgery zone. You have to write the module specifications that will enable the builders to actually build the system.

Who is going to build the modules? It may be that you, as the designer of the application, will also build the modules that make it up. If so, you might be tempted to write a minimal specification and get coding as soon as possible, or maybe even code first, then write the specification afterwards (or not at all!). This temptation is particularly strong in a RAD development.

We recommend very strongly that you record your design as early as possible, because failure to do so will come back to haunt you. Suppose that you get pulled off your development task to do some other design. You'll then try to hand over to a colleague a piece of half-written code with no comments and no specification. This doesn't make you popular, highly regarded, or successful.

The more likely scenario is that you run short of time so the specification is forgotten and never gets written. Those of us who have attempted to maintain undocumented code already know what a nightmare this can turn into. We must discipline ourselves to always assume that another person will have to take our design specification and turn it into code. For anything other than trivial modules, or those that are generated from a code generator and never modified, we need to write a module specification.

There are some other temptations that may hinder you in producing a module specification. One of the most popular, most expensive, and most completely pointless is to assume that the person who will be writing the code is incapable of writing code himself or herself—so you do it for them. In other words, you create a "specification" written in *pseudocode.*

Pseudocode is a disaster. By its very nature, it is dictating the structure of the real code and not allowing the developer to solve the problem. It is *very* prone to errors, both syntactic and logical. You can't syntax check it, you can't compile it, and you can't run it, so you can't test it.

And *nobody* gets code right without testing it. So what you have is code (the pseudocode) which you can be absolutely certain contains errors. But it is also the specification for part of your system, so if the programmer follows the pseudocode, we can guarantee that the module will contain errors.

If you must supply algorithms, keep them general. The only (arguably) allowable exception is the specification of some complex mathematical calculation with lots of dependencies between the steps where it may not be possible to express the calculation precisely enough without using a formal language. By all means, use an algorithm, but make sure that it is one that you can syntax check and execute within your environment, test, and publish in a form that the programmer can install on his or her own workstation. In other words, if you are determined to code, then finish the job and ship the solution to the build team for integration into their output.

Frankly, if you find that you cannot avoid writing specifications that contain pseudocode, we suggest you pick one of the two following alternative courses of action:

- Get a job as a programmer and write some real code, or

- Go work in a different industry

Some designers tend to include SQL statements ready-coded in the module specifications. Again, we must stress that if your programmers cannot write SQL statements, you should fire them and hire some who can. It is quite an easy language to learn and several million people already know it. Also, it is quite possible that in the time between writing the specification and developing the code, the database schema may undergo several alterations. At this point, the SQL may no longer be optimal and may even not be valid. On the other hand, SQL is a well-defined language and anything that you write in it can be tested. So our advice is: *do not write SQL in a module specification* unless the data design has been based on the premise that the programs will employ a particular approach and this approach has been tested.

Having told you not to put SQL in your module specifications, we must point out that it is easy to conceal your SQL by pretending that you are writing in English. Example 17-1 shows an example; again, the solution here is to assume that the developer has a brain and simply to specify what data is required.

Example 17-1. SQL Statement Dressed Up as Descriptive Text in an Extract from a Specification

> Select the Quantity and Customer Name from the Order Items, Order and Customers table, where the Customer Number on the Order table matches that on the Customers table for the Customer already retrieved...

Example 17-2 shows another variation on the theme of wasting time and paper by telling developers things they do not need to have explained to them. 3GL programmers know that to process sets of data you write a loop, and they know that at the end of a loop they must instruct the program to go off and do something else. If you really do have to tell your programmers these things, you need better programmers, not longer specifications.

Example 17-2. Redundant Instructions from a Specification

> Loop through the set of rows returned by the query checking for end of fetch; if this is encountered, then proceed to the processing described below, under...

A good module specification should list the tables and columns that are accessed and should state which are queried, inserted, updated, and deleted and which are used as predicates in a WHERE clause. As we've mentioned, this is sometimes referred to as a *CRUD matrix* because it has columns for *C*REATE, *R*EAD, *U*PDATE, and *D*ELETE. Most CASE products that support module definition expect this level of information and generally provide a structured means of entering it. One big advantage of these matrices (particularly if you are using a CASE tool) is that the impact of a proposed database change can be assessed by referencing the module specification to see which modules will be affected by the change.

Finally, you must review every module specification in the light of all design decisions and standards. Consider the interaction between the module and rules enforced as database objects, with particular emphasis on providing a good human interface. For example, is it acceptable to a user to spend a couple of minutes keying data only to have it all rejected on commit with a message that says, "Check constraint SYS_00023 violated"? The answer is probably not. An acceptable solution probably involves a number of steps, possibly including some template code for handling Oracle Server-generated errors.

In summary, remember that a good module specification should tell the builder, and the rest of the world, what the module is expected to do rather than exactly how it should do it.

Specifying Screens and Reports

For modules that are screens or reports, it is sometimes helpful to include a layout or format with the design. This may include the name of the source column for all fields that originate from the database. However, it is more important to have the following details:

- Statement of what the screen or report does (e.g., "Change of Customer Status" or "Aged Debt Analysis Summary")

- Navigation (where is it called from, what does it call)

- Parameters (what input parameters are there, what are the default values)

- Processing (what events may occur within the module, how are they handled)

- Errors (what errors are raised during the processing and what is the consequence)

- Security (who can run it, who has restricted actions available)

In most applications, once the first two or three screens and reports have been built, then the formats for most of the rest can be "specified" by simply referencing one of those that already exists. This is a particular benefit that can be derived from a prototyping exercise.

Specifying Batch Processes

For batch processes, the majority of the description focuses on the processing, but remember to incorporate the following items:

- Statement of what the screen or report does (e.g., "Change of Customer Status" or "Aged Debt Analysis Summary")

- Parameters (what input parameters are there, what are the default values)

- Recovery (what to do if the job fails part way through processing)

- Locking (use of table locks or preemptive locking to ensure that the job is not held up)

- Mutual exclusion (with any online functions or other batch routines)

- Logging (where does the run log go)

- Expected database state, before and after the run

- Errors (what errors are raised during the processing)

- Security (who can run it, who can submit it, and who has restricted actions available)

Batch processing is described in greater detail in Chapter 20, *Designing Screens, Reports, Batch Programs, and More.*

18

Locking

You use *locking* in database applications to try to keep people from doing things you don't want them to do. But while we usually lock a safe to prevent a potential and almost certainly deliberate crime, we lock database rows and tables to prevent an accidental loss of data or data integrity. In a true single-user application, one in which only one session will ever be connected to the database at any point in time, traditional locking is irrelevant. But as soon as we support multiple users, then we start to encounter potential errors that can be prevented by appropriate locking strategies.

The use of the word "prevented" in the previous paragraph is entirely deliberate. Although the lock on a cash box may not be enough to deter or defeat a determined burglar, a database lock will, in fact, be honored by the database for as long as the lock remains validly in force.

Locking Strategies

When we developed our original outline for this book, we pictured writing a long chapter on locking. When we actually came to write it, though, we found that the chapter was quite short. Why? Because in almost all cases, Oracle's default locking strategy is an entirely adequate solution. We caution, however, that for good multiuser performance you must remember two simple rules: *lock little* and *lock late*. This is in contrast to the tendency of most tools, especially Oracle Forms, to lock early. We'll explain what we mean by these rules as the chapter progresses.

Locks prevent other users from doing things, and that doesn't always please them. Those users would probably appreciate being allowed to go about their legitimate business and not to be told that they cannot, for example, change a customer's credit rating because an order is currently being entered for that same customer. Indeed, credit control might well feel that if an order is being entered for the customer and they need to reduce his credit, then their update has even *more* right to go through immediately than it normally would.

The real question here is why the order entry screen has locked the customer record in the first place. The answer given by most builders (at least those who have sat through one of Oracle's courses) is that if you retrieve a row and plan to update it (or even think that you might update it) then you should retrieve it with a FOR UPDATE clause and take a row-level lock on it. This guarantees that the row will remain unchanged for the duration of your transaction, and that it will therefore be safe to use the values that you retrieved as the basis for an update.

However, if all you need to do is to update a balance, then there really is no need to ever explicitly lock the record. The balance can be updated using a statement such as the following one:

```
UPDATE customers
   SET account_balance = account_balance - :this_amount
     , latest_trans_id = :this_trans_id
 WHERE cust_id = :this_cust;
```

Of course, as soon as the program issues this UPDATE statement, Oracle will acquire a row-level lock that will be held until the end of the transaction. But at least we have delayed taking the lock until the last possible moment (that is what we mean by "lock late"). By default, Oracle Forms locks rows as soon as the user enters a change, even though it may be several minutes before the user commits the changes. We recommend against this approach—we prefer to acquire the lock at the last possible moment and then to check to ensure that the record (the row) has not changed in the meantime.

Locking Later

Row version numbers offer a simple way to check whether a row has changed since you selected it. Every table on which you wish to lock late can be given a column that defaults to zero when the row is inserted, and that is updated by one on every update. If we call this column *row_version* and make a note of its value when we first display data from the row, then we can code our UPDATE with an additional predicate clause, as in the following:

```
UPDATE customers
   SET account_balance = account_balance - :this_amount
     , latest_trans_id = :this_trans_id
 WHERE cust_id        = :this_cust
   AND row_version    = :version;
```

If the UPDATE returns no rows processed, we know that either the row has been deleted in the interim or that it has been updated. In either case, we must re-query before proceeding, and the application must handle this.

Techniques which lock late, rather than early, and which therefore run the risk of encountering an error condition are usually called *optimistic locking*. We prefer to refer to the technique as *optimistic not locking* to stress its advantages—though to be fair, Oracle will eventually apply a lock whether we like it or not.

Rollback Segment Usage

Oracle's default locking strategy comes with the intriguing claim that:

> Readers do not block writers and writers do not block readers.

This is completely true, but it comes at a significant cost. In Oracle, you will normally see committed changes which have been made since the start of your transaction. Of course you can use the SQL command:

```
SET TRANSACTION READ ONLY;
```

to supply a read consistency point that remains unchanged until you either commit or roll back. This is essential if you are going to navigate a master-detail structure using nested queries rather than a join. Why? Because otherwise you will eventually get inconsistent results because the query on the master table has a different read consistency point from each of the queries on the detail table.

The longer the read-only transaction runs, the more likely it is to encounter the error "SNAPSHOT TOO OLD," which means that Oracle no longer has the roll-back segment information required to reconstruct some block the way it was at the read consistency point. At this point, your query dies; this can happen to any long-running query. Larger rollback segments will help reduce the incidence of the problem. However, the only way it's possible to guarantee that a long-running query will not encounter this problem is to block DML on the table—that is, to lock the table in share mode before starting to execute the query. This is a drastic measure to have to take, and it is yet another reason why long-running queries may be better supported by a copy database which is not subject to continual update traffic.

Foreign Keys

Foreign key constraints have an unexpected effect on Oracle's default locking strategy. If you build a simple table such as that created by the statement:

```
CREATE TABLE emp_assigns
( emp#    REFERENCES employees
, proj#   REFERENCES projects
```

```
, PRIMARY KEY (emp#, proj#)
);
```

then you might be very surprised to find that when you perform any DML activity on the table *emp_assigns*, the transaction which issues the DML acquires a share lock on the table *projects* (but not, in later versions, on the table *employees*). Now, provided that the table *projects* is only rarely maintained, this is unlikely to be much of a problem. However, when both tables are volatile, these share locks can dramatically affect throughput.

This anomaly is caused by the absence of an index on *emp_assigns*, which has *proj#* at its leading edge. Briefly, the problem is this: when any user tries to change or delete a primary key in *projects*, then that change can only be permitted if the key is not referenced from *emp_assigns*. With an index (and a nontransactional internal lock), Oracle can quickly and easily check whether the operation is legal. However, if no such index exists, then Oracle has to scan the *emp_assigns* table looking for a reference (which can be a lengthy operation). It does this using recursive SQL, whereas the index operation is performed using internal calls within the database engine. The recursive query is subject to read consistency and cannot see any uncommitted changes which have been made to the child table. Even if it could see them, there would be an ambiguity because they are uncommitted. Oracle's own designers elected to solve this problem by preventing it: the share lock means that you will not be able to make changes to the parent while the child table has uncommitted transactions. If you have an index on the foreign key in the child table, this restriction does not apply.

TIP   Every foreign key that references a volatile table should be indexed in its own right or should be at the leading edge of an index.

Deadlocks

Sooner or later, any complex multi-user application will encounter a deadlock. Although Oracle has extremely good *deadlock detection,* it leaves *deadlock resolution* entirely to the user. The designer and programmer can either resolve the problem in the application (which is the correct approach) or leave it to the end user to work out what to do (which is inviting trouble). The problem is that when Oracle raises the "DEADLOCK DETECTED" error, the only feasible action that can be taken is to roll back the current transaction and try again. As a marginal sophistication, it may be worth waiting for a few seconds before starting to retry. If the deadlock is encountered more than, say, three times on the same transaction, then we would recommend that the application report this as a fatal error.

At one time, Oracle internal project standards called for the imposition of a standard locking order which, it was claimed, would prevent deadlocks from occurring. This is a fine principle, but it simply does not work in practice for a number of reasons:

1. It can be extremely difficult to write code that locks in the required order, and code that is difficult to write tends to be both expensive and difficult to maintain.

2. In some cases, such as multirow forms, the update order may effectively be user-controlled. To be fair, it is possible to code around this problem, but doing so is tedious.

3. Oracle sometimes encounters benign deadlocks which are the result of competition for internal resources. One known cause of this situation was discussed in Chapter 14, *Designing for Parallel Processing*.

TIP   We recommend that all of your update processing should contain the simple code required to check for deadlocks and immediately roll back the transaction. Depending on the circumstances, the process may then give an error message, or retry the transaction a fixed number of times before finally conceding that all is not well and that an error message is required.

Unfortunately, Oracle's deadlock detection does not extend to distributed deadlocks, and the instance parameter, DISTRIBUTED_LOCK_TIMEOUT, is used instead. This instructs the Oracle server how long it should wait for another server to respond to a lock request before simply giving up and returning an error to the user. It is important for all code that might be required to take distributed locks also take this "error" into account.

Serializability

By default, Oracle does not provide serializability—that is, it cannot guarantee that if you were to issue exactly the same transactions in the exactly the same order against exactly the same starting data contents, then you would always get exactly the same answer. The reasons for this surprising statement are a little outside the scope of this book. Nevertheless, you will be forced to address this issue if, for some reason, you try to base recovery or restart logic on reapplying transactions rather than using Oracle's redo logs. It has been our experience that project teams which attempt this approach invariably fail, in part because of the serializability issue.

If you do need to be able to take this approach (and we suggest that you do almost *anything* to avoid having to address this problem), then you will need to run with the INIT.ORA parameter, SERIALIZABLE=TRUE, and, contrary to our previous advice, you will now *lock large* and *lock early*. Each query will take a table-level share lock before it starts. In Version 7.3, this level of isolation can be set at transaction level, but with a different effect. Rather than taking table-level share locks, which prevent anyone else from updating any table you have queried, a query that has issued the command:

```
SET TRANSACTION ISOLATION LEVEL SERIALIZABLE;
```

will fail with an appropriate error if it visits a row in a block that has been changed since the start of the transaction. This is almost certainly not what you want!

Other Design Issues

This section contains information on several additional locking issues that may impact your design.

User Locks

Oracle's procedural option contains a little used but extremely useful package called DBMS_LOCK, which allows the designer to create a *cooperative* locking strategy which may be based on anything. Using the package, processes can compete for locks on 32-bit numbers to which meanings are assigned by the application. One major feature of these locks is that they need not be transactional— that is, they can survive across a commit, although all the user locks held by a session are released when the session disconnects.

User locks are an effective way for an application to reserve resources. We have used them to reserve a primary key for later use within a transaction; we have also used them to signal that a particular table should not be used because a primary key reorganization (one which spans several transactions) is taking place.

Lock Efficiency: Block Cleanout and Table-Level Locks

When a user takes a row-level lock on a row in an Oracle table, then an *interested transaction entry (ITE)* is made in the block header to reflect this fact. One ITE in the block header allows the user to lock any number of rows in the block and, by default, each block has a single ITE in its header for this purpose (INITRANS 1). If one user has already locked a row in the block, and another user wants to lock a different row in the same block, the second user will be able to proceed only if there is enough space left in the block to create a second ITE. Otherwise, that user will have to wait for the first transaction to complete.

The real problems, however, start on commit because in versions prior to 7.3, the locks are not removed but are simply left in place. Even with Version 7.3, the locks are only removed if the blocks containing the locks are still resident within the SGA and the INIT.ORA parameter DELAYED_LOGGING_BLOCK_CLEANOUTS = FALSE. The locks are normally still in the SGA for online systems, but this is less likely for long batch runs. The next user to visit the block for any reason incurs the cost of checking to see if the lock is still in force and, if so, removing it. At sites where CPU is charged to the user, this situation can cause great resentment since ad hoc query users end up footing the bill for the block cleanout.

WARNING   Block cleanout slows down the first reference to data after recoverable DML upon the blocks. This is the cause of many misconceptions about Oracle performance that may arise when a "performance specialist" loads up some data and then tries two different ways of accessing it. The first approach is very likely to be slower than the second simply due to the overhead of block cleanout.

We have seen designers try to avoid the effects of block cleanout by using table-level locking instead of row-level locking. Trust us: locking a table in exclusive mode does not help. When you insert or update, you still place the row-level lock entry in the block header, and the next SQL statement to visit the block after you commit will still have to clean it out. Such is life. It may be intuitively obvious that table-level locking ought to use fewer resources than row-level locking but it just ain't so.

If your application has a relatively short table against which there are many row-level locks taken (for example, a BRANCHES table in which a balance is being maintained), then it may be worth setting the INITRANS parameter to a value higher than 1 to ensure that users do not have to wait for locks simply because there is not enough space to record the ITE. The ITEs are more than 20 bytes long, so values in double figures would be quite extraordinary. Very few applications need to set this parameter, and those that do might be better served by adopting the solution outlined in the next paragraph.

The need to maintain balances is a fairly common cause of lock contention. One effective, if highly artificial, solution is to have many sub-balances of each widely maintained balance. Suppose that we were trying to hold a running total of the total value of orders posted in a large online system. We would expect the row in which this total was held to quickly become the subject of a lock queue. We could, however, have 10 such rows and some arbitrary method by which each process decided which row to update, as shown in the following example:

```
UPDATE order_bals
    SET total_value  = total_value  + :this_order_total
    , total_orders = total_orders + 1
  WHERE sub_balance_id = MOD(uid, 10);
```

The only penalty is that in order to retrieve the balances we have to code a summary operation, but this can be encapsulated in a view:

```
CREATE OR REPLACE VIEW order_balances (total_value, total_orders) AS
    SELECT SUM(total_value)
         , SUM(total_orders)
      FROM order_bals;
```

The example is deliberately oversimplified—in a real application we would expect to see some form of date effectivity applied to the balances. To avoid errors, it might be a very good idea to withhold SELECT privilege on the table from all ad hoc users to ensure that they reference the view and do not encounter the sub-balances.

Note that tables (and indexes) where many sessions may need to update rows or index entries in parallel tend to suffer from block-level contention (*buffer busy waits* in Oracle tuner-speak). Block contention occurs principally on multiprocessor platforms. If the table concerned is genuinely short, then it can be trivially eliminated by forcing the database engine to only put one row into each block; you do this by setting the PCTFREE parameter to an artificially high value such as 95. This "wastes disk space," and indeed consumes more cache space in the SGA than would otherwise be the case, but for a table with only a few tens of rows, the waste is insignificant compared with the throughput benefit of eliminating block contention.

NOTE   You may wonder why block contention can impact throughput on a multiprocessor platform but is not regarded as a potential concern on a uniprocessor. The answer lies in Oracle's approach to database block references. Because *any* type of reference can result in a change being made to the block, Oracle takes a short duration lock called a *pin* on each database block just for the duration of any reference to it by the database engine. Oracle is also designed to relinquish the CPU as soon as it encounters any wait state, and ensures that it never voluntarily waits while holding a pin. So with only a single processor, even if two processes are querying or updating the same block, they should never see each others' pins.

But in a multiprocessor environment, particularly with symmetric multiprocessing where the processors can proceed independently, there is a statistical chance that

Oracle running on one processor will collide with a pin held by Oracle running on another processor. The more frequently any given block is referenced, the more likely this is to occur.

19

Selecting the Toolset

In this chapter:
- *Types of Tools*
- *Which Selection Criteria Are Important?*
- *Client/Server Tools*
- *Designing for the World Wide Web*

This chapter focuses on selecting the development tools or languages that you will use to maintain and query the data in your database. Of course, not every project goes through this process—sometimes it is a "given" that you use certain products. Many organizations are standardizing on development tools so they have consistency between their applications and so that they don't spread the load of skills and development staff too thin. We will look at the categories of tools that you can use (screen development tools, report writers, etc.), how you should go about selecting one, and specific issues for client/server developments.

Types of Tools

Most applications will require a mixture of tools to perform different functions within the system. The salesman for the Acme Development Tool Company may have convinced your management that absolutely anything can be efficiently coded in the latest release of Acme Express, but typically you will need a mixture of tools to handle the following types of module:

Forms
> Screen-based forms for data entry, maintenance, and inquiry

Reports
> Printed and possibly screen-based reports

Batch processes
> Processes supporting data feeds and bulk data processing

Ad hoc queries
> Support for ad hoc queries

Integration tool

Tool pulling the various components together into a seamless application

Although you are likely to have some input into the selection of tools, the final choice doesn't usually lie with the designer; often there are external influences and preferences at a site. Many corporations now have a list of "strategic" products that are used for every development unless a very good justification can be given for an alternative. You have to ensure that the strategic product set can fulfill the requirements of the system and (successfully) challenge the corporate standards if it cannot. We recommend that when you are proposing alternatives, you dwell more on the productivity gains and cost savings that you are going to achieve, rather than the aesthetics of the various options.

One of us has a vivid memory of trying to persuade a consulting client to code just one module (out of about 750) in Pro*C rather than PL/SQL. The project manager's view was that PL/SQL was the corporate standard and that therefore PL/SQL would be used. The relevant section of the consultant's report read:

> I agree with your development staff that it is not technically possible to write the ratings module in PL/SQL and meet the stated performance requirement. In addition the development effort for the PL/SQL variant is approximately ten times that of the C variant.

After more than a year of trying approach after approach in PL/SQL to overcome their performance problems, the manager who had replaced the original project manager finally authorized the rewriting of the module in Pro*C. This took one programmer a week to code and test, and solved the performance problems.

We have a saying:

> If the tool does not do what you want, then change what you want.
> If the tool does not do what you need, then change the tool.

Which Selection Criteria Are Important?

If the choice of tools is not dictated to us, then we must have a valid formal method for making our decision. The first step is to decide what criteria are important to us. The following list contains some likely criteria:

- Portability of the code across hardware and software platforms.

- Ability to support client/server features outlined in Chapter 11, *Designing for Client/Server.*

- Degree to which the product is *database aware.* (This is a reflection of how much work it takes to allow the programs to interact with the database. Tools

that have high levels of database awareness have default database functionality already built into all applications.)

- Support for code generation from a CASE tool.

- Skill set of the development staff, or the availability of consultants with knowledge of the tools.

- Degree to which the product is considered "state of the art" and the likelihood that it will remain supported for many years to come.

- Complexity of the tool and the speed with which programs can be written
  and debugged.

- Ability to support a multi-user development and test environment, including
  the degree of integration with source control tools.

- Reputation and financial stability of the tool developer and/or vendor and, in
  particular, the help desk and support facilities that are available.

When making an evaluation, you should make your own list (possibly based on
our template list) and prioritize the items on it, ranking the candidate products
against each item. When you have conflicting requirements or priorities, you may
end up choosing more than one tool. In particular, it is fairly common to have
one tool for writing the main database-oriented applications and another as an
integration tool to provide the wrapper in which the applications operate. License
costs should not be a major issue, though overall cost of ownership should.

If a decision is to be made on development and ad hoc query tools, then it may
be beneficial to get evaluation copies of the candidate products. The evaluation
can be combined with the prototyping exercise. You can develop the prototypes
in each of the tools or possibly divide the prototypes between the products. Obviously, this process will affect the timescales of the prototyping exercise. Most
software vendors will make free copies of their software available for trial
purposes, but you must make sure that you run the trial objectively and without
bias. Don't worry if a particular vendor refuses to give you a free trial; you will
find that the cost of a single evaluation copy of most software is insignificant
compared with the cost of mounting a properly structured trial of it.

Client/Server Tools

There are some specific issues that you will need to investigate when you
perform an evaluation for a client/server environment. The communication
between the client and the server will fall into one of the following three
categories:

- Direct SQL connect through SQL*Net

- SQL Connect through an ODBC driver

- RPCs to application servers that issue all the database requests

In reality, only the first two are currently widely available. The third is starting to look like the route of choice for both Web applications and for deployment of Oracle's Network Computing Architecture (NCA). There are doubtless those within Oracle who believe that these two are the same thing and that every Oracle site which is deploying Web applications will automatically adopt the NCA.

Some products, such as Powerbuilder from Powersoft Corporation, offer a choice of either of the SQL connections, and it is important to be aware of the differences. First, to use ODBC, you will need an ODBC driver if you cannot use direct connect, although the required drivers are quite often bundled with the tools. To use SQL*Net, you can freely write SQL that contains Oracle extensions to the ANSI standard. With an ODBC driver, the driver may attempt to parse the SQL and reject any SQL which is not ANSI compliant.

This restriction results in problems when we try to design a screen that enables the administrator of the application to maintain users, since commands such as ALTER USER and DROP USER are not ANSI standard. This restriction applies to almost all Oracle7 DCL and DDL. *The Oracle7 Server SQL Reference Manual* contains a list of Oracle extensions to standard SQL and the Version 7.2 manual lists more than 60 SQL commands supported by Oracle7 but not part of standard SQL. For those not familiar with the restricted scope of the SQL standard(s) we should point out that the list includes CREATE SYNONYM.

The ANSI restriction can be overcome in most ODBC drivers by setting an option called *pass through mode*. This mode causes the driver to pass the SQL directly through to the server, without attempting to interpret it. This allows non-ANSI SQL to be used, but negates one of the main advantages of using ODBC, which is that if pass through mode is not used applications can be made database-independent. This means that, in theory, the application should work against Oracle7, Sybase, SQL Server, Informix, etc. If this is important—for example, if your project is developing a product that is to be sold to a wider market than just Oracle7 servers—then ODBC without pass through should be your standard. But if that is the case, then very little of this book (aside from the section on pseudocode) will be of assistance to you!

People sometimes enable pass through mode because of the perception that the middleware (ODBC driver interpreting the SQL) is too much of an overhead and renders the application too slow. However, this depends heavily on the ODBC driver that is used: ODBC itself is merely a standard, and there are many drivers available on the market. Some have a reputation for speed regardless of the mode. Again, evaluation by prototype and benchmarking of the various drivers can be a valuable exercise. One thing to bear in mind is that if the ODBC driver is interpreting and rewriting the SQL, then it may strip out embedded comments, including those that are really hints to the Oracle7 optimizer. This will severely restrict your ability to influence the server in optimizing performance of individual SQL statements.

One final word about ODBC: in the first ODBC standard (ODBC 1) a program can call a database-resident stored procedure or function, and can pass parameters to it. However, it is not possible for the procedure to return values back to the calling program. This limitation severely restricts the design of the client/server interface, since stored procedures normally play an important role. The ODBC 2.0 standard rectifies this omission.

If you are considering the use of Microsoft Visual Basic or Visual C++ as your front end, there is an alternative to using ODBC (or embedded SQL), which is to use Oracle Objects for OLE (OO4O). This product has a very similar programmatic style to ODBC, but is written specifically for an Oracle7 server and is therefore optimized for Oracle.

Some client development tools have a built-in database engine. This can be useful for PC-based development, since otherwise we need access to an Oracle7 server (or Personal Oracle7 if we have enough memory on our PC). Here are some examples:

- Oracle Power Objects Version 1.x with Blaze
- Oracle Power Objects Version 2.x with Oracle Lite
- Microsoft Visual Basic with Jet
- Borland Delphi with Interbase
- Powersoft Powerbuilder with Watcom SQL

These engines do not support anything like the full functionality of Oracle7. In particular, they do not support database-resident constraints or code components such as triggers or stored procedures. These limitations dictate the level to which development can usefully progress on a standalone configuration, and makes using Personal Oracle7 appear to be a much better option. Oracle recently introduced Oracle Lite, which is capable of running in 1 megabyte of memory, but again this is a seriously restricted engine aimed much more at the embedded systems market than the applications market.

We can describe the previous category as "client development tool with built-in database engine" where the development tool can also access a remote database on a server, usually via ODBC. There is another type of developer tool/database combination, products which may be categorized as "client database engine with built-in development tool." Examples of this second category are Microsoft Access and Borland Paradox.

There is a trap that we need to be wary of when designing client/server systems around such tools. We may (sensibly) choose to use the local database to hold certain nonvolatile data such as reference data. When we join local tables to server tables, we find ourselves effectively in the twilight zone of distributed database. We want the server database to be in control, since that is where the bulk of our data and the heavy processing power resides. However, sometimes the client database initiates a power struggle and attempts to take control. Large tables are downloaded from the server database to the client, often the entire table, to be joined to a local table on the client (see Figure 19-1). Obviously, such strategies have a disastrous effect on performance.

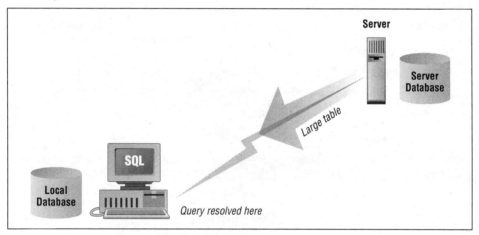

Figure 19-1. Problems when client database manager tries to take control

Some client development products generate code that is unable to use either public or private synonyms within the database. Some may work only for the user who owns the table since they do not support table references that are prefixed with the schema name (*schema.table*). If this is the case with a tool that you are evaluating, you need to consider the implications on your security policy if, for instance, everybody has to connect to the database with the same user id.

Designing for the World Wide Web

Many new applications are going to be developed for deployment through Web browsers. In organizations where prospective users already have a Web browser, it's difficult to see why a new application might want to use any other user interface tool. In saying this, we are not suggesting that all of your new applications be opened up to the entire Web community worldwide. We're simply pointing out that browser technology makes for a very convenient way to deploy a new application over *an intranet* rather than *the Internet*. Ensuring that there is a difference between the two means either not connecting your internal network to the Internet at all, or ensuring that you have an effective firewall.

However, if you are proposing to take this route, then we urge you to look at three-tier architectures, and to remove from the user interface code all direct references to the database. Instead, place these references in the application server(s). In Figure 19-2, we have shown only a single application server and two databases, which may be maintained in isolation by some applications, or together by other applications.

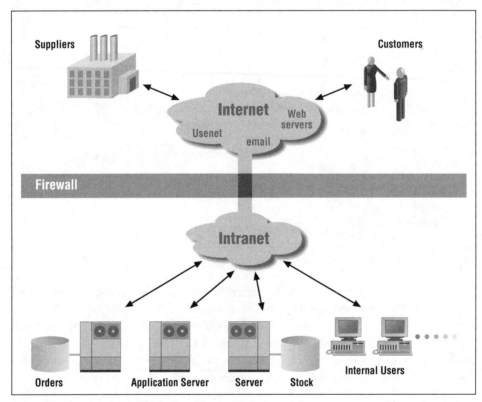

Figure 19-2. Using the World Wide Web

20

Designing Screens, Reports, Batch Programs, and More

The application screens and reports that use and access your database are the shop window of your application. Like a shop window, they create an immediate impression in the user's mind that is not easy to change. It is, therefore, of great importance that your screens and reports be professional, good-looking, and easy to use. The batch processes are the engine room of the operation. Nobody cares what they look like or how they work, but we all expect them to continue to function reliably and efficiently. We also describe design issues for error handling, navigation, and online help.

In this chapter, which has less to do with databases than most, we spotlight the issues that might make or break your system. If you don't get them right, then next time you might not have a database to design!

Designing Screens

The most important aspect of screen design is to make the screens intuitive and able to lead the user through some particular process without being intrusive.

These days, pretty much every user is familiar with other products. Most people have a PC on their desks and are likely to use a word processing or spreadsheet package. When they are asked about an interface to a product, it is only natural that they will refer to their familiar applications. You should try to do the same. When designing, try to fit in as best you can with the existing standards in the user's own environment (such as using the F1 key for help in a Microsoft Windows application). We should also be consistent with any other applications that they happen to run.

On the other hand, it's easy to get hung up on this point and end up designing a program to resemble something that it isn't. Spreadsheets and word processors may be good for many situations, but they are not ideal as database front ends, particularly when it is necessary to update the database. Don't fall into the trap of trying to make a data entry screen look and behave like Lotus 1-2-3 or Microsoft Excel! It doesn't take that long to familiarize a user with a new format or style. You can spend weeks making a relocatable button bar, when it would suffice to simply educate the user that the bar will be permanently positioned along the top of the screen. Also although graphical user interfaces (GUIs) are likely to be available, fully exploiting their features may not be the best option for all users.

It is helpful to categorize our user community into various types of users. Some possible categories are these:

- Data entry personnel who will be using the system frequently and heavily but will not be making inquiries

- Regular inquiry users with low data entry volumes

- Ad hoc users who perform the occasional lookup and (even more occasional) update

- Decision support users who want ad hoc query capabilities but rarely or never update

- Operators who schedule and monitor reports and batch jobs

Let's consider the data entry users for a moment. It is worth taking time out to observe these people at work on the current system. The rate at which they bang in the data can be awesome! So what? Well, if we are planning to replace the old system, we had better be sure not to impact their productivity levels, especially if they are working under a volume-based incentive scheme. It is quite likely that they are using an archaic character-based screen which they have become quite fond of over the years. Now we come along, as knights in shining armor, and tell them that what they need is a GUI!

The problem is that our brave new world has no benefit to them, except that during their rest breaks they may get to play either Solitaire or Minesweeper. The last thing they want is to have to take their hands off the keyboard to use a mouse when inputting data. This doesn't mean that all screens built with a GUI are inappropriate for data entry users. What it does mean is that we have to design screens and interfaces with empathy towards our users.

Now let's consider our regular inquiry users. They may find that a mouse is ideal for their purposes, especially if they typically have a phone in one hand. In this case, they will probably find it easier to operate a mouse than a keyboard with their free hand.

This is another area where a quick prototype can be invaluable. The users can be given the prototype screens to "test drive." With the feedback from the prototypes (which should encompass a wide user community), you can design your user interface with users' requirements in mind. However, be wary of the feedback from this exercise. Most people have a natural resistance to change and will make only negative comments. The new computer system may be just a small part of a business restructuring exercise, and the screens may reflect new working practices. The users may take the opportunity of being asked for feedback to raise their objections to the process rather than to the specific system functions within it (especially if they think that they personally are going to be restructured!). Remember these points when assessing the feedback from users and determining which of their concerns you can (and should) address.

The general principles of screen design are:

- All screens should have a unique and meaningful title.

- All fields should be clearly labeled with further detail available when online help is invoked.

- The default cursor navigation should generally be left to right, and then from top to bottom.

- Mandatory items should generally appear at the top. Items should be ordered on the screen by importance.

- The screen should detect and report entry errors at the earliest possible point, rather than deferring validation (unless we are designing screens that will run over a slow network such as a dial-up line).

- Screens should use consistent locking methods and should detect and resolve conflicts.

- Screens should not span multiple pages (back to the megamodules again!).

- Users should only have to enter a code once and should never have to remember or write anything down when moving between screens.

- The minimum number of special effects should be used; if you are determined to have a professional look to your screens and reports, then employ a professional graphic designer. Even an average graphic designer will do a better job than any of your designers, analysts, or users, and a *much* better job than your programmers (even if the designer cannot code recursive structures in C++).

- Getting more on the screen by reducing the character size only works to a limited extent.

- Most people can cope with vertical scrolling a lot better than they can cope with horizontal scrolling, especially if scrolling to the right causes primary key data and legends to disappear off the left of the screen.

Designing Reports

"Reports" used to mean jobs that were run at the end of the month and would produce a rain forest's worth of printout on lined computer paper that was stored in a filing cabinet and never looked at. Those were the days! Nowadays, the results are as likely to be displayed as a graph on a screen as they are to be printed as text on paper. This change has deeper implications than simply requiring us to design smarter presentations of our data. The old-style reports could generally run overnight for the listing to be picked up in the morning. However, it is unlikely that a user will find it acceptable to wait several hours for the graph to display!

The subject of reports covers a broad range of requirements. There are still quite often requirements for the "old fashioned" style of reports, in addition to the newer variety. Here are the basic categories of reports:

- Statutory (required) reports
- Periodic reports (e.g., month end, year end)
- Reports on preprinted stationery (e.g., invoices)
- Letters
- Ad hoc and immediate reporting
- Graphical reports
- Multimedia reports with embedded sound and video clips

Often two separate reporting products are employed on a project, one to support the ad hoc requirement and the other to support all the other requirements.

Many reports simply regurgitate the data that was input, applying suitable formatting to it. For instance, we may take orders for our products throughout the day and then print invoices during the night. These reports simply collect the order and pricing information and format it into an invoice. They are fairly easy to design. All we have to do is to design the template for the format and indicate where all the data in the various fields is sourced from the database.

Most other reports require some form of aggregation. Let's consider management information reports. Even though we may have our ad hoc reporting tools, we still generally have to produce these reports both on a regular basis and on demand. These reports tend to require a different perspective on the data from the way in which it was input. Often they will require a breakdown by department, geographical area, or some other category. If the database has been designed to optimize data entry, then it may not be trivial to provide such breakdowns. It will be slow and, in some cases, it may not be possible at all to generate the report directly from the data. These observations may lead us to suspect that what we really need is a data warehouse (see Chapter 13, *Designing for Data Warehouses.*)

If a data warehouse is not a viable option for your system, we might consider using a common reporting technique, the *report extract.* This is a facility that extracts the data from the database and loads it into derived tables that are optimized for reporting. The advantage of the extract is that it is run prior to the report and can populate the tables in a single pass. This can include calculation of aggregates.

A report that is attempting to "swim against the tide" by trying to report against the original tables in a single SQL statement may have to repeat projection and aggregation operations involving several tables for every row in the report. By adding preprocessing to our reports, we can improve runtime performance of the report by several orders of magnitude. If the same aggregates are used by many reports, these advantages will be further multiplied.

As with all design areas, there are costs and cautions that we must mention for reports; in this case, they are mainly cautions:

- You may have problems with the consistency of the derived data if updates take place while you are performing the extract and if the extract requires more than a single SQL statement. Although you can always extract a consistent set of data by using the SQL statement SET TRANSACTION READ ONLY, this is scarcely an option if you specify an extract process that directly loads into the derived tables.

- The extract tables represent a particular point in time and will become progressively more and more out of date. This can be a major advantage when users need to be able to run many mutually consistent reports, but it can also cause problems for users in interpreting the reports.

- You must be careful when designing the reports that need to join the derived tables to the live tables because the live tables may have changed in the time between running the extract and running the report. Running the reports immediately after the extract and running the entire process at night would minimize the risk as long as there is no likelihood of interference from any batch jobs running at that time.

- Unless you are prepared to specify a highly complex change tracking mechanism, you must ensure that the derived tables are empty before you perform each extract. The SQL statement TRUNCATE...REUSE STORAGE is ideal for this purpose, particularly if the extract tables are unindexed (you would do well to avoid bulk loading into indexed tables).

- Where the extracts are performed on demand you must exercise some concurrency control. In particular, unless you have one set of extract tables per user, you must use a mechanism that ensures that two users do not perform the same extract at the same time. Such an operation is likely (maybe even certain) to result in duplicate data in the extract tables. This, in turn, will lead to reports with incorrect and misleading data in them. The package DBMS_LOCK, which is supplied with Oracle7, may be of help in implementing a *cooperative locking strategy* to apply concurrency control.

NOTE   A cooperative locking strategy is one which works only if all the users (in this case, programs) play by the published rules. A mandatory locking strategy is one that works even if some users try to ignore it. Thus, if one session issues the SQL statement LOCK TABLE contracts IN EXCLUSIVE MODE, no other session will be able to make changes to that table until the session which holds the lock either commits or rolls back.

Unless Oracle is run with the initialization parameter SERIALIZABLE = TRUE (which we do not recommend for performance reasons), the server has no mandatory locking mechanism that can apply a transactional read lock to a table.

- You should log all runs of the extract process so that reports can always determine the precise effective date and time of the extract against which they are running. It is good practice to put the extract date and time in the header of the report. Put another way, it is indefensible not to do so. Every time you report from data which may be out of date, you have a responsibility to tell the user the read consistency point of the data.

Designing Batch Programs

Even in these days of high availability online systems, batch processing is still alive and kicking. Most application suites have either a nightly schedule of runs or a series of bulk processing steps which are run as and when required. Even in the world of the Internet, where (at least in theory) information can always be exchanged in real time, there are at least three compelling reasons why batch processing is still used so extensively:

- It is invariably more efficient than transaction processing.

- It is considered easier to audit and control than transaction processing.

- It removes the need for event-driven software.

Batch processing is often not given the attention it deserves. We think that too much emphasis is usually placed on the visual and tangible components of a system—the screens and reports. However, batch processing is as important today as it ever was, and it shows no signs of going away.

In many applications, the batch jobs are the critical success factor of the entire application. For instance, a payroll system will have a periodic payroll run; it is probably vital that this run completes overnight and that it produces accurate output so the employees get paid on time. Similarly, a billing system will have periodic billing runs that produce invoices. If this goes wrong one night and cannot be rerun until the next night, then the money comes in later, potentially squeezing your organization's cash flow.

It becomes clear that maximizing throughput and ensuring robustness of batch processing is very important indeed. Every long-running batch program must allow for interrupts, failures, and recovery, and the design of our batch processing must address any concurrency issues which arise. We mention the importance of maximizing throughput in some batch programs in this chapter. Be aware, though, that you may need to use parallelism to get the throughput required. Chapter 14, *Designing for Parallel Processing*, deals with this subject in detail.

Tracking Jobs

Most of the advice given in this book applies to the design of batch programs as much as it does to the design of online processing, but batch processes (including reports) have some special characteristics that result from their bulk and inter-dependency. The main problem with many of the batch programs that we have come across is that they start, they run, and they (eventually) end. While they are running they do nothing other than run, and when they complete they do nothing other than end. We do not think this is sufficient. In our opinion, all batch processes should also do the following:

- Log their start to the database

- Log their progress to the database

- Log their completion to the database

The following CREATE TABLE statements show the design of a simple master-detail structure to handle this type of logging. In an open systems environment we don't believe that simply writing messages to the standard output stream is an adequate alternative to logging to the database. On a mainframe which preserves a machine-readable copy of the console log, database logging is less important.

But it is still very useful and allows the normal database reporting tools to be used to report batch throughput and report on failures.

```
CREATE TABLE run_log
   ( run_id           NUMBER          NOT NULL /* from run request  /*
   , task_name        VARCHAR2(16)    NOT NULL /* might want path    /*
   , command_line     VARCHAR2(255)   NOT NULL /* gives the arg list /*
   , invoked_by       VARCHAR2(30)    NOT NULL /* requesting user    /*
   , started_at       DATE            NOT NULL
   , ended_at         DATE
   , completion_code  VARCHAR2(72)
   , rows_processed   NUMBER                   /* from driving table /*
   , cpu_used         NUMBER                   /* if available       /*
   , memory_used      NUMBER                   /*       "            /*
   , io_used          NUMBER                   /*       "            /*
   , CONSTRAINT run_log_pk PRIMARY KEY (run_id)
   );

CREATE TABLE run_step
   ( run_id           NUMBER          NOT NULL /* from run request /*
   , stage            VARCHAR2(16)    NOT NULL
   , rows_processed   NUMBER          NOT NULL
   , reached_at       DATE            NOT NULL
   , cpu_used         NUMBER                   /* if available /*
   , memory_used      NUMBER                   /*       "      /*
   , io_used          NUMBER                   /*       "      /*
   , CONSTRAINT run_step_pk
              PRIMARY KEY (run_id, stage, rows_processed)
   , CONSTRAINT run_step_pk
              FOREIGN KEY (run_id) REFERENCES run_log
                );
```

In additional to the logging of progress through the job, the job must be designed to produce diagnostics on demand so that you can turn on much more detailed logging if you start to experience problems with a specific component. You must be able to enable such logging via some form of control that is easy to set: this may be a system environment variable, an attribute in a control table, or a persistent variable in a package.

NOTE   The common practice of conditionally including debug code, as shown in the next code extract, is simply not acceptable because it means that the version in which a problem is first experienced will be different code from the version used to debug the problem. This is a particular issue when you are trying to track down pointer corruptions in C programs. In such cases, *any* change to the program, even by conditional compilation, can move the point where the problem is occurring.

```
#ifdef DEBUG
/* where am I diagnostic */
fprintf(f_logfile, 'About to update customer totals'.;
#endif
```

The next code extract shows the acceptable approach. Many application programmers will dismiss this as "inefficient" because, they claim, the IF statement is "unnecessary in normal operation." This is, sadly, arrant nonsense. Why? First, the statement is totally necessary because one day we may need to trace what the program is doing, and second, each execution of the conditional test is going to take a few tens of nanoseconds at most. If we were to make ten million of these tests in the course of our batch job (assuming that we have ten logging points per record), then we might add as much as one CPU second to the load. In our experience, adding one CPU second to a batch job which processes a million records will not make any observable difference to the elapsed time of the job.

```
debug_flag = getenv("DEBUG");
..

..
IF (*debug_flag == 'Y'.
{
  /* diagnostic stuff */
  fprintf(f_logfile, "About to call function lb_commit");
}
```

In PL/SQL, you may switch diagnostics on by use of a package variable as follows:

```
IF l_debug.debug_mode THEN
  -- diagnostic stuff
  DBMS_OUTPUT.PUT_LINE('.bout to insert 100 new orders'.;
END IF;
```

This example is interesting because without inspecting the package *l_debug*, we cannot tell whether *debug_mode* is a function which returns a Boolean value or a globally visible persistent package variable which has type BOOLEAN. We hope that it is a function, for the reasons discussed elsewhere in this book.

In any normal application suite, many of the batch jobs are, in fact, reports. It clearly can be as useful to record these in our logging table as it is to record the updating jobs, but you are likely to find that you are committed to a reporting tool that simply does not support DML in any way, shape, or form. This is a real shame, because it is very often your reporting load which is the most variable part of the batch window, and you may have a real need for data on *who* is running *which* components, *what* values the parameters are being set to, *how many* rows are being processed, and *how long* the jobs are taking.

A partial solution may be to invoke report jobs from a relatively simple logging program, which logs the job start before starting the reporting tool, and logs completion on return from the reporting tool. The more data that is returned by

Diagnostic Output from PL/SQL

The DBMS_OUTPUT package is supplied with the procedural option of Oracle7. It mimics file I/O functions, allowing the user to write and read a "work file." However, as implemented in current versions of Oracle7, it uses SGA memory rather than the file system to buffer the data, and allows only the same connection to retrieve it.

This has a number of consequences: the two most important are that the data which has been "put" will be lost if the database connection is lost before it can be retrieved, and that there are limits on how much memory it is sensible to tie up on such activities. The default buffer size is only 2K bytes, which is normally grossly inadequate; it is extremely annoying to have your run fail simply because you failed to (or were unable to) allocate enough memory to buffer the diagnostic data.

An alternative is to load such logging and debug information into a database pipe using the Oracle package DBMS_PIPE; this is only effective if you can be sure of having a daemon or server process waiting for these pipe messages and (immediately) making a permanent record of them.

In Version 7.3, Oracle supplies the package UTL_FILE, which allows serial operating system files to be written and read from PL/SQL. This may be an attractive mechanism for producing diagnostics, but the security model used is very weak.

What you absolutely must not do with diagnostics is to insert them directly into a logging table in the database. Why? Because if any transaction rolls back, then any uncommitted diagnostics will roll back with it. Nor is it acceptable for the program to commit after inserting each diagnostic; this will invariably alter the nature of the transaction boundaries. By sending the diagnostic text through a pipe, the receiving process can safely insert and immediately commit each message.

These issues are discussed further under "Error Handling," later in this chapter.

the reporting tool to standard output or a console log, the more data the calling program has to work with, and potentially to log.

The sections that follow contain a deceptively short discussion on batch techniques. The brevity is due, in large part, to our strong feeling that many of the issues that surround the successful management of batch processing have nothing whatever to do with the data management software being used. We resist the notion that matters such as job control are best addressed from within a database engine, whatever advantages of portability that may bring. It is unfortunately true that open systems platforms do not arrive with mainframe-style job management systems, but that industrial strength support in this area will be a critical success factor in many applications. This is, however, outside the scope of an Oracle design book.

Choosing a Tool

Even with the many improvements made in Versions 7.2 and 7.3, we wouldn't really recommend PL/SQL as the implementation tool of choice for high performance batch processing. As you will have seen from the many examples in this book, we are committed to the use of PL/SQL as the language for stored procedures and triggers, but it has a series of restrictions that make it too expensive for use when processing large volumes of data; these include the following:

- Support for file I/O is absent in versions prior to 7.3.

- The security model for file I/O in Version 7.3 is extremely weak.

- Memory management for PL/SQL tables, although improved in Version 7.3, is not adequate for the handling of large-scale arrays and data caches; such techniques are normally an essential part of high performance batch processing.

- PL/SQL is an interpretive language, although to be fair it is compiled to an intermediate form before it is interpreted.

- Complex PL/SQL running in the server is a nightmare to debug.

We recommend that batch processing be written in a 3GL running on the server, passing data to and from the database engine using Oracle's array interface. Further, we recommend that database operations be restricted to include only those things which either must be done within the database or which do not need to be externalized. Thus, if we need to add 1 to a database value but have no need to see the value in the controlling code, we should use a simple relative update such as:

```
UPDATE emp
   set SAL = round(SAL * (1 + :increase_pct/100);
```

This example is a double-edged sword because it is likely that we will have to report not only how many increases were granted (the update will return the number of rows processed), but also the total amount of increase. So we almost certainly should have externalized the values. This example also shows another of the major errors routinely made: it uses the SQL engine to perform arithmetic which is much better performed in a 3GL (in this case, dividing by 100 and adding 1). Keep in mind that Oracle performs all SQL arithmetic in decimal floating point to 38-digit precision. And you can't do that in a single hardware instruction on very many machines!

For non-time-critical jobs, PL/SQL does have certain advantages, namely:

- It is a well-structured language that is easy to read and closely integrated to SQL.

- It is the language of choice for Oracle Corporation, which has invested heavily in it and will be around for a long time.

- It allows you to have compiled code nicely packaged and encapsulated on the server.

Control Break Processing

The other major recommendation that we have to make about the design of batch jobs is to make maximum use of control break processing, and to couple this with the soft disabling of triggers while the process is running.

If we were posting cash movements to accounts, the smart approach would be to sort all of the incoming records into account number order so that we can process all of the cash movements for a single account together. Provided that we have a robust locking strategy, this means, in turn, that we need not update the account balance until we have processed the last cash movement for that account. Change of account number becomes our control break.

If the account balance is normally maintained by a trigger, we want to disable it for postings made by our batch process because this process has undertaken to maintain the balance itself in order to reduce the number of updates performed. The art of design, in a situation such as this one, is to decide whether the performance gain is worth the effort and the risk (if any). In this case, correct implementation should render the approach risk-free; the key is to make sure that no commit is performed during the processing on an account until the balance has been updated.

Commit Interval

We have found that the commit interval is a major issue in the design of batch processing. Too many designers either leave the decision to the programmer or (worse) specify that the program will commit once at the end. We recommend that every batch process commit at least once every five minutes if at all possible, and that it should leave enough information in its log so it can resume from the most recent commit.

There is the obvious disadvantage that a job which commits once, after four hours of processing, may lose up to three hours and 59 minutes of work if there is a media failure or some other instance crash. However, what is often not considered during design is the size of the rollback segment that will be required to support the single commit model, as well as the time that will be taken by the recovery start-up following an instance crash. If your program is using ten gigabytes of rollback segment in use at the time your job crashes, then Oracle will have to apply ten gigabytes of rollback segment entries when you restart. This can "materially increase the duration of the resulting outage."

The longest start-up that either of us has ever seen following an uncontrolled shutdown was six hours; a number of architectural improvements in later Oracle versions would have reduced that considerably. The instance had been running a long batch job when a shutdown abort was issued. If the batch job had committed approximately once every five minutes, then the recovery time could have been held down to about the same interval or less (and we would not have had to repeat five hours processing!).

Introducing more frequent commit points will normally have only the most marginal effect on throughput; at each commit the process will wait for the redo log writer to catch up, which should only take a few tens of milliseconds. This is not a major cost once every few minutes. A difficulty arises, however, where the process is coded as a set statement like this:

```
INSERT TABLE live_orders
SELECT *
  FROM orders
 WHERE dead_flag IS NULL
UNRECOVERABLE;
```

This is, without a shadow of a doubt, the fastest way of moving rows from one table to another. In the latest version, the CREATE TABLE...AS SELECT... form can also be given the attribute UNRECOVERABLE, meaning that the problems with rollback segment usage and instance recovery time are overcome. There is still the risk that an instance, operating system, or hardware crash could lose a great deal of work and, of course, the operation is not recoverable if a later problem necessitates a restore and roll forward recovery. So you may decide not to use the UNRECOVERABLE option in production jobs, but reserve it for major housekeeping operations which are immediately followed by a backup. The statement below is the second fastest way of moving the rows:

```
INSERT TABLE live_orders
SELECT *
  FROM orders
 WHERE dead_flag IS NULL
/* UNRECOVERABLE we need recoverability */;
```

but this form will use rollback segment space in direct proportion to the number of rows copied. However, in many cases, we can quite simply turn this into a multistep operation by adding a driving table which selects a key range from orders. Then, by using a loop we can transfer one key range at a time, logging end of step and committing at the end of each range. An outline implementation of this solution in PL/SQL is shown below:

```
DECLARE
  CURSOR c1 IS
    SELECT deptno
         , dname
      FROM dept
     ORDER BY dname; -- makes the log look more logical
BEGIN
  INSERT INTO run_log (id,    start_at)
            VALUES  ('.X'. SYSDATE);
  FOR this_dept IN c1
  LOOP
    INSERT INTO new_emp
    SELECT * FROM emp WHERE deptno = this_dept.deptno;
    INSERT INTO run_steps (id,    step,            ended_at)
            VALUES   ('.X'. this_dept.dname, SYSDATE);
    COMMIT;
  END LOOP;
  UPDATE run_log SET ended_at = SYSDATE
   WHERE id = 'XX'.
  COMMIT;
END;
/
```

This is one of the few cases where we feel able to recommend the implementation of a major batch process in PL/SQL, because almost all of the execution time will be spent in the SQL engine and the demands on the procedural language are minimal (and because PL/SQL makes it so easy to code CURSOR FOR loops!).

The technique that we've shown here will add a modest amount to the cost of creating the job, and will mean that it has to be implemented in PL/SQL or a 3GL rather than as a simple SQL*Plus script, but it will also save a huge amount of rollback segment space and allow much faster recoveries.

We are not generally impressed by sites whose batch processing is coded in SQL*Plus.

Note that if this example is converted into a stored procedure, which we would almost certainly recommend, then the session must have COMMIT IN PROCEDURE enabled. Oracle's own tools, most notably Oracle Forms, tend to issue an ALTER SESSION command to disable this. They do this so they can rely on locks which they have taken still being in force. If COMMIT IN PROCEDURE is enabled, then any stored procedure or function which a process calls may issue a COMMIT or ROLLBACK which will cause the expiration of all transactional locks held by the session.

Doing Things in the Right Places

What does "doing things in the right place" actually mean? It requires judgment and experience to get things exactly right, but we can recommend a set of general principles that will lead you to an acceptable solution in almost all cases:

- Try to acquire each piece of data only once—that is, use caching where appropriate; this requirement alone often rules out PL/SQL as the implementation vehicle.

- Don't be afraid to sort files and ORDER BY in queries so that you can take advantage of control break processing; the overhead of the sort will usually be more than is recouped by being able to move some processing to the control break rather than doing it per entry in the driving table or file.

- Do not filter data in the control logic unless the data must be externalized for other reasons; there is a high overhead in externalizing data. Consider this example:

```
DECLARE
  CURSOR c1 IS
    SELECT deptno
         , dname
         , active
      FROM dept
     ORDER BY dname;  -- MAKES THE LOG LOOK MORE LOGICAL
BEGIN
  INSERT INTO run_log (id,    start_at)
             VALUES   ('.X'. SYSDATE);
  FOR this_dept IN c1
  LOOP
    IF this_dept.active = 'Y'
    THEN BEGIN
      INSERT INTO new_emp
      SELECT * FROM emp WHERE deptno = this_dept.deptno;
      INSERT INTO run_steps (id,    step,           ended_at)
             VALUES   ('.X'. THIS_DEPT.DNAME, SYSDATE);
      COMMIT;
    END;
    END IF;
  END LOOP;
  UPDATE run_log SET ended_at = sysdate
   WHERE id = 'XX'.
  COMMIT;
END;
/
```

In this example, it would be much simpler and more efficient to put the condition (department active) in the WHERE clause.

Error Handling

Most of us have at one time or another been greeted by a message such as "Unexpected condition has occurred" or even "04FD63-unknown reference". We are left wondering what on earth they mean and are frustrated by the fact that we don't know what we did wrong, if indeed we did anything wrong. We nevertheless just regarded these types of error as a fact of life and would normally try again. Today's users demand messages that they can identify with and react to—another fact of life. A third fact of life is that any two programmers handling the same exception without a design which tells them how to handle it are highly unlikely to do so in exactly the same way, and can be guaranteed to come up with different error message texts. Hence the need for a generic and consistent approach.

We recommend that all possible error conditions be allocated completely meaningless codes (we are deadly serious about this) and that these codes be stored with the severity level and a textual description of the error either in the database or in a file. It is absolutely vital that issuing new error numbers be easy, because otherwise programmers will recycle existing numbers.

The next step is to provide standard routines for reporting errors. The coder hands the routine the error number, and any required parameters and the error handler does the rest. If the severity is fatal (or higher), then the program does not get control back; otherwise, it does. Where the error-handling routine reports the error is its own business (more encapsulation), but it is probably going to log it into a file (the database may be inoperable) and (if it can find a screen or report stream) show the descriptive text to the user.

Applications that encounter errors really should issue a rollback, but there are two dreaded design bugs that may occur when rollbacks are required.

The first bug occurs when you do anything else before issuing the rollback, particularly putting a modal window on the user's screen that says something like:

```
Fatal error encountered
Press OK to abort process
```

or worse

```
Severe error encountered
Press Abort or Retry
```

Now if you've just spent ten minutes entering the data and you get this second modal window, what do you do? You press Retry—again and again and again in the hope that it will eventually work and you can avoid losing your work. Unfortunately, if the program has taken out a series of important locks before putting these messages out to the user, the result can be a complete application lock-out.

The second, and even more humorous, bug is to log the application steps to the database to assist in debugging the fatal error. It is relatively obvious that when your program rolls back, it rolls back all of its log entries as well. The solutions are simple: commit instead of rolling back (can we be serious?) or log to files instead of logging to the database. The file solution is somewhat easier with Version 7.3 than previously because PL/SQL can now write to files on the server although the security aspect "leaves a little to be desired" since these files may contain sensitive data in the diagnostic information that a casual user may happen upon. With earlier versions, if the bulk of the error handling is through stored procedures, then file-based logging can be achieved by use of DBMS pipe messages to a dedicated server process. Don't be tempted to use DBMS alerts; they are transactional, which is the formal way of saying that they are subject to commit and rollback.

Some people think the commit solution is acceptable on test systems, but we regard it as indefensible under any circumstances. If you have not completed the transaction (for example, you had only made three of the five inserts when you got "Duplicate value in index," then committing the incomplete transaction and compromising database integrity is not a professional solution.

NOTE   You can create a listener process written entirely in PL/SQL which can listen for messages sent using the DBMS_PIPE package. When the process receives such a message, it logs the message to the database, commits, and goes back to waiting for another message. A further level of sophistication is to add a "Stop" message so that you can tell the listener to exit.

By having the events logged within the database, you can use any SQL-based reporting tool to extract and collate the data, and this can be a major benefit. However, before using this approach to log high numbers of events in applications which are subject to stringent response time or throughput requirements, you must test the impact of sending more than one or two pipe messages per second using your particular platform and version of Oracle7.

Navigation

The ease with which users can navigate around the screens and facilities of the system can be the make-or-break of the entire system. If the users have to steer a torturous path to get from one screen to another or key in data more than once or remember a code or piece of information between dialogues, their main feeling about the system will be that it is cumbersome.

Navigation is particularly crucial when creating a GUI application. There are so many controls on a GUI that can perform navigation. It is essential that you have a set of stringent standards that enforce a level of consistency. Here are some of the controls which can be used for navigation:

- Menus

- Icons on a button bar

- Icons

- Icons within windows

- Non-iconic buttons in windows

- Tab dialogue boxes (where clicking on a tab reveals a different panel of the box)

- Hot keys

We mentioned that users must not have to remember or rekey information. This leads us to the concept of navigation with and without *context*. Navigation without context is where you go from one screen to a completely unrelated one. For instance, you are processing a transaction but you want to go and take a quick look at a print queue to see if your job has printed yet. A navigation with context implies going from one screen to a related one. One common example is traversing a relationship in the database, such as zooming in to order lines from a screen of orders; you wouldn't expect the user to have to remember which order he was looking at and key it in again.

This concept can be taken a step further. Consider an insurance claims system. A user working on a claim might want to pull up many different screens when determining the validity of a claim. Things that might be of interest are policy information, policy exclusion clause and excesses, previous claim history and policy holder details. A flexible navigation system might let users bring these screens up in an order all within the context of the claim they are working on. However, context can sometimes be constraining. Our user is suddenly interrupted by a phone inquiry and now wants to look at a different policy (that of the caller). Clearly our "with context" navigation is no longer a help but becomes a hindrance. What the user would like is to "park" the current claim somewhere, start on a different claim (which becomes the in-context claim), and at a later point in time bring the parked claim back into context and continue where he or she left off.

When you are piecing together navigational dialogues, you must have a comprehensive view of the working practices of users, particularly their workflow practices. We strenuously urge you to test (prototype) all required interfaces between tools both to ensure that they are technically feasible and to check on the performance and software licensing implications. If you call one tool from another, you'll encounter a common problem: both tools will require connections to Oracle; even if this does not exceed license limits, it is likely to impose a major memory overhead on your database server.

You also need to consider security issues within your navigation subsystem. The navigation mechanism must be aware of security privileges and must be able to prevent violation of access rights. If at all possible it should also avoid externalizing user names and passwords. In other words, it is a security hazard to run another product by dynamically creating a script file with the run command, which includes the user name and password.

Online Help

These days good software, especially desktop products, tends to come with sophisticated online help. It is now quite common to distribute software with no manuals (or with the manuals available only in machine-readable form) and for users to rely almost completely on online help. For users, finding information via online help takes a bit of getting used to, but can be better than a manual if the search facilities are powerful enough to ensure that you can always quickly find the entry you need. However, the help subsystem must be well designed, and be logical and easy to use. In most cases, it should also be *context sensitive*—that is, the help system should be accessible from anywhere within the application and should (by default) present help on the part of the application from which it was invoked.

When you are designing online help for your application, there are several factors you need to consider:

- Presumably, the user is on a screen and presses a key or clicks a button to invoke help. What the user expects at this point is for context-sensitive help to pop up that provides information about the field on which the cursor is positioned. This is known as *field-level help*. Some systems only offer *screen-level help* in which context for help is the entire screen rather than specific fields. Whatever level of help you provide, the help text should guide the user through using the screen. It should give a business or functional overview of the purpose of the screen and should describe the meaning of each field. It should also contain hypertext links to related topics.

- For complex systems, and applications where users may not receive thorough training, you should consider providing tutorials that guide the user through the basics of using the system. In many cases, the content of these may have much more to do with the way the business works than with the way the application works.

- *Cue cards* that can be switched on for an inexperienced user are another popular form of help. These pop up on top of the screen and describe the actions that the user must take to achieve the desired results. For instance, there might be a set of cue cards for "Entering an Order."

- There is a synergy between errors and help. Most errors (with the exception of system errors) arise as a result of the user's doing something incorrect. After informing a user that he or she has entered an incorrectly formatted order number, an integrated application will go on to offer help on how order numbers are composed.

- Context-sensitive help demands that the help text have at least some of the properties of hypertext. Hypertext allows you to jump around between related subjects within the help subsystem. It is a good way of learning about a system. The application calls the help system, passing the context in which the help is required. In a simple file-based system, the context may be based on section headings within the help text.

- The help system should be familiar to the user. Had we written this chapter, two or so years ago, we would have almost certainly included advice on the design of help text tables, but the world has moved on and we no longer believe that help systems should be implemented at the project level. They need to look and feel similar to the help systems that the user accesses from other applications and products. The best bet is to use the native help tool of the client platform, even though doing so means distributing the help files down to at least the file server level within the enterprise. For instance, on Microsoft Windows clients, you should use Microsoft Help. As soon as you adopt the use of a standard help system, then powerful and easy to use help authoring tools become available to help your project to produce professional looking help files.

- You may need to design a layer of code (middleware) that sits between the application and the help facility. This code interprets or is passed the context (for example a form name and a field name), translates the context into a valid reference, and calls the help facility, quoting this reference. The obvious place to hold the mapping between the screen context and the help system reference is in the database, and if standardization is not rigidly imposed on the naming of contexts, then the resulting help system will never really meet the objectives of usability and predictability.

- Version 1.2A and higher of Oracle Designer/2000 has a generator that creates help in Microsoft Help format based on table and module descriptions. This will, of course, degenerate into a classic example of GIGO (garbage in, garbage out) unless the table and module descriptions are written in a way that makes them comprehensible to users. In most projects, it is enough of a battle to get them written in a way that makes them comprehensible to the programmers!

- It is usually best to get a user or, better yet, a professional technical writer to create the help text. If an IT designer or builder writes it, it tends to have too much of a system bias, and be based on the developers' understanding of how the system should be used. The help text should be written in plain language and use the standard terms of the business. What a developer might explain in terms of blocks and functions can better be explained by a user in terms of business processes.

V

Appendixes

The appendixes describe the following:

- Appendix A, *Off-the-Shelf Packages*, compares the merits of buying a packaged solution with those of developing a complete application from scratch.

- Appendix B, *Tricks of the Trade*, focuses on three specific design techniques. We suggest a method for avoiding the annoying "mutating table" problem in Oracle7 triggers; we look at the problems presented by the imminent change of century (the millennium problem); and we take a brief tour into extensible SQL.

Off-the-Shelf Packages

For many applications, there is an alternative to an expensive development project—you can buy a packaged solution that will do part or all of the job for you. Buying a packaged solution is often a relatively inexpensive option simply because of economies of scale; since the vendor is developing a product for many user communities, they all effectively share the cost.

There are a multitude of products out there. In fact, there are so many that trying to select a suitable one may feel like trying to walk across a minefield. Please note that we say "trying to select a suitable one" rather than "trying to find the best" or "trying to find the most suitable." This field is difficult enough without making it completely impossible by trying to achieve perfection!

You can buy solutions for such applications as Accounting and Finance, Manufacturing, Management Information (MIS), Executive Information (EIS), Payroll, Personnel, Help Desk Management, Electronic Document Management, and Workflow (along with many others). It is trivially easy to get vendors fighting each other to sell you the features of their products, and it is correspondingly hard to make an informed decision.

NOTE   There is no doubt that a project based around a purchased solution is a very different beast from one produced as the result of a traditional design, build, and test. Indeed, many die-hard developers find it inconceivable that consultants who specialize in applications can command large fees without ever dirtying their hands writing code. The fact is that buying the product is the easy part. Integrating and customizing a product can be a long and highly complex job. We point out as many pitfalls as we can in this appendix.

In this appendix we explore some of the issues and opportunities that arise when you purchase software solutions or components. It is a short appendix since much of the content, by its very nature, is general to all applications rather than specific to Oracle.

Evaluating a Package

The first thing you need to decide is whether a purchased solution can do the job that you require. If there is one that genuinely can do what you need, it will be difficult to find any sustainable argument for writing your own application. Often the project analysis team will perform an initial valuation of available products against the requirements of your system. It's important at this stage to make a distinction between features and benefits. The vendors will attempt to attract you with *features* (often gimmicks that look good in demonstrations). What you must concentrate on are the *benefits* that the product can deliver in terms of helping you meet your specific requirements. We have all been duped by a convincing demonstration in our time! The role of the designer in such an evaluation team is usually to perform a technical evaluation and feasibility study, leaving cost and functional evaluation to the project management and analysis team, respectively.

Our opinion is that this traditional approach is unsafe. We believe that the analysis should be undertaken in full, as for a traditional development project. The requirements should be fully documented in a requirements specification prior to evaluating any off-the shelf products. Once the requirements have been agreed upon, the evaluation should be performed by a combined analysis and design team. You should produce a short-list of candidate products and (if the list has more than a single entry) carry out a time-boxed evaluation of each, splitting the time evenly between them. If you are also considering a home-grown solution, this solution must be given the same allocation of time.

WARNING   We must warn you, in passing, that if (as in many projects) your analysis makes design assumptions about mechanisms, then it is extremely unlikely that anything other than a custom development will match your requirements.

When you have completed the evaluation (seen the demos, read the books, and watched the movies), the team should produce a cost/benefit analysis, comparing both the packages evaluated and a home-grown solution. As a designer, you'll find it tempting to be biased towards the home-grown solution because you know you can design and build it, and you want to! We understand this temptation (we have been there), but we advise you to try to be objective about it. How can you really justify building your own custom email system when the market is full of relatively cheap "open" products that are fully tried and tested?

Of course, the products that you evaluate may not all be based on an Oracle database. For the purpose of this book, though, we're assuming that Oracle is the chosen database technology for your corporation and, therefore, that support of Oracle is a prerequisite. If the package runs with a variety of database servers, you may want to check quite carefully how well it exploits Oracle features.

Let's consider what aspects of a solution we should be looking at in our part of the evaluation:

Does It Fit?

There is no such things as a "technology island" these days! No application can run in blissful isolation from the world around it. You have to consider how the proposed package will fit in with your current operations.

Hardware and Operating System

First, you need to determine the hardware and operating system platform(s) on which the application can run. Just because the product uses Oracle as its data store, don't assume that it is as portable as Oracle itself, and at all costs do not assume that package functionality is identical on each platform. For instance, there are many Oracle-based products which will run only on UNIX, and some that run only on certain flavors of UNIX. There are also products which will run under both UNIX and proprietary operating systems such as VMS and Windows/NT.

You will need to compare the platforms on which a proposed solution can run against your own particular hardware and operating system strategy and your current installations. If there is not a match, don't necessarily dismiss the product out of hand—after all, the vendor may plan to port to your platform in the near future. If your order is likely to be a large one, many vendors will offer to port to your selected platform to secure your business. We caution, however, that buying a software version that does not yet exist removes perhaps the greatest advantage of purchasing off the shelf.

When establishing the hardware requirements, you need to consider disk, memory, and processor specifications and compare these against any spare capacity that you already have on existing systems. The additional hardware requirements must be fed into the cost. There may be major upgrades required to both servers and clients. Don't rely on the hardware requirements quoted by vendors; these tend to be "minimum configurations" and may be completely inoperable.

Some products have specific networking requirements, and these have to be evaluated against the capability and capacity of your existing networks. Make sure to verify all sizing using observed tests, and remember that most product vendors use high-specification machines for demos and benchmarks. In particular, in client/server demos, the clients normally have at least 32 megabytes of memory and communicate with the servers over switched Ethernet. If you can afford to replicate the demo environment in production, that's fine. But don't be surprised if real-world performance using 8-megabyte 486-based clients connecting over a wide area network is orders of magnitude slower than the demo that persuaded your Chief Executive to sign the order.

Applications

Most applications have to interface with other applications in some way. This is especially relevant if the package you are evaluating does not provide the entire solution to your requirements, and will have to coexist with some inhouse code or with a component of another third-party package. There are a number of ways that applications can interface to each other:

1. Database objects in one application are replicated into another in either batch or real time.

2. The application provides an output data feed (usually a flat file) that is used as input to another application.

3. The applications share some common database objects either as a means of communication or as simply shared data items.

4. Applications may call other applications (probably passing parameters).

5. Interface modules may be used to connect to both applications and act as the communication buffer. This is roughly how Microsoft Dynamic Data Exchange (DDE) works.

6. An application can contain an object belonging to another application using a technology such as Object Linking and Embedding (OLE) or ActiveX.

Let's take a look at how some of these features work in practice.

Suppose that you buy an Sales Ledger or Accounts Payable package. Chances are that it will have a Customer table in its database. It is most unlikely that this table will look anything like any Customer table which you already have in terms of the columns or structure. You ideally want to avoid maintaining two Customer tables, with all the problems that entails, so you decide to replicate from one into the other. You would first have to nominate one (we hope your original table) as the master, through which all changes are made, and ensure that the changes are propagated to the slave table. This sounds easy in theory, but there are some complications.

The first issue to tackle is how open the vendor of the package is about their database structure. Sure, you can go into SQL*Plus and DESCRIBE the tables, but this only gives you the column names and their datatypes. The names may not be at all meaningful and can leave a lot to guesswork (what exactly is NOT_CUST_ PARENT_FLAG in the Customer table? Worse, what is C012 in T047?). The next problem is how to populate any mandatory columns on the slave table that don't exist on the master; you may be reduced to using a special value (not a null, obviously) to represent "not yet known."

You need to decide on a mechanism for keeping the slave table current, although you first need to define what is meant by "current" in your environment. Does the slave Customer table need to be updated in real time, that is, whenever the master table is updated, or would a periodic refresh suffice? If the update has to be immediate, then you have to write triggers on the master table that apply the changes to the slave. If it is not critical that the two are fully synchronized, then you could batch changes up by writing them to a holding table or file and apply them periodically (overnight, for instance).

You might decide that you are willing to sacrifice your own Customer table so that customer details are held in only a single place. A brave decision, indeed! One of the authors worked at a site that made such a decision. However, when they realized that the new Customer table lacked certain data that they wanted to hold, they added their own columns to the table. They justified this action on the basis that additional columns couldn't affect the working of the packaged software. Then they wrote their own form for maintaining the altered Customer table and replaced the supplied form with their own. It all seemed to work, but they really were walking a tightrope!

Many application software suppliers have realized that customers want integrated systems and have tackled the issue by delivering the software in component form. Some packaged software comes with a set of standard screens, but also a comprehensive set of Application Programmatic Interfaces (APIs) which enable you to develop your own screens around the "engine" supplied with the product. We feel that products offering an API are generally at an advantage. Not only does an API give you the flexibility to be able to develop your own front-end screens, but it also provides a door into the application for batch programs and custom reports (one that isn't a "back door"). An API-based package may take slightly longer to implement if you develop your own screens, but it is a cost that is often worth absorbing; it guarantees a standard look and feel.

Oracle Designer/2000 has a set of APIs that are implemented as a series of PL/SQL packages. These routines let you perform functions that aren't necessarily implemented in the Repository Object Navigator or other tools and that, in previous versions, you may have had to perform by updating the repository tables directly.

NOTE   In the not-so-distant future, we foresee application development evolving into an art of knitting together many different objects supplied by various vendors, rather akin to controls such as VBX and OCX (which are available now) but on a much more global scale. Programming, as we know it now, will become a lost art and a new breed of "integrators" will emerge!

      This is the space which Oracle hopes will be filled by its Network Computing Architecture with the objects being implemented as cartridges.

A product with an API allows you to develop your own screens and thus make the integration more seamless to the end user, but it does not really solve the problem of maintaining two Customer tables. You may be able to update the customer in the packaged application by calling an UpdateCustomer method, but there are still two Customer tables!

A really sophisticated application might let you embed an accounting "object" such as a set of books, an account, or a posting within a row in the database (stored in a LONG or LONG RAW column). The embedded object would expose a series of methods and properties that can be accessed. For instance, you might be able to adjust a posting by altering its "amount" property, or pop up a window showing an account summary by calling its "display" method.

Let's summarize what you should be doing at this stage. In addition to a requirements matching exercise, you need to undertake an integration feasibility study. Never underestimate the importance or complexity of integration issues. It is highly unlikely that you can evaluate how well a product will integrate by reading technical specifications or marketing collateral or by watching well-scripted demonstrations. You really need to get hold of an evaluation copy of the software and to run a well-organized pilot or research project. Unfortunately, though, the cost of this project is likely to be so much that your employer won't be willing to fund a study of each possible contender.

System Support Functions

As soon as you are committed to bringing in a solution from the outside, you lose some control over your destiny. Third-party tools may end up violating, or at least compromising, any policy or practical decisions that you have made in the past. The issues we discuss in Chapter 10, *Safeguarding Your Data*, are particularly relevant here. Whatever you have decided to do about archiving of data, auditing, security, and backup, be aware that consistent handling of errors and batch processing may not be compatible with what the package does. You are likely to have to reach a sensible compromise and either relax the rules or move the rules to conform with the package.

Can It Be Tailored?

Face it, no package that you buy off the shelf is going to meet 100% of your requirements. However, this may not be a major problem if the package fully supports customization. As a first task, you need to perform what is sometimes known as *gap analysis*, where you identify the requirements that the product doesn't support. Then you develop a functional specification of what is needed to plug the gaps. The task of the designer is then to turn the functional definition into a workable solution given the constraints of the products.

Remember our observation in the previous section that the best way to extend is via a set of supported API routines that are provided by the original developer. If there are no such APIs, what then? You could always read and update the base tables and views of the application directly, but we certainly do *not* recommend this. There are a number of self-evident reasons:

1. The structure of the database is likely to change between releases. When you upgrade the product, your custom add-ons may stop working. You certainly would need to retest them all after every upgrade.

2. The supplier of the software probably won't support you anymore. Even if they do, they will be naturally suspicious of any problems you encounter that other users haven't experienced. The natural reaction is to blame your "extensions" before looking at their own code.

3. You may compromise the integrity of the underlying data, especially if any constraints are enforced in the product's application code rather than in the database. This is normally the case unless the product was originally designed to operate with a data server with both triggers and declarative constraints.

In the previous section we discussed the problem of maintaining the same data both within and outside the packaged product (our Customer table). Some packaged applications overcome this problem by having a set of interface tables that we are at liberty to read from or write to without fear of compromising any of the live data. However, this solution works best for one-way traffic and does not guarantee an immediate response to keep the data inside the application perfectly synchronized with the equivalent data on the outside. Another method of keeping the data in step would be to write database triggers on the Customer table within the application that duplicate any actions into the external Customer table. This is facilitated in Version 7.1 and higher where there can be multiple triggers of the same type on a table; you can write your triggers independent of any triggers that the original developer created. Of course, if in the next release some of the columns have changed their name or format, then you will still have a problem.

Some projects get over the lack of an API by persuading the developer of the packaged product to hand over some (or all) of the source code. This practice should come with a serious health warning! Think about it. (Actually, those of us who have worked in a so-called "parallel development environment" won't have to think about it—we come with a built-in revulsion to it!) While you develop your custom add-ons to the code, the original developer is both fixing bugs and adding lots of new functionality. You, of course, want these changes running at your site. When the new release with all the fancy new features is released, it doesn't contain your modifications, so you have to add them again—in some cases, you have to rewrite them because the original code has changed so much. Someone now has a job for life, making the custom amendments each time a new release comes along, and it gets progressively harder and more complex each time around!

Some software developers have attempted to make their products extensible by means other than API. For instance, Oracle Financials has a concept known as "flex fields" that are basically spare columns on some of the main tables in the application that the users can adapt for their own use. These can be used as links to other tables, but they are really only intended to add your own descriptive fields to the table. They are also totally unsupported by many development tools.

What about the look and feel of the product? If it has a GUI front-end, was it developed to the same GUI standards as the other products and home-grown applications that you use? The answer is generally "no," since no two GUIs are identical and no two design teams ever quite come to the same conclusions about the rules for an interface. This may be an issue for users who would have to get used to different toolbars, menus, alerts, and all kinds of other GUI controls when in different applications. However, some applications come with a powerful set of macros and customization tools that enable you to modify the appearance of the application. It is possible to customize some products so much that they look nothing at all like the original product!

When you are considering the look and feel of an application, don't get too concerned about the reference data maintenance screens that come with the product. Income tax rates, for instance, do not change that often and you (and your payroll department) can probably cope with having to visit the documentation each time they need to be updated. Concentrate on the core application screens that the everyday users will be using. Under some circumstances, you may even decide to change your own screens to fit in with the standards of the product that you buy.

To tackle the customization problem, you need to first decide on which ways you want to bend it. Do you want to change only the appearance of the application, or do you need to alter the underlying functionality in some way? Are you looking at simply bolting some of your own functionality onto the product to make up for a shortfall in functionality—and, if so, are the additions data, functional, or both? It is certainly worth asking your product developer or reseller whether they would consider putting your requirements into the core product, either now or in the future. If the answer is yes, you may decide to hang on and save yourself the trouble particularly if your MoSCoW analysis (described in Chapter 1) has classed these "requirements" as *should have* or *could have* rather than *must have*. We repeat our earlier warning that buying a package in order to get a feature which has not yet been implemented does vitiate one of the best reasons for buying a solution—to get something that can already be shown to work.

In summary, let's reiterate the pitfalls of making modifications to packaged software:

- Beware of accessing the database directly; it is not guaranteed to remain static between releases, and vendors don't tend to look favorably on you if you do this.

- Don't start modifying the source code without giving serious attention to the maintenance headache you are creating for yourself.

The Big Data Model Issue

As we said at the beginning of this appendix, applications are no longer islands. To achieve interoperability (yet another buzzword of the '90s), data analysts (and, to a lesser extent, designers) are creating corporate data models. In the past, most organizations would have separate definitions of corporate data in separate applications (often referred to as application-centric models). There would be a Customer table in the Sales application, another one in the Billing application, yet another in Support, and so on.

One of us once worked for a client who had seven different Customer models! Not only was the data inconsistent, but the structure of the tables was variant. Address formats were so completely different that it was virtually impossible to use a postal address to verify that "Serious Cybernetics Corporation" in one application was the same company as "Serious Cybernetics Corporation" in another!

This corporation was losing money by providing free servicing on customer equipment because they simply couldn't tell if the equipment was still under warranty (that information was in the Sales database).

So-called *corporate* or *enterprise data models* take an enterprise-wide conceptual view of data and derive all new data models from this view. The model will normally be contained in a CASE repository. With this approach, at least a Customer table on one system has similar attributes with similar names to another system. Now enter into this highly organized brave new world a packaged application that, of course, has a Customer table. What are the chances that this table fits nicely into your corporate data model?

Whether or not the problem is solvable depends on the package vendor. If they deliver to you an active data model in the CASE format of your choice, then you can start to compare the models and design bridges to make them meet. If they don't deliver such a model, then you may be able to go some way towards a bridge by reverse engineering. Most modern CASE products support reverse engineering, that is, the creation of objects in the CASE repository from tables in the database. Of course, this model will be, by its nature, a totally physical one. On the other hand, your corporate data model should be, by its nature, a totally logical one. It is not easy to turn a physical model back into a logical one, and it is certainly not desirable to turn your corporate data model into a physical one. So you still have a problem. CASE vendors make much of their reverse engineering support, but the payback from it is questionable in the extreme.

If the package vendor can provide you with a complete logical model, that's very good. However, you still have your work cut out for you. It is likely that the model was produced to different data quality standards and methodologies. The sad fact is that most are unwilling to supply a data model for fear that:

- They will disclose proprietary information and lose competitive advantage.

- Their users will see all the questionable design and other "dirty linen" inherent in the product.

- Their users will come to rely on the model remaining unchanged in future releases.

You may decide that you can live without a design dictionary for your application, especially if it is largely used standalone or as a "black box". If you are supplied with one (or worse, have to reverse engineer one from the table schema), remember that there will be a lot of hard work involved which you have to balance against the benefits of an integrated model. Finally, remember that nothing in life is static and that you are not in control of the application; next month's new release may well have a radically different database design to this month's.

B

Tricks of the Trade

This appendix describes three special design problems and our tricks for getting around them. These are mutating tables, the millennium (year 2000) date problem, and extensible SQL.

Fixing Those Mutating Tables

What do we mean by a *mutating table?* The term conjures up an image of a part of your database transforming itself into a green monster that jumps out of your screen to attack you. The reality is even worse! A mutating table is simply one that is being changed by the current statement, and it represents a severe restriction in Oracle trigger functionality.

We define table triggers based on database events. These events occur at one of two levels: row level and statement level. Remember that a single statement can process many rows. For instance, DELETE FROM MY_TAB will process all of the rows in MY_TAB in a single statement; thus, any BEFORE DELETE trigger would fire once, but any BEFORE DELETE...FOR EACH ROW would fire once for each row in the table. The mutating table problem occurs when you attempt to reference a table in a FOR EACH ROW trigger that is (even potentially) being changed or mutated by the same statement.

Let's look at a simple practical example, using the ubiquitous EMP table. Suppose you want to enforce the rule that if a manager is deleted, all of his direct reports have the *manager* column set to NULL. The relationship between an employee and his manager is self-referential from EMP to EMP. We cannot enforce this relationship declaratively (with a foreign key constraint) because Oracle7 only supports RESTRICT (the default) and ON DELETE CASCADE. What we are developing here is a third option, ON DELETE NULLIFY, which some other relational database management systems support as standard. Bear in mind that whenever we do not (or cannot) specify constraints to enforce relationships, we must write our own code to enforce *all* the rules.

Let's try the obvious solution first to see why it is flawed. Here is the complete code listing that creates the database objects and illustrates the problem. Our trigger *emp_bdr* has failed due to a mutating table error—it cannot access the table that caused the trigger to fire (EMP).

```
CREATE TABLE emp ( empno NUMBER(4) NOT NULL
                 , deptno NUMBER(4) NOT NULL
                 , ename VARCHAR2(10)
                 , job   VARCHAR2(9)
                 , mgr   NUMBER(4)
                 , CONSTRAINT emp_pk PRIMARY KEY (empno));

INSERT INTO emp VALUES(111,10, 'Big Boss'. 'Manager ',NULL);
INSERT INTO emp VALUES(123, 11,'.ittle Guy'. 'Janitor ',111);

CREATE OR REPLACE TRIGGER emp_bdr BEFORE DELETE ON emp
FOR EACH ROW
BEGIN
    UPDATE emp SET mgr = NULL WHERE mgr = :old.empno;
END;
/

DELETE emp WHERE EMPNO = 111;
/* The following error occurs :
ERROR at line 1:
ORA-04091: table SCOTT.EMP is mutating, trigger/function may not see it
ORA-06512: at line 2
ORA-04088: error during execution of trigger 'SCOTT.EMP_BDR'
*/
```

Why does Oracle have this restriction? There is a general, and quite theoretical, property of SET statements or statements that can operate on many rows with a single statement. SQL does not guarantee the order in which the rows described in the statement will be visited. The immediate consequence of this is that if it is known that a table is mutating during a SET statement, then any reference to that table in a trigger might occur before or after any given change actually takes place. Because the order in which changes are made is not guaranteed, you will not necessarily get the same results each time you run identical statements against identical data.

Whether or not you are convinced that this restriction is to protect you against yourself, how do you overcome it and achieve what you set out to do? We have seen various types of attempted solutions to this problem, some using shadow tables, others using a dedicated server process that is waiting to be signaled to perform the update that would cause the error. Since these solutions are highly complex and fraught with danger, we will present two simple alternatives.

Let's first consider an approach that is highly inefficient and therefore not recommended—but one that will work! You wait until after the delete has taken place and then examine the entire table for rows whose *mgr* column now reference a nonexistent employee. If you find any, then you nullify their manager. The next example shows the code required:

```
DROP TRIGGER emp_bdr;
CREATE OR REPLACE TRIGGER emp_ad AFTER DELETE ON emp
BEGIN
    UPDATE emp
    SET     mgr = NULL
    WHERE NOT EXISTS (SELECT NULL
                             FROM emp emp2
                             WHERE emp2.empno = emp.mgr);
END;
/

DELETE emp WHERE EMPNO =111;
SELECT * FROM emp;
>
>    EMPNO    DEPTNO ENAME       JOB           MGR
>--------- --------- ---------- --------- ---------
>      123        11 Little Guy Janitor
>
```

```
ROLLBACK;
```

This solution, although somewhat inefficient, has the interesting property that it will repair earlier referential errors which might be the result of having run for a few hours (or weeks) with the trigger accidentally disabled. The first delete of any employee will fire the trigger that will nullify *mgr* for *all* employees referencing a nonexistent manger, not just those that referenced managers deleted in the current statement.

This "self-correction" of data may appear at first glance to be a good thing, but it has consequences which are less than desirable. Every time a single employee is deleted, the entire EMP table is scanned for employees working for a nonexistent manager. On our example table with two rows, this matters not one hoot. But in a table with several thousand rows, performance would be dire! We need to somehow restrict the search to only those rows that reference the deleted manager, without causing the mutating table problem.

What other options do you have to solve this dilemma? The second (and recommended) option involves a clever trick of simply recording the deleted EMPs during the row-level triggers and deferring the checking for EMPs who had the deleted EMP as manager until the AFTER statement-level trigger. For temporary storage of deleted *empno*s, you need to use a persistent PL/SQL table.

What is a persistent PL/SQL table? PL/SQL packages have the option of containing *persistent package variables*. These are simply declared either in the package (if they are to be visible from outside the package) or in the package body but outside all procedures and functions, in which case they can be seen only from inside the package. Both types are instantiated when the package is first referenced (for whatever reason), and remain in memory until the Oracle session disconnects. Although PL/SQL Version 2.3 allows entries in tables to be destroyed, for any site using Oracle7 Version 7.2 or earlier the gradual accretion of memory for persistent package variables is a potential problem that must be considered during design; the workaround is to assign a completely empty table of the same type to the table whose memory is to be released.

Code to implement a solution using persistent package variables is shown in Example B-1. The code consists of a package with three procedures and three triggers on the EMP table, each one fired by a different event and calling one of the packaged procedures. One of the package variables is a table of deleted *empno*s, the other is an index into it. The BEFORE DELETE statement-level trigger simply calls a procedure that sets the index to zero, thereby logically emptying the table. The BEFORE DELETE row-level trigger passes the primary key (*empno*) of the record being deleted, which is added to the end of the table. The AFTER DELETE statement-level trigger goes through the table and nullifies the *mgr* column of any employees that had the deleted employee as their manager.

NOTE   Example B-1 uses package procedure calls within the trigger so the
            package persistent variables can remain private to the procedure.
            The same technique can be implemented with less code by simply
            putting the persistent package variables into the package itself (rath-
            er than the package body) and manipulating them directly from the
            triggers. As you might suspect if you've read the rest of this book,
            we strongly prefer the encapsulated approach.

Example B-1. Avoiding Mutating Tables by Deferring Action to Statement Level

```
DROP TRIGGER emp_ad;

CREATE OR REPLACE PACKAGE pk_emp_mgr as
    PROCEDURE clear_count;
    PROCEDURE add_mgr (p_empno IN emp.empno%TYPE);
    PROCEDURE nullify_reporting_emps;
END pk_emp_mgr;
/
CREATE OR REPLACE PACKAGE BODY pk_emp_mgr AS
```

Example B-1. Avoiding Mutating Tables by Deferring Action to Statement Level (continued)

```
   TYPE tab_empno_type IS TABLE OF emp.empno%TYPE INDEX BY BINARY_INTEGER;
   g_empno tab_empno_type;
   g_empno_ind BINARY_INTEGER;

PROCEDURE clear_count IS
BEGIN
   g_empno_ind := 0;
END clear_count;

PROCEDURE add_mgr(p_empno IN EMP.EMPNO%type) Is
BEGIN
   g_empno_ind := g_empno_ind + 1;
   g_empno(g_empno_ind) := p_empno;
END add_mgr;

PROCEDURE nullify_reporting_emps IS
l_empno emp.empno%TYPE;
BEGIN
   FOR I IN 1..g_empno_ind LOOP
      l_empno := g_empno(g_empno_ind);
      UPDATE emp SET mgr = NULL WHERE mgr = l_empno;
   END LOOP;
END nullify_reporting_emps;
END pk_emp_mgr;
/

CREATE TRIGGER emp_bd BEFORE DELETE ON emp
BEGIN
   pk_emp_mgr.clear_count;
END;
/

CREATE TRIGGER emp_bdr BEFORE DELETE ON emp
FOR EACH ROW
BEGIN
   pk_emp_mgr.add_mgr(:old.empno);
END;
/

CREATE TRIGGER emp_ad AFTER DELETE ON emp
BEGIN
   pk_emp_mgr.nullify_reporting_emps;
END;
/

DELETE emp WHERE empno = 111;
SELECT * FROM emp;

>EMPNO     DEPTNO ENAME      JOB              MGR
>--------- --------- ---------- --------- ---------
>     123        11 Little Guy Janitor
>
ROLLBACK;
```

Although this may seem like a large number of individual code units, it is a proven and effective technique. But there is also a subtle extension to this problem.

What will happen if rows are deleted from EMP not directly as a result of the user issuing a DELETE statement against EMP, but as the result of cascading deletion from a parent table? We illustrate this by introducing the equally ubiquitous DEPT table to the equation. We attach our employees to different departments and then delete the department of the manager (Big Boss), which will delete Big Boss and, in turn, should render anyone who worked for Big Boss "managerless". A script to test this mechanism is illustrated in Example B-2.

Example B-2. The Mutation Problem is Back—Caused by a Cascaded Delete from a Parent

```
CREATE TABLE dept(deptno NUMBER(4) NOT NULL
                 ,dname VARCHAR2(20) NOT NULL
                 ,loc   VARCHAR2(20) NOT NULL
                 ,CONSTRAINT dept_pk PRIMARY KEY (deptno));

INSERT INTO dept VALUES(10, 'DIRECT SALES ', 'BOSTON ');
INSERT INTO dept VALUES(11, 'CLEANING ', 'NEWARK ');
ALTER TABLE emp ADD CONSTRAINT emp_fk1 FOREIGN KEY (deptno)
REFERENCES dept(deptno) ON DELETE CASCADE;

DELETE FROM dept WHERE deptno = 10;

>ERROR at line 1:
>ORA-04091: table SCOTT.EMP is mutating, trigger/function may not see it
>ORA-06512: at "SCOTT.PK_EMP_MGR", line 19
>ORA-06512: at line 2
>ORA-04088: error during execution of trigger 'SCOTT.EMP_AD'
```

The surprising result is that our original mutating table problem has now re-occurred, and this time it is reported on the statement-level trigger. The reason is that Oracle considers a table to be mutating (in an inconsistent state) during recursive SQL. *Recursive SQL* is defined as any SQL statement that is executed internally by Oracle when executing another SQL statement. In this case, Oracle has internally generated a DELETE statement against the EMP table to enforce the ON DELETE CASCADE.

Now we have identified a further problem, so let's solve it. What we need to do is duplicate the statement-level code for EMP so that it also fires on deletion of a DEPT, and to prevent the statement-level code around EMP from firing if it is invoked as a result of recursive SQL. The solution can be found in Example B-3, where we change the package header to incorporate a persistent variable (*n_ cascade_ind*) to tell us if we are in ON DELETE CASCADE mode. We change the statement-level triggers on EMP so they don't fire if the package variable is set. We add a BEFORE DELETE and an AFTER DELETE trigger for DEPT to set, and

---

Recursive SQL

Although it is rather more important to managing the performance of Oracle than to understanding the design process, experienced Oracle DBAs should note that the definition of recursive SQL changed fundamentally with the introduction of Oracle7. In earlier versions, with no triggers and no stored procedures, recursive SQL was always the result of Oracle itself issuing SQL—for example, to perform space management operations when a table needed another extent.

In Oracle7 there are three quite different types of recursive SQL:

- The traditional type of SQL statements that Oracle has decided to issue for its own management purposes and that are always parsed as the user SYS.

- User SQL that has been executed from within PL/SQL.

- SQL that has been generated by Oracle to support declarative constraints—this class is surprisingly rare as most of these operations make direct calls to the required functions inside the server. ON DELETE CASCADE is an exception.

---

reset the package variable and fire the *nullify_reporting_emps* procedure. All the new and revised code in Example B-3 is shown in bold.

Example B-3. The Solution Extended to Handle Cascade Operations

```
CREATE OR REPLACE PACKAGE pk_emp_mgr AS
    in_cascade_ind BOOLEAN := FALSE;
    PROCEDURE clear_count;
    PROCEDURE add_mgr (p_empno IN emp.empno%TYPE);
    PROCEDURE nullify_reporting_emps;
END pk_emp_mgr;
/

CREATE OR REPLACE TRIGGER emp_bd BEFORE DELETE ON emp
BEGIN
    IF NOT pk_emp_mgr.in_cascade_ind THEN
       pk_emp_mgr.clear_count;
    END IF;
END;
/

CREATE OR REPLACE TRIGGER emp_ad AFTER DELETE ON emp
BEGIN
    IF NOT pk_emp_mgr.in_cascade_ind THEN
       pk_emp_mgr.nullify_reporting_emps;
    END IF;
```

Example B-3. The Solution Extended to Handle Cascade Operations (continued)

```
END;
/

CREATE OR REPLACE TRIGGER dept_bd BEFORE DELETE ON dept
BEGIN
    pk_emp_mgr.in_cascade_ind := TRUE;
    pk_emp_mgr.clear_count;
END;
/

CREATE OR REPLACE TRIGGER dept_ad AFTER DELETE ON dept
BEGIN
    pk_emp_mgr.nullify_reporting_emps;
    pk_emp_mgr.in_cascade_ind := FALSE;
END;
/

DELETE FROM dept WHERE deptno = 10;

SELECT * FROM EMP;

>EMPNO     DEPTNO ENAME      JOB            MGR
>--------- --------- ---------- --------- ---------
>     123         11 Little Guy Janitor
>
ROLLBACK;
DELETE FROM EMP WHERE EMPNO = 111;
SELECT * FROM EMP;
/* should give same results */
ROLLBACK;
```

We've conquered the mutating table! We now have a pretty comprehensive solution which gets us around the problem. And although our example dealt with a DELETE operation, we can, of course, extend this technique to UPDATE as well. It provides a robust and efficient workaround to the problem of mutating tables and has no significant impact on performance.

TIP   You may also encounter a restriction on triggers within Oracle concerning *constraining tables*; this is a mutating table in reverse.

Within the processing of a statement, a reference has been made from a child table to a parent table to enforce a referential integrity constraint, and now a SQL statement in a trigger is trying to modify the parent table. The solution to this problem is the same as to the mutating table problem; note in persistent PL/SQL variables the changes that need to be made, and then apply them in an AFTER statement trigger.

Dealing with the Millennium Date Problem: An Oracle Perspective

There are many legacy computer systems in production operation today that are a time bomb waiting to explode. Many of these bombs will explode simultaneously when we humans are out celebrating the turn of the century! In fact, a large majority will start to falter much sooner than that, many too close for comfort. We are talking about the millennium, or year 2000, date problem.

Background

What is the millennium date problem? When older systems were originally designed and written, nobody worried about the need to use at least three significant digits (preferably four) in representations of the year to make it unambiguous. To illustrate the issue, consider what happens when you write checks. We generally write the date in a format such as "01/01/96", "01 JAN 96", "1st January 96," etc. When the year 2000 comes around, will we be writing "01/01/00", or even "01/01/000"? We may, but it would look a bit strange; probably, we will write "01/01/2000". Many computer systems don't show the century in date fields on the screens, nor do they allow the user to enter the century when entering the date. Furthermore, they generally assume that all dates are in the twentieth century, so that when the user enters "01/01/96" the system implicitly assumes that what he means is "01/01/1996". To take the argument to its logical conclusion, if he enters "01/01/00", then the system assumes that he means "01/01/1900", which (in nearly all cases) is not what he means at all. This is the heart of the problem.

The image of all the computers in the world suddenly going wrong in unison on New Year's Day 2000, is good science fiction, but it is fiction rather than future fact. Many systems already have to handle items such as expiration dates that may be several years into the future; for example, applications to handle home mortgages or pension schemes have already had to take this issue into account. The problem is creeping up on those of us who have not addressed the problem, and some will be affected sooner than others.

The problem described above illustrates potential pitfalls with application software. There will undoubtedly also be problems with computer hardware, operating systems, and system software (including most database management systems).

All computers have an internal clock that holds and maintains the current date and time. This is held in a dedicated place in the computer hardware and is usually in an internal format. In older machines, where memory was at a premium, it may well be held in as compact a form as possible. One technique for compacting it would be to not hold the century. If you are running on older hardware, the only way you can be sure that you don't have this problem is to speak to your hardware vendor or try an experiment and set the date forward to the year 2000.

Most operating systems provide function calls that allow user-written programs to extract the system date from the hardware; the operating system has to reformat the date from the internal value to a more readable format for the program. This is another potential source of error, particularly on older operating systems.

Database management systems store dates in their internal structures so users of the database can call them back or base queries around them. Once again, an internal format is usually used for storage, and translation occurs between the database and the user application, managed by the database management system. No doubt, some of these internal formats and translation processes will fail when it comes to supporting dates in the next century.

What are the consequences to the users of these systems, who are sitting on these time bombs? They are potentially disastrous, or at least very costly! Let's consider a simple example of a billing system for consultants' time. At the end of a billing period, the system works out the number of days that a consultant spent at a client site and multiplies it by the billing rate. Suppose that consultant Smith works at client Jones Industries for the period 29 December 1999 to 02 February 2000. The billing system misinterprets the second date, entered as "02-02-00", and assumes that it is 02 Feb 1900. During the billing calculation it subtracts the first date from the second, comes out with a large negative number, and multiplies that by the consultant's rate. This, of course, gives an even larger negative number.

So instead of sending out a modest invoice for the consultant's time (consultants never send out *small* invoices), we send out a huge credit note for more money than our small consultancy is worth. Is this far-fetched scaremongering? Maybe, but it is indicative of the type of error that could occur.

Now that we've explored in general the type of problems that will occur if the issue is not addressed, let's consider the implications for systems that use an Oracle database. As we discussed in Chapter 7, Oracle has a DATE datatype that is designed to hold a date and time, with the time held to the nearest second. The range of dates supported by this datatype is from "01-JAN-4712 BC" to "31-DEC-4712 AD". Internally, Oracle holds a date as an seven-byte integer that represents the date in packed format with one byte each representing the century, year, month, day, hour, minute, and second. Given this internal format Oracle implicitly records the century in all dates that are held in DATE columns.

It is extremely rare for dates to be stored in character or numeric format in Oracle tables since there is no good reason for avoiding the DATE format. The one exception to this rule is the case in which only the year is recorded, for example, the year of registration of a car. The year could be in a number or a character column, with either two or four significant digits.

The main problem with software written for an Oracle database is the conversion of dates between internal and external (display) format. Oracle provides a mask facility to allow the programmer to specify the required external date format. This is achieved by pasting together a set of components. Examples of masks are "DD Month YYYY", "DD-MON-YY", "DD/MM/YY", "MM/DD/YY", and so on. Problems are bound to arise when the year component of the mask omits the century, since it is always assumed to be 19. Oracle had the foresight to anticipate the problem as early as 1993 when Oracle7 was first released and the mask "RR" introduced. RR assumes the twentieth century if the year is greater than or equal to 50, and the twenty-first century if it is less than 50. Thus, TO_DATE('.4-JAN-05'. 'DD-MON-RR'. yields a date in the year 2005, and TO_DATE('.1-MAR-68'. 'DD-MON-RR'. yields a date in the year 1968.

Unfortunately, designers and programmers have not been particularly quick to pick up on the significance of this new technique, and use of "YY" in date masks continues to proliferate. Perhaps the year 2000 still seems a long time in the future, especially in computer terms. Even where sites have been disciplined enough to enforce the use of "RR", where appropriate, or to enforce a standard of "YYYY", this practice has typically only been put into effect in new developments or in rewrites of existing code. There are still many lines of code out there in production Oracle systems that employ the "YY" mask for dates or that use no masks at all.

Management is only just now realizing the enormity of the millennium date problem and the potential cost of solving that problem. The task of locating all source code (in whatever format) and checking every line for potential problems is a huge logistical task, as well as a labor-intensive process. Inevitably, some source code will have been misplaced, and in those cases a rewrite will be the only viable alternative.

What do you do when your manager tells you, the designer, to sort out the problem and ensure a smooth passage into the new millennium? First of all, don't underestimate the enormity of the task involved. But how can we alleviate the potentially huge cost of simply keeping our current Oracle systems functional as we approach the millennium? Here are some thoughts.

Can We Fix It in the Database?

The answer to this question is that we can only fix it to a very limited degree in the database without having to delve into application code.

Imagine a screen where the user enters a date into the typical Oracle nine-character field (no century). We take this screen out of the production environment into a test arena and experiment with it. We enter "31-DEC-00" into the field, commit, and requery the record—it still shows as "31-DEC-00". But when we go into SQL*Plus and query the date field including the century, we see that it is "31-DEC-1900". We conclude the form does not use the "RR" mask for the century.

Let's suppose that the date in question is an expiration date; we can assume that it will never be in the past. Given this rule, we can write a trigger on the table that checks for a date in the past and converts it to a date in the twenty-first century. The code of this trigger is:

```
create or replace trigger POLICIES_BIUR
before insert or update of EXPIRY_D on POLICIES
for each row
Begin
  If :new.EXPIRY_D < trunc(sysdate) And :new.EXPIRY_D is not null
  Then
     :new.EXPIRY_D := Add_Months(:new.EXPIRY_D,1200);
  End If;
End;
/
```

This code works well, but we have some strong reservations about it:

- Are we 100% sure about our assumption that we *never* back-date a policy expiration? Do we ever retrospectively load details of old policies? If so, they may become active again, which is potentially embarrassing if we start billing premiums to policy holders who died many years ago.

- By altering the value of the expiration date between the form and the database, we have created an inconsistency between the two. The form believes that the policy expires on "31-DEC-1900", while the database considers the expiration date to be "31-DEC-2000". If we amend another field on the form, causing an update, without first requerying, we are likely to be informed by the application that the record has been changed by another user. It hasn't really, but the form has spotted the inconsistency and has assumed that another user is responsible.

- We were able to write a "fix-up" trigger for this column because we had a firm rule that we could base our logic on (expiration cannot be in the past). With many fields, we can't safely assume either way. Take date of birth, for example: in the first year of the century, "01-DEC-00" could be a very young person or a very old one. We could possibly look at other fields, such as Social Security number, and assume that a baby won't have one, but we are treading on dangerous ground here.

- User input is only part of the problem. Within the code of the form there is likely to be conditional logic based around date values. There may be dates hard-coded into the logic, but this is rare and unlikely to be ambiguous with regard to century. Typically, it would be something along the lines of:

```
IF :creation_date > To_Date('01-DEC-90','DD-MON-YY')
    THEN Process_New_Policy;
    ELSE Process_Old_Policy;
END IF;
```

What is much more likely is that the program will contain local variables that hold representations of date values that are retrieved from the database. Example B-4 contains some extracts from a live system indicating some areas of potential problem in the millennium.

Example B-4. Some Code Extracts Indicating Potential Problem Areas

```
initialization
:B1.S_START_TIME :=to_date ( to_char(sysdate,'DD-MON-YY HH:MI:SS'),
                                       'DD-MON-YY HH:MI:SS') ;
:global.stage_date   := TO_CHAR(SYSDATE,'DD-MON-YY');
:b1.generation   := TO_NUMBER(TO_CHAR(:b1.application_date,'YY'))


conditional logic
IF :ORG2.DELETED_DATE > TO_DATE(TO_CHAR(SYSDATE,'DD-MON-YY')) THEN


predicates
.... and     to_number(to_char(sch_date_started,'YY')) < 85

.... order by to_date(hci_month,'MON-YY') desc

.... and     hist_date < trunc(to_date(to_char(sysdate,
                               'DD-MON-YY')),'YEAR')


in cursors
cursor count_dates is
select count(distinct(to_char(hom_offer_of_cover_date,'DD-MON-YY'))),
       count(distinct(to_char(hom_date_issued,'DD-MON-YY'))),
       count(distinct(to_char(hom_date_cp_notice,'DD-MON-YY'))),
       count(distinct(to_char(hom_date_final_cert,'DD-MON-YY')))
from   homes
where (:b1.service_type = 'HB3'
       and hom_hb3_service_request_no = :b1.service_request_no);


problems with boundary crossing?
ELSIF TO_CHAR(launch_datetime,'DD-MON-YY HH24:MI:SS') <
              TO_CHAR(SYSDATE,'DD-MON-YY HH24:MI:SS') THEN


use in keys - problems when ordering
.... order by claim_no; -- claim_no is YY/nnnnn
```

The problem is not restricted to screen-based programs; we should also consider the impact on reports, batch programs, and database-resident code. Reports should not present too much of a problem since they don't usually update the database; also, if they show only a two-digit year, the user will probably be able to interpret it correctly within the report context. However, certain periodic reports may update the table that records the last time the report was run—and this will surely include a date field. Also, it is possible that a date column selected from the database into a field on the report that does not include the century is bound into the predicate of a subsequent query. The other area to watch for in reports is the handling of parameters that are dates.

Batch programs tend to have problems where date columns are fetched into character variables without the century and are later converted back into date columns in the database or are bound into predicates in SQL statements. It is relatively straightforward to increase the size of the variables by two characters and to alter the masks from "YY" to "YYYY".

The conclusion to be drawn here is that it is highly unlikely that we can avoid digging up and delving into the old application code of our Oracle systems. Of course, this may the opportunity that we've been waiting for to rewrite a lot of this code (maybe to take it from character-based to GUI). However, is it a practical proposition to rewrite all the current production systems? There may be no choice if we cannot locate all the source!

Leaving a total rewrite aside, for now, let's consider how best to undertake the task of searching for potential problem areas of our code and fixing them.

The Search Begins

How do we locate the sections of code that will be problematic in the new century? First of all, we will probably put our source files into a common directory (or one directory per source type). Next, we need to identify a search tool. UNIX has a rich set of tools and utilities to search for occurrences of strings within files (*grep*, *sed*, and *awk*, to name but three).

What do we search for? Finding all the occurrences of "YY" would be a good first attempt. Finding all the occurrences "'Y'" in a string enclosed in single quotes might reduce the number of false hits (but might possibly mean that we miss some useful comments). Finding all the occurrences of "YY" that are not within a "YYYY" string will cut out some more false hits, but would any instances slip through the net? We could extend the search criteria to include occurrence of the type "..-...-.." where "." is a wildcard character representing any single character. Unfortunately, SQL has very weak data typing, so it is possible to convert to and from the DATE datatype without specifying either a mask or a conversion function; these are going to be difficult to find using simple searches.

There may be elements of our code that have potential problems with dates that have no connection with Oracle. For instance, we may search for an operating system file based on its creation date. Part of our application might be a UNIX shell script that utilizes the *date* utility, in which case we have to look for instances of "%y". Without a thorough understanding of our application, we will never find all these until things start to go wrong. This is one reason why thorough testing is important.

If all our source code is held in text files, then the output from these searches will be single lines of code. These can be examined, and some of the output eliminated on site. Source code held in binary format is unlikely to produce decipherable output from the search, although such pattern matching is still a useful way of finding out if any of the SQL embedded in the application contains the alarm signals we've discussed. At the end of the search we will have a list of "at risk" source files that may need attention. This will give some indication of the scale of the problem. All we have to do now is to roll up our sleeves and fix it!

Fixing It

Unfortunately, each case must be evaluated on its own merits. We cannot go blindly replacing all occurrences of "YY" with "RR". First we would have to ascertain if we can correctly assume that any date in which the year is less than 50 belongs in the twenty-first century. We certainly cannot replace all instances of "YY" with "YYYY" without carefully considering the effect of the increase in size when making an assignment to a variable or screen field. If we increase the size of all date fields on the screen, we may have to reorganize the entire screen.

Automating It

If the scale of the problem is significant, you may hope to automate at least some of the changes, especially if you are starting to see recurring patterns in the code. Again, UNIX utilities such as *awk* are ideal for this purpose. If you use an operating system that doesn't have string manipulation utilities, you may have to resort to writing a 3GL program (maybe C or COBOL) that reads a file or set of files, makes a series of well-defined amendments, and write them out again. Here are some general guidelines on automation:

- Back up or keep a copy of all the source before you start.

- Test the replacement code on a single source file before applying major surgery to the entire source directory.

- Tackle recurring problems that are relatively easy to fix first.

- Periodically rerun the search facility to consolidate.

- Make absolutely sure that any automated approach alerts you to potential
  knock-on effects, and make sure that you follow up any warnings! For
  instance, if in an Oracle Forms module we amend the line:

```
global.cur_date := to_char(sysdate, "DD-MON-YY")
```

  to:

```
global.cur_date := to_char(sysdate, "DD_MON-YYYY")
```

  we must then check where else the variable *:global.cur_date* is used. Worse,
  this check cannot necessarily be restricted to the same form, so other source
  files need to be searched. If we find it used in an assignment such as

```
:b1.cur_date := :global.cur_date
```

  then we must look at the definition of *:b1.cur_date* and ensure that it is large
  enough to house the longer value. We now have a new trail to follow in that
  we have to examine the form for other references to *:b1.cur_date* and so on.

Testing It

A good test strategy is key to the success of the entire exercise. If you can prove
that everything is going to be hunky-dory, then you will be able to sleep (or
party) in complete confidence on New Year's Eve 1999! One strategy would be to
test all of the modules identified in the search phase with the date set forward to
2000 to see what will happen if the code is not changed. This will give you a
handle on the effects of the problem, as well as confidence when retesting after
the fix, that it was required and effective.

Subject each source module that you change to a full unit test. You should follow
the unit test plan for the module (if one exists) and should certainly add tests to
the plan to specifically test dates in 2000 and beyond.

Now rerun the entire system and integration test suite, and again add new tests to
specifically test date functionality.

Set up a specific Oracle instance for testing the millennium problem. Using a separate instance allows you to set the date to a fixed value (using the Oracle
initialization parameter FIX_DATE. Note that this will only affect the Oracle date—
SYSDATE) when fetched from the server. Client/server applications may use the
local clock on the client, and you will have to check for operating system calls to
get the date. Oracle Forms has a subtle difference between $$DATE$$ and
$$DBDATE$$; the first is the local operating system date, and the second is the
server database date.

As we mentioned previously, there may be elements of our code that rely on dates outside of the Oracle sphere, such as file creation dates. The safest mechanism for testing is to have a dedicated machine and to put the clock forward. Obviously, this is not always practical.

A Generic Solution

A truly generic solution would be great, but is probably just a pipe dream! If you can invent one, you will probably make yourself a lot of money at the time that panic begins to set in when management pull their heads out of the sand and realize that they are going to miss the deadline no matter how many bodies they throw at the problem!*

There are a number of tools creeping onto the market that claim to automate the process. We remain dubious and have yet to learn of any that are specifically targeted at the Oracle marketplace.

Millennium Summary

It is never too early to start planning and investigating. Try to assess the scale of the problem in your applications and, if you have packaged products, speak to your vendors. Work methodically, identifying areas of risk, fixing them, and testing them. Above all, test the fixes so you can sleep easily into the next century.

Providing User Extensibility

As we said right at the beginning of the book, design is about finding an affordable way of meeting functional requirements with the tools available. We've included a short discussion on this, extensible SQL, because we have each seen a number of projects take very expensive approaches to meeting the "simple" requirement—users should have some control over the action of their system. It's clear that such features need to be designed in; it's our experience that trying to add them after the fact can be extremely difficult (for reasons similar to those discussed previously). The first problem is finding all the dependencies.

When to Consider Extensibility

You can easily provide a great many customization options using entirely normal design and build techniques. If we are told that prices might change, we store the

---

* We were going to put a short section in here about how assigning more staff to a task does not necessarily mean that it completes sooner, but we decided that if you have even started to read this book you probably already knew that!

prices in a PRICES table. If we are told that discount levels might change, we store the discount levels in a DISCOUNT_LEVELS table, and so on. As we remarked in Chapter 3, identifying such cases should be part of the analysis work and the results should be in the entity relationships model.

But what if we are told that the marketing department wants the ability to automatically apply discounts and that they need to be able to vary the rules on 24 hours' notice. Actually, the 24 hours part will be the result of frantic negotiation on your part—what they will initially ask for is to be able to vary the rules on demand, by which they mean instantly.

Whenever you are told that a *rule*, rather than the *value of a term* within a rule, is subject to change, then you may be looking at a requirement for extensibility. If you are then told that there is no current knowledge of the future rule, there is no doubt that you can't code it right now. Either you build in extensibility, or you must rule the requirement out of scope. This gets right to the heart of the matter: you have to decide whether the requirement is so open-ended that you cannot guarantee to meet it.

There is nothing more frustrating than spending two or three person years designing extensibility into an order discount system only to discover that you did not make it quite extensible enough—because, for example, you never dreamt that anyone would want to use the first three or four digits of the customer's telephone number as part of the discount rule.

For purposes of this brief discussion, we'll ignore a whole series of issues that need to be addressed in the real world (and which are frequently ignored), like:

- Who is responsible for checking the system impact of a proposed change?
- Who is responsible for testing that the change is working as expected?
- Who is responsible for backing out the effects of any change made in error?

We could dedicate an entire book to this subject, and perhaps one day we will, but for the moment we just want to end this book with a short section explaining the techniques that can be used within Oracle applications to provide extensibility, and to identify some of the pitfalls for you.

Types of Extensibility

When we are dealing with requests to deploy extensibility, there are two separate types of requirements which are often not well distinguished by the users or, indeed, by the systems staff. These are:

- Algorithmic extensibility, where new processing rules are required to supplement or replace existing rules

- Schema extensibility, where new attributes are required for existing entities or, more complex, entirely new entities are required along with supported relationships to the existing entities

Schema extensibility is invariably accompanied by algorithmic extensibility as the existing code is unlikely to reference objects that were unknown when it was written, and there is little point in introducing new data objects if none of the logic is going to refer to them. It is also invariably data-driven, that is, the basis for it is to store within the database the definitions of the new data items for algorithms to retrieve and use to generate dynamic SQL.

Within an Oracle environment, there are three basic approaches to providing users with algorithmic extensibility: data-driven, view-driven, and procedure- or function-driven. We describe these in the following sections, and contrast them with the traditional approach.

Data-Driven Extensibility

Most projects that we have seen attempt algorithmic extensibility have used the data-driven approach. Example B-5 shows a DDL fragment from a table design which is attempting to implement a data-driven rule of some type:

Example B-5. DDL Extract of Table to Store Parts of a Calculation Rule or Formula

```
CREATE TABLE RULE_ELEMENTS
( RULE#   NUMBER
  CONSTRAINT rule_element_rule# REFERENCES rules
, step#  NUMBER  NOT NULL
, OP     CHAR(1) NOT NULL
  CONSTRAINT rule_element_op CHECK (OP IN ('+', '-', '*', '/', '%'))
, type   CHAR(1) NOT NULL
  CONSTRAINT rule_element_type CHECK (type IN ('literal', 'column'))
, literal NUMBER
, CONSTRAINT rule_element_literal CHECK
    (  (type = 'literal' AND literal IS NOT NULL)
    or (type <> 'literal' AND literal IS     NULL))
, colname VARCHAR2(30)
, CONSTRAINT rule_element_colname CHECK
    (  (type = 'column' AND colname IS NOT NULL)
    OR (type <> 'column' AND colname IS     NULL))
, CONSTRAINT rule_element_pk PRIMARY KEY (rule#, step#)
);
```

From a trivial examination of this code, we can predict that although it will let us handle simple rules involving only columns of a single row, it is going to run into difficulties when we need to reference other tables. In addition, it seems unable to handle parentheses or arithmetic functions such as ROUND( ). With a little more effort, we could come up with a design that handles these features, and possibly one that contains an IF capability as well. We then have to find a way not only of implementing the table and its maintenance, but also of implementing the rules that the table describes.

You would normally do an implementation of this kind through a simple project-written code generator which produces dynamic SQL or dynamic PL/SQL. The CPU usage of the PL/SQL compiler may mitigate against the use of dynamic PL/SQL, although if most cases are going to generate the same anonymous block, the shared SQL area may come to your rescue. This is unlikely if column values are being inserted into the generated code as literals, and unfortunately very few project-written generators use bind variables.

A much more serious problem with this type of approach is that the users have to be trained how to maintain the RULE_ELEMENTS table when they probably want to simply express their solution the way they would have expressed it in a spread-sheet. It might be easier to teach them how to write SQL and PL/SQL than to teach them how to decompose their solution into the step-by-step RULE_ELEMENTS. If you really want to spend money to no good effect, then you can also write a compiler to take expressions written in some notation you have just devised and translate it into RULE_ELEMENTS, remembering that you have also had to write a generator to turn RULE_ELEMENTS into SQL.

We hope that this discussion illustrates the futility of this level of engineering as a project-level approach. In general, both the cost and delivery lead time will be too high without any guarantee that the users will be able to handle every extension that could conceivably be required. However, there is a more direct approach which can be more flexible.

The tables shown in Table B-1 contain not the individual elements of formulae, but the formulae themselves plus the derivation of formula terms. The formulae are coded in PL/SQL and the derivations in SQL.

There are still a number of tricky implementation issues, and the overall performance of the solution will depend on how well the solution is able to manage caches to ensure that it does not find itself continually revisiting the same rows. For this reason it might be better to redefine *formula_params* as a two-level structure with SQL statements capable of returning many values so that a single visit to the database can acquire all of the data likely to be needed from any rows that it has to visit.

We have some sympathy with the more direct approach, which stores SQL or PL/SQL clauses within rules tables, and which uses dynamic SQL to insert these fragments into the required context during processing. Again, however, there may be efficiency problems with the amount of parsing required. Also, the approach is useless unless someone in the user community is capable of executing accurately all of the development stages of the mini-project required to implement a new rule. These, of course, are:

- Analysis
- Design
- Code
- Test
- Transition

Normally the only one tackled is code, with the result that we have equipped the users with a sophisticated and expensive weapon with which they proceed to massacre their own data.

Table B-1. Stored PL/SQL and SQL to Implement Discount Rules

Formulae

NAME	RETURNS	FORMULA
| CREDLIM | BOOLEAN | ```
IF (cur_cred > 1000)
THEN
    return (&cur_cred + :order_value) < 500;
ELSE
    return (&cur_cred + :order_value) < 250;
END IF;
``` |
| CREDLIM2 | BOOLEAN | ```
return (&cur_cred + :order_value) <
                &orders_last_year * 0.125;
``` |

Formula_Params

NAME	S_SQL
| cur_cred | ```
SELECT SUM(ord.order_price)
  FROM orders ord
 WHERE ord.status NOT IN ('PAID', 'CANC')
   AND ord.cus_id = :customer_id
``` |
| orders_last_year | ```
SELECT SUM(ord.order_price)
  FROM orders ord
 WHERE ord.status = 'PAID'
   AND ord.order_d BETWEEN SYSDATE AND SYSDATE - 365
   AND ord.cus_id = :customer_id
``` |

Case study: screen design

The data-driven approach to design is not always a panacea. It has to be controlled; otherwise, it's possible to go overboard with this approach and design something so abstract that it either can't be coded by mere mortals (like you and us), or it becomes horribly inefficient. Or both.

One of the authors recently inherited some code that could only be described as a case of "soft-code overload". Every field on the screen was placed in exactly the same location and had exactly the same size. When he went into the screen painter component of the development tool, his immediate reaction was "What a strange looking screen!" After much searching through the procedural code, it became apparent that each field was resized and repositioned dynamically. The size was based on the size of the column in the database, and the positioning code ensured that the fields were neatly spaced. The field prompt was derived from the name of the field. This code worked and had the advantage that a column could be resized in the database or a new column added to the screen without having to worry about the positioning of fields. However, it was desperately slow and impossible to maintain! The same system had the menu structure and sequence held in database tables and created all the menus dynamically, even though the tool itself had a perfectly adequate menu maintenance facility. Overkill!

Some designers will tend to be far too abstract in their data modeling; they have a tendency to create a kind of meta-model that simply can't be made to run efficiently. How can you identify such dangerous designers? Watch out especially for any column that contains the name of another table or column. For instance, a large arc in a conceptual information model can be implemented as a single foreign key and a column naming the table that the foreign key refers to. The problem with the solution that involves holding the name of the table that the foreign key references is that the only way to issue a runtime query against such a structure is by fetching each row from the master and querying the detail separately for each row. This is inefficient and difficult, especially from a tool such as Oracle Forms or Powerbuilder.

Case study: Oracle Payroll

Oracle Payroll is part of the Oracle Financials suite of applications. The original product brief called for the calculation engine to be able to calculate pay for any organization by allowing (demanding) payroll formulae to be entered as part of the onsite customization *without changing any code that was part of the base product*. In addition, it had to be possible to quickly change the rules when the customer was confronted with a change to (local) tax law or collective labor agreements.

The solution recommended by one of the authors of this book, and adopted and adapted by the project team, was to use PL/SQL expressions stored in user tables to hold the calculation rules. It was also necessary to implement a meta-dictionary within the application so that an expression in a formula such as "employee age" or "qualification level" could be mapped to a *table name, column name,* and *primary key.* At runtime, the required formula was fetched and scanned to find out what variables it required; these variables were then selected from the database. The formula could then be executed as a PL/SQL anonymous block. In an organization with complex pay rules, more than 100 formulae might have to be executed for a single employee, and under Oracle Version 6 the only way in which we could execute the PL/SQL was as an anonymous block.

Functionally, the approach was almost completely successful; we say *almost* because the mechanism was sufficiently complex that end users had great difficulty with the set-up, which often had to be performed either by in-house IT staff or by payroll consultants. It also had tremendous performance problems during its early life. In Chapter 14, *Designing for Parallel Processing*, we describe some of the techniques which had to be used in order to get adequate performance from this approach.

View-Driven Extensibility

Without getting into the depths of relational calculus, we'll point out that using SQL it is always possible to retrieve any well-ordered set of data from any set of tables. So simply by providing views you can, at least in theory, extend the query rules at any time by adding to the views that are used for retrieval—that is, if we also use these views within the triggers and procedures used in our update logic.

Unfortunately, there are very real problems. Writing the required views can be difficult, and in many cases writing an efficient view will be impossible. To amend any view, users must not only have a good knowledge of both SQL and the data structures, they must also have been granted at least some DDL privileges. And finally, even with the extensions in the latest versions of Oracle, very few join views are updatable.

Generators are not a solution, as very few (if any) generators are capable of producing the type of view definition required to perform complex conditional calculations.

Procedure- and Function-Driven Extensibility

Let's assume that we may have to deploy conventional programming skills to implement new functionality. In this case, we may try to limit the number of discrete changes that will have to be made to the application by ensuring that each atomic action taken by the application appears once and only once within the source code. This, in turn, will mean that all of the application process rules (as distinct from display rules) are held within the data dictionary as stored procedures (or functions).

This is nothing more than yet another plea for encapsulation; carried to its logical extreme, it will result in an application with a very high number of very small units of code. This, in turn, causes both performance and project management problems. However, in certain areas the overhead of having many small functions may have a dramatic payoff as simple changes and extensions to functionality can be made in one place (the online data dictionary) and be guaranteed to be immediately applied system-wide.

Thus, application-wide values, such as the maximum length of an account code, can be implemented as functions within a package specific to the application. For example:

```
CREATE PACKAGE acc_values AS
CREATE PACKAGE acc_values AS
...
FUNCTION max_acno_len RETURN NUMBER;
...
END; -- acc_values

CREATE PACKAGE BODY acc_values AS
...
  FUNCTION max_acno_len RETURN NUMBER IS
  BEGIN
    IF (sysdate >= '01-JAN-98'.
    THEN RETURN 10; -- see change req 4374
    ELSE RETURN  8;
    END IF;
  END;
...
END; -- acc_values body
```

Syntactically, functions without arguments are interchangeable with persistent package variables. In this example, the value could be provided using a persistent package variable and a constructor in the package (assuming that no application is connected to the database at midnight on New Year's Eve 1997). However, the function approach is more general because it allows a constant value to be replaced by one that requires a database lookup although in many cases the database lookup will require parameters to be available. These should always be passed as part of the function call or retrieved inside the function by calling other functions such as *acc_values.curr_acno*, which would return the account number of the account currently being processed by the application.

Such techniques, though powerful, involve changing the code generated by the original project and may thus be considered to be simply a carefully restricted form of traditional application extension, discussed below. They can also become highly complex as apparently simple application functions start to rely on the cooperation of perhaps several hundred specific functions.

Traditional Extension

The traditional approach is to simply ask the IT department or application supplier to make the changes required to support the new requirement. This technique is well known to, and widely mistrusted by, user departments because the lead times frequently run into years. Users make their requests, there are endless negotiations, and eventually something is built and shipped which may or may not meet their needs. It is for these reasons that users request the flexibility to change the rules for themselves.

Extensibility Summary

If there is no way out of providing fully general extensibility of algorithms, then we strongly recommend the use of PL/SQL procedures and functions despite their potential performance problems.

We have both worked on applications that featured both self-describing data and data-driven rules. These applications worked (within limits), but we cannot wholeheartedly recommend any approach other than handling all genuinely new requirements as application maintenance. What we can do within the design (to take our users at least one step further forward) is to clearly document what can be achieved within the design using data-driven techniques, and the precise limits of this flexibility. Coupled with comparative cost estimates of limited versus more generous flexibility, this may be enough to persuade the project sponsors to opt for a less ambitious specification.

We'd like to end this book with a statement that we suggest you recall whenever your task as a designer seems to be impossible, just in case it identifies the true cause of your problem:

> It really is absurdly difficult to design a piece of code that will completely meet a totally unknown requirement.

Index

About the Authors

Dave Ensor is manager of Worldwide Solutions, PATROL R&D with BMC Software, where his roles are assisting customers in their use of both BMC's PATROL product and the Oracle Server and feeding the results of his field work back into product planning. He has more than 30 years of IT experience and has been involved with the design and performance issues surrounding Oracle since 1987. For many years he led Oracle Worldwide's Performance Studies Group based in the U.K., which provided consultancy support to both customer and internal projects with critical performance requirements. Dave is well known as a speaker on performance management and design; he presents his papers at user conferences and writes and delivers one-day seminars. He lives in the U.K. just outside London, but spends much of the year travelling to user sites and meetings. In his spare time he also travels, but in this case without his laptop and with his wife. He can be reached at *dave_ensor@compuserve.com.*

Ian Stevenson is a freelance consultant specializing in database design and development. He has worked with database technology for 19 years, starting with early hierarchical models. He worked for Oracle (UK) for two years in Post-Sales Support and Human Resources Development. This is where he formed his friendship with Dave Ensor. Ian has a first class honours degree in Mathematics from the University of Southampton and is a member of the British Computer Society. He is married to Brenda and has two children, Todd and Tara. He is a fanatic supporter of the Southampton football club. He can be contacted at *ian@westmail.demon.co.uk.*

Colophon

The insects featured on the cover of *Oracle Design* are a dragonfly and a damselfly. These two insects comprise the order Odonata. Dragonflies and damselflies are quite similar—both are predatory insects, aquatic when young, and excellent flyers as adults. They are able to fly as fast as 35 miles per hour, and to perform impressive mid-air acrobatics. A primary difference between them is the way they hold their wings while at rest. Dragonflies spread their wings out when resting, while damselflies fold their wings together over their backs.

Young dragonflies are equipped with a unique "jet propulsion" ability. By drawing water in through their gills, which are located in the posterior of their abdomens, and quickly forcing it out again they are able to powerfully propel themselves across the water surface. This technique is used in emergencies when a quick getaway is called for.

Adult dragonflies and damselflies catch and eat their prey while flying. They fly with their long, bristle-covered legs bent in front of them, forming something like a basket, which they use to scoop up other insects. Dragonflies are quite popular with humans both because of their beauty and grace and because their diet is largely made up of mosquitoes and flies.

Edie Freedman designed the cover of this book, using a 19th-century engraving from the Dover Pictorial Archive. The cover layout was produced with Quark XPress 3.3 using the ITC Garamond font.

The inside layout was designed by Nancy Priest and implemented in FrameMaker by Mike Sierra. The text and heading fonts are ITC Garamond Light and Garamond Book. The illustrations that appear in the book were created in Macromedia Freehand by Chris Reilley. This colophon was written by Clairemarie Fisher O'Leary.

How to stay in touch with O'Reilly

1. Visit Our Award-Winning Web Site

http://www.ora.com/

★ "Top 100 Sites on the Web" —*PC Magazine*
★ "Top 5% Web sites" —*Point Communications*
★ "3-Star site" —*The McKinley Group*

Our web site contains a library of comprehensive product information (including book excerpts and tables of contents), downloadable software, background articles, interviews with technology leaders, links to relevant sites, book cover art, and more. File us in your Bookmarks or Hotlist!

2. Join Our Email Mailing Lists

New Product Releases

To receive automatic email with brief descriptions of all new O'Reilly products as they are released, send email to:
listproc@online.ora.com
Put the following information in the first line of your message (*not* in the Subject field):
subscribe ora-news "Your Name" of "Your Organization" (for example: subscribe ora-news Kris Webber of Fine Enterprises)

O'Reilly Events

If you'd also like us to send information about trade show events, special promotions, and other O'Reilly events, send email to: **listproc@online.ora.com**
Put the following information in the first line of your message (*not* in the Subject field):
subscribe ora-events "Your Name" of "Your Organization"

3. Get Examples from Our Books via FTP

There are two ways to access an archive of example files from our books:

Regular FTP

- ftp to:
  ftp.ora.com
  (login: anonymous
  password: your email address)
- Point your web browser to:
  ftp://ftp.ora.com/

FTPMAIL

- Send an email message to:
  ftpmail@online.ora.com
  (Write "help" in the message body)

4. Visit Our Gopher Site

- Connect your gopher to:
  gopher.ora.com

- Point your web browser to:
  gopher://gopher.ora.com/

- Telnet to:
  gopher.ora.com
  login: gopher

5. Contact Us via Email

order@ora.com
To place a book or software order online. Good for North American and international customers.

subscriptions@ora.com
To place an order for any of our newsletters or periodicals.

books@ora.com
General questions about any of our books.

software@ora.com
For general questions and product information about our software. Check out O'Reilly Software Online at **http://software.ora.com/** for software and technical support information. Registered O'Reilly software users send your questions to: **website-support@ora.com**

cs@ora.com
For answers to problems regarding your order or our products.

booktech@ora.com
For book content technical questions or corrections.

proposals@ora.com
To submit new book or software proposals to our editors and product managers.

international@ora.com
For information about our international distributors or translation queries. For a list of our distributors outside of North America check out:
http://www.ora.com/www/order/country.html

O'Reilly & Associates, Inc.
101 Morris Street, Sebastopol, CA 95472 USA
TEL 707-829-0515 or 800-998-9938
(6am to 5pm PST)
FAX 707-829-0104

O'REILLY™

Titles from O'Reilly

Please note that upcoming titles are displayed in italic.

WEB PROGRAMMING
Apache: The Definitive Guide
Building Your Own Website
CGI Programming for the World Wide Web
Designing for the Web
HTML: The Definitive Guide
JavaScript: The Definitive Guide, 2nd Ed.
Learning Perl
Programming Perl, 2nd Ed.
Mastering Regular Expressions
WebMaster in a Nutshell
Web Security & Commerce
Web Client Programming with Perl
World Wide Web Journal

USING THE INTERNET
Smileys
The Future Does Not Compute
The Whole Internet User's Guide & Catalog
The Whole Internet for Win 95
Using Email Effectively
Bandits on the Information Superhighway

JAVA SERIES
Exploring Java
Java AWT Reference
Java Fundamental Classes Reference
Java in a Nutshell
Java Language Reference
Java Network Programming
Java Threads
Java Virtual Machine

SOFTWARE
WebSite™ 1.1
WebSite Professional™
Building Your Own Web Conferences
WebBoard™
PolyForm™
Statisphere™

SONGLINE GUIDES
NetActivism
Net Law
NetLearning
Net Lessons
NetResearch
NetSuccess for Realtors
NetTravel

SYSTEM ADMINISTRATION
Building Internet Firewalls
Computer Crime: A Crimefighter's Handbook
Computer Security Basics
DNS and BIND, 2nd Ed.
Essential System Administration, 2nd Ed.
Getting Connected: The Internet at 56K and Up
Internet Server Administration with Windows NT
Linux Network Administrator's Guide
Managing Internet Information Services
Managing NFS and NIS
Networking Personal Computers with TCP/IP
Practical UNIX & Internet Security. 2nd Ed.
PGP: Pretty Good Privacy
sendmail, 2nd Ed.
sendmail Desktop Reference
System Performance Tuning
TCP/IP Network Administration
termcap & terminfo
Using & Managing UUCP
Volume 8: X Window System Administrator's Guide
Web Security & Commerce

UNIX
Exploring Expect
Learning VBScript
Learning GNU Emacs, 2nd Ed.
Learning the bash Shell
Learning the Korn Shell
Learning the UNIX Operating System
Learning the vi Editor
Linux in a Nutshell
Making TeX Work
Linux Multimedia Guide
Running Linux, 2nd Ed.
SCO UNIX in a Nutshell
sed & awk, 2nd Edition
Tcl/Tk Tools
UNIX in a Nutshell: System V Edition
UNIX Power Tools
Using csh & tsch
When You Can't Find Your UNIX System Administrator
Writing GNU Emacs Extensions

WEB REVIEW STUDIO SERIES
Gif Animation Studio
Shockwave Studio

WINDOWS
Dictionary of PC Hardware and Data Communications Terms
Inside the Windows 95 Registry
Inside the Windows 95 File System
Win95 & WinNT Annoyances
Windows NT File System Internals
Windows NT in a Nutshell

PROGRAMMING
Advanced Oracle PL/SQL Programming
Applying RCS and SCCS
C++: The Core Language
Checking C Programs with lint
DCE Security Programming
Distributing Applications Across DCE & Windows NT
Encyclopedia of Graphics File Formats, 2nd Ed.
Guide to Writing DCE Applications
lex & yacc
Managing Projects with make
Mastering Oracle Power Objects
Oracle Design: The Definitive Guide
Oracle Performance Tuning, 2nd Ed.
Oracle PL/SQL Programming
Porting UNIX Software
POSIX Programmer's Guide
POSIX.4: Programming for the Real World
Power Programming with RPC
Practical C Programming
Practical C++ Programming
Programming Python
Programming with curses
Programming with GNU Software
Pthreads Programming
Software Portability with imake, 2nd Ed.
Understanding DCE
Understanding Japanese Information Processing
UNIX Systems Programming for SVR4

BERKELEY 4.4 SOFTWARE DISTRIBUTION
4.4BSD System Manager's Manual
4.4BSD User's Reference Manual
4.4BSD User's Supplementary Documents
4.4BSD Programmer's Reference Manual
4.4BSD Programmer's Supplementary Documents
X Programming
Vol. 0: X Protocol Reference Manual
Vol. 1: Xlib Programming Manual
Vol. 2: Xlib Reference Manual
Vol. 3M: X Window System User's Guide, Motif Edition
Vol. 4M: X Toolkit Intrinsics Programming Manual, Motif Edition
Vol. 5: X Toolkit Intrinsics Reference Manual
Vol. 6A: Motif Programming Manual
Vol. 6B: Motif Reference Manual
Vol. 6C: Motif Tools
Vol. 8 : X Window System Administrator's Guide
Programmer's Supplement for Release 6
X User Tools
The X Window System in a Nutshell

CAREER & BUSINESS
Building a Successful Software Business
The Computer User's Survival Guide
Love Your Job!
Electronic Publishing on CD-ROM

TRAVEL
Travelers' Tales: Brazil
Travelers' Tales: Food
Travelers' Tales: France
Travelers' Tales: Gutsy Women
Travelers' Tales: India
Travelers' Tales: Mexico
Travelers' Tales: Paris
Travelers' Tales: San Francisco
Travelers' Tales: Spain
Travelers' Tales: Thailand
Travelers' Tales: A Woman's World

International Distributors

Europe, Middle East and Northern Africa (except France, Germany, Switzerland, & Austria)

INQUIRIES
International Thomson Publishing Europe
Berkshire House
168-173 High Holborn
London WC1V 7AA, United Kingdom
Telephone: 44-171-497-1422
Fax: 44-171-497-1426
Email: itpint@itps.co.uk

ORDERS
International Thomson Publishing Services, Ltd.
Cheriton House, North Way
Andover, Hampshire SP10 5BE, United Kingdom
Telephone: 44-264-342-832
  (UK orders)
Telephone: 44-264-342-806
  (outside UK)
Fax: 44-264-364418 (UK orders)
Fax: 44-264-342761 (outside UK)
UK & Eire orders: itpuk@itps.co.uk
International orders: itpint@itps.co.uk

France

Editions Eyrolles
61 Bd Saint-Germain
75240 Paris Cedex 05
France
Telephone: 33 1 44 41 46 16
Fax: 33 1 44 41 11 44

Australia

WoodsLane Pty. Ltd.
7/5 Vuko Place, Warriewood NSW 2102
P.O. Box 935, Mona Vale NSW 2103
Australia
Telephone: 61-2-9970-5111
Fax: 61-2-9970-5002
Email: info@woodslane.com.au

Germany, Switzerland, and Austria

INQUIRIES
O'Reilly Verlag
Balthasarstr. 81
D-50670 Köln
Germany
Telephone: 49 221 97 31 60 0
Fax: 49 221 97 31 60 8
Email: anfragen@oreilly.de

ORDERS
International Thomson Publishing
Königswinterer Straße 418
53227 Bonn, Germany
Telephone: 49-228-97024 0
Fax: 49-228-441342
Email: order@oreilly.de

Asia (except Japan & India)

INQUIRIES
International Thomson Publishing Asia
60 Albert Street #15-01
Albert Complex
Singapore 189969
Telephone: 65-336-6411
Fax: 65-336-7411

ORDERS
Telephone: 65-336-6411
Fax: 65-334-1617
thomson@signet.com.sg

New Zealand

WoodsLane New Zealand Ltd.
21 Cooks Street (P.O. Box 575)
Wanganui, New Zealand
Telephone: 64-6-347-6543
Fax: 64-6-345-4840
Email: info@woodslane.com.au

Japan

O'Reilly Japan, Inc.
Kiyoshige Building 2F
12-Banchi, Sanei-cho
Shinjuku-ku
Tokyo 160 Japan
Telephone: 81-3-3356-5227
Fax: 81-3-3356-5261
Email: kenji@ora.com

India

Computer Bookshop (India) PVT. LTD.
190 Dr. D.N. Road, Fort
Bombay 400 001
India
Telephone: 91-22-207-0989
Fax: 91-22-262-3551
Email: cbsbom@giasbm01.vsnl.net.in

The Americas

O'Reilly & Associates, Inc.
101 Morris Street
Sebastopol, CA 95472 U.S.A.
Telephone: 707-829-0515
Telephone: 800-998-9938 (U.S. & Canada)
Fax: 707-829-0104
Email: order@ora.com

Southern Africa

International Thomson Publishing Southern Africa
Building 18, Constantia Park
240 Old Pretoria Road
P.O. Box 2459
Halfway House, 1685 South Africa
Telephone: 27-11-805-4819
Fax: 27-11-805-3648

O'REILLY™

TO ORDER: **800-998-9938** • **order@ora.com** • **http://www.ora.com/**
OUR PRODUCTS ARE AVAILABLE AT A BOOKSTORE OR SOFTWARE STORE NEAR YOU.
FOR INFORMATION: **800-998-9938** • **707-829-0515** • **info@ora.com**

O'REILLY™

O'Reilly & Associates, Inc.
101 Morris Street
Sebastopol, CA 95472-9902
1-800-998-9938

Visit us online at:
http://www.ora.com/
orders@ora.com

O'REILLY WOULD LIKE TO HEAR FROM YOU

Which book did this card come from?

_____

Where did you buy this book?
- ❏ Bookstore
- ❏ Direct from O'Reilly
- ❏ Bundled with hardware/software
- ❏ Other _____
- ❏ Computer Store
- ❏ Class/seminar

What operating system do you use?
- ❏ UNIX
- ❏ Windows NT
- ❏ Other _____
- ❏ Macintosh
- ❏ PC(Windows/DOS)

What is your job description?
- ❏ System Administrator
- ❏ Network Administrator
- ❏ Web Developer
- ❏ Other _____
- ❏ Programmer
- ❏ Educator/Teacher

❏ Please send me O'Reilly's catalog, containing a complete listing of O'Reilly books and software.

Name _____ Company/Organization _____

Address _____

City _____ State _____ Zip/Postal Code _____ Country _____

Telephone _____ Internet or other email address (specify network) _____

Nineteenth century wood engraving
of a bear from the O'Reilly &
Associates Nutshell Handbook®
Using & Managing UUCP.

POST CARD

BUSINESS REPLY MAIL
FIRST CLASS MAIL   PERMIT NO. 80   SEBASTOPOL, CA

Postage will be paid by addressee

O'Reilly & Associates, Inc.
101 Morris Street
Sebastopol, CA 95472-9902